Pharaoh's Land and Beyond

Pharaoh's Land and Beyond

ANCIENT EGYPT AND ITS NEIGHBORS

Edited by Pearce Paul Creasman
and
Richard H. Wilkinson

OXFORD
UNIVERSITY PRESS

OXFORD

UNIVERSITY PRESS

Oxford University Press is a department of the University of Oxford. It furthers
the University's objective of excellence in research, scholarship, and education
by publishing worldwide. Oxford is a registered trade mark of Oxford University
Press in the UK and certain other countries.

Published in the United States of America by Oxford University Press
198 Madison Avenue, New York, NY 10016, United States of America.

Library of Congress Cataloging-in-Publication Data
Names: Creasman, Pearce Paul, 1981- editor. | Wilkinson, Richard H., editor.
Title: Pharaoh's land and beyond : Ancient Egypt and its neighbors / edited
   by Pearce Paul Creasman and Richard H. Wilkinson.
Description: New York, NY, United States of America : Oxford University
   Press, 2017.
Identifiers: LCCN 2016059037 | ISBN 9780190229078 (hardback) |
ISBN 9780190229092 (ebook)
Subjects: LCSH: Egypt—Foreign relations. | Egypt—Civilization—To 332 B.C.
   | Egypt—History—To 332 B.C.
Classification: LCC DT83 .P52 2017 | DDC 932/.01—dc23
LC record available at https://lccn.loc.gov/2016059037

9 8 7 6 5 4 3 2 1
Printed by Sheridan Books, Inc., United States of America

TABLE OF CONTENTS

LIST OF ILLUSTRATIONS

LIST OF PLATES

1 Maiherpri as depicted in his *Book of the Dead.* **Image courtesy of Udimu,** <https://commons.wikimedia.org/wiki/File:**Maherperi.JPG>; Creative Commons—Attribution 3.0 Unported (**<https://creativecommons.org/licenses/by/3.0/us/legalcode>).

2 Map of main overland routes in Egypt, with the primary important routes marked in red. Adapted from T. Kendall, *Kerma and the Kingdom of Kush 2500–1500 BC: The Archaeological Discovery of an Ancient Nubian Empire* (Washington: National Museum of African Art, 1997), xvi (map); J. Baines, J. and J. Malek, *Atlas of Ancient Egypt*, revised ed. (Oxford: Phaidon Press, 2000), 31 (map); C. Rossi and S. Ikram 2013, "Evidence of Desert Routes across Northern Kharga (Egypt's Western Desert)," in F. Förster, Frank and H. Riemer (eds.), *Desert Road Archaeology in Ancient Egypt and Beyond* (Köln: Heinrich-Barth-Institut, 2013), 266 fig. 1. **Drawing by G. Mumford and C. Childs.**

3 Map of main overland routes in Palestine, with major routes marked in blue and additional, important through secondary routes, indicated in red. Adapted from Y. Aharoni, Yohanan, *The Land of the Bible: A Historical Geography* (London: Burns and Oates, 1979), 44 map 3. **Drawing by G. Mumford and C. Childs.**

4 Map of main Middle Bronze/Late Bronze Age overland routes in Near East with main routes marked in red, a potential Assyrian merchant route from Ashur to Kanesh noted in green, and selected maritime route(s) shown in blue. Adapted from M. Roaf, Michael, *Cultural Atlas of Mesopotamia and the Ancient Near East* (New York: Facts on File, 1990), 113 and 179 (maps). **Drawing by G. Mumford and C. Childs.**

5 Bowing foreigners watch as the ingots of precious metal they have brought as gifts/tribute to Egypt are weighed. Theban Tomb 39 (Puyemre); Eighteenth Dynasty, reigns of Thutmose III and Hatshepsut. Detail from N. de G. Davies, *The Tomb of Puyemrê at Thebes* (New York: Metropolitan Museum of Art, 1922), pl. I.

6 Map with images from Thera (Museum of Prehistoric Thera), Byblos, Abu Simbel, and Napata/Gebel Barkal. **Image from Thera courtesy of Olaf Tausch, CC BY 3.0 (**<https://creativecommons.org/licenses/by/3.0/us/legalcode>**); image from Byblos courtesy of Satak Lord, CC BY-SA 2.5** (<https://creativecommons.org/licenses/by-sa/2.5/legalcode>**); images of Abu Simbel and Napata/Gebel Barkal by Stuart Tyson Smith.**

xv

ACKNOWLEDGMENTS

The editors are grateful for the effort and expertise that its many authors have brought to this work, as well as to the University of Arizona Provost's Author Support Fund and the Institute of Maritime Research and Discovery's publication program. Bettina Bader would like to thank D. Aston for improving the English of her chapter, and Vera Müller for discussing some of the points presented as well as for her expertise on the Predynastic period, noting that any remaining mistakes are solely the author's responsibility. Orly Goldwasser is grateful to Annick Payne and Yoram Cohen for their remarks, also noting that any remaining mistakes are solely the author's responsibility. Inspiriation for the cover design was provided by Noreen Doyle. Thanks are also due, from editors and authors alike, to Stefan Vranka and his team at Oxford University Press for their enthusiastic support of the new perspective offered by this volume.

The Editors
Tucson, Arizona & Luxor, Egypt

LIST OF CONTRIBUTORS

Noga Ayali-Darshan is Lecturer in the Hebrew and Semitic Languages Department, Bar-Ilan University (Israel).

Bettina Bader is Principal Investigator of the Austrian Science Fund START Project Beyond Politics hosted by the Institute for Oriental and European Archaeology, the Institut für Orientalische und Europäische Archäologie, Austrian Academy of Sciences (Austria).

Vanessa Boschloos is a Post-Doctoral Assistant in the Department of Archaeology, Ghent University and Researcher in the Antiquity Department of the Royal Museums of Art and History (Belgium).

Judith Bunbury is a geologist in the Department of Earth Sciences, University of Cambridge (England).

Izak Cornelius is Professor and Chair of the Ancient Studies Department, Stellenbosch University (South Africa).

Pearce Paul Creasman is Associate Professor of Dendrochronology and Egyptian Archaeology, and Curator, University of Arizona (USA).

Rosalie David is Professor in the Faculty of Life Sciences, University of Manchester (England).

Noreen Doyle is Research Associate with the University of Arizona Egyptian Expedition (USA).

Orly Goldwasser is Professor and Head of Egyptology, Ancient Near Eastern Languages and Cultures, Institute of Archaeology, Hebrew University of Jerusalem (Israel).

James A. Harrell is Professor Emeritus of Geology, Department of Environmental Sciences, University of Toledo (USA).

Kathryn Howley is Lady Wallis Budge Junior Research Fellow in Egyptology, Christ's College, University of Cambridge (England).

Nanno Marinatos is Professor and Department Head of the Department of Classics and Mediterranean Studies, University of Illinois at Chicago (USA).

Samuel Mark is Professor of Maritime Studies, Texas A&M University at Galveston (USA).

Gregory Mumford is Associate Professor of Anthropology, University of Alabama at Birmingham (USA).

Thomas Schneider is Professor of Egyptology and Near Eastern Studies, University of British Columbia (Canada).

Ian Shaw is Professor and Head of the Department of History and Archaeology, University of Chester (England).

Stuart Tyson Smith is Professor and Chair of the Department of Anthropology, University of California, Santa Barbara (USA).

Anthony Spalinger is Professor of Classics and Ancient History, University of Auckland (New Zealand).

Richard H. Wilkinson is Regents Professor of Egyptian Archaeology Emeritus, University of Arizona (USA).

Introduction

Pearce Paul Creasman and Richard H. Wilkinson

Few societies in human history excite the mind as ancient Egypt does and, indeed, has for millennia, but the popular concept of pharaonic Egypt as a unified, homogeneous, and isolated cultural entity is misleading. The Egypt of antiquity was, rather, a rich tapestry of social, religious, technological, and economic interconnections among numerous cultures from disparate lands. Foreign influence pre-dates the pharaohs, continued throughout their rule, and saw the pharaonic period to a close. Although the Egyptians themselves seemingly maintained an extremely "Egyptocentric" worldview, the glory of the pharaohs would not have existed such as it did without the resources and influence of the societies around them. However much the ancient Egyptians may have looked down upon foreigners as culturally inferior peoples or as dangerous agents of chaos, Egyptian society was on many levels deeply entangled with those of its neighbors.

The connections between ancient Egypt and its wider world has long been a topic of lively interest and study, but much remains to be explored. Most book-length publications on the subject of Egypt's relations beyond its borders are tightly focused, typically on a geographical region, chronological period, or mode (e.g., diplomacy or trade). Often, these works are written for the specialist academic reader, which renders them less accessible to a more general readership not already in command of other specialist literature. *Pharaoh's Land and Beyond: Ancient Egypt and Its Neighbors* represents a comprehensive effort to bring together, for a broad readership, the multifaceted aspects of the interdependent, international agents, ideas, and forces that shaped Egypt and its neighbors through the centuries.

Foreign influence within Egypt pre-dates the unification of the state, as does the spread of Egyptian influence beyond its traditional borders of the Delta and first cataract. Interconnections in the ancient world were dynamic and fluid, crossing time, space, and cultures. The long period between the First and

Thirtieth Dynasties, during which the Bronze Age arose and transformed into the Iron Age, witnessed the flourishing of international trade across vast distances of land and sea. Desire for, and even dependence on, foreign resources led in antiquity—as today—to concerns for security and by extension warfare, but this period was also a nascent age of diplomacy and "international" art styles. Coincident with the migrations and other travels of people with their goods were exchanges of ideas and language and disease. Such socio-cultural interactions occurred in an active geological context likewise subject to influence beyond its borders, as weather far to the south and natural catastrophes elsewhere had profound impact on the fortunes of Egypt and its neighbors. The scholars of Egyptology, Near Eastern studies, and related disciplines assembled here explore Egypt's fortunes in light of all of the above based on multifaceted lines of evidence: the intertwined archaeological, artistic, and textual records of some 3,000 years.

The chapters are arranged in five thematic groups. The first three chapters detail the geographical contexts of interconnections through examination of ancient Egyptian exploration, maritime routes, and overland passages. The next three chapters address the human principals of association: peoples, with the attendant difficulties differentiating ethnic identities from the record; diplomatic actors, with their complex balances and presentations of power; and the military, with its evolving role in pharaonic expansion. Physical manifestations of interconnections between pharaonic Egypt and its neighbors in the form of objects are the focus of the third section: trade, art and architecture, and a specific case study of scarabs. The fourth section discusses in depth perhaps the most powerful means of interconnection: ideas. Whether through diffusion and borrowing of knowledge and technology, through the flow of words by script and literature, or through exchanges in the religious sphere, the pharaonic Egypt that we know today was constantly changing—and changing the cultures around it. Natural events, too, played significant roles in the pharaonic world: geological disasters, the effects of droughts and floods on the Nile, and illness and epidemics all delivered profound impacts, as seen in the final section.

Thus from the unique perspective of interconnections, *Pharaoh's Land and Beyond* provides insights into a wide scope of pharaonic culture. Many topics are addressed here for the first time or for the first time from within such a context. The editors present this volume as a foundation upon which future work from similar frames of reference may build. And they hope, too, that this volume will prove to be a valuable resource for scholars and students of ancient Egypt and its contemporaries while remaining fully accessible to the enthusiast.

SECTION I }

Pathways

1 }

Finding the Beyond
EXPLORATION
Thomas Schneider

Introduction: *Terrae Incognitae* and *Terrae Cognitae*

Exploration has been defined as a determining part of human identity, an innate human instinct. At the same time, exploration as a political and cultural concept and practice is historically embedded in the European history of colonialism and is today widely seen as symbolizing state power, scientific progress, and national exceptionalism. In his exposé on the historical structure of the ancient Near East published in 1965, Siegfried Morenz subscribed to this idea of European exceptionalism when he credited the ancient Greeks with the willingness to explore and to learn from abroad, a willingness that he regarded as opposed to the Egyptian way of life. Although Morenz's assessment can today no longer be seen as valid, this still leaves the question open as to whether the modern concept of exploration is applicable to ancient Egyptian expeditions abroad or how it should be defined. In their introductory chapter to the volume *Mysterious Lands*, David O'Connor and Stephen Quirke say about the opening lines of one of the Egyptian guides to the underworld from the royal tombs in the Valley of the Kings, the *Amduat*, that "the European expansionist claim to possess time and space is alive here in the 15th century BC, but as knowledge appropriate to divine kingship" (O'Connor and Quirke 2003, p. 2). This is hardly the case. The deceased king of the *Amduat* is not the earthly king; his knowledge as described there is that of somebody initiated into the mysteries of the cosmos and not a knowledge instrumentalized for the colonization and exploitation of the inhabited earth. While the *terrae incognitae* of the real globe, of fiction, and of the underworld can certainly overlap, and while perceptions about them can influence each other, this contribution will focus on the Egyptian exploration of the physical world of the Mediterranean, Africa, and the Middle East.

In the context of this volume, the editors describe "exploration" very broadly as the acquisition by the Egyptians of knowledge about areas beyond ancient

Egypt's own territory and civilization. To establish for Egypt the extent and process of acquisition of the knowledge about what was "beyond Pharaoh's land" is exceedingly difficult for a variety of reasons. First, the reduced scope and type of preserved evidence makes it in a very fundamental way impossible for modern scholars to know what the Egyptians actually knew. Secondly, it is also difficult because the nature of this knowledge must have been very varied and will have changed over time, as did the locales and milieus where knowledge could be acquired. Thirdly, what was seen as areas beyond ancient Egypt's own territory and civilization changed over time, both geographically and culturally.

These introductory remarks will thus attempt to look at three fundamental questions: What are the limits of our modern knowledge about what the Egyptians knew about the "Beyond"? How could knowledge about this "Beyond" have been acquired by the Egyptians in the first place? And what was the "Beyond" that the Egyptians would have found and explored? This chapter will thus be not so much a description of the Egyptian exploration of *terrae incognitae*, but an exploration of the challenges that modern research into Egypt's exploration encounters. *Terrae (in)cognitae* is therefore also a metaphor for our (lack of) knowledge of the Egyptian realm of knowledge of what was beyond "Pharaoh's land."

Terrae Incognitae: The Limits of Modern Knowledge about Egyptian Exploration

Our knowledge of the past is extremely fragmented. Paucity of evidence as an epistemological problem determines all areas of the Egyptological endeavor. This is also true for the topic of Egyptian exploration. New finds such as the Red Sea harbors of Wadi el-Jarf and Wadi Gawasis, serving maritime expeditions across the Red Sea and likely as far as Punt in the Old and Middle Kingdoms, or the Abu Ballas trail leading from Dakhla Oasis in the Western Desert of Egypt toward central Africa, attested in the Old and Middle Kingdoms, are changing our perception of Egyptian exploration in a fundamental way (fig. 1.1). More specifically, they change the parameters in which we have to conceptualize Egyptian exploration abroad. Oric Bates's dictum of 1914 (p. 48; MacDonald 2003, p. 100), claiming that "the whole of Africa west of the Nile was, to the Egyptian, a *terra incognita* which stretched away from the familiar haunts of men to the realm of the dead," is more a reflection of the lack of modern knowledge than of the absence of Egyptian knowledge of the Western Desert. Similarly, David O'Connor and Stephen Quirke held in 2003 (p. 4) that "Anatolia and the Tigris-Euphrates region appear to be *terra incognita* to Egypt prior to the Late Bronze Age, when they play a dominant role in the international relations for which correspondence survives in the form of the

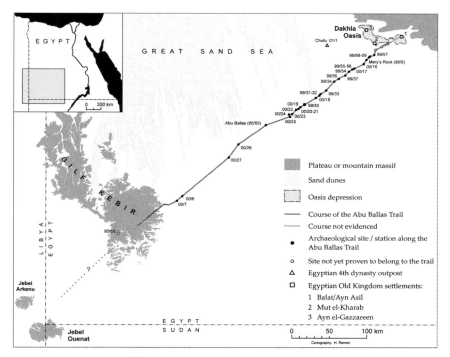

FIGURE 1.1 Map showing the chain of archaeological sites along the Abu Ballas trail.

Amarna Letters of the 14th century BC and similar material." This statement at the very least speaks about what "appears" to be the historical situation as derived from the "surviving evidence." It also pertains only to the time of the Early and Middle Bronze Age, since late fourth millennium interaction between Mesopotamia and Egypt is well documented in the artistic and intellectual repertoire. For the Middle Bronze Age, the objects of the long-known foundation deposit of the Montu temple at Tod and a military campaign described on fragments of records of royal deeds found at Mitrahina (both from the reign of Amenemhat II, Twelfth Dynasty), as well as a passage in the *Tale of Sinuhe* probably mentioning a royal title from Anatolia, may enjoin scholarship to caution, however. A recently found fragment of a letter sent to the Hyksos residence at Avaris by one of the last kings of the First Dynasty of Babylon proves that Middle Bronze Age correspondence from Anatolia and Mesopotamia to Egypt has simply not been preserved. For the Old Kingdom, the lapis lazuli trade from Afghanistan (fig. 1.2) across the Iranian plateau and Mesopotamia was channeled to Egypt through Ebla in north Syria, where fragments of Egyptian stone vessels would become deposited in Palace G. It is unlikely that the lapis lazuli was traded to Egypt from the Far East without any accompanying knowledge about its provenance and the mediating centers, and indeed, either the place of

FIGURE 1.2 Lapis lazuli inlay in the form of a falcon, New Kingdom.

origin or a main trading point of the stone is mentioned on a relief from the time of Khufu. Is it on any account historically plausible that the full-fledged bureaucratic state of the later Old Kingdom and the empire of Sargon of Akkad were not interacting with each other? Sargon captured the Lebanon and reached the Mediterranean Sea, where the Egyptian state had a trade emporium at Byblos and was maybe involved more intensely; so rather than becoming known in Egypt only in the Amarna Age, it is most probable that Sargon was well known in contemporary Egypt. The inscribed clay tablets found at the Egyptian western oasis residence of Balat/Ayn Asil seem to be indirect evidence for the knowledge of cuneiform tablets in Egypt, and a more intense cultural influence of Egypt on Mesopotamia has been suggested. These examples from the Early and Middle Bronze Age, in support of the view that Anatolia and Mesopotamia were by no means unknown to the Egyptians prior to the Late Bronze Age, indicate that knowledge or absence of knowledge about the "Beyond" cannot be determined by the coincidence of preserved evidence. It must instead rely on arguments of plausibility that take into account the historical context and the diminished state of sources.

Terrae Cognitae: How Would Egypt Acquire Knowledge about the "Beyond"?

As John K. Wright outlined in 1947 (p. 2), "whether or not a particular area may be called 'unknown' depends both on whose knowledge and on what kind of knowledge is taken into account." He continues (pp. 2–3):

As used literally on the early European maps, the words *terra incognita* signified a land unknown to the map maker after he had presumably consulted all available sources of information; but if such "unknown territories" were beyond the ken of the geographers and cartographers of Western civilization, they were known to their inhabitants, if any, and frequently to peoples of other civilizations as well. [...]

[...] Hence, depending on our point of view, there are personal, community, and national *terrae incognitae:* there are the *terrae incognitae* to different cultural traditions and civilizations; and there are also the *terrae incognitae* to contemporary geographical science.

The meaning of *terra incognita* depends no less on the kind of knowledge that we are considering. There are two grades of geographical knowledge: knowledge of observed facts and knowledge derived by reasonable inference from observed facts, with which we fill in the gaps between the latter.

The difference of observed and inferred knowledge is reminiscent of philosopher Bertrand Russell's distinction between knowledge by acquaintance and knowledge by description. Knowledge by acquaintance is the "foundational knowledge of truths," while knowledge by description is ultimately based on knowledge by acquaintance, too, but is mediated, indirectly acquired through informants and intercalary sources. In ancient Egypt, exploration in the form of military and trade expeditions would have been the primary means to acquire observed knowledge, to which individual reconnaissance (e.g., by royal messengers) and exploration from local bases (Egyptian trade emporia, governors' residences and garrisons) must be added (fig. 1.3).

The acquisition of such knowledge was carried out in the interest of economic and political interests, although scientific interest is not absent. Animal menageries served royal legitimation but at the same time also showcased fascination with and knowledge of the exotic. This was also believed to be true for the "cabinet of curiosities" of Thutmose III, his botanical garden at Karnak, with depictions of species of animals and plants from Egypt to Anatolia, Iran, and the Caucasus, although it has now been suggested that those rooms with their decoration may have been used ritually for priestly initiation into cosmic knowledge. On a temple pylon at Armant from the reign of Thutmose III, a rhinoceros brought to Egypt as booty is depicted, including the measurements for its body and its horn. That manuals of foreign topographical knowledge for military and administrative use existed can be inferred from topographical lists of conquered towns and territories on temple walls, from onomastica, and a document such as Papyrus Anastasi I that presents problems of military logistics, the topography of Syria-Palestine, and incidents from an elite soldier's life.

In past scholarship, Egyptian exploration would have often been portrayed as following an evolutionary scheme, with the New Kingdom being most

FIGURE 1.3   The expedition leader, Iny.

engaged in international exchange and contact, most vividly highlighted by the 2002 book title *Amarna Diplomacy: The Beginnings of International Relations* (Cohen and Westbrook 2000). It now appears plausible that the extent of Egypt's exploration was similarly robust throughout history until Egypt became part of global empires in the first millennium, and that what differed was rather the degree of appropriation and type of management of the territories behind that frontier.

Precisely the archetypal example of Egyptian exploration abroad, iconic in the history of human exploration, can be cited here to illustrate the revision of views: the journey to the country of frankincense, Punt, on the Eritrean coast of the Red Sea, as described and portrayed in great detail in the mortuary temple of Queen Hatshepsut at Deir el-Bahari. As late as 1988, Howard R. Lamar (p. xi) singled it out as an example of the human heroic saga of discovery and exploration:

> Discovery, that is, the documented (e.g., on a map) initial contact with the unknown, and exploration, the understanding of discovery, have together constituted a heroic dimension of the human saga from its very beginnings. The first recorded expedition was sponsored by Queen Hatshepsut, Bronze Age Egypt's only female pharaoh, to Punt (Somalia) for the purpose of trade in the middle of the fifteenth century BC.

Within the last years, an assessment of the Punt reliefs as authentic records of the Eighteenth Dynasty has given way to a view of Hatshepsut merely aligning her trade mission with a tradition of Punt expeditions one thousand years earlier. It seems now likely that the depictions at Deir el-Bahari were copied from an Old Kingdom template. This is buttressed by Fifth Dynasty reliefs of King Sahure at Abusir that may have belonged to a Punt expedition, apart from the archaeological support provided by the newly discovered Wadi el-Jarf harbor and textual evidence from the Fifth Dynasty. In her expedition to "the god's land" Punt, Hatshepsut thus emulated a historical precursor from the distant past. She aligned herself with a tradition of exploitation to legitimize her rule, not with exploration per se. Since Egyptian kings by definition were rulers of "what the sun encircles," a phrase attested first in the early Middle Kingdom (*Sinuhe* B213; stele of Horus from the Wadi el-Hudi), and were "the sun god by whose rays one sees" (*Loyalist Instruction*), exploration would not appear to be a category of royal achievement although actually reaching those distant regions of royal power and knowledge could have constituted a feat of royal pride. In turn, traveling into foreign territory was a category of self-presentation and achievement for private individuals, most famously the expedition leaders of the Old Kingdom, and royal messengers in the New Kingdom. Expeditions in the Old Kingdom were sent far into the (at the time, more hospitable) southwestern desert, the Red Sea, and the Levant, part of a large state system of revenue and trade featured in biographical accounts by expedition leaders (most famously the expeditions of Harkhuf to Irem/Yam), to which more recently, administrative documents can be added.

In the Middle Kingdom, the prototype of an Egyptian royal envoy abroad is Sinuhe, the protagonist of a story who fled Egypt and had a successful career in the Levant before returning to Egypt in his old age; he at the same time set a literary model for living abroad within the well-explored and culturally appropriated frontier. In the New Kingdom, as shown by the determinatives used after place names (hieroglyphs that indicated the category of meaning of a word or name), "to a certain extent, 'Egypt' and 'abroad' cease to be distinct entities: the former has lost hierarchical prominence over the latter" (Loprieno 2003, p. 45). While the Egyptian army in this age reached and secured militarily geographical areas never attained before, such as the Euphrates River in Syria and the region of Kerma in the Sudan between the fourth and fifth cataracts of the Nile, royal envoys in diplomatic missions traveled as far as the capital cities of the Hittite and Babylonian empires. We can mention here Egypt's ambassador Netjeruimes (Nemtimes?)/Pirikhnawa, who brought the original silver tablet with the Hittite-Egyptian peace treaty to Egypt, and the royal envoy Huy, who "went up to Hatti and brought her Princess," apart from Egyptian physicians, translators, and other specialists employed at the Hittite court. With regard to envoys to Kassite Babylonia, Amarna letter EA 7 provides an unusual "lesson in geography" (as labeled by Moran 1992, p. 13):

> From the time the messenger of my brother *ar[rived here]*, I have not been well, and so *on no occa[sion]* has his messenger eaten food and [drunk] spirits [in my com]pany.... [Furthermore], since I was not well and my brother [showed me no] con[cern], I for my part became an[gry] with my brother, saying, "Has my brother not hea[rd] that I am ill? Why has he sho[wn] me no concern? Why has he sent no messenger here and *visi[ted me]?* My brother's messenger addressed me, s[aying], "(It) is not a place close by so your brother can hear (about you) and send you greetings. The country is far away. Who is going to tell your brother so he can immediately send you greetings? Would your brother hear that you are ill and still not send you his messenger?" I for my part addressed him as follows, saying, "For my brother, a Great King, is there really a far-away country and a close-by one?" He for his part addressed me [as] follows, saying: "Ask your own messenger whether the country is far away and as a result your brother did not hear (about you) and did not send (anyone) to greet you." Now, since I asked my own messenger and he said to me that the journey is far, I was not angry (any longer), I said no [more].

Since the Babylonian Great King was most likely aware of the actual distance in the first place, this letter can also be read as an ironical critique of Egyptian royal pretense and an appeal to his status obligations. Does the Egyptian king not claim to be the lord of the universe? And would he not do whatever was in his power to prove that he was a great king? Explicitly, however, this letter also attests to professional conversations among messengers and thus a network of inferred knowledge about the "Beyond" that would allow for a more global exploration by description. Such knowledge by description could, as in this case, be gained abroad, but would often have been acquired in Egypt itself, from people of foreign origin who resided temporarily or permanently in Egypt. Egyptian society attests to a large immigration of foreigners on all social levels, from kings and king's wives to workers, who originated across the Middle East, the Mediterranean, and northeast Africa (pl. 1). One of the most intense exposures to knowledge about the "Beyond" on a state level was likely provided in the New Kingdom by the foreign wives of Egyptian kings from the Hittite, Babylonian, and Mitanni empires who moved to Egypt with their entourage and households and thus arguably also carried with them literary texts for their personal perusal in their own "Beyond," which was Egypt.

Knowledge about those regions is also indirectly reflected by the extensive nature of technological and cultural innovation from abroad visible throughout the second millennium BCE, from weaponry, textile industries, and glass production to loanwords, borrowed literary texts, and adopted deities. The "Beyond" provided narrative fiction—such as the *Doomed Prince*—with exotic settings, and at times faraway regions such as Punt and the Aegean show up in the artistic repertoire. This is testament to the wide-ranging degree of intellectual exploration and the fact that Egyptian civilization had culturally appropriated features of the "Beyond."

Terrae Incognitae: What Was the "Beyond" that the Egyptians Explored?

Egyptian political ideology maintained a strict distinction between Egypt and the outside world, and between inhabitants of Egypt, who conformed with the order perpetuated here by the pharaoh, and inhabitants of the chaotic world beyond its boundaries. Ideologically, Egypt was defined by a strict model of inclusion and exclusion that combined the existence or lack of acculturation with the notion of territorial authority and power hierarchy. "Pharaoh's land" by this definition was restricted to the Nile Delta and Nile Valley up to Aswan on the first cataract of the Nile, the country's traditional southern border, despite the fact that foreign culture proliferated within Egypt and Egyptian culture abroad. If "exploration" pertains to knowledge of the unknown, then the degree of knowledge determines if and when we can speak of exploration. In that respect, the areas "beyond Pharaoh's land" are as much part of a space of knowledge and imagination as they are geographical areas.

In his classic book, *The Great Frontier* (1952), Walter Prescott Webb portrayed the relationship between the known world and the "beyond" as a sequence of circles, of which the innermost circle, "the metropolis," meant Europe around 1500 CE, and the area between the metropolis and the limits of knowledge were the "frontier":

> The inner circle represents the area of accurate knowledge. The outer circle represents the limits of knowledge. The area B [between the inner and the outer circle, TS] is the region known of but not understood. It is here that imagination has free play, that mystery and romance abound, that inquiry and investigation go on. Gradually the inner circle is enlarged. If it could expand until coterminous with the outer circle there would be no mystery, little room for imagination and nothing to investigate. The greater the distance x–y [the space of area B, TS] the greater the opportunity for the imagination, literary and scientific.
>
> (Webb 2003, p. 349)

The relationship between the "metropolis of Egypt" and its frontier was always complex. At all times, Egypt comprised areas populated by non-Egyptian groups behind its official political boundaries, such as the first Upper Egyptian province north of the first cataract ("Nubian land"), the eastern mountains of Egypt that continue to be populated by Bedja tribes today up to the geographic latitude of Thebes, the western Nile Delta and the Egyptian Western Desert with a large frontier zone of Egyptian, Libyan, and Nilo-Saharan interchange. Large-scale immigration occurred from the frontier (as evidenced in the case of the Nubian Pan-grave culture, as well as Palestinian settlement in the eastern Nile Delta; both *c.* 2000–1500 BCE). In turn, both Nubia (Lower Nubia since *c.* 2000 BCE, Upper Nubia since *c.* 1500 BCE) and Palestine/southern Syria (since *c.* 2000 BCE) underwent substantial Egyptianization and became cultural and political colonies of Egypt. The existence of topographical lists, onomastica, and handbooks of topographical knowledge mentioned above indicate that those regions had become well-known areas of knowledge and thus did no longer lie "beyond" as a target of exploration, although they could still be a source of wonder and literary imagination (fig. 1.4).

This development is paralleled by a change in literary narratives, where the border that the protagonist has to pass is no longer between Egypt and a foreign country, but rather between the "real" and the "imaginary" spheres. The colonized areas were subjected to a system of political and economic exploitation, formally implemented through a specialized administration of military control and resource management. By contrast, areas such as the Eastern Desert of Egypt were always an area of knowledge but still remained an area beyond human civilization, "god's land", as they were called. They were the place where miracles could occur (under Mentuhotep IV in the early Middle Kingdom, inscriptions tell us about the miraculous appearance of a gazelle

FIGURE 1.4 Part of a topographical list. Luxor Temple, New Kingdom.

and a well in the midst of the desert) and where miraculous objects could be found (like a petrified sea urchin found by a priest Tjanefer and described as a "wonder"),

The actual area of exploration, the little-understood "Beyond," had come to lie beyond the frontier already claimed and acculturated, where one could sail a river to the south but at the same time downstream (the Euphrates, inverse to the Nile, in Mitanni territory) and where birds would be laying eggs every day (chickens, as presented to Thutmose III in Lebanon by a Near Eastern country whose name is not preserved). This was a space not necessarily beyond civilization, but beyond either sufficient knowledge or understanding.

Where the actual limits of Egypt's exploration must be drawn on a map is impossible to determine, due to the limits of preserved evidence and modern knowledge. New evidence keeps coming forth, such as the recently found first Egyptian graffito in Saudi Arabia from the reign of Ramesses III, at the oasis of Taima. At present, the farthest points from Egyptian territory for which observational knowledge through Egyptians who were present at the place can be ascertained are: to the southwest of Egypt, the Gebel Uweinat, at the modern Egyptian-Libyan-Sudanese state border; to the southeast of Egypt, the Eritrea coast of the Red Sea (the probable location of Punt); to the northeast, Babylon (through the envoy mentioned in El Amarna letter 7); to the north Tarhuntassa (where the Egyptian envoys to Hatti and other specialists were

sent). A famous topographical list of Aegean place names from the reign of
Amenhotep III also mentions, for the northwest, cities in mainland Greece
such as Thebes in Boeotia. In view of the extremely reduced situation of source
preservation, it is epistemologically unlikely that these coincidental mentions
of most distant places attested would be congruent with the most distant places
actually known to the Egyptians by personal observation or, even more so, by
indirect knowledge. There was very certainly a beyond known to the Egyptians
that was further than our current knowledge of Egyptian exploration.

The most famous text about ancient Egyptian exploration abroad, apt to
illustrate the problems highlighted in the previous pages, is the one preserved in
Herodotus' *Histories*, about the circumnavigation of Africa allegedly commissioned by Necho II in the Twenty-sixth Dynasty. Willi Müller (1891, pp. 109–
10) praised it as the climax of human exploration:

> The history of geography, and in particular, of discoveries, is not short of
> momentous events; never was there a lack of motives of the most noble
> or less noble kind that impelled brave men to explore unknown parts on
> our planet's surface. Hardly, however, has there been or will there ever be
> any deed greater than that Phoenician journey.

The account itself is recorded in *Histories* 4.42 and runs as follows:

> As for Libya (= Africa), we know it to be washed on all sides by the
> sea, except where it is attached to Asia. This discovery was first made
> by Necos, the Egyptian king, who on desisting from the canal which
> he had begun between the Nile and the Arabian Gulf, sent to sea a
> number of ships manned by Phoenicians, with orders to make for the
> Pillars of Hercules (= the Strait of Gibraltar), and return to Egypt
> through them, and by the Mediterranean. The Phoenicians took their
> departure from Egypt by way of the Erythraean Sea, and so sailed into
> the southern ocean. When autumn came, they went ashore, wherever
> they might happen to be, and having sown a tract of land with grain
> waited until the grain was fit to cut. Having reaped it, they again set
> sail; and thus it came to pass that two whole years went by, and it was
> not till the third year that they doubled the Pillars of Hercules, and
> made good their voyage home. On their return, they declared—I for
> my part do not believe them, but perhaps others may—that in sailing
> round Libya they had the sun upon their right hand. In this way was
> the extent of Libya first discovered.

This claim is not supported by any other document, a fact that has made
scholars doubt its reliability: in the twentieth century, inscribed scarabs were
forged to provide the missing proof. While no independent proof for the

historical authenticity of the expedition can be provided, both the 1891 treatise by Willi Müller and the recent reassessment by Jan Moje (2003) have confirmed the basic plausibility of the account. From an epistemic point of view, even our knowledge about the "metropolis," Egypt itself, is dramatically underdetermined. By definition, the frontier was situated outside the realm of precise knowledge that was peculiar to the metropolis. It would appear inconsequent to expect an Egyptian proof precisely for knowledge of this realm beyond knowledge.

As we attempt to map Egypt's knowledge of what lay beyond the pharaoh's land, we also map the modern scholarly frontier.

Paths in the Deep

MARITIME CONNECTIONS

Pearce Paul Creasman and Noreen Doyle

The ubiquity of boats in the iconography of the Predynastic and pharaonic periods underscores the importance of water transport for the ancient Egyptians. Essential tools for the consolidation and administration of Egypt as a distinct cultural and political entity along the Nile, wooden watercraft likewise facilitated the export of the royal will beyond Egypt's borders, farther upstream on the river and along the shores and sea-lanes of the Mediterranean and Red Seas. These bodies of water provided Egypt and its neighbors with complex flows of traffic ferrying people, animals, products, and ideas.

The Nile—generally navigable for 1,100 km between the first cataract at Aswan and the Mediterranean shore—appears to be an ideal medium for unifying the settlements that developed along its fertile floodplain. However, its northward flow complicated long-distance upstream traffic. Efficient travel had to be mastered in both directions to consolidate that vast length of river into a single political unit. In the Nile Valley, the prevailing winds blow from the north, that is, upstream, which presented Nile boatmen, and their rulers, with an opportunity. Unlike some later nautical technologies, the sail (fig. 2.1) probably developed on the Nile, rather than being introduced from elsewhere. Although not strictly necessary for seafaring, the sail makes long-distance transportation easier than human propulsion, which originally was paddling, a technique that later developed into mechanically more efficient rowing. During unification, armies and settlers, as well as materiel and intelligence, would need to travel regularly in both directions; afterward, the river would facilitate the exploitation and administration of resources. It can be no coincidence that the Egyptians' ability to harness the wind to propel a boat upstream evolved during the Predynastic Period before or perhaps in tandem with the development of the state.

FIGURE 2.1 The earliest known depiction of a sail on an Egyptian painted pot. Probably Naqada IIc.

Watercraft thus predictably feature in the earliest records of state formation and kingship. Boats appear with the names of early kings in the mining regions of the Sinai Peninsula, Eastern Desert, and Nubia. The Protodynastic Narmer Palette, one of the earliest records of a king in control of both Upper and Lower Egypt, features among its images a boat (behind a wooden door) above two rows of decapitated foes. The inclusion of a watercraft here, as elsewhere, informs the viewer that the king possesses the tools to impose and maintain his will wherever necessary. A host of other lines of evidence paint a convincing picture that Egypt had developed its nautical capabilities well prior to those of neighboring societies. Indeed, the old hypothesis that a Mesopotamian group, the "Followers of Horus," found their way to Egypt via the Red Sea and established the foundations of pharaonic culture in the Nile Valley has long been discredited. Egypt's early nautical developments, using native timbers, were indigenous, and its first maritime connections, developed as it sought to exploit territories beyond its geographical borders, were self-initiated.

Egypt's earliest boat-borne influences may have come from and flowed back to not the Near East but rather its neighbors on the Upper Nile, above the first cataract. Egypt's Predynastic proto-kingdoms had one or more coeval counterparts among the Nubian A-Group peoples. One of the A-Group proto-kingdoms was centered just north of the second cataract at Qustul. Two incense burners found here are Nubian artifacts with iconography developed by their Egyptian trading partners downstream, including a falcon deity perched on a *serekh*, a palace façade, a man wearing the white crown, a harpoon, and two boats. One of these boats features an early example of a sail, very much like one that appears on an Egyptian pot of late Naqada II (c/d) date (fig. 2.1). These Nubian rulers deployed Egyptian symbols—including nautical iconography— to express their own power.

Ties between the Nilotic states forming north and south of the first cataract, which included exchanges of goods as well as ideas, were close but not entirely peaceful. A petroglyph (fig. 2.2) at Gebel Sheikh Suleiman (near the second cataract), likely of First Dynasty date, shows a prisoner bound with the glyph of a bow (used in the writing of Ta-Seti, "Land of the Bow," the earliest Egyptian name for Nubia) before a falcon-mounted *serekh*. To the right of this group are two "town" glyphs and a second prisoner tethered to a boat that seems to pass over corpses of the (drowned?) enemy. Whatever the historical specifics of its date and meaning, both of which are debated, this petroglyph demonstrates the effective reach that the river gave even earliest Egypt: deep into foreign territory, Egyptian kings could carry with them the power to confront and subdue an indigenous population. This advanced nautical prowess facilitated the extirpation of the A-Group as the budding pharaonic state expanded and increasingly administered its geographical holdings.

Judging the degree to which early trade between Egypt and its nearest Asian neighbor, Canaan, was maritime in nature during such antiquity is difficult. Egyptian trading colonies established in the Predynastic Period (abandoned in the First Dynasty) might have been supported at least in part by the maritime route, but no shipwrecks by which this likelihood could be evaluated are known for any culture of this period. Nonetheless, pottery dating to the Proto- to Early Dynastic Periods (Early Bronze Age I) of both Egyptian and Levantine manufacture has been recovered from deep water off the coast of Israel, and Egyptian pottery of this date has been found in Atlit Bay (Israel). Excavations at Tel Ashkelon (Israel) suggest the existence of a port through which the products of sites farther inland entered a maritime trading network in the Early Dynastic Period/Early Bronze Age I; however, rising sea levels and the seaward

FIGURE 2.2 Commemoration of an Egyptian victory in Nubia. Petroglyph at Gebel Sheikh Suleiman, near the Second Cataract (Nubia). Probably First Dynasty.

extension of the Delta coastline have drowned and otherwise obscured the Mediterranean shoreline of the Proto-Dynastic through Old Kingdom period, along with many settlement sites of this time and later periods as well.

Lack of direct archaeological evidence notwithstanding, large-scale importation of Levantine/Canaanite wine to Egypt at this period does suggest conveyance by watercraft rather than caravans, simply as a matter of feasibility. Likewise, the importation of large pieces of non-native timber to Egypt strongly suggests a robust maritime trade network. Smaller pieces of imported coniferous wood, probably from the Levant or possibly Sinai, appear in earlier contexts, but the First Dynasty king Aha had access to logs large enough to provide his tomb with architectural beams some six meters long. In the Proto- and Early Dynastic Periods, construction of increasingly large and more complex monuments and other buildings in Egypt required larger timbers. At some sites, the timbers are reported to have been of non-native genera (especially conifers), and almost certainly these arrived in Egypt by ship. There were, very likely, ports—Ashkelon among them—that served not only as points of transshipment for inland products but as way stations for a trade route that extended farther to the north, where the best quality timber was to be had. Similarly, wood obtained from conifers growing in Sinai is likely to have been transported across the Gulf of Suez by boat, as were the peninsula's mineral resources.

By the end of the Second Dynasty, if not earlier, Egyptian kings shifted the geographical center of their Asiatic interests northward of Canaan. Perhaps lured by the availability of better coniferous timber and resins that played an essential role in Egyptian rituals, and also by a decline in settlements along the Canaanite coast (which may have had significant environmental causes), Egypt made Byblos its major trading partner. A close relationship that would persist through much of the pharaonic period formed. So deep was the association of this port and its timber with Egyptian shipbuilding that the Egyptians called some of their own vessels, including those that sailed the Red Sea, "Byblos ships."

Timber provides the most convincing evidence for early maritime trade. Prized for its minimal shrinkage, ready workability with copper tools, resistance to decay, and availability at lengths greater than other trees could provide, the wood of Lebanese cedar (*Cedrus libani*) and other coniferous species that do not grow in Egypt were heavily imported. The royal annals of the Palermo Stone record the "bringing of 40 ships full of(?) coniferous wood" (*int dpt 40 mḥ[?] ʿš*) during the reign of Snefru of the Fourth Dynasty. Byblos is generally assumed to be the source. Certainly at this time Egypt received substantial volumes of *Cedrus libani*, which is not native to Sinai. More than 30 tons of it had to be imported to build each of the two boats buried beside the Great Pyramid at Giza, belonging to Sneferu's son and successor, Khufu.

Egyptians likewise pursued their interests in resources available via the Red Sea. Separated from the Nile Valley by the Eastern Desert, even the nearest shore of the Red Sea was a land as foreign as any in the Levant. Until perhaps the Ramesside Period, the Egyptian presence anywhere on these shores was to one degree or another persistent but ephemeral: mission-specific outposts that remained dependent upon the valley for even basic food supplies, although local marine resources supplemented the diet. The earliest (secondary) evidence for Egyptian ships operating on these waters comes from the region of the southern Sinai turquoise mines, exploited first during the Naqada IIIa Period. Here too, as in Nubia, Egyptian inscriptions feature boats, strongly suggesting that ships crossed the Gulf of Suez to deliver expeditions even at this early time.

The Egyptians were not alone in occupying these lands. Although the region lacked settlements such as those encountered along the Mediterranean shore, local nomadic populations challenged the maritime expeditions, which were putting additional pressure on precious subsistence resources and disrupting the nomads' own trade. An early expression of the situation from the Egyptian point of view may be seen at Wadi Ameyra (a site 18 km inland from the Sinai's western coast). Here a graffito with the name of King Iry-Hor shows a boat above a scene depicting the smiting of a bound captive, a northern echo of the roughly contemporary graffito at Gebel Sheikh Suleiman (see fig. 2.2). Defenses such as hilltop lookout positions and the small fortress at Ras Shamra indicate the difficulties that the Egyptians continued to encounter in this region during the Old Kingdom. The Sixth Dynasty autobiography of Pepinakht Heqaib mentions that somewhere along the Red Sea shore nomads massacred an Egyptian expedition that was constructing a Byblos ship destined for Punt, a land far to the south.

Supporting Red Sea naval expeditions was more complex than doing so for those that traveled up the Levantine coast. While the Nile Delta offered water routes directly from the Nile Valley to the Mediterranean, Egyptian ships had to reach the Red Sea overland, through the wadis of the Eastern Desert. Accordingly, a driving philosophy behind Egyptian shipbuilding was ease of disassembly and reassembly, so that ships could be carried, timber by timber, across the desert. Indeed, the Red Sea-based maritime activities, which focused on obtaining mineral resources and on long-distance trade, were so essential to the Egyptians through the New Kingdom that their shipbuilders apparently forwent certain construction techniques in order to retain the overland transportability of their watercraft. Shipwrights are notoriously conservative; ultimately, adherence to this tradition may have prevented native Egyptian shipbuilders from applying certain technologies—such as pegged mortise-and-tenon joinery, which Egyptian carpenters used in the construction of other objects (including boat cabins) and which Egypt's Mediterranean trading partners used for ship hulls—that would have improved the carrying capacity and performance of their ships. This failure to adopt very likely contributed significantly toward Egypt's reliance on foreign shipbuilding traditions and mariners from the late second millennium BCE onward.

The earliest known Egyptian Red Sea port, at Wadi el-Jarf on the Gulf of Suez, dates to the reign of Khufu (fig. 2.3). Situated about 150 km south of Suez, at the eastern end of the Wadi Araba, Wadi el-Jarf took advantage of a local spring for freshwater to support the port itself and the expeditions it launched in search of the vast amounts of copper required for the tools used in the construction of Khufu's pyramid at Giza. It featured well-developed infrastructure, including administrative buildings and a jetty that provided about 3 ha of protected anchorage. In addition to constructing buildings near the shore, the Egyptians cut long, narrow "galleries" into the neighboring hillsides. These artificial caves served as workspace and as storage for supplies such as timber for future expeditions. They became standard features of Red Sea port facilities. Nearly a hundred abandoned stone anchors, some with inventory markings, attest to what must have been seasonally intense and strictly controlled use of the port.

Wadi el-Jarf supported a coastal fortress across the Gulf of Suez, at Tell Ras Budran, which in turn provided security and support for Egyptian mining expeditions in Sinai. Construction of the fortress probably made use of a small fleet of five or so boats to carry stone 4–6 km from a quarry. Wadi el-Jarf and Tell Ras Budran enjoyed only a brief period of use. In the end, Wadi el-Jarf was formally closed and supplanted by a location farther to the north, at Ayn Soukhna, which was in use by the reign of Khafre.

FIGURE 2.3 The jetty at Wadi el-Jarf on the Egyptian Red Sea coast. Fourth Dynasty.

Ayn Soukhna, too, launched expeditions to the Sinai Peninsula, but this, or its predecessor, may have also given Egypt its marine access to the land of Punt, a region to the south and east of Egypt. Although the specifics of its boundaries, which probably fluctuated, are subject to debate, Punt certainly included a portion of the Red Sea coastline of Africa and very possibly of Arabia as well. The Palermo Stone provides the earliest known textual trace of Punt, recording, among other goods, the arrival of 80,000 measures of Punt's most prized export, *ꜥntyw* (perhaps myrrh), during the reign of Sahure (Fifth Dynasty). The decorative program of this king's funerary complex includes imagery of a maritime fleet just returned from the region with incense trees for transplant, a practice that began no later than the reign of Sneferu, founder of the Fourth Dynasty.

The Red Sea allowed the Egyptians to bypass intermediaries who controlled the trading route(s) between Punt and the Upper Nile Valley in Nubia. This river route was most likely the first way by which these regions connected, and Puntite and other Sub-Saharan exotica—including Pygmies—continued to flow into Egypt via the Nile. This was one of the many facets of Nubian trade that prompted Old Kingdom rulers to directly dominate Lower Nubia. A repopulation of Lower Nubia by descendants of the A-Group, referred to archaeologically as the C-Group, began in the Fifth Dynasty, and in Upper Nubia, the kingdom of Kerma was on the rise. The transportation and support of Egyptian troops (for example, those stationed at the riverside fortresses at Buhen and Kuban), as well as the extraction and conveyance of building stone and other wealth obtained within or through Nubia to the Egyptian royal centers, were boat-intensive ventures. To facilitate them, in the mid-Sixth Dynasty navigation canals were cut at the first cataract.

Egyptian trade with all of its neighbors dwindled as the Old Kingdom declined into the First Intermediate Period. The autobiography of a local warlord, Ankhtifi, in his tomb at Mo'alla (south of Thebes) declares the export of barley from his territory to Lower Nubia, but Egyptian goods appear not to have reached Upper Nubia. In the *Admonitions of Ipuwer*, a later Middle Kingdom text perhaps reflecting back on First Intermediate Period circumstances, the failure of ships to sail to Byblos signifies how far Egypt had fallen. While evidence of contact between Egypt and the Aegean during this time suggests that Egypt's maritime trade did not entirely cease, its ebb during this period almost certainly resulted from the absence of a strong centralized state entity. Currently there is little evidence that private individuals could amass the resources—and, indeed, assume the risks—necessary to launch private seaborne trading ventures with regularity or on a large enough scale to compete directly with the enterprises of kings and temples before the New Kingdom. Seafaring endeavors carry an inherently high risk, as every ship that sets sail may be lost.

With the reunification of Egypt and rise of the Middle Kingdom after a century or so, vigorous exploitation of the seas and the upper reaches of the Nile resumed. Middle Kingdom rulers sailed up the Nile "to vanquish Lower Nubia" and even farther, into Kush, and they returned victorious on the current. The establishment of a string of river fortresses—expanding on those of the Old Kingdom—provided for a permanent Egyptian presence that could once again exploit the regional resources and control trade. For example, after a campaign in Nubia in his eighth year, Senwosret III ordered cleared what was probably an Old Kingdom canal. This eased the transport of wealth resulting from his expansion of Egypt's reach into Nubia and enabled more efficient provisioning of the fortresses. These were positioned along the river as far south as Semna, at the southern end of the second cataract; Semna became a transshipment point beyond which no Nubian *k3i* boats were allowed to travel unless bound for the fortress at Mirgissa for trade. One portion of the second cataract posed a particularly difficult navigational challenge. This began at Mirgissa, so here the Egyptians undertook construction of a mud-surfaced, overland slipway across the desert that ran perhaps 5 km northward. In operation for centuries, it allowed teams of animals or men to drag watercraft around the worst of the rapids.

Egypt's naval power extended northward as well. In the Sixth Dynasty, ships had delivered troops to a trouble spot in Canaan, and such naval activity in the Levant resumed with the Middle Kingdom. In the late Eleventh Dynasty, during the reign of Nebhepetre Mentuhotep, a ship-borne expedition overthrew Asiatics in a place called Djaty (probably an Egyptian locality, but potentially in Asia). Amenemhat I, first king of the Twelfth Dynasty, sent a fleet of twenty warships built of coniferous (*ʿš*) wood against those who resisted the reunification, possibly holdouts in the northeastern Nile Delta. The Mit Rahina inscription of Amenemhat II describes the dispatch and return of several expeditions along the Levantine coast, as well as the cargos (nominally tribute) and captives with which they returned. Some of these traveled indisputably by sea. The substantial amount of *ʿš* wood brought back testifies to the continued Egyptian need or desire for quality timber. Interestingly, this wood came not specifically from Egypt's ancient trading partner Byblos but rather from Khenty-She (probably Lebanon).

The nature of Egypt's contact with some foreign localities is conjectural. One of the place names in the Mit Rahina inscription is *I3sii*, which has been suggested as precursor of "Alashiya," that is, Cyprus. Although the island lay easily within the reach of Egyptian shipping technology of the period, evidence for direct trade between Middle Kingdom Egypt and Cyprus is lacking. Similarly, whether the exchanges that resulted in the presence of Aegean wares in Egypt were primarily direct, with ships that traveled between the Aegean and Egyptian Delta ports, or took place at an intermediary site such as Byblos, as was likely the case in the Old Kingdom, remains a subject of much speculation.

The trade that Byblos itself enjoyed with Egypt was sufficiently important that its rulers Egyptianized their titulary, monuments, and other significant aspects of their worldview.

The renewed sea trade was a factor that spurred changes in settlement patterns in the Levant. Here, during the Middle Kingdom (Middle Bronze Age IIA), coastal sites came to dominate and once again draw material resources from internal regions into the cycle of eastern Mediterranean trade. Egypt's participation in these networks resulted in archaeologically attested use of Lebanese cedar for boats (fig. 2.4) and coffins, Asiatic and Aegean goods dispersed along the length of the Nile, and, to a lesser extent, Egyptian exports in foreign locations. In Egypt, this economic growth benefited not only the king but also an expanded bureaucratic class. However, the extremely Egyptocentric nature of the Egyptian worldview likely accounts for a relative scarcity of textual evidence for sea-based foreign engagement. Iconographic sources are even rarer, although the funerary temple of Nebhepetre Mentuhotep at Deir el-Bahri may have featured maritime scenes comparable those to his ancient predecessor Sahure (at Abusir) and his much later successor, Hatshepsut (also at Deir el-Bahri).

The Egyptians reestablished their Red Sea trade as well during this period. Perhaps as early as the Eleventh Dynasty, coincident with quarrying expeditions in the Eastern Desert, activity resumed at Ayn Soukhna, reopening the Old Kingdom route to obtain the turquoise and copper of Sinai and to access the southern Red Sea trade with Punt. But the flourishing nexus of Middle Kingdom operations on the Red Sea became *S3ww*, the sheltered natural bay available in ancient times at a site today known as Mersa/Wadi Gawasis, far south of Ayn Soukhna. First used during the Old Kingdom, this site was reached from Koptos via the Wadi Qena. As at other pharaonic Red Sea ports, infrastructure included galleries cut into the limestone cliffs, but here no

FIGURE 2.4 Boat built of imported cedar. From the pyramid complex of Senwosret III at Dahshur, now in the Egyptian Museum, Cairo; Twelfth Dynasty.

constructed architecture was provided other than shrines, which incorporated stone anchors and the local coral conglomerate. Expedition personnel were, instead, housed in temporary structures, perhaps tents. Administrative and other texts reveal that the institutions and individuals responsible for supporting these expeditions extended beyond the palace to include the king's funerary establishment and the mayor of Thebes.

Finds of Canaanite and Minoan pottery hint that the crews might have included foreign sailors. However, because the Minoan wares were found only as votive offerings, Egyptians themselves might have deposited these objects, as this practice is known elsewhere in Egypt. Nubians and southern Arabians seem to have been present here, too, as indicated by cooking wares, although their purpose (crew? traders? nomadic visitors?) remains open to conjecture. Regardless of the specifics, even at a remote bay on the Red Sea shore without permanent habitation, human activity had a distinctly international flavor.

Eventually the Red Sea facilities fell into disuse: as the Middle Kingdom waned, so did Egypt's maritime activities. No expeditions to Sinai are known for this period after the reign of Amenemhat IV. At Ayn Soukhna, someone—perhaps Egyptians, perhaps nomads—destroyed the timbers for two boats stored in the galleries. But if Red Sea trade ceased in late Middle Kingdom, Mediterranean did not.

In the northeastern Delta, a rival dynasty of Asiatics had taken hold. Coexisting with the Egyptian Thirteenth Dynasty, this foreign Fourteenth Dynasty might have had its capital at Avaris (Tell el-Dab'a), which would become an important Nilotic port with access to the Mediterranean. Despite this presence, the Thirteenth Dynasty was able to maintain its ties to the Levant, including Byblos (from which it was able to obtain timber), but the wider eastern Mediterranean perhaps lay beyond its reach.

The Thirteenth Dynasty did, via the Nile, have direct access to Nubia and its rich resources, but the Egyptians had begun to scale back their presence there even in the Twelfth Dynasty. The burgeoning Kushite kingdom, centered at Kerma, gained the loyalties of Egyptians who had lived for generations at some of the Nubian forts, while Nubian populations settled into others that the Egyptians had abandoned. Although the Thirteenth Dynasty had territorial control over the Nile River Valley, the Kushites and the Fourteenth Dynasty traded and even participated in diplomatic marriage.

The Second Intermediate Period that followed the Thirteenth Dynasty is not well understood. Another Asiatic dynasty, the so-called Hyksos, now ruled the northeastern Delta from Avaris. The Hyksos made significant territorial advances southward but seem to have lost the river connection with Kerma: native Egyptian rulers remained stubbornly in control of the Nile between Abydos and the first cataract, but these dynasties, centered at Thebes and briefly at Abydos, were effectively landlocked. An expedition through the Eastern Desert to the Red Sea remained the only potential access for Egyptian maritime traffic, and no evidence of Red Sea travel for this period has yet been recovered.

But for the Hyksos, Mediterranean maritime trade flourished. For the first time, Cyprus became a major trading partner with Egypt. In the harbor at Avaris might be found "hundreds of ships of new cedar filled with gold, lapis lazuli, silver, turquoise, bronze axes without number, apart from the moringa-oil, incense, fat, honey, *itrn*-wood, *ssndm*-wood, spny-wood, and all their [other] precious woods, and all the good products of Retenu (i.e., Canaan and Syria)." This is the treasure captured by Kamose, a native Theban king who sailed his navy from Upper Egypt to Avaris to vanquish his Hyksos rivals. It is telling that one of Kamose's acts against the Hyksos was destruction of every ship in the harbor, not all of which would have been Hyksos. Whatever wealth foreign polities might have lost during this violent reentry of a reunified Egypt into the eastern Mediterranean, the resulting market would more than compensate. The great international economy of the Late Bronze Age was about to blossom.

Nonetheless Egypt's first major military push remained on the Nile: the second king of the Eighteenth Dynasty, Amenhotep I, sailed upstream to seize Nubia and thereby secure a stream of revenue—most importantly, gold—from its nearest neighbor. Naval operations, which ultimately reached as far as the fourth cataract, necessarily supported Egyptian campaigns that left the river to penetrate the desert wadis in search of raw minerals. Amenhotep I's successor, Thutmose I, renewed a Middle Kingdom canal (itself perhaps an Old Kingdom remnant) that had become blocked with stones due to neglect during the Second Intermediate Period. With its southern border secured and passage cleared, for the first time Egypt sought to control lands far beyond the Nile.

Records of Egyptian maritime contacts at this time are the most plentiful in all of pharaonic history. Expeditions to Punt via the Red Sea played a significant role in New Kingdom politics. Thutmose I's daughter, Hatshepsut, declared that the god Amun had ordered her to launch a Red Sea fleet to reopen trade with Punt. This was part of an ambitious program of legitimation for her rule that incorporated an array of domestic institutions: the priests of Amun, the army, and the administration of Lower Egypt. Puntite incense and other exotica brought back from the shores of the southern Red Sea benefited particularly the cult of Amun and its growing social and political prominence. Just as important, this grand maritime undertaking provided a practical exhibition of her ability to exercise royal power. Successful organization of such an expedition—ships, crews (sailors, soldiers, administrators), provisions—could not be achieved by a weak monarch. The Punt trade continued through subsequent reigns, but the religious pretext offered by Hatshepsut dissipated. Her ships carried goods purported to be divine offerings, but by the reign of Ramesses III in the Twentieth Dynasty, the Red Sea fleet sailed on trade missions "laden with the products of Egypt without number and of all kinds." The reappearance of Egyptian ships in the southern Red Sea may have spurred the

Puntites themselves to seek to trade with Egypt. Puntites had been known in Egypt since they arrived on Egyptian ships in the Old Kingdom, but the New Kingdom provides the earliest evidence that they might have traveled aboard their own watercraft to either Egypt or a region controlled by Egyptians.

While Hatshepsut's activities concentrated on the south, her co-regent and stepson, Thutmose III, actively engaged in military exploits in the Mediterranean region. He campaigned from the Sinai to as far north as modern Turkey and far inland, beyond the Euphrates River in modern Syria. During most of these campaigns Thutmose III used ships, including those captured in enemy harbors. His army was even able to construct, or have constructed, in the field boats that carts then transported (as individual timbers or perhaps sections) to the Euphrates riverbank, where the troops used them for crossing into Mitanni. It is under Thutmose III, with his robust navy, that Egypt's borders reached their greatest extent.

The degree to which military operations in the Levant were naval—that is, reliant on ships for transport of infantry, chariots, prisoners, booty, and so on—is not explicit in the monumental texts that commemorate Egyptian military campaigns there. The sea and foreign shores and islands appear in the pharaonic vocabulary of dominance, which asserted that the Egyptian king's mastery extended over them. The extremes of these claims—domination of the Aegean, for example—are rhetorical only, but they relied on a genuine potential represented by the Egyptian fleet. The ships that would have been employed in either actual or metaphoric military engagements were not warships in the later, Classical sense of, for example, triremes outfitted with rams; rather, they were ships of logistics. The relatively scanty references to boats in the "Annals" of Thutmose III likely belies their fundamental role in Egyptian successes in eastern Mediterranean territorial expansion. Jar sealings found at sites along the Ways of Horus (the land route that traced the coast between the northeastern Nile Delta and the Levant) give the names of ships that must have plied these waters. Such names, shared with military units, reflect a close association between soldiers and their transports. To better administer Egypt's holdings in Asia, and to guard its vulnerable northeastern border, for much of the New Kingdom pharaohs occupied royal cities in this region. The Ramessides even moved the capital to Piramesse (Qantir), a harbor city immediately downstream of the old Hyksos city of Avaris on the Nile's easternmost branch, the Pelusiac, in the Delta.

The ships that came and went from these Nile ports were not limited to naval vessels on military expeditions (fig. 2.5). Egypt was a significant economic participant in the Mediterranean's dynamic, multicultural maritime traffic both as supplier (especially of gold and grain) and consumer (of almost everything). The Late Bronze Age Uluburun shipwreck, lost off the southwestern coast of Turkey in the second half of the fourteenth century BCE, provides the clearest example of the complexity of maritime trade networks of this time. Study of

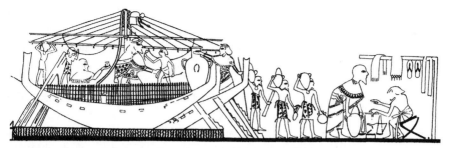

FIGURE 2.5 Syrian merchant ships arriving at an Egyptian market. Wall painting from Theban Tomb 162 (Kenamun); Eighteenth Dynasty.

the ship and its cargo has redefined our understanding of the vast interconnections in the eastern Mediterranean during the late Eighteenth Dynasty.

The ship was lost with a full cargo, consisting of thousands of items from Cyprus, Greece, the Levant, Egypt, and other regions as far away as northern Europe. It appears to have been a royal dispatch westbound from the Carmel Coast (northern Israel) to a single but unknown destination, laden with a rich cargo of both raw and manufactured goods. Exotic raw materials aboard included glass ingots, ostrich eggshells, and hippopotamus tusks from Egypt. The small but significant manufactured luxury cargo included gold jewelry (for example, a scarab naming Nefertiti), worked ivory, beads of glass and faience, and semiprecious stones. Bulk cargo included more "everyday" commodities such copper (10 tons) and tin (1 ton), likely intended for bronze production, as well as Cypriot pottery and various foodstuffs. The entire cargo appears to have been under the escort of two armed Mycenaeans, likely aboard to see the ship to harbor somewhere in the Aegean. While this ship was neither Egyptian nor carrying an Egyptian crew nor intended for an Egyptian destination, the wreck exemplifies the totality of interconnected life among Mediterranean cultures—including Egypt—at the time. None lived, struggled, or thrived independent of the others.

Egypt's Mediterranean network was based on exchange with the Syro-Canaanite coast (modern Lebanon and Syria) and the Aegean. While most of this trade seems to have focused on ports in the Nile Delta, the site of Marsa Matruh, far to the west in coastal Marmarica (near the modern border of Libya and Egypt), demonstrates that even Western Desert nomads participated directly in maritime transactions. At this isolated harbor, ships—seemingly often of Cypriote origin—likely sailing down from Crete could stop to engage in small trade and probably refit and resupply. During the reign of Ramesses II and perhaps into that of Merenptah, the Egyptians established and maintained at least one fortress along this coastline. Supported in part by deliveries that arrived by sea, the fortress at Zawiyet Umm el-Rakham perhaps controlled the coastal land route westward of Marsa Matruh, which new Libyan populations might now have threatened. It is at Marsa Matruh, on Bates's Island, that rare evidence of private trade, undertaken by sailors or passengers accompanying what were likely state-sponsored maritime missions, can be found. Such commerce must have been commonplace, but in the archaeological record it is all but invisible.

Since the Egyptians were often engaged in hostilities in the Levant, the Aegean connection became increasingly important. Although Egyptian transport jars have been found in the Aegean only at the Cretan harbor of Kommos, these two regions had established regular, direct trade by the early Eighteenth Dynasty. This led to increased cultural and technological diffusion, well evidenced by archaeological finds in both areas. During the reign of Amenhotep III, an Egyptian diplomatic mission traveled throughout the Aegean. The Egyptians hired Aegeans as mercenaries and also appeared to provide them with significant access for trade within Egypt. Several private Egyptian tombs depict Aegeans (Minoans and Mycenaeans) presenting their goods in Egypt. When not hostile to Egypt, Syro-Canaanite city-states were likewise allowed substantial access to the Nile for trade. They, too, are depicted in tombs, conducting ship-based trade in the heart of Egypt.

The appearance of foreign merchant ships in Egyptian tombs largely ignores the export activities of Egyptian ships and crews. Export tends to be neglected in iconography focused on expressing what was coming *into* Egypt. The Papyrus Harris I hints at the extent of the Egyptian merchant fleet under Ramesses III not only with its description of Red Sea ships laden with goods but also with its mention of more than eighty seagoing ships of different types, complete with crews, granted to the temple of Amun in Thebes. These *krr, mnš,* and bꜣr ships were to "transport the goods of the land of Djahy [i.e., Asia] and lands at the ends of the world" to the temple treasury. These ships explicitly carried armed contingents. The conditions in which international commerce took place in the eastern Mediterranean were changing.

Texts and temple reliefs from Medinet Habu dating to the eighth year of Ramesses III's reign depict a great naval battle in which foreign tribes conventionally called the "Sea Peoples" attempted to invade but met with defeat. A conglomeration of ethnic groups from the Aegean and Anatolia, the Sea Peoples had threatened shipping in the region for generations. This particular battle may have taken place in the lagoon at the end of the ancient Pelusiac branch of the Nile, near the fortified site of Tell el-Borg on the Ways of Horus. The commemorative scene of the battle, a relief on an outer wall of Ramesses III's temple at Medinet Habu, depicts the Egyptian navy visually as ships of perhaps foreign influence manned by foreign mercenaries. (The scene shows only one of the three Egyptian ship types—perhaps the ꜥḥꜥ—specified in the accompanying text.)

The presence of foreign shipwrights and sailors in New Kingdom Egypt is little doubted. The worship of Baal and Astarte at Perunefer, a (or the) major harbor of the New Kingdom, suggests the involvement of Levantine individuals in operations there even during the mid-Eighteenth Dynasty, for example, but the degree to which Egyptian shipbuilding at this period had adopted significant foreign elements remains uncertain. No seagoing ships from the New Kingdom, Egyptian or otherwise, have yet been recovered in Egypt.

Despite Ramesses III's Red Sea fleet, during this time maritime trade with Punt dwindled, perhaps as overland routes down the Arabian Peninsula took precedence. Half a millennium later, Punt was little more than legend.

The literary composition known as *The Report of Wenamun* provides further evidence of the disintegration of Egyptian maritime capability and consequent dominance by Egypt's former vassals. Set at the opening of the Third Intermediate Period, it purports to be an account written by an Egyptian priest who meets with robbery and further disrespect while on a mission to obtain timbers to build a sacred boat. His treatment at the hands of local rulers and the difficulty he experiences in his mission at Byblos suggest that Egypt's navy posed no credible threat, nor was its maritime trade particularly valued, even by its longtime partner.

During the Late Period, a series of invasions often with naval components resulted in a periodic succession of foreign rulers laying claim to Egypt. Ships were instrumental in the subjugation of Egypt by Piye of Kush, and, later, by Ashurbanipal of Assyria. The native Egyptian kings of the Twenty-sixth Dynasty regained some of Egypt's former maritime status, but only with the aid of foreign mercenaries and shipbuilding technology in the form of warships, including triremes. International trade, highly regulated and carried out chiefly by Greeks and Phoenicians, formed an important component of Egypt's flourishing economy; trading settlements, including notably Thonis (Herakleion) and its upstream counterpart, Naukratis, through which Greek trade was obligated to pass, were established in the Delta during this period.

In the 6th century BCE Egypt fell prey to the Achaemenid Persian Empire, which likewise had Greek warships and crews among its forces. So that ships might travel directly between the Persian Gulf and Nile River, Darius I completed a canal between the eastern Delta and the Red Sea, a feat of engineering perhaps initiated and abandoned in the Twenty-sixth Dynasty. This endeavor seems to have contributed little to Red Sea commerce and likely played a greater political and military role. International trade continued to thrive not only through the Delta but also at the Nubian border; documents written in Aramaic reveal details of private, state, and temple shipping ventures at Aswan (Elephantine), a cosmopolitan community that in this period included Persians, Jews, Carians, and others. This First Persian Occupation was followed by less than a century of native Egyptian rule during which international maritime trade was again strictly administered and taxed and the Mediterranean coastline was increasingly fortified. Nonetheless, the Persians reclaimed Egypt, but only for a decade or so; in 332 BCE they succumbed to the overland advance of Alexander the Great and his supporting fleet. Claimants to the pharaonic tradition, Ptolemaic Greek rulers would give Egypt the largest navy in the region (purportedly 1,500 ships), its farthest reach of direct trade (India), and its most famous maritime accomplishment (the lighthouse of Alexandria).

Thus Greek and other foreign seafaring practices largely eclipsed those that had developed on the Nile, but Egypt's coveted glory—which remained undiminished until its loss at the naval battle of Actium in 31 BCE reduced the kingdom to a Roman province—was the legacy of its most ancient pharaonic maritime traditions.

3 }

Pathways to Distant Kingdoms

LAND CONNECTIONS

Gregory Mumford

Introduction

Despite Egypt's frequent exploitation of the Nile, its diverse other waterways (e.g., lakes, ponds, marshes), and the Red Sea and Mediterranean for local through long-distance interactions with the surrounding world, the Egyptians and other peoples actually used overland routes quite commonly and increasingly for passage between a broad network of near-to-distant regions, polities, and peoples, often combining riverine, maritime, and overland transport (e.g., portaging boats around impassable stretches in the Nile; ferrying personnel across rivers, lakes, and sea). Although the nature, scope, routes, and carriers of overland interactions changed over time, from prehistory to the pharaonic period (and later), these local through long-distance ventures included such objectives as obtaining and redistributing non-indigenous raw materials and products, mining metals and minerals, quarrying stone, prospecting for new resources, scouting and securing key areas and regions (e.g., desert patrols), maintaining communications (e.g., keeping in touch with remote garrisons, desert patrols, and expeditions), diplomacy (e.g., dispatching regular messengers and special emissaries; escorting foreign dignitaries, princesses, and their entourages to Egypt), trade, transitory military activities (e.g., small-scale raids, campaigns), and long-term settlement and colonization (i.e., imperialism in Nubia, the Levant, and western oases). The means employed for traveling overland also varied widely according to the specific locality, distance, time period, and their varying requirements, including foot traffic, transportation in litters, chariots, and other vehicles, riding donkeys, horses, and (later) camels, and utilizing porters, pack animals, and ox-drawn sleds, carts, and wagons for carrying heavy loads. The types of overland routes, terrain, and cultural landscapes varied greatly too, ranging from deserts to savannah lands, marshes, forests, cultivated lands, and plains and mountains, encompassing infrequent to well-traveled ways, natural and prepared roadways, and traversing routes with minimal natural amenities (e.g., springs, oases) to better-appointed trails containing artificial wells, way stations, forts, villages, towns, and cities. This paper examines Ancient Egypt's land connections and relations with Nubia and sub-Saharan Africa, the Western Desert, Eastern Desert, Sinai, Arabia, and Near East, providing a synthesis on the diverse land routes, travel, travelers, objectives, interactions, and commodities exchanged between Egypt and its neighbors, and addresses some changes in the relations between these regions during the Predynastic through pharaonic periods.

* * *

Egypt interacted with its neighbors using different and frequently complex routes that combined land and water travel across northeast Africa, Arabia, and the Near East (southwest Asia). The routes varied and changed, and included complex networks of alternate and separate trails running parallel to and away from the Nile: trails traversed Nubia and parts of sub-Saharan Africa; overland paths headed into the Western and Eastern Deserts, and crossed the Sinai Peninsula; some land routes incorporated maritime stretches across the Red Sea and east Mediterranean to reach Arabia, parts of sub-Saharan Africa (e.g., Punt), the Levant (Syria-Palestine), and more distant regions (e.g., Anatolia, Mesopotamia). A wide range of peoples, materials, and products traveled these routes and regions, both departing from and entering Egypt, with merchants and others carrying commodities that might originate ultimately from a single source (e.g., Sinaitic turquoise; lapis lazuli from Afghanistan), or multiple sources (e.g., copper from the Eastern Desert of Egypt and Nubia, south Sinai, Timna, Feynan, Cyprus, and elsewhere), often incorporating a complex history of past re-dispersals, ownership, and recycling of various materials and products.

Nubia and Sub-Saharan Africa

Although the Nile played a major role in Egypt's relations with Nubia and parts of sub-Saharan Africa in past millennia, overland travel served a significant role, often in conjunction with riverine transport, but also separate from it (pl. 2). Although Egypt desired the various metals, minerals, flora, fauna, and people available in and via Lower Nubia, Egyptian travel through and often control of this region provided more direct access to Upper Nubia and sub-Saharan Africa (e.g., Yam, Punt, and elsewhere), which furnished greater quantities and more diversity of such wealth, plus choice aromatics and other exotica. During the Predynastic through pharaonic periods, Egyptians, Nubians, and desert tribes utilized several overland routes between southern Egypt and Nubia (e.g., Darb el-Arbain, Elephantine to Sai Island via Selima Oasis), a number of trails from the Nubian Nile to the adjacent desert resources and other destinations (e.g., Kubban to Wadi el-Allaqi, Toshka to diorite quarries), and trails that bypassed several bends in the Nile (e.g., Meheila Road from Kawa to Gebel Barkal/Nuri, Bayuda Road from Nuri to Meroe, Wadis Allaqi and Cabgaba from Kubban to Kurgus). Many Old Kingdom expeditions to Nubia from Elephantine used donkey caravans to head upstream along the Nile, going through less hospitable, arid, narrower, and stony flood plains, bypassing less navigable stretches of the Nile (e.g., the cataracts), and sometimes encountering hostile populations. In some cases Egyptian missions went overland through arid wastelands to several oases, diorite quarries (Gebel el-Asr), gold mines, and other destinations in the adjacent deserts and hill country (e.g., Harkhuf's "Oasis Road"). Egypt controlled and colonized Nubia increasingly during the Middle and New Kingdoms, while in post–New Kingdom Egypt, the Kushites of the Twenty-fifth Dynasty ruled Egypt, intensifying interactions between both cultures. The early Saite kings may have held Lower Nubia, while Psamtik II dispatched a transitory military expedition, including overland segments, as far south as Gebel Barkal in Upper Nubia. Regarding Punt (most likely in/near Eritrea), some pharaonic maritime expeditions along the Red Sea, such as Hatshepsut's famed Eighteenth Dynasty expedition, disembarked and headed inland, navigating forests and hills to harvest aromatics, transplant myrrh trees, fell trees, and obtain other inland, Puntite resources (e.g., minerals, metals, animal skins). In Third Intermediate Period, Kushite, and Saite Period inscriptions, contact with Punt is implied by references to myrrh from it, while one assumes long distance interactions entailing both ships and overland passage into the mountains via either the Red Sea or eastern Sudan and Eritrea.

EGYPTIAN EXPORTS

Egyptian exports to Nubia varied, fluctuated, and increased generally over time. Beginning in the Predynastic to Early Dynastic Period, much Egyptian contact appears in Nubia: pottery containers (for grain, wine, beer, dairy products, and vegetable oils), stone vessels, stone incense burners (e.g., the famed Qustul example), cosmetic utensils (e.g., palettes, unguent jars), weaponry (maceheads, axes), jewelry (e.g., beads, amulets), copper tools (e.g., chisels, adzes, fishhooks, harpoon points), and other things, people, and influences. By the Old Kingdom, Egypt had established a fortified settlement for trade and copper working at Kor (Buhen South) near the second cataract, with further activity at Sai (south of the second cataract) and the Gebel al-Asr diorite quarry (to the west). A late Old Kingdom Meidum bowl sherd appears at Laqiyat al-Arba'in in northwest Sudan, suggesting further overland interactions. In the Middle Kingdom Egypt annexed Lower Nubia, building pairs of fortified settlements along the Nile, and exploited the adjacent deserts for gold, copper, stone, and other resources. Egypt secured Lower Nubia with strategic walling systems at Aswan and the second cataract, multiple forts in the second cataract region, overland slipways for bypassing cataracts (e.g., Mirgissa), and alternated between trading with and periodically fighting the kingdom of Kerma (Kush/Upper Nubia). Egyptian items actually increased at Kerma in this period, including much pottery, stone containers, cosmetic sets, bronze utensils, daggers, and other items, suggesting mostly peaceful and flourishing relations. During the Second Intermediate Period, Egyptian artifacts and influence continued in Lower Nubia, with a greater Nubian presence and material culture among the Egyptian residents in the second cataract forts, which had switched allegiance to the ruler of Kush; Egyptian material culture also reached Kerma and elsewhere in Upper Nubia, consisting of trade items, booty, gifts, art and architecture, and probably Egyptians. The Classic Kerma city and cemetery contain much Egyptian material (e.g., pottery), including statuary and other items probably looted from Lower Nubia and southern Egypt (late Seventeenth Dynasty), plus Hyksos scarabs and Levantine and Aegean pottery. The Kermans also adopted some superficial Egyptian-type forms, motifs, and customs in architecture (e.g., a temple, palace, some burials), construction (e.g., vaulting), decoration, sculpture, furniture, jewelry, utensils, and other artifacts.

At the advent of the New Kingdom, Egypt re-occupied the Middle Kingdom forts in Lower Nubia, creating temple towns and colonies and absorbing the indigenous populace. Egypt expanded settlement in Upper Nubia, but it remained less Egyptianized and more autonomous. The Egyptian state continued exploiting Nubia's Western and Eastern Deserts, building wells, shrines, temples, and other installations along desert trails such as Wadi el-Allaqi. New Kingdom pottery and other items (e.g., seals, calcite vessels) are also found at riverine and inland sites 200–700 km south of Egypt's frontier at Kurgus, to the south and east of Khartoum at Jebel Ardeb, Khor Shangerite, the northern Gabati Plain, Isnabir, Doleib Hill, the Gash region, Mahal Teglinos (near Kassala in eastern central Sudan), and elsewhere. By the late Ramesside period Egypt's occupation of Nubia retreated rapidly toward Aswan. In the post–New Kingdom (Napatan-Meroitic) period, Egyptian-type architecture, statuary, art, iconography, material culture, and other influences emerge in an autonomous Nubia, including temples (e.g., Gebel Barkal), religion and deities (especially the Amun cult), and other components; Egyptian-derived pyramid tombs and chapels are used by Napatan royalty, featuring sarcophagi, religious texts, canopic jars, perhaps mummification, shabtis, scarabs, and other artifacts, with potential exports and influence much farther south, and to the east in Eritrea (e.g., faience amulets, calcite alabastra). These Egyptianizing traits continue into the Meroitic period, with Egyptian/Napatan-type amulets and other artifacts reaching distant inland and riverine sites over 250 km south of Khartoum, such as Gebel Moya (35 km west of the Blue Nile), Abu Geili, Sennar, and elsewhere.

AFRICAN IMPORTS TO EGYPT

During late prehistory through the pharaonic period (and later), Egypt received a wide range of items from Nubia and sub-Saharan Africa (e.g., Yam, Punt), including exotic lumber (e.g., African blackwood; cork wood), transplanted aromatic trees, resins, plants, live animals, animal byproducts, metals, building stone, obsidian, precious and semi-precious stones and minerals, weaponry, utensils, musical instruments (e.g., drums), pottery vessels, leather containers, basketry, furniture, jewelry, and people (e.g., Pygmies; captives; migrants). Many of these items often reflect multiple sources (Nubia, Punt, sub-Saharan Africa, elsewhere) and diverse transmissions via caravans, ships, and combinations of waterways and overland segments in their delivery to Egypt.

The Western Desert and Beyond

Egypt's relations with the Western Desert (pl. 2) extend far back into prehistoric times, when much of this region was wetter and contained savannah land, while reduced and fluctuating interactions with the Sahara and sub-Saharan Africa continued during the increasingly drier and less hospitable pharaonic and later periods. Aside from ancient Egypt's exploitation of the Western Desert's adjacent fringe for burials and quarries, many Egyptian expeditions went much deeper into the Sahara, navigating a range of environments consisting of arid plateaus, sand dunes, hill country, and valleys, including springs, oases, and nomadic desert tribes. Several primary routes and destinations exist by the Old Kingdom and later, including: (1) traffic to Wadi el-Natrun, Khargeh, and Dakhla oases (e.g., Darb el-Tawil route from Beni Adi to eastern Dakhla Oasis); (2) a north–south network of trails traversing these oases to Nubia (e.g., Darb el-Arbain); (3) other more remote routes, such as the Abu Ballas trail leading to Gilf el-Kebir and perhaps northeast Chad and sub-Saharan Africa, and another pathway from Sai to Wadi Uwaynat (which contained a text of Mentuhotep II). Second Intermediate Period and New Kingdom traffic and routes intensified across the Western Desert, and expanded along the Mediterranean coastline to Marsa Matruh (e.g., Bates's Island), including Ramesside forts (e.g., Kom Firin, Zawiyet Umm el-Rakham). Post–New Kingdom and Late Period trails led increasingly to settlements in Farafra Oasis, Siwa Oasis, and Cyrene (Twenty-sixth Dynasty). However, prior to the Ptolemaic–Roman period, the ancient Egyptians apparently seldom traveled farther west than these oases (including Wadi Uwaynat and perhaps Gilf el-Kebir). Instead, Egypt relied mainly upon intermediaries and other networks to reach Kufara Oasis, Cyrene, and other distant places.

Egypt's direct interactions with the Western Desert are still being clarified but involved fewer sources of stone, minerals, and metals than the Eastern

Desert (see below). The ancient Egyptians do not appear to have traversed or settled the Western Desert and its oases until mainly the Old Kingdom (and later). Instead, various semi-nomadic indigenous peoples (e.g., Sheikh Muftah culture, Dakhla Oasis) served as the main means of early communication and trade with the Nile Valley during the Predynastic (c. 5000 BCE) through early Old Kingdom (and in other periods as well). Around 3000 BCE, the Sheikh Muftah culture (Dakhla Oasis) and affiliated desert peoples ranged widely throughout the eastern Sahara. Their activity is attested via "Clayton rings" (enigmatic small pottery tubes and perforated disks) found at oasis sites, along Western Desert routes, and some Eastern Desert localities. In the late Old Kingdom, the Abu Ballas Trail may have extended to Gebel Uwaynat, and possibly onward as an alternate Egyptian overland route to Yam in Nubia. This trail features a series of depots spaced roughly three days' journey apart (75–90 km) and stocked by donkey caravans with a few dozen to sometimes hundreds of large pottery jars (mainly for storing about 30 liters of water, but also attested holding barley and perhaps other provisions), alongside occasional baskets of locusts and other items, to enable travel across an otherwise mostly barren landscape. A few depots also contained temporary shelters, hearths, bread vats, drinking cups, flint tools, and Senet game boards. Egyptian activity increases in the Middle Kingdom (e.g., cultivating the Fayum) and New Kingdom, while traces of a New Kingdom temple lie beneath a Late Period temple at Hibis in Kharga Oasis. In the Late Period, Egypt expanded its Western Desert activities, building temples in Kharga, Dakhleh, and elsewhere, and influencing the indigenous peoples in Siwah Oasis: Egyptian architectural and decorative elements are evident in a small chapel and mortuary temple built for the Ammonian ruler, Wenamun, at Umm Ubaydah (temp. Nectanebo I–II), but it was built by Greek stonemasons and artists from Cyrenaica. In contrast, both the Egyptian and Greek languages were reportedly used in Late Period Siwah.

EGYPTIAN EXPORTS

During much of the pharaonic period, Egyptian Nile Valley culture is transplanted to and flourished in key localities in the Western Desert oases, including the establishment of Egyptian administrative and related settlements at Ayn el-Gazzareen (near el-Qasr), Mut el-Kharab, and Balat (Dakhla Oasis), Hibis (Kharga), and elsewhere. Egypt also interacted with the indigenous peoples of the oases and surrounding desert. Egyptians settled increasingly in key places in the Western Desert, utilizing seasonal camps, small outposts, police patrols, and large fortified settlements with administrative quarters, housing, workshops, shrines, tombs, and a full range of material culture such as at Balat in Dakhla Oasis during the late Old Kingdom and subsequent periods. These Egyptian residents initially brought much of their material culture with them and settled, utilizing both local fabrics (oasis ware) and provisions alongside continuing influxes of Nile Valley technology, products, commodities, and culture.

WESTERN DESERT IMPORTS TO EGYPT

In the later Holocene, during which the Western Desert had a wetter and more savannah-type environment, cattle domestication occurs in Nabta Playa and the Western Desert in general. During the post-Holocene period of increasing aridity, such innovations, plus apparently some sub-Saharan flora and migrants, shifted to and settled in the Nile Valley. The oases remained fairly fertile in fauna and flora, however, and served as rich resources for the Nile Valley in pharaonic times. The Middle Kingdom *Tale of the Eloquent Peasant* summarizes the typical oases products sent to the Nile Valley from both the Wadi Natrun (Sekhet-Hemat / "Field of Salt"), and other Western Desert commodities: salt, natron, stones, wood from Hestiu?-country, reeds, many types of plants, herbs, berries(?), *inst*-seeds, birds, animal hides, and staves of Ta-Menment ("Cattle Country": Farafra Oasis). Additional typical Western Desert exports known in the pharaonic period include various types of salt, some wood, plants (e.g., silphium), diverse agricultural products, especially wine, mineral pigments, "shining stone" (*thnt*), Libyan "desert glass" (perhaps *mf3t?*), livestock (e.g., sheep and goats), animal byproducts (e.g., leopard skins; ostrich eggs and feathers), and some finished products (e.g., decorated containers). Sub-Saharan products were also obtained via the Western Desert and included such things as gold, ivory, ostrich feathers, and perhaps slaves, all of which are attested in trans-Saharan trade in the late pharaonic through more recent periods.

The Eastern Desert and Beyond

The ancient Egyptians utilized the adjacent Eastern Desert (pl. 2) for burial grounds and quarries along its fringes (e.g., Tura, Gebel el-Silsila), but forged much deeper into its wadis and hills to quarry stone, mine metals and minerals, and hunt wild game. Despite its misleading appellation, the Eastern Desert hill country and valleys also contain a wide range of fauna, flora, springs, oases, and Bedouin residents. Multiple wadi networks offered natural, hard-packed, stony "roadways" and access to the Eastern Desert's resources, including a series of interconnecting valleys from (1) Memphis/Helwan to Ayn Soukhna, (2) Beni Suef and Wadi 'Araba to Wadi el-Jarf, (3) Koptos and Wadi Qena to Gebel Zeit, (4) Koptos via Wadi Hamama to Safaga (near Mersa Gawasis), (5) Koptos and the Wadi Hammamat to Quseir, (6) Edfu to Mersa Alam, (7) Kom Ombo to Mersa Alam, and (8) Elephantine to Wadi el-Hudi. In addition, many expeditions traversed the Eastern Desert to reach key points along the Red Sea coastline (e.g., Ayn Soukhna, Wadi el-Jarf), from which they often crossed the Red Sea to el-Markha Plain in south Sinai, and resumed overland travel to mine copper, malachite, and turquoise inland at Wadi Maghara, Wadi Kharig, and Serabit el-Khadim. Other Red Sea destinations included the southern Arabah (Ramesside Atika?), Eritrea / northern Ethiopia (Punt), and perhaps Arabia (via Mersa Gawasis), which incorporated both maritime and overland routes. Red Sea expeditions to Punt commonly utilized overland travel from the Qena Bend (Koptos) to Red Sea ports (e.g., Mersa Gawasis) and often continued overland passage from various landing points in Punt, heading inland to the hill slopes ("terraces") to obtain myrrh and other resources from "God's Land."

EGYPTIAN EXPORTS

During much of the pharaonic period, the bulk of Egypt's exports to the Eastern Desert consisted of transitory expeditions, equipment, and supplies, some construction of permanent and seasonal installations (e.g., wells, shrines, monuments, forts, camps), and varying associations with the indigenous inhabitants of this region. The interactions with the local Bedouin ranged from peaceful (i.e., non-hostile), to the inclusion of some Bedu guides and labor in other expeditions, to open hostility, such as Egyptian pre-emptive and retaliatory attacks upon Bedouin campsites and wells (e.g., Sety I; Ramesses II).

EASTERN DESERT IMPORTS TO EGYPT

The Eastern Desert hill country, wadis, and coast served as sources and conduits through which Egypt obtained many different products: metals (e.g., copper; electrum; gold), minerals (e.g., malachite; galena), semi-precious and precious stones (e.g., amazonite; Roman emerald mining), building stone (e.g., limestone; sandstone; basalt; granite; calcite ["alabaster"]), wild game (e.g., antelopes), animal byproducts (e.g., hides), Red Sea items (shells; coral; sea urchin spines), and Sinaitic, Puntite, and southwest Arabian products (see above and below). The Bedu also pastured their flocks in the flood plain.

The Sinai Peninsula and Beyond

Egypt's eastern Delta had direct access to the Sinai land bridge, which, like Egypt's neighboring "deserts," also contained diverse topography (e.g., mountains, plains, valleys), flora (e.g., scrub land, savannah, some forests), fauna (e.g., gazelles, ostriches, giraffes, hyena), water sources (e.g., springs, oases), and micro- to macro-environments and climatic conditions (e.g., arid desert plains to snow-capped mountains). The Sinai Peninsula joined northeast Africa to southwest Asia and contained three significant routes (pl. 3). The two southernmost routes appear to have been used periodically as an alternate means of traversing the Wadi Tumilat and southern Isthmus of Suez, especially in the Ramesside Period (see below). Egyptian travel to southwest Sinai began in the late Predynastic period, continuing throughout the Old, Middle, and New Kingdoms, and departed mainly from the Memphite region (including Middle Kingdom Itj-tawy), to cross the Eastern Desert, Red Sea, and Markha Plain to reach the turquoise and copper mines at Maghara, Kharig, Serabit el-Khadim, and other sites. During the Ramesside Period, overland expeditions left from the residence at Piramesse in the northeastern Delta, or Tjaru, passing by a well at Gebel Mourr (where Ramesses II erected a commemorative stela) and a small stone shrine and well at Gebel Abu Hassa (built and maintained during the reigns of Sety I and Ramesses II), to reach a Ramesside coastal fort at Kom el-Qolzoum (Suez). This southern terminus facilitated Ramesside missions to south Sinai, the southern Arabah, and northwest Arabia. A stela from Gebel Abu Hassa mentions "Hathor, Mistress of Turquoise." This attests to some Ramesside travel to the turquoise and copper mining region in south Sinai, including Wadi Maghara, Serabit el-Khadim, and Reqeita. The presence of some copper working at a Late Bronze Age site in western Sinai, roughly midway between Kom el-Qolzoum and Markha Plain, suggests that some travel took place overland; other ventures may have used ships for a portion of the trip. In addition, a reference to one or more turquoise and copper mining expeditions led by a mayor of Tjaru, which is now equated with Tell Heboua in northwest Sinai, reveals greater complexities in the network of routes used to reach south Sinai and other destinations. The Ramesside fort at Kom el-Qolzoum (Suez) also apparently facilitated some overland travel along the Tih Plateau and central Sinai to the Timna copper mining region in the southern Arabah during the reign of Ramesses III: His expedition(s) are attested by rock-cut texts at Wadi Abu Gada (southeast of Kom el-Qolzoum) and Themilat Radadi (Borot Roded, site 582; northwest of Aqabah). The recent discovery of rock-cut cartouches of Ramesses III near Tayma' Oasis, plus Egyptian containers, figurines, and a scarab from a shrine/structure in Area O at Tayma', implies that at least one or more Ramesside expeditions traveled fairly far overland into northwest Arabia, presumably to obtain southwest Arabian aromatics from one or more intermediary.

North Sinai, however, served as the most important long-term and continuously used overland route, called the "Ways of Horus," linking northeast Africa and southwest Asia. This northern land passage began near the mouth of the Nile's Pelusiac branch and a series of lagoons ("the Dividing Waters") and crossed a 220 km long coastal stretch until reaching the region of Gaza, at which point travelers could utilize a wide combination of coastal and inland trails to reach different objectives in the plains, foothills, and hill country of the Levant (and beyond). The sand dunes that typify North Sinai today are mainly a post-pharaonic development, while this coastal region featured various springs, wadis, oases, and other natural rest stops, including Wadi el-Arish.

North Sinai also received a variety of defensive, administrative, and other support facilities over time for travelers, including Early Bronze Age and Old Kingdom campsites, the more elusive Middle Kingdom "Walls of the Ruler," a Hyksos stronghold at Tjaru (Tell Hebou I), New Kingdom campsites, outposts, forts, magazines, granaries, and reservoirs along the Ways of Horus (e.g., Heboua, Tell Borg, Bir el-Abd, Haruba [near el-Arish], Raphia, Deir el-Balah), Assyrian forts (Abu Salima/Sheikh Zuweid), Saite and Persian Period fortifications, canals, and sites (e.g., Tell Defenneh, Tell Qedwa, Tell el-Herr, Tell el-Ghaba, Tell er-Ruqeish), a Bronze Age through Iron Age anchorage and later stone quay at Tell Ridan and offshore Jezirat Ridan (which probably facilitated seaborne supplies), and other Late Period installations and fortifications (e.g., Tell Abu Sefah, Pelusium).

EGYPTIAN EXPORTS

Most Egyptian exports to Sinai facilitated Egyptian outposts, way stations, seasonal mining camps, cultic complexes (e.g., the Hathor temple at Serabit el-Khadim), and other installations, with relatively few items reaching the indigenous population. However, some Predynastic Egyptian-type artifacts (e.g., carnelian beads) may occur in the Chalcolithic *nawami* tombs in southeast Sinai, while late Predynastic to First Dynasty Egyptian graffiti (Wadi 'Amayra) and calcite containers, pottery vessels, and their contents (i.e., presumably unguents and foodstuffs) are attested at several indigenous seasonal campsites in southwest Sinai. During the late Chalcolithic to Early Bronze Age I, some Egyptian and Egyptian-type items appear at Tall Hujayrat al-Ghuzlan near Aqaba (e.g., Nile shells, incense burners?, a macehead, some flint tools). During subsequent periods, Egyptian products appear in varying quantities alongside Canaanite and other material culture at sites across north Sinai and the Negev. Much Middle through New Kingdom activity is attested in south Sinai, especially in the Hathor temple at Serabit el-Khadim, and the Ramesside Hathor shrine at Timna, to which mining expeditions brought numerous votives. Otherwise, Egyptian material culture in Sinai coincides with the main periods of Egypt's domination of various parts of this region, especially during the New Kingdom. The newly attested Ramesside overland foray into northwest Arabia (i.e., Tayma) via the southern Arabah, and other Egyptian items from Western Arabia (e.g., New Kingdom and later ex situ seals and amulets) suggest an early emergence of trade with Arabia, particularly in southwest Arabian incense.

SINAITIC AND ARABIAN IMPORTS TO EGYPT

Egypt's main imports from the Sinai Peninsula appear to be turquoise from south Sinai, some copper from southwest Sinai (e.g., Maghara, Bir Nasb) and areas farther to the east (e.g., Timna, Feynan), selected minerals and stones (e.g., malachite, rock crystal), and Red Sea shells, sea urchin spines, and coral (e.g., Ras Budran). In addition, Ramesses III's direct contact with Tayma Oasis (northwest Arabia) probably obtained southwest Arabian aromatics and other products. Southwest Arabian ("Yemenite") pottery appears in Middle Kingdom and New Kingdom contexts at Mersa Gawasis but arrived via Red Sea shipping with little evidence for overland dispersal to the Nile Valley. During the Late Period, Arabian overland caravans traverse western Arabia and the Negev, carrying aromatics and reaching Gaza and other destinations, including Egypt.

The Near East

Ancient Egyptian overland routes and travel through the Near East are far more complex and varied, from prehistory through the pharaonic period (pls. 3–4). Their usage and frequency depended upon the mixed, changing, and fluctuating geo-political infrastructures, including semi-nomadic pastoralists (e.g., Chalcolithic and Early Bronze Age IV Palestine), tribal societies (e.g., Iron Age I Palestine, Edom, Moab, Ammon), chiefdoms and emerging city states (e.g., Early Bronze Age I–III Levant), multiple city states (e.g., Middle Bronze Age–Late Bronze Age Canaan), larger kingdoms (e.g., Iron Age Philistia, Israel, Judah), and empires (e.g., Hatti, Mitanni, Assyria, Babylonia, Persia). The Egyptian rationale for contact with and sometimes control over the Levant varied widely, including commerce, wider spread international relations (e.g., diplomacy), security (e.g., pacifying the Hyksos and their allies [at Sharuhen/Tell el-Ajjul?], subduing potential and current foes: Bedouin, city states, kingdoms), imperialism (e.g., safeguarding and administering garrisons, vassals, travel, communications, and access to key sites, resources, tribute, and allies), and other factors, such as repelling Assyrian, Babylonian, and Persian incursions into southwest Palestine and pending invasions of Egypt.

Aside from maritime travel along the Levantine coast, Egyptians and others used three main north–south roads: (1) a coastal road ("the Way of Horus", "Way of the Sea") from Tjaru (northwest Sinai) to the Carmel Range, which turned eastward to Galilee; (2) a hill country route (via Jerusalem), which joined the first road at Galilee and headed north to Hazor and northeast to Damascus; and (3) the eastern "King's Highway," which ran from Aqaba through the Transjordanian Plateau to Damascus, and further north. Several east–west roads linked coastal towns to inland settlements and the eastern route, while other pathways connected the remaining towns and villages. Papyrus Anastasi I provides a detailed summary of the Egyptian familiarity with and nature of key places, topography, routes, logistics, hazards (e.g., animals, bandits), and travel through Canaan. The road network further north elsewhere in the Near East is far more complex (see pl. 4). A few transit routes also linked the southern Levant with the Gulf of Aqaba, and northwest Arabia, such as Iron Age routes from Wadi el-Arish, Gaza, Ruqeish (an Assyrian trading *karum*), and elsewhere to Kadesh Barnea, and onward to a Red Sea fortified port at Tell el-Kheleifeh. Egypt's travel through and presence in the Levant changed dramatically in its nature, geographic scope, and intensity in relation to its commercial, diplomatic, and political needs and capabilities. These circumstances included late Predynastic to First Dynasty periods of intense Egyptian trade, military raids, and potential settlement in the southwest part of the Levant; increasing raids during the late Old Kingdom into Palestine; Middle Kingdom commerce with the Levant; a Levantine (Hyksos) occupation of Egypt during the late Middle Kingdom to Second Intermediate Period; the New Kingdom imperial expansion into Syria-Palestine; a late New Kingdom post-imperial decline and Third Intermediate Period decentralization and weakness; a brief Saite resurgence in imperial ambitions; and concurrent and later periods of Near Eastern empires and increasing aggression and/or expansion into Egypt by the Assyrians, Babylonians, and Persians.

EGYPTIAN EXPORTS

Egypt exported a wide range of materials, products, animals, people, and influences to Sinai and the Near East during the late Chalcolithic through Persian periods. The nature, quantities, and specific means of transmission for such dispersals vary broadly over time and in geographic coverage. These items can be grouped into broad categories for Early Bronze Age I–II Palestine and Early Bronze Age I–III Syria: raw metals, some flints, stone statuary, stone containers (unguents, other contents), faience vessels, pottery containers, clay sealings (from containers and other items), jewelry, cosmetic palettes (Predynastic to Early Bronze Age I), Nile mollusks (utensils?), weaponry, tools, and food (e.g., Nile catfish). Egyptian influence materialized through local copies of many of these aforementioned categories, while an Egyptian presence is attested in the southwest Levant during Early Bronze Age IB via similar building types (e.g., en-Besor, Ereini), locally made Egyptian-type pottery, and other evidence (e.g., "African"-type human remains in Early Bronze Age I burials). Late Old Kingdom products are well attested in Syria at Byblos, Ebla, and elsewhere. After an economic decline in Syria, and virtual de-urbanization and minimal trade in Palestine during Early Bronze Age IV, Egyptian contact is revitalized in Middle Bronze Age II. For instance, Byblos contains Egyptian-type royal tombs, a temple, monuments bearing hieroglyphs, antique statuary and stelae, vessels of stone, glass, and faience, and jewelry (beads, seals). Egyptian artifacts and materials appeared elsewhere in the Levant (e.g., Qatna), and continued in the Middle Bronze IIB–C period of Canaanite prosperity.

During Egypt's New Kingdom Empire, an Egyptian presence and influence intensified and includes several headquarter cities, places featuring hieroglyphic monumental texts (e.g., Beth Shan, Nahr el-Kelb, Kadesh), Egyptian traders, soldiers, and other residents (e.g., Ugarit, Beth Shan), a full range of Egyptian-type structures (e.g., forts, houses, temples, shrines) unspecified "gifts" to city-state rulers (e.g., Thutmose III's Megiddo campaign), and diverse material culture among the elite Canaanites and others. Egypt also dispersed representatives and many materials and commodities to kingdoms beyond its imperial boundaries: emissaries, gold, containers of metal, stone, and faience, furniture, linen, and grain (e.g., famine relief for the Hittites, temp. Merenptah). In the post-imperial period, the nature, quantity, and scope of Egyptian materials and products decreased but still featured migrants (Egyptians and Kushites), some monuments, pottery, luxury containers, jewelry, seals, game boards, weights, fauna, and other exotica (including some recycled items). Naturally fluctuations occur in the nature and scope of such interactions during these changing times: Egypt's decentralized Third Intermediate Period; a strengthened Kushite-ruled Egypt (Twenty-fifth Dynasty); the early Saite Period of renewed imperialism; Phoenician transmissions of Egyptianizing artifacts and motifs; and the expanding domination of the Levant by the Assyrian, Babylonian, and Persian Empires. These empires also fought against and occupied parts of Egypt and/or its adjacent territories, often extracting tribute, booty, many items, exotic animals, prisoners, and other influences to Mesopotamia and beyond (e.g., Persepolis).

NEAR EASTERN IMPORTS TO EGYPT

During this time frame Egypt variously desired, sought, and obtained a wide range of materials, commodities, and influences from the Near East via the aforementioned separate and interlinked overland, riverine, and maritime routes. During the late Predynastic and First Dynasty (Late Chalcolithic to Early Bronze Age I), Egypt displayed an intriguing influx in art and architectural items and influences from Syria and Mesopotamia (e.g., niched facades, cylinder seals, hero-figure separating two animals). Near Eastern imports continued in the Early Dynastic and Old Kingdom periods (Early Bronze Age I–III), consisting of lapis lazuli, silver, copper ore, salt, sulfur, and bitumen, lumber, agricultural produce and byproducts, stone vessels, some flints, pottery containers, jewelry, weaponry, animals, and Asiatic males, females, and children (migrants, captives, and transients). After an apparent brief reduction in international relations during the First Intermediate Period, Egypt increased its interactions with the Near East in the Middle Kingdom (Middle Bronze Age IIA) through Second Intermediate Period (Middle Bronze Age IIB–C). Levantine-style courtyard housing, shrines, flexed burials, donkey burials, Canaanite material culture (weaponry, pottery), a large statue of an Asiatic (Hyksos) ruler, and other influences appear increasingly at Tell el-Dab'a (Avaris), which expands its domination and rule over northern Egypt (Hyksos); some east Delta towns may adopt Levantine-type embankment/mound fortifications (e.g., Tell el-Yahudiyeh; Heliopolis [this is debated]); Canaanite migrants are attested increasingly in northeast Egypt (e.g., people bearing Semitic names [including high officials]) and elsewhere (e.g., Levantine female weavers and tutors in southern Egyptian households). In the Second Intermediate Period, southern (Theban) Egypt also adopts Canaanite chariots, horses, composite bows, and musical instruments (lyres, lutes).

The Theban defeat of the Hyksos and the subsequent advent and intensification of Egypt's New Kingdom Levantine Empire realizes a dramatic increase in Levantine and other imports and influences entering Egypt: royal gifts from neighboring kingdoms, annual tribute from vassals; captives, hostages, mercenaries, merchants, messengers and emissaries, foreign princesses (i.e., marriage alliances with Egypt), transitory pastoralists, and others (especially captives assigned to royal, cultic, and private estates and workshops). Many Levantine deities, some of whom had already appeared in the Middle Kingdom through the Hyksos period (e.g., Sopdu, Baal), became more popular, including Reshef, Qedeshet, Baal, Anat, Horon, and other deities and some cult centers. During the post–New Kingdom periods, Egypt experienced expanding influxes of foreigners, material culture, and other cross-cultural influences, including Libyan incursions, Levantine refugees (e.g., Judeans, Edomites), Assyrian and Persian invasions and occupation forces, Greek and Phoenician merchants, mercenaries, and other cross-cultural exchanges.

Other Aspects of Overland Travel

OFF THE BEATEN TRACK

Other overland routes requiring consideration include new and irregular trails, reconnaissance, and scouting in more remote or less-traveled regions. For instance, the Egyptian state often dispatched patrols along key border regions and in fringe areas to monitor movements by desert tribes (e.g., Middle Kingdom Semna dispatches). Egyptian police are also reported tracking and pursuing fugitives along the Wadi Tumilat and into northern Sinai (Papyrus Anastasi V). Military scouts and affiliated spies might traverse rough terrain, not usually used for regular traffic, in order to reconnoiter enemy movements and positions. This is implied in various narratives such as Thutmose III's year 22 campaign to Megiddo and Ramesses II's year 5 expedition against Kadesh; Egyptian armies and other travelers also sometime crossed difficult mountain paths and more remote trails during military campaigns through hostile territory (Papyrus Anastasi I). Some routes also emerge, shift, or become abandoned in relation to individual circumstances, including changes in the environment, socio-political circumstances, commercial ties, technological needs, and other factors (e.g., Abu Ballas trail). Egyptian prospectors also searched the adjacent deserts for new sources of metals, minerals, stone, and other resources, presumably consulting local informants and entering new terrain beyond already depleted and exhausted resources. For instance, a distinct increase in Ramesside prospecting for and exploiting copper sources in the Eastern Desert, south Sinai (e.g., Reqeita), and southern Arabah (e.g., Timna) may relate to a temporary decline in and/or loss of access to Cypriot copper during the Egypto-Hittite wars, an insufficiency in other regional copper sources, and an increased demand for copper by the Egyptian state.

EXPEDITION TYPES AND COMPOSITION (STAFF)

An expedition's size and composition varied depending upon its specific route, nature, scope, and objective(s), including military expeditions, mining, quarrying, mercantile, diplomatic, and other ventures, which range from well-attested "royal missions," temple expeditions (e.g., cults of Amun, Re, and Ptah), to provincial endeavors (e.g., Djehutyhotep), and less well-known, private commerce (e.g., *The Eloquent Peasant*, Hyksos caravans across north Sinai, Bedouin/Asiatics bringing galena to Beni Hassan). Overland missions could contain: a single messenger (e.g., a Hyksos courier traveling to Kush through the Western Desert); scouts reconnoitering enemy territory; a royal emissary, charioteer, and escort (noted in the Amarna Letters); or larger groups numbering a few hundred (e.g., some expeditions to Sinai), thousands (e.g., mining, quarrying, military, and other groups), and up to 40,000–50,000 personnel (e.g., Ramesses II's campaign against Kadesh). The leadership of such groups encompassed state and military leaders (e.g., the pharaoh, princes, generals, officers, Medjay scouts), non-military officials with specific expertise or broader qualifications (e.g., expeditions to Nubia led by Elephantine's nomarch and/or his sons, treasury officials in Sinai, broadly qualified and trustworthy high officials), and others (e.g., employees of temple cults). Likewise, the staff of such expeditions also differed according to specific requirements, including larger contingents of unskilled personnel/conscripts (e.g., quarrying, mining, military conscripts), skilled labor (e.g., engineers, prospectors, masons, naval contingents), more specialized staff (e.g., officers, scribes, masons, architects, priests, guides, interpreters), and foreign auxiliaries (e.g., Nubians, Levantines, Mycenaeans[?], some Sea Peoples).

EXPEDITION EQUIPMENT AND SUPPLIES

Many expeditions required the transportation of additional provisions, supplies and personnel (fig. 3.1) to traverse difficult and often hostile desert terrain, including walking sticks, bags of bread, water skins, spare sandals, pack donkeys with supplies, indigenous Bedouin hunters and bodyguards, and armed police escorts against potential Bedouin attacks. An Eleventh Dynasty steward, Henu, needed to dig fifteen wells in three areas for an expedition of 3,000 men dispatched to the Wadi Hammamat and Red Sea. In friendly foreign polities an

FIGURE 3.1 Establishing a military campsite; from Horemheb's Memphite tomb.

expedition's leadership and some staff could be billeted in outposts, towns, and cities. One New Kingdom official (Intef [Theban Tomb 155]) is attested traveling ahead of the army in Canaan to prepare the pharaoh's daily quarters and other amenities in vassal city-states (see also Papyrus Anastasi IV). Otherwise, the personnel of most large expeditions camped in the open, reusing old campsites and shelters or sometimes establishing new camps, tents, campfires, and other transitory facilities (e.g., North Sinai). In crossing enemy territory, the New Kingdom military foraged and harvested its foe's crops, making temporary enclosed camps with an outer shield wall, an area for soldiers' tents, pack donkeys, chariots, and horses, wagons, and oxen, and an inner enclosure with the leaderships' tents and pavilion (e.g., Ramesses II's campaign scenes). Aside from the ubiquitous and hardy pack donkeys, Egypt's New Kingdom military used chariots and ox-drawn carts and wagons in Canaan (e.g., Ramesses II) and along Eastern Desert roads (e.g., Ramesses IV); carts transported heavier materials and supplies, thereby moving more slowly according to the requirements of the oxen (8 miles [almost 13 km] per day). Some Egyptian and Near Eastern texts, models, and depictions indicate litters and chariots with sunshades and covered wagons, suggesting a variety of means to improve the comforts of overland travel for the elite and others. Camel caravans are not attested until later in the ninth century BCE in the Near East, albeit earlier in Arabia and with varying usage in Mesopotamia, the Near East, and elsewhere.

TRAVEL PERIODS, PERMITS, AND FACILITIES ALONG ROUTES

Overland travel (fig. 3.2) is attested year round, especially during the winter in the adjacent drier desert landscapes, while a reduction in sea and land travel occurred in the winter months in northern regions owing to frequent storms, rainfall, mud, snowfall (in Anatolia), and less easily navigated roadways in parts of the Levant and Anatolia. Regarding other travel restrictions, inscriptions note travel permits and papers for entering, staying, and leaving Egypt, for city-states within the Levant, and elsewhere, during the Middle Kingdom (e.g., tomb of Khnumhotep II), Eighteenth Dynasty (Amarna Letters), and late Twentieth Dynasty (Wenamun). Travelers often required diverse adaptions for overland passage across difficult and different terrain (e.g., deserts, forests, plains, mountains), geo-political landscapes (e.g., chiefdoms, city-states, kingdoms, empires), and specific circumstances (e.g., peaceful regions, hostile territory). For instance, a rough sandstone roadway ran 12 km across Egypt's Western Desert to Lake Moeris (Fayum) to enable dragging basalt blocks to a quay for shipment to the Nile. The Hittites maintained "royal roads," including some paved segments, to facilitate winter travel to Hattusas (central Anatolia) and elsewhere; North Sinai reportedly had a mud-brick road. Most "roads" represented well-traveled paths and tracks (e.g., Canaan), firmer, winding desert wadi beds (e.g., Wadi Hammamat, Ras Budran to Wadi Maghara), or less well-defined, broader trails across wide landscapes (e.g., north Sinai, Western Desert). Regarding Egypt's adjacent deserts and north Sinai, small to large expeditions followed wider trails and worn routes between natural springs, oases (e.g., Wadi el-Arish), wells, and reservoirs; they stopped at regularly established supply depots (e.g., Bir el-Abd granaries), way stations and shrines (e.g., Gebel Abu Hassa, Beit el-Wali), administrative and fortified outposts (e.g., Deir el-Balah), and anchorages or ports with both seasonal and permanent installations (e.g., Tell Ridan, Tell er-Ruqeish).

NAVIGATING ACROSS FOREIGN LANDSCAPES

Egyptian expeditions used different methods to navigate across unfamiliar or confusing terrain, including local guides, experienced expedition members who knew the terrain, and papyrus maps illustrating key landmarks and features (e.g., Sety I's replication in Karnak temple of a map of north Sinai [fig. 3.2]; the Wadi Hammamat map [fig. 3.3]); expeditions also followed well-marked human, donkey, and other visible trails across the desert (e.g., camel trails in the seventh century BCE and later), and established stone cairns (*alamat*) and other key landmarks to aid in navigation across different and remote landscapes (e.g., Wadi al-Jarf, Mersa Gawasis, Dakhla Oasis). Other navigational aids might include celestial observations, such as using the stars at night. In addition, Egyptian travelers left rock-cut texts and

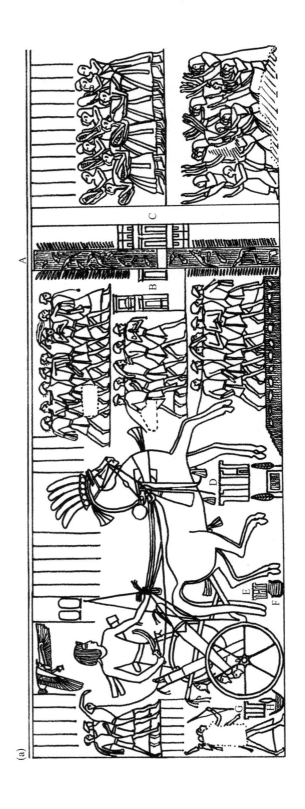

(a)

(b)

A = "The dividing waters"; B = "The fortress of Tjaru"; C = (?); D = "The-dwelling-of-the-lion"; E = "The-migdol-of-Men-maat-re"; F = "The well Ḥ-p-n";

G = Buto-of-Sety-Merneptah"; H = "The well Tract-of-…"; I = "The-castle-of-Menmaatre-The-…-is-his-protection"; J = "The-stronghold-of-Sety-Nerenptah";

K = "Town-which-(his)-Majesty-built-(newly)"; L = "The well 'Ib-s-ḳ-b"; M = "The well of Sety-Merenptah"; N = "The well Menmaatre-(is)-great-in-victories";

O = "The well (called) sweet"; P = "Town which his majesty built newly at the well Ḥ-b(?)-?-t"; Q = "The-stronghold-of-Menmaatre-heir-of-Re";

R = "?-b(?)-r-b-t"; S = "The well of Menmaatre"; T = "N-ḫs of the prince"; U = The-town-of-[Raphia]" (after Gardiner, 1920: 113 Karnak list of names, images pls 11 and 12.

FIGURE 3.2 a&b: Sety I's north Sinai forts and way stations. From Karnak temple.

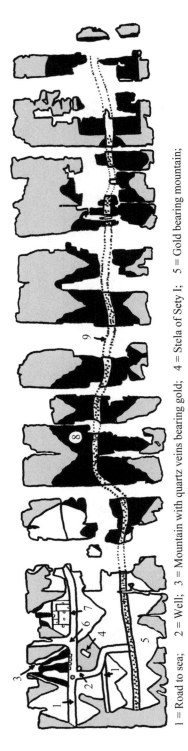

1 = Road to sea;   2 = Well;   3 = Mountain with quartz veins bearing gold;   4 = Stela of Sety I;   5 = Gold bearing mountain;

6 = Gold mining settlement;   7 = Shrine of Amun;   8 = Mountains;   9 = Main trail along the Wadi Hammamat.

FIGURE 3.3   Ramesside papyrus map of the Wadi Hammamat.

graffiti at shaded rest stops (e.g., Rod el-Air) and other localities along routes and various destinations, attesting to their passage and presence in remote areas. Egypt also relied upon foreign overland caravans at different periods and various geographic areas to export and import goods between the Nile Valley, intermediate zones (e.g., Dakhla Oasis), and distant regions (e.g., Gilf el-Kebir and farther south).

EXPEDITION HAZARDS

Travel outside the Nile Valley and Delta entailed a wide range of both feared and real dangers, spanning natural through supernatural and human threats. One late Old Kingdom text notes the Bedouin massacre of an entire expedition and its leader on the shores of the Red Sea, presumably near Mersa Gawasis (or possibly Ayn Soukhna; probably not Wadi al-Jarf), while they were preparing ships for embarkation to Punt. Another Sixth Dynasty text deals with the arrangements for the retrieval of the body of an expedition commander, Sabni, who had been killed in Nubia along with his personnel. The Middle Kingdom *Satire of Trades* emphasizes that couriers made wills before setting out owing to dangers from lions and Asiatics. Other prospective travelers made offerings to various protective deities (e.g., Horus *cippi*) and wore amulets to protect themselves against potential snakebites, scorpion stings, and other dangers. The higher death rates experienced by missions outside the Nile Valley is underscored by boasts by expedition leaders that their ventures did not suffer any deaths or other misfortunes. The Amarna Letters and other documents also refer to Shasu, Habiru, and other Bedu attacks on and robberies of mercantile caravans and other travelers traversing Canaan and the Near East in general. A Twentieth Dynasty text cites the loss of over nine hundred personnel (10 per cent) from a mining and quarrying expedition of approximately nine thousand persons dispatched by Ramesses IV into the Wadi Hammamat. A late Ramesside literary piece, *The Report of Wenamun*, mentions the tomb of Khaemwas' emissaries, who languished seventeen years in Byblos without completing their mission. Hence, these accounts and other data imply that foreign travel commonly held many dangers, spanning adverse climate (e.g., flash floods, sand storms, sea storms), natural causes (e.g., wild animals, pestilence, diseases, poisonous stings and bites, heatstroke, dehydration), to particular circumstances (e.g., poor planning, misfortune ["fate"]), plus caravan robberies, attacks (e.g., Bedouin/other raids, ambushes, skirmishes, and battles) and other factors.

EXPEDITION CARGO AND GOODS

In addition to the personal requirements for expedition personnel and draught animals during their overland travels (be it a military expedition, mining/

quarrying venture, trading caravan, diplomatic mission, or another form of travel), such expeditions also carried additional cargos and other things intended for their destinations both outside Egypt and for journeys to Egypt. Naturally, the specific materials, product types, animals, peoples, and their quantities and influences differed widely over time and with their varying destination(s) (see above).

SAFEGUARDING ROUTES AND TRAVELERS

The Egyptian state frequently dispatched armed escorts to accompany travelers and expeditions in remote and hostile regions outside the Nile Valley (e.g., twenty-five Nubian troops escorting a gold mining expedition in the reign of Ramesses IX [Papyrus Cairo C-D]), while foreign city states and kingdoms normally assumed the responsibility for safeguarding routes, overland travelers (including Egyptians), and cargoes travelling through their territories (e.g., Amarna Letters). The Egyptian state also implemented additional security measures: For instance, Dakhla Oasis has yielded evidence for police patrols and posts during the Old Kingdom. Middle Kingdom patrols and trackers are attested frequenting the desert fringes in Nubia to monitor, intercept, question, and report the movements of the desert tribes. In the Middle Kingdom, Amenemhat I built a 47 by 59 meter fort at Wadi el-Natrun to secure this region from Libyan incursions. In the Second Intermediate Period, the Theban kingdom apparently established and administered a 218 acre settlement at Umm Mawagir (110 miles to the west of Thebes), which contained Nubian troops and formed a major Western Desert trading hub straddling the east–west Girga road and a north–south overland route between the delta and Nubia. In the Ramesside period of increasing troubles along Egypt's frontiers, Ramesses II and other rulers built and maintained a series of forts along the edge of the west delta to deter further Libyan incursions (e.g., Kom Firin, Zawiyet Umm el-Rakham), while Sety I and his successors fortified the "Ways of Horus" across North Sinai, and established military garrisons at key places in Canaan (e.g., Gaza, Tell Farah South, Tell Sera', Tell es-Sa'idiyeh, Beth Shan). The Saite rulers also founded a few military bases abroad, including a major Egyptian garrison at Carchemish in Syria (i.e., to aid the declining Assyrian Empire), and probably the fortress at Dorginarti in Lower Nubia.

Conclusion

The succeeding Ptolemaic and Roman Periods witnessed a dramatic increase in overland travel to, exploitation of, and interactions with Egypt's Eastern and

Western Deserts (e.g., Wadi Hammamat, Siwah Oasis, Cyrenaica), a combination of riverine and overland trade with sub-Saharan Africa (e.g., Meroe, Gebel Moya, Aksum), and expanded maritime commerce with Eritrea/Ethiopia, southwest Arabia, East Africa, and India. As in the pharaonic period, such interrelations frequently combined riverine, maritime, and overland routes (e.g., Red Sea ports of Abu Sha'ar, Myos Hormos, Bernike), but included alternate, overland routes as well (e.g., Abu Ballas trail).

SECTION II }

People

4 }

Children of Other Gods

SOCIAL INTERACTIONS

Bettina Bader[*]

Introduction

In order to discuss the ancient Egyptian attitude towards non-local and "foreign" people in the best possible way it is necessary to start with some considerations of the current situation of the "interpreters." It is clear that research questions such as the topic of this chapter are driven by modern/current interests and problems as well as by our own life experiences. Before it is possible to ask questions such as "how did Egyptians treat people from abroad and interact with them," it must be clarified that our modern world and personal situations influence the way we look at the evidence. Currently we take this topic so seriously for obvious reasons. Moreover, we must remain aware that our worldview is heavily influenced by the tradition of western philosophy.

Another important point is the consideration of post-colonial research undertaken in other parts of the world, because early Egyptian archaeology was also driven by a desire to acquire objects of art worthy to be displayed in European and North American museums. Most governments of "developed" western countries were attracted by the possibility to combine cultural efforts of research and collecting with political/colonial aims of the respective period. "Egyptomania" of the late nineteenth and early twentieth century CE boosted this field. At the same time the discipline of Egyptology developed a colonial and male viewpoint on the ancient culture. While such and similar factors have been identified and theorized at length in social anthropology and archaeologies of other parts of the world, Egyptology is becoming aware of its lack of theoretical (self-)scrutiny.

[*]Bettina Bader currently leads the Austrian Science Fund financed project Beyond Politics—Material Culture in Second Intermediate Period Egypt and Nubia hosted by the Austrian Academy of Sciences (FWF—Y754-G19).

The indebtedness of Egyptology to the culture-historical approach to the ancient past needs to be mentioned. This approach goes back even past V. G. Childe, a famous prehistorian, who maintained that recurring combinations of artifacts and a distinct material culture reflects "cultural" groups of people or "peoples." In consequence, the Egyptian culture, which appears as uniform and very coherent, was viewed as self-created, self-sufficient, and "pure." Such concepts have been severely criticized and largely abandoned, because they do not take into consideration that cultures do not exist in isolation. It is clear that any of these underlying concepts directly influences the way we interpret "cultural contacts" between Egyptian people and the rest of the world.

Important for understanding is the fact that, besides the archaeological record that does not supply names and views on the self, the Egyptian sources provide only limited material about the view of self of higher-status individuals and even less on non-Egyptians. Here the tomb stelae may be mentioned, which represent beside the physical bodies the only record of individuals and their identities (gender, age, profession, ethnicity, and so forth) and how they (or their relatives) wanted them to be seen by posterity. It remains largely unknown which rules applied to the composition of such stelae besides the artistic canon for the depiction of the tomb owner (if there was one) and if they were the same for Egyptians and non-Egyptians. This is more than the neighboring archaeological cultures can offer, but it is necessary to be aware that this information is through the eyes of a literate male Egyptian elite that may have fostered a generalized and stereotyped picture.

A Combination of Sources: Archaeology, Texts, and Pictorial

Egyptology offers the advantageous situation that allows us to consult and combine archaeology, textual, and pictorial evidence for most periods except the very early ones. While this additional information provides a better chance for reconstruction and interpretation of the past, it must not be forgotten that these different source types need different approaches and source criticisms. Texts may be used to advantage on a meta-level. Also, for some periods not all source types exist in triple to complement each other, but rather they are to be used alternatively. Thus, for eras not covered by one source type the other is used to extrapolate, which is far from ideal and sometimes stretches the existing sources. Some reliefs of the Old Kingdom, for example show quite clearly which commodities were brought back into Egypt (e.g., relief of a Syrian bear with some vessels from the Fifth Dynasty pyramid temple of Sahure, Berlin ÄM 21828, [Abusir]). Such fragments were used frequently for far-reaching interpretations even though some are lacking inscriptions and may therefore be ambiguous especially in the social implications.

An example of a lost chance to combine archaeology and texts to advantage is the Middle Kingdom settlement of Lahun, where (among many other documents) a number of papyri have been found with lists of Asiatics and other Egyptian unfree people (perhaps similar to serfs, but not equivalent to Roman slaves) in the employ of certain institutions and individuals. They are identified by name, given Egyptian name, origin (*ꜥꜣm*), occupation, gender, and filiation. The fact that many of them were given Egyptian names makes them frequently disappear from the records. Although the settlement was extensively excavated in 1890–1891, the material culture of co-habitation of Egyptian and Asiatic people is not sufficiently preserved to decide whether the non-local presence indicated by the texts had any influence on the material culture in general. However, there are a few exceptions: for example, a weaving implement (British Museum 70881) with an unknown (pseudo)inscription that Sass has ascertained to be not Proto-Sinaitic. Torques and ivory box inlays with concentric circles are not necessarily Syro/Palestinian products. The truly imported pottery known from Lahun, as well as the locally produced pottery, which shows influences from abroad (e.g., the Aegean), cannot give any hints to the physical presence of non-Egyptians because the local industry might have been influenced just by the presence of the original product. Aegeanists have stated that those pottery vessels/fragments would have been immediately apparent as local imitations. The same can be said about faience stirrup jars from the Late Bronze Age/New Kingdom, where the idea of the vessel type is apparent but the execution is clearly non-Aegean and deeply rooted in Egyptian production.

Archaeologically Proven Contacts and Their Interpretation

From the first archaeological endeavors in Egypt onwards, finds from countries abroad were noted and discussed. At first, from the Chalcolithic, such contacts were pinpointed by the appearance of raw materials that do not naturally occur in Egypt and thus must have come from abroad, such as lapis lazuli, obsidian, silver, or bitumen. Some of the most famous works of early art such as the Gebel el-Arak knife and palettes carry artistic motifs that show influences from Mesopotamia. For these early incidents it remains quite unclear how the contact situation and the social framework within which it took place are to be imagined. Whether a regular exchange took place, or if the contact was all but indirect via a long line of unknown intermediaries, can only be hypothesized. It is clear, however, that in Egypt a stratified society existed and not everybody had access to such items due to their rarity, especially in Upper Egypt. This also suggests that the main contact line ran through the Egyptian Nile Delta, but future finds may change this picture.

Over time more objects, often pottery, especially in prehistoric archaeology, attest to intense contacts from earliest times onward. For example, the hundreds of imported storage jars found in large elite tombs in cemetery U at Abydos in Naqada IIIA need to be mentioned, as well as the so-called wavy-handled jars that underwent a typological development in Egypt quite separately from those found in the Levant. These containers were not imported for their own sake but for specific and sought-after contents, such as vegetable oils, figs, and wine. While on the receiving Egyptian side—the context suggests the highest stratum of society—it remains unclear what, if anything, was given in return and to whom exactly.

Notably, during the same time a number of settlements existed in the southern Levant, such as Tel Halif, En Besor, and Tel Lod, at which a proportion of pottery was found exhibiting certain traits in typology and manufacturing technology that are labeled "Egyptianizing" or "Egyptianized," with all the baggage and unspoken implications such terms carry. In very few cases is it known how the proportions of Egyptian versus local material relate to one another or if these vessels cluster in certain contexts. Also the consideration of what constitutes "Egyptian" and "Egyptianizing" material seems to have changed over the last decades and making a coherent interpretation based on a range of reports difficult. While Tell el-Sakan was described as a fortified settlement with a larger amount of such pottery and Egyptian-type buildings, Tel Erani yielded a more differentiated view on these locally made Egyptian finds and (parts of) buildings, which included architectural features known from the Egyptian Naqada culture. Renewed fieldwork and analysis changed the picture in that "Egyptian" and "Egyptianizing" pottery started later than previously thought (Early Bronze Age IB2). Besides pottery, notably chipped stone tools exhibit traces that can be interpreted as peculiarly Egyptian or Levantine. The chipping traditions of these areas seem to be quite different. The interpretations of these findings center on some form of Egyptian hegemony or colonization. Here variants range from Egyptian colonial posts in one case to peaceful settlements with Egyptian presence (no arrowheads at Erani) of civilian nature. Both types may have served for trading purposes in the form of merchant colonies, military stations, or fortified sites.

The presence of so-called "hybrid" pottery at Erani is noteworthy, including southern Palestinian shapes made from chaff-tempered fabrics and Egyptian-style finish, Egyptian forms with southern Levantine plastic ornaments, and Egyptian shapes made from Canaanite-type fabrics. This is a feature of material culture that seems to occur in areas and periods where people of different origin meet, such as the Delta and southern Palestine and probably also on the southern border of Egypt. The material culture and any changes it might have undergone are only now being studied and contextualized. Thus, it is perhaps a bit fortuitous to speak of straightforward Egyptian colonies. A thorough comparative study of the material culture from both areas is needed in order to pinpoint differences and similarities and to come to a consensus about the cultural assignation. The fact that the contexts differ—tombs versus settlements—might also distort the interpretational framework.

Another example for an archaeological contact situation can be found in the first half of the second millennium BCE at Tell el-Dab'a—ancient Avaris—in the northeastern Nile Delta. This site has a habitation history that ranges from the beginning of the Twelfth Dynasty to the Late Period. This longevity makes the site a valuable source of information because it is possible to study the development of the material culture of a purely Egyptian site after cultural influences from the north—Syria/Palestine. As in prehistory, the names of the majority of the individuals living at this site remain unknown and the few Hyksos king's names inscribed on stone fragments were found out of context.

After a lengthy period of settlement in orthogonally planned housing (no cemeteries have been found for the earlier part of the Twelfth Dynasty) with a material culture that shows only scant evidence of commodity exchange in the form of ceramic containers of so-called Levantine Painted Ware and very few Canaanite jars, the volume of imported material rises sharply in the late Twelfth Dynasty. At the same time tombs with some characteristics of the northern Middle Bronze Age culture appear at the site in one area. This concerns mainly some types of grave goods (toggle pins, Syro/Palestinian weapons, burial of articulated animals before the entrance of the tomb) and the burial positions of the bodies (on the back with legs flexed). Typically Egyptian objects, such as kohl pots and other stone vessels, beads, scarabs, and a few statues are found in the same tombs. At the same time the tomb architecture is no different from that in other parts of Egypt, where mud-brick chamber tombs set into pits and simple pit tombs occur. The pottery found in those tombs consists of Egyptian as well as imported Syro/Palestinian ceramics (amphorae and juglets). While such combinations (with the addition of Syro/Palestinian diadems, and Egyptian coffins, palettes/mullers, and mirrors) in tomb contents continue until the end of the Second Intermediate Period, there is also an increasing number of previously imported and later locally produced pottery, at first mainly small juglets presumably containing some precious commodity, and then several Middle Bronze Age pottery types.

In the course of the late Middle Kingdom and the Second Intermediate Period the settlement architecture provides no indications of any outside influence either in the house plans (with one exception in the late Twelfth Dynasty) or in the building technology or the lay-out. Religious architecture is represented by temples/chapels, two of which show a typical tripartite arrangement as do other Egyptian chapels, and two Near Eastern types (one broad-room temple and one with bent axis). Finally the presence of a huge palace of an agglutinating plan dating to the late Second Intermediate Period with close similarities to Near Eastern types such as at Mari and Ebla needs to be mentioned. An interesting absence is to be noticed in direct evidence for non-Egyptian gods in this period. They seem to mostly appear during the New Kingdom.

As for the objects of daily use, the pottery corpus shows over time an amalgamation of Egyptian and Syro/Palestinian typological traits such as surface treatment, manufacturing technology, and shape repertoire. The products of this very regionally confined development cannot unequivocally be assigned to one or the other tradition, because the pottery represents an intricate mixture of both. To a limited extent a similar process can be observed in scarab production.

The interpretation of this archaeological situation usually focuses on the presence of people from Syria/Palestine and explains it by means of re-settlement of prisoners of war by the Egyptian central administration in the late Twelfth Dynasty or more generally as immigrants who sought the "bread baskets" of Egypt who later on became more powerful and extended their political influence toward the Nile Valley and farther south. While the first option is derived from more or less contemporaneous texts (annals of Amenemhat II, Stela of Sobekkhu, Lahun papyri), the archaeology does not suggest any means of suppression or forced presence. However, while the development of the material culture has been frequently used for studies of acculturation (a collection of divergent theories without unified definition, sometimes of colonial spirit), it is clear that both cultural components were present and continued to exist for some time soldered together in a new form, albeit in a spatially very confined region. This continued co-existence of both cultural elements also makes it difficult to pinpoint an ethnic identity in a cultural sense of the buried people at the site, because it is a situational-fluid social concept, defined through real or perceived similarities and differences of culture, history, and language. These perceptions may have changed during the lifetime of a person and need not be in congruence with genetic factors. As neither any names of the inhabitants of the Second Intermediate Period nor the language/vernacular that they spoke is known, it seems impossible to go beyond the assertion of a mixed cultural tradition at this site. Whether the non-elite inhabitants considered themselves as Egyptians, Levantines, or a third (mixed) grouping cannot be fathomed. Also it remains unknown whether this question played a major role in the daily reality of these ancient people.

The sensational find of the Minoan wall paintings at the same site in a trash layer of an early New Kingdom palatial context needs a quite different explanation.

Contrast between Official Ideology and Daily Routine with Neighbors

The dichotomy between the Egyptian stereotypes of foreigners (skin color, dress, hair style, accessories, epithets) and references to individual non-Egyptians was explained by means of Loprieno's concept of *topos* and *mimesis* initially developed from Egyptian literature, where the (mostly negative) stereotype represents the topos and individual realism stands for mimesis. This concept has also been transferred to pictorial sources and archaeology. The motif of "slaying the enemy/prisoner" (fig. 4.1) was entrenched in Egyptian iconography since the prehistoric period, as can be seen in tomb 100 at Hierakonpolis and the Narmer palette. It was still used on temple fronts in Roman times. While for the earliest attestations no inscription names the "enemy," the later tradition clearly identifies the habitual underdog (Asiatic/Syrian or a triad of a Syrian, Nubian, and Libyan), ethnic stereotypes created to represent the Egyptian worldview in a positive light. The famous Narmer palette shows an inhabitant of the Delta as the enemy slain, while an ivory tablet depicts a non-Egyptian desert-dweller with long hair. By the time of the Old Kingdom a phenotypical distinction between the main groups of non-Egyptians (Nubians, Asiatics, Libyans) seems to have been in place in the artistic conventions. Nevertheless, until at least the Eleventh Dynasty some enemies have identical faces and were distinguished only by their inscriptions or attributes. Even Upper Egyptians were among them. Thus in the first instance all people seem to have been on an equal footing and whether they rebelled against the "mighty cosmological power"—the ruler or *mꜣꜥt*—was the only decisive factor in their slaying, not their origin. Interestingly in the New Kingdom icons a predominance of

FIGURE 4.1 Slaying of the enemies. Karnak temple.

FIGURE 4.2 Slain enemies. Karnak temple.

Asiatics in the choice of victims perhaps as prototypes for foreigners (fig. 4.2) can be noticed, while Nubians are also frequently mentioned and shown in pejorative terms ("vile" or "wretched" Nubians). Libyans seem to occur more rarely, and the Aegeans, namely the people from Keftiu and Hau-nebut, are not found in such a context (but see below, for the Theban tomb scenes), perhaps because no major confrontation occurred before the depiction became so deeply rooted. The action behind the icon, namely the killing of the enemies by cutting off heads and other body parts, was most probably real, as some archaeological finds and temple scenes suggest (cut-off hands and heads in a pit at Tell el-Dab'a; a cruelly bound and killed prisoner in the area of the Mut temple in Luxor; heap of cut-off hands at Medinet Habu) (fig. 4.3).

Another icon to be mentioned here is the "stepping on the nine bows" by the pharaoh as a symbolic action for the overcoming of rebellious enemies against the all-ruling power. These nine bows are depicted below the feet of the pharaoh on footstools or pedestals of statues or even on the underside of sandals. As in the execration texts, a magical means to defeat enemies, Upper and Lower Egyptians are included in the list, as well as oasis dwellers. Thus, the origin of the person was again not particularly relevant, but rather if (s)he took action against the pharaoh, who controlled everything on earth and crushed any unlawful resistance.

FIGURE 4.3 Counting the hands of the fallen enemies. Medinet Habu.

Archaeologically, several situations where people from abroad lived together with local Egyptian people can be brought forward: for example in the late Middle Kingdom and Second Intermediate Period settlement at Tell el-Dab'a/ Avaris. There is no evidence to suggest that any segregation or suppression was in place, but it also remains unclear what sort of record we are looking for. The papyri from Lahun and Thebes, lists of unfree workers fulfilling a range of specific tasks such as singing or weaving, on the other hand show a very different picture. It is very difficult to know how such "slaves" were treated and if this label is actually justified. As lists naming fugitives (Papyrus Brooklyn 35.1446) exist, forced labor was involved and it concerned foreigners as well as Egyptians.

Similarly it is difficult to ascertain why and how the owners of the "pan-graves" of the late Middle Kingdom and the Second Intermediate Period found at several sites in southern Egypt fit into the Egyptian social fabric. Known primarily by their round, shallow pit tombs with side-flexed burials and a distinct range of burial gifts (items such as jewelry from certain shells, pottery, painted animal crania, and so forth), they are quite dissimilar from Egyptian customs. There are cemeteries where "pan-graves" are isolated, while in others they are interspersed between Egyptian ones. Moreover, in other instances objects commonly considered Egyptian are found together with non-Egyptian ones. Some burial customs, such as rectangular shafts and extended body position, were also taken over. These variants are often ascribed to a development. Whether relational and material entanglement developed needs detailed research. The archaeological material of the "pan-grave culture" is currently undergoing a fresh contextual analysis. This group of people was identified with the Medjay of Egyptian texts, who lived in a non-specific area to the east or southeast of the Nile Valley. The "ethnic identity" of this group is an Egyptian creation and therefore a stereotype, with which not necessarily any nomad from the Eastern Desert themselves identified at first. The textual sources suggest that over time the Medjay became an important part of the Egyptian imperial military system and in the New Kingdom the term signified a type of specialized military unit, whose members considered themselves proudly to be Medjay. Recently awareness has been raised about the long-standing connection and extrapolation between the (textual) Medjay and the (archaeological) "pan-grave culture" without giving critical thought on the nature of the source types.

Perhaps different again is the situation at the southern end of the country at Elephantine, where there is continuous evidence for contact with Nubians. (The definition and distinction of the material culture of the C-group, "pan-grave", and Kerma especially in the earlier phases is currently not finalized.) It seems that small amounts of Nubian-derived pottery made up part of the ceramic repertoire of Elephantine settlement and burials from the third millennium BCE onward, representing a close relationship. Whether a real mix existed is at present hard to say but may be expected. So far only for the Middle Kingdom evidence of Nubian influence on the local ceramic repertoire (mostly in terms of decoration) in the settlement provides hints for a close contact. Straightforward importations from Lower Nubia alone cannot be considered to represent the physical presence of people, and the same holds true for similar situations at other sites. The massive presence of Nubian cooking pottery at the fortress of Askut amid an otherwise Egyptian ceramic repertoire points to a presence of Nubian cooks (female, probably). The most difficult task in archaeology is to provide proof for the physical presence of non-local people, because it would necessitate the assignation of certain objects to certain "ethnicities" and this remains problematic in most cases.

The cemetery of Tombos in Nubia, however, in use from the early Eighteenth to the Twenty-fifth Dynasty seems to cater for Egyptian colonists and local Nubians and shows a situation where tombs reflecting Egyptian as well as Nubian burial customs appear side by side. It became obvious that the local population chose between Egyptian and Nubian burial customs, but which factors influenced this choice remains unclear. Resistance was suspected as possible motivation. In Napatan times Egyptian and Nubian traits became intricately mixed, a feature known from the late Middle Kingdom and Second Intermediate Period cemeteries at Avaris.

Egyptians as Nationalists?

Closely connected to the view of the "other" is the view of the self and the question whether Egyptians considered themselves to belong to a "state" or a "nation" in a supra-local sense. Recent research into the connection between modern "nationalistic" concepts and a possible equivalent in ancient Egyptian views doubts that such a notion ever existed in antiquity. In the search for a national identity (only one of many) expressed in texts it appears that stress is regularly laid on the local perspective rather than on any "national" notions. Nation states and discourse connected to them have existed only since the nineteenth century CE. The hometown seems to be of major importance to the owner of inscriptions in general in a wide range of periods. Within this framework fits the Egyptian desire expressed in literature to be buried in one's hometown. Thus, this might have implications on the view toward the "other"— namely, foreign—people, too. In principle there should, then, be no difference between a person from the next town (which is not one's own) and a town in Retjenu or Kush. Nevertheless, one may recall the instructions of Ptahhotep (Old Kingdom) and Ani (New Kingdom) to take a wife who is known in the town and to beware of an "outsider woman" who is not. This would then also concern people from abroad, unless it is meant misogynistically.

In the Amarna period, all persons, animals, and things on earth were the creation of the sole god, and the great Amarna Hymn (Lichtheim 1976, p. 98) specifically mentions:

> O sole God beside whom there is none!
> You made the earth as you wished, you alone,
> All peoples, all herds and flocks;
> All upon earth that walk on legs,
> All on the high that fly on wings,
> The lands of Khor [Syria/Palestine] and Kush [Nubia],
> The land of Egypt.
> You set every man in his place,

> You supply their needs;
> Everyone has his food,
> His lifetime is counted.
> Their tongues differ in speech,
> Their characters likewise;
> Their skins are distinct,
> For you distinguished the peoples.

This particular verse has been taken to mean that there is no hierarchical difference between Egyptians and other peoples during this time, but that they are only of different appearance. This is in contrast to the—later—story of Wenamun, where Amun-Re is said to have founded Egypt first, although he still created all other lands as well. It remains difficult to decide whether the purported "outside" view of Egyptian literature refers there to Egypt as a geographic unit only or to an identity.

Contact Situations Known from Depictions and Their Interpretations

In the following some pictorial scenes are discussed with a focus on their social implications and interpretational difficulties.

A relief block from the Old Kingdom pyramid temple of Sahure of the Fifth Dynasty shows Asiatic sailors and their families on seagoing ships returning from the Levant or the Red Sea, who perform a gesture of adoration to the pharaoh just like the Egyptian part of the crew (the superiors). Interestingly, these Asiatics are only shown on the return journey; thus it has been assumed they were brought back by the expedition. While the destination remains unmentioned, Byblos has been assumed. Asiatics constitute the majority of people on the ship, which do not seem to be treated like prisoners or slaves, as shackles and ropes are not shown. Thus, it seems as if they are treated as equals to Egyptians, but the inscriptions remain silent on this. The presence of Egyptian interpreters (^cw) is also remarkable. A similar scene in the Unas causeway a few generations later shows a larger majority of Asiatics but without families on board seagoing ships. Bietak has drawn the conclusion that by that time the presence of Asiatic sailors with their special expertise has become a usual occurrence in Egypt and that they had found a place in the Egyptian social system.

The famous caravan of Asiatic men, women, and children depicted in the Middle Kingdom tomb of Khnumhotep II at Beni Hassan (tomb 3) in Middle Egypt from the reign of Senwosret II has frequently been used as an illustration for infiltration and settlement of Asiatics in Egypt. If this is indeed so, it would mean that such a process was not restricted to the liminal Delta/southern Palestine zone. Moreover, there is no contemporary (archaeological) evidence in Middle Egypt for Asiatic settlement. Khnumhotep was "overseer/administrator of the Eastern Desert" and it is in this capacity that the ʿ3mw of šw were presented to him by two Egyptian officials, an overseer of the hunters and a scribe, in year 6—a very concrete date for the event. They were "brought because of black eye paint" or "bringing the black eye paint" (i.e., lead sulfide, galena), according to the inscriptions. Except for the bellows, which may be connected to lead production, no specialized tools are shown. Whether they were supposed to bring galena or work with it there remains unknown. The leader of the group, Ibsha (Abishar), is mentioned by name and as ḥḳ3 ḫ3st "ruler of the foreign lands." Although only fifteen people are depicted, the accompanying text on the "presentation slip" of the scribe mentions thirty-seven; thus the scene in the tomb has been adapted perhaps to the available space. The clothing of the men and women, the tools, musical instruments, and weapons they carry, as well as their hairstyles, diadems, and beards, seem to represent the dress and equipment in use by Aamu at the time. Some of these implements were identified in the archaeological record, while the scene on the whole was used for pinpointing the origin of the people and their socio-economic situation. The use of the scene as a chronological link between Egypt and the Levant is also noteworthy. As is frequently the case, the geographical information is vague, so it is not reasonably possible to assign a specific origin for this group of Aamu. It remains simply unclear if they were nomads at all, came from the Eastern Desert (as the galena might suggest), Sinai, (southern) Levant, or somewhere else. Doubtful associations with (much later) biblical references have also been suggested. If these people originally came from the Eastern Desert, a connection to the southern Levant is not supported. This example demonstrates that the interpretation of scenes, even if they carry inscriptions, needs care and context. Moreover, there are scenes with Asiatic warriors in other tombs at Beni Hassan.

For the New Kingdom, a group of Theban tombs of high officials (Senenmut, Useramun, Rekhmire, Menkheperreseneb, and others) from the reign of Thutmose III are important, because they contain scenes where foreign people from Nubia, Libya (in later tombs), Syria/Palestine, and the Aegean bring a variety of gifts. This type of scene also occurs on royal monuments and continues to exist until the Twentieth Dynasty. Although foreign people mostly occur in sizeable tableaus mistakenly called "tribute" scenes, Aegeans appear in only a few tombs but have gained greater notoriety because historical and chronological clues were drawn from these scenes for the synchronization between Egypt and the Aegean. Based on various details some scholars distinguished Minoans and Mycenaeans, based on a traditional culture-historical interpretation that seems unwarranted due to the vagueness of the associated geographical terms. It is noteworthy that in later tombs the inscriptional identification of the peoples does not always fit the iconography. This may mean exactitude and knowledge about the people diminished or was not particularly important.

First we shall consider the context of the scenes as the presentation of a variety of gifts to the respective tomb owners as intermediaries between the processions and the pharaoh. Recent holistic study of the genre and the accompanying texts suggests that in the absence of concrete occasion and dates for the processions and the presence of all the "great ones" of then known foreign peoples these scenes represent a variation of Egyptian ideology. The pharaoh ruled over the whole (known) world and its inhabitants. The scenes in the private high-status tombs of the Eighteenth Dynasty seem to stress the social role of the tomb owner as an important intermediary between such processions and the receiving pharaoh (sometimes accompanying gods), demonstrating their personal place in that world order. Besides the social standing of these officials, we also get a glimpse through Egyptian eyes on the increasing contact with neighboring peoples and the core knowledge available about them, including some typical objects these scenes contain. Some of them may be identified archaeologically. It has been maintained that the scenes show the Egyptian view of a gift-exchange re-interpreted for the Egyptian audience as a "tribute" in a propagandistic appropriation according to the prevailing decorum. Some of the Amarna letters provide a (later) counter picture for the Egyptian part of this exchange, which appears much more modest. The extent of historical facts in these scenes remains disputed.

Libyans, semi-nomadic people from areas west of the Nile Valley, only moved into the focus of Egyptian power during the later New Kingdom, when wars and punitive skirmishes with them were mentioned for example by Merenptah and Ramesses III (fig. 4.4). During this time it seems as if Libyan people moved increasingly into Egypt, especially in the north. In the Third Intermediate Period the political fragmentation of Egypt created a favorable situation for the heads of Libyan chiefdoms (Libu, Meshwesh, Ma, and others) to come to power from within. A high degree of acculturation was assumed because archaeologically it is hitherto not possible to distinguish their material culture. But interestingly the Libyans are always depicted with the typical dress and feathers on their heads, so their acculturation was considered to have only been superficial.

Finally, the following Libyan and Nubian Twenty-second to Twenty-fifth Dynasties adapted to a certain extent to the Egyptian iconography of power and pharaonic rule in order to demonstrate their legitimacy, but in contrast to the earlier rulers they did not seem to conceive or present themselves as Egyptians.

FIGURE 4.4 Libyans. Medinet Habu.

The Social Situation of Migrants/Non-Egyptian People Living in Egypt

Because archaeology does not inform explicitly on the social situation of the early pre-historic immigrants in Egypt or the Egyptian presence in southern Palestine, some hypotheses have been proposed to explain the finds of the respective material culture in the other area. While the Egyptian materials in southern Palestine were explained as a "humane" colonial arrangement by Egyptian powers, did the people arriving in the Egyptian Delta do so as specialized workers or as members of a "trade mission" but certainly not as colonizers themselves? In the absence of textual evidence to provide a background for these hypotheses, the circumstances of these contacts must remain subject to further research and publication of archaeological data. The later sources often mention prisoners of war or people (men and women) brought back in the course of expeditions to distant lands both north and south. Some of these people were "awarded" to especially renowned military men as booty. This surely suggests an enforced and asymmetrical power relationship between the immigrant and his/her master. The individual situations would have strongly depended on the personality of the individual, but for Egyptologists it is hard to imagine that the subject of our study should have been cruel when the wisdom literature shows the ideals of a well-lived and just life. But perhaps these texts existed exactly because the reality was quite different? What the lives of these people were like in the course of their forced stay remains largely unclear except that some lists named fugitives. This must mean that their life could not have been easy, or else they would not have fled. For the lowest social stratum, besides names in lists no more information on their life circumstances comes forward, so to "prove" archaeologically their non-Egyptian-ness is fraught with severe problems. In the New Kingdom, texts indicate that prisoners of war were part of royal building projects, were assigned to temples, and especially served as mercenaries. The tomb of the three foreign wives of Thutmose III provides a high-status example that only their foreign personal names reflect their foreign-ness, not the archaeological artifacts from their tomb.

Inclusion into Egyptian Society and Different Ways of Dealing with Identity

Only if funerary stelae or tombs give clues of a non-Egyptian origin it is possible to gain insights into their social situation, but this also means that they would have belonged to an elevated social stratum able to afford such a monument. At the same time this implies that they were part of Egyptian society and knew the decorum of what was appropriate to be said and shown in order to belong. This may mean that an additional "Egyptianizing" filter existed. Insufficient clarity in the Egyptian terminology for family relationships adds to the problem of identifying non-Egyptians securely, as some changed their names during their lifetime.

The sources show that it was possible for non-Egyptians to climb the social ladder under different circumstances, be it the Nubian mercenaries from the First Intermediate Period in Gebelein, some of whom were shown as Nubians with the prefix ḥsy added to their Egyptian names, or the New Kingdom high official Aperel, who was not required to change his name or his appearance in the depictions in his tomb at Saqqara. A more subtle approach to self-identity is shown by Maiherperi, a royal fan bearer buried in the Valley of the Kings (KV 36) in an utterly Egyptian manner with exclusively Egyptian objects. Only the depiction of him in the *Book of the Dead* with very dark skin color and his mummy itself exemplify his non-Egyptian ancestry.

In contrast, Hekanefer, a contemporary of Tutankhamun, had himself depicted in his Nubian tomb at Toshka as an Egyptian, but in the so-called "tribute" or "procession" scene in the Theban tomb of Amenhotep-Huy, the viceroy of Nubia, Hekanefer is shown in the usual Nubian *topos* with dark skin color. This amply exemplifies that there was no escape from the ideology even if the tomb owner considered himself as Egyptian. On a larger scale, the Egyptian pharaoh had to be the cosmological ruler with Egypt at the center, whether this was a historical fact or not.

5 }

Between Brothers

DIPLOMATIC INTERACTIONS

Richard H. Wilkinson and Noreen Doyle

Diplomacy forms one of the central and ultimately most important facets of the interconnections exhibited between ancient Egypt and her neighbors. As a mechanism of the coexistence of states, diplomacy not only protected but also advanced Egyptian interests at home and elsewhere, and its reach and importance is seldom overestimated in assessments of Egyptian history.

To understand the true importance of diplomacy for ancient Egypt, we must carefully define its role. Diplomacy is often defined as communication between two or more parties at the official level, often in times or situations of tension. But tension is not a secondary issue—it is often of central importance, because where there is no tension there is no real need for diplomacy. In the following sections we outline some of the key aspects of diplomacy as understood and practiced by the ancient Egyptians, and it will be seen that in virtually every area the mitigation of tension is central to what was being pursued. Although we find evidence for Egyptian diplomatic interaction from Old Kingdom times forward, most of the extant evidence comes from the period of the New Kingdom, and it is on this era that the present chapter will primarily focus.

Foundations of Egyptian Diplomacy

PSYCHOLOGICAL FACTORS

At the most basic psychological level, diplomacy can be seen to stem from an understanding of the needs of populations regarding their own shared identity versus that of other groups. Shared versus "other" identity causes a juxtaposition of not only us and them but also our space and their space (a dichotomy commonly attested linguistically in the ancient Near East —as in Sumerian *kalam* and *kur.kur*, Egyptian *t3* and *ḫ3swt*, as well as *kmt* and *dšrt*), our resources and their resources, our activities and their activities. It is an underlying tension often existing beneath the surface when no overt tensions are visible, and it was primarily responsible for the formation of city-states and eventually nation states—both of which require diplomacy to survive and flourish.

This situation must be combined with the fact that, for the ancient Egyptians, interaction with other groups was usually seen through the lens of their own presumed centricity. Although such a viewpoint is held by many cultures, it was reinforced in Egypt by the geographical, topographical, and ecological realities of a fertile, populated, and easily navigated area largely surrounded by relatively barren and difficult terrain. As a result of this semi-isolated and centrist attitude, "The geographical elements and cultural characteristics of the inhabitants of the peripheral world [were] considered not only different but inferior to those in the central country" (Liverani 2001, p. 19). This is a truism, yet it underlies not only the concept of dominance in general relationships between core and periphery areas but also the specific attitude implicit in the way Egyptian diplomacy was often conducted. This is not to say that diplomacy was always viewed as a one-sided affair for the Egyptians, but it is an attitude that is clearly evident in Egypt's dealings with its less powerful neighbors and can often be seen to be present, if only subtly so, when Egypt's parity relationships are closely examined.

DOMINANCE AND PARITY

The relational background to most Egyptian diplomatic interactions is most clearly understood from the perspective of dominance and parity relationships. While New Kingdom Egypt fulfilled a dominant role in interactions with many of its smaller neighbors for much of its history, its relationship with other areas was not so clear-cut, and in some cases Egypt and other nations interacted on the basis of understood (if not always mutually admitted; fig. 5.1) equality. The roots of this pattern ran centuries deep: Lines B219–222 of the Twelfth Dynasty *Story of Sinuhe* are traditionally interpreted as a list of vassal princes whom the Egyptian king could summon, but this passage may instead reflect a proposed call for diplomatic gifts from distant kingdoms independent of (in parity with?) Middle Kingdom Egypt. Our understanding of the number of nations interacting with Egypt on a parity level has increased in recent years as we have come to more fully grasp the nuances of ancient diplomatic interchange and the underlying factors affecting the relationship between Egypt and other states.

In the past, the understanding of the basis for dominance and parity relationships between states was sometimes tied to concepts such as topographical, ecological, and climate factors (e.g., fertile riverine areas versus arid desert). While these factors are obviously important, they may also have been

FIGURE 5.1 Stela commemorating the marriage of Ramesses II and the daughter of the Hittite king Hattusili: directed at a domestic audience, the iconography and text affirm Egypt's superiority. Note that even in the presence of her father the princess is already Egyptianized. Great Temple of Rameses II, Abu Simbel; Nineteenth Dynasty, reign of Ramesses II.

overstressed at times. On the other hand, some have looked at dominance interactions largely as a result of "military might" (our army is larger than yours, so we call the shots), workforce numbers (with enough slaves you can do anything), or other societal vectors of power, but these and other factors are now usually considered to be the results of economic dominance rather than its cause. In embracing this reality, however, we must be careful not to undervalue other factors that were influential.

In classic World Systems Theory, the "core" countries of the modern world are the industrialized capitalist nations on which periphery countries and semi-periphery countries depend to some degree, but this model is based almost entirely on economic realities. In the ancient world it is clear that peripheral states might depend on Egypt (or Egypt on her neighbors) for a number of reasons—including, for example, transportation, resource access, protection, and even simple good will.

It would also be naïve to presume that Egyptian relations with other states were developed for the same reasons and in the same ways in all similar cases. Egypt's non-parity relations with Nubia to the south and Canaan to the north were often based on entirely different desires and expectations, as their diplomatic interchanges reveal.

Diplomacy was involved, of course, in the initiation and continuation of these and many other areas of interaction precisely because so many of them involved tensions of some kind. For both the Egyptians and their neighbors, stability at home was frequently established and maintained through diplomatic activity, and we can see the importance of that factor by surveying—even at a surface level—the great deal of information that has survived to us regarding the agents and instruments of diplomacy.

Agents of Egyptian Diplomacy

THE KING

When Egypt (or any other ancient core power nation) felt itself to be in a position of dominance vis-à-vis the nations around it, that dominance was invariably expressed by means of the verbal and representational depictions of the king produced for both domestic and foreign consumption. It is well known, for example, that royal titles and epithets suggesting universal dominance are found in a number of the more powerful cultures of the Late Bronze Age Near East, and the Egyptian *nb n ḫꜣswt nbt* "Lord of all the Lands" is a prime example. (See also the Akkadian *šar kiššati* "king of the universe," etc.)

Beyond the assumption of universal titles and epithets, there were also other means of projecting the Egyptian kings' power relative to other cultures. One such was the act of crossing the boundaries of other nations and publishing the fact—as in the erection of stelae by Thutmose III in the area of the Euphrates confirming that "the king [...] crossed the Euphrates [...] seeking that miserable enemy in the foreign lands of the Mitanni" (Cumming 1982, p. 3). This was, of course, a statement of dominance for the benefit of the local populace more than for readers back home. Even physical representations of the king—striking enemies on the battlefield or dispatching foreign captives at home—could be, and doubtless were, used as diplomatic messages of dominance available for view by foreign ambassadors and others visiting Egypt. The example is often given of the manner in which the colossal statues of Ramesses II at Abu Simbel on Egypt's southern border were carved to be imposingly visible to all who ventured down the Nile from the south.

The concept of Egyptian centrality and supremacy worked well, of course, in asymmetric situations, in dealing with subjugated or submissive nations, but the conceptual basis of diplomatic interaction had to be adjusted when dealing with cultures that also saw themselves as central and powerful. At the dawn of the New Kingdom, for example, power along the Egyptian Nile was essentially shared between the native Egyptian dynasty at Thebes, the Hyksos in the Delta, and the Nubians who controlled the area below the First Cataract. As Egypt grew in power and influence during the New Kingdom, those balances of power rapidly changed; but Egypt then more closely encountered more distant groups as its influence spread beyond its earlier borders.

This increased contact with parity- and non-parity-level cultures led to a great deal of diplomatic correspondence (see below) based on the relationship usually termed "diplomatic brotherhood," in which the kings of the various states, although not physically related at all, addressed each other as "my brother" or "my father" or "my son." This fraternal ideology was the hallmark of Late Bronze Age diplomacy. Although in some cases these terms were used in situations where older individuals addressed younger ones, or vice versa, in other cases the language of brotherhood was clearly used as an expression of mutually (or unilaterally) understood (or hoped-for) parity or non-parity relationships. We see this, for example, in the way Assur-uballit, first king of the Middle Assyrian Empire, only uses the term *šarru rabû* ("great king") of himself and calls the Egyptian pharaoh "my brother" as he becomes independent of Mittani. When the king of the relatively minor state of Alashiya addressed the pharaoh as "my brother," it was based on the knowledge that he had resources the pharaoh wanted and needed, not on any diplomatic misconception of actual levels of parity. The brotherhood metaphor is particularly appropriate for political relationships because, as has been pointed out, it does not deter "brothers" from quarrelling, and a great deal of diplomatic exchange was based on exactly that kind of interaction—rooted in disputes over everything from territory to trade, from extradition to exorcism requests.

Yet even at the height of Egypt's "brotherly" relationships with other symmetric powers, the tension between what the Egyptian king was forced to accept and what he desired is clearly seen. To mitigate that tension the pharaoh often clung to his ideologically mandated position of supremacy by means of power-related terminology in diplomatic contexts. We shall see this clearly below in considering treaties between the powers.

Although the king was the supreme agent of diplomacy throughout the ancient Near East, we should not forget the role of the queen. During the reign of Akhenaten, his mother Tiye received correspondence from Tushratta of Mittani asking her to intercede with her son. Even Ramesses II adapted the Hittite practice of involving the queen in royal correspondence in parallel to the role of the Hittite queen Puduhepa as part of diplomatic negotiations.

ENVOYS AND OTHER DIPLOMATIC PERSONNEL

If in the ideal kings communicated with each other directly, in reality bureau-cracies of envoys, scribes, and other court officials intervened. While diplo-matic appointments of a specific envoy to a specific place are known, kingdoms neither hosted nor stationed permanent embassies; perhaps the closest such institution might have been the commissioners Egypt included among its foreign-based garrisons, who visited vassal courts in the region. When a delega-tion had to stay at all—some received orders not to linger even overnight—two to three weeks seems to have been acceptable.

There was no career diplomatic corps, although diplomatic personnel might regularly serve their king in that capacity. The men appointed as envoys of the pharaoh (*wpwtyw nsw r ḫ3st nb* "king's messengers to every foreign coun-try," *wpwtyw nsw r t3 nb* "king's messengers to every land") held other, non-diplomatic positions as well. During the Amarna Period, merchants commonly performed the duties of diplomatic messengers, while most of the known (Egyptian) envoys of the Ramesside era had military backgrounds, particularly that of charioteer. A connection between charioteers and envoys existed among the Hititites as well. Men of these professions would have had the experience of foreign travel, with its exposure to languages, customs, and geography desirable in an agent acting as his monarch's eyes and ears abroad. Lesser kings might visit the Egyptian court personally, and foreign rulers occasionally sent their sons or brothers as envoys to Egypt. This was an ancient practice; "children" of Asiatic rulers arrived at the court of Amenemhat II to present (obsequiously, in the Egyptian record) precious metals, animals, and slaves. Hishmi-sharruma, son of Hattusili III, joined the Hittite delegation more than once and was even invited back by Rameses II.

As intermediaries responsible for conveying messages and gifts between courts, envoys personally felt the hospitality of a grateful host or the wrath of a disappointed one. Ideally, a king entertained foreign messengers with food and drink, and he was further expected to provide them with precious gifts in addition to those they were to bring home for their lord. When Babylonian messengers complained to their king, Kadashman-Enlil, that Amenhotep III had shirked this duty, the pharaoh assured Kadashman-Enlil that these men were lying.

Deceit was expected of envoys, but honesty remained the ideal: "If you are a man of entry (i.e., trust), sent [by] a great man to [another] great man, be utterly precise [when] he sends you. Perform for him the mission as he says. [...]. Seize the truth; do not transgress it" (*The Instruction of Ptahhotep*). Through execution of their duties individual messengers gained—and lost—good reputations at home and abroad.

Written correspondence, although potentially a tool of deceit, authenticated the messenger and his message. But the envoy did not necessarily know the content of the letter he was delivering either from or to the king he served; some letters thus had to speak for themselves. An envoy might, on the other hand, know more than the written message he conveyed and might have to defend his king's position or negotiate terms with his host.

Not all messengers or their messages reached the court to which they were sent. Their hosts might keep them waiting months or years. Although Thutmose III professed immunity from such hindrances, later in the Eighteenth Dynasty, while gifts were prepared, Egyptian delegations suffered detention because of plague or even to secure the release of a likewise detained Mitanni contingent. Compromise of speed heightened tension between royal courts. It not only delayed the completion of a mission but also, perhaps even more importantly, could signal a deteriorating relationship between "brothers."

Who gained admittance to the royal court was part of the diplomatic game. Some letters indicate that an Egyptian scribe, rather than the foreign envoy, would deliver the message to the pharaoh on behalf of its sender. Allies were expected to reject envoys from a mutual enemy, and failure to do so risked retaliation. Even rulers of lesser states might request that a great king not receive messengers from their foes.

Diplomatic missions only occasionally included a translator. The standardization of Akkadian as the diplomatic lingua franca may have allowed envoys to become conversant in the requisite language regardless of which (northern) court they visited. Similarly, evidence from the Place of the Correspondence of the Pharaoh at Amarna suggests that the scribes in charge of the cuneiform documents there were very likely Egyptian rather than foreign.

Instruments of Egyptian Diplomacy

DIPLOMATIC CORRESPONDENCE

Egyptian diplomacy utilized a number of instruments in fulfilling its purposes. Perhaps primary among these was the use of diplomatic correspondence. By the nature of the situation, we have more information regarding this correspondence than any other form of diplomatic interaction. Nevertheless, most Egyptian diplomatic archives were destroyed when Egypt was invaded at various times, the major exception being the Amarna Letters (fig. 5.2), which, although extensive and of great value, present a chronologically narrow window into the world of Egyptian diplomacy. Fortunately, for the time they cover, the Amarna Letters do supply us with a good deal of the correspondence between Egypt and the rulers of the major powers, as well as letters to and from many

FIGURE 5.2 One of the Amarna Letters (EA 27), from Tushratta of Mitanni to Akhenaten of Egypt, reminding the pharaoh of his obligations.

smaller states within the sphere of Egypt's direct influence. From these sources we can get a sense of the range of diplomatic interaction extant during the time in which the archive flourished. Diplomatic interaction is seen in the Amarna Letters in no fewer than six distinct areas: legal diplomacy, trade diplomacy, economic diplomacy, social diplomacy, disaster diplomacy, and political diplomacy. In practice, combinations of several of these areas of concern could occur, of course, at the same time.

Although we have relatively fewer diplomatic letters from earlier and later in the New Kingdom, an abundance of Thutmoside and Ramesside monuments and other textual sources shows that the Egyptian self-concept of centrality and supremacy was the norm that was maintained where possible in diplomatic correspondence. This is seen particularly in the presentation of the person of the king, yet the underlying reality of the situation, as the New Kingdom progressed, is also seen in several areas of diplomatic interchange. That Egypt could not deny, in fact, that it was only one of a number of strong centrist powers in the Late Bronze Age is seen in the adoption and continued use of Akkadian as the lingua franca of international correspondence, a practice perhaps inherited from the Hyksos period, as well as the many clues apparent in the parity relationships exhibited within the terminology of "diplomatic brotherhood," frequent examples of "ideological abandonment" (such as the avoidance of supremacist monarchial terminology), and, of course, the treaties, diplomatic marriages, and other examples of parity behavior detailed in the correspondence itself.

Archived cuneiform tablets found at a number of sites in the Near East have also thrown light on Egyptian diplomatic interaction with her neighbors. The site of the Hittite capital Boghazkoy, for example, contained correspondence between Hattusili III and Ramesses II—some of which discusses the nature and provisions of the great peace treaty that the two powers eventually ratified.

TREATIES

Treaties between Egypt and neighboring groups and states were among the most important products of diplomatic activity. For the New Kingdom, the earliest evidence is that of the treaty established between the Egyptians and the Hyksos, allowing the latter to leave their besieged capital of Avaris and guaranteeing them safe passage out of Egypt. (This treaty is recorded by the historian Josephus, quoting Manetho, in *Antiquities of the Jews.*) This was to be the first of a number of treaties and treaty-like agreements the rulers of New Kingdom Egypt would conclude as her power increased and her sphere of influence expanded.

In the case of non-parity relationships, such as those formed between Egypt and minor states in the Syro-Palestinian region, we find one-sided arrangements (rather than formal treaties) by which the lesser parties swore to be subject to the pharaoh and never to rebel, while the pharaoh, for his part, essentially promised nothing. This situation differs from the more common form of the Asiatic vassal treaty in which both vassal and suzerain subscribed to the agreement and the latter usually promised at least token protection or goodwill in return for submission. Egyptian diplomacy in this type of case also involved setting the tribute to be paid to Egypt, when it was levied.

But Egyptian relations with parity states such as those of the Hittites, Mitanni, Assyrians, Babylonians, and others were, of course, decidedly different. In some cases Egypt had no choice but to submit to parity-style treaties of the types regularly employed by the more powerful of her neighbors. Yet even in these cases, the underlying tensions caused by Egyptian monarchial ideology—which we have noted repeatedly—were the cause of much subtle diplomatic language manipulation. Ramesses II, for example, in the parity treaty established with the Hittites, styles himself as *ḥḳꜣ* ("great king") while referring elsewhere in the treaty to Hattusili III as a *wr* ("great chieftain"), despite the fact that the details of the treaty reveal a clearly symmetrical political situation. In fact, the documentation of the treaty is carefully written up so that Ramesses is depicted in one part for an Egyptian audience—as the king who "establishes his boundary as far as he desires, in any foreign land" (Kitchen 1996, p. 64)—while in the content of the treaty itself we find the admission that Ramesses "will not transgress against the land of Hatti to take anything from it, forever" (Kitchen 1996, p. 64). In this way diplomacy was served for both of the treaty's groups of readers, those at home and those abroad. Although the *pax aegypta-hethitica* is only a single example, it clearly demonstrates the way tension between the position of the Egyptian king and that of his foreign peers was achieved through the diplomatic presentation of the treaty to its respective audiences.

DIPLOMATIC EXCHANGES OF MATERIAL GOODS

The Egyptocentric ideology evident in the Egyptian language of treaties extended to official exchanges of goods. On the one hand, vassal states of a greater kingdom were required to present local commodities and other goods to their suzerain in recognition of, and to enhance, his authority (pl. 5). The gravitation of material resources to a great king was essentially recognized as a cosmic principal.

On the other hand, the giving and receiving of material objects and living things was also a "brotherly" practice of parity relationships. Abundant wealth (to share) correlated with peaceful international relations. Participation in exchanges of goods and, as we will see shortly, of people was an element of communication that eased tensions between kingdoms. A king was expected to behave as his predecessor(s). Failure to participate in established exchanges of gifts and other communications signaled an end to diplomatic fraternity. This is the reason for the apparent preoccupation with material goods in the

Amarna Letters. The importance of *things* comes not (only) from the value of the objects themselves but (also) from the meaning the act of gift giving imbues upon them. One does not send a present to one's enemy, but one does to a brother; a brother, but not an enemy, will reciprocate.

The act of exchange separates "gift" from "tribute." Reciprocity—a foundation of diplomacy—was required between peers. This is not to say that *giving* particularly could be assumed. Kings often wrote to one another to request specific gifts, sometimes pleading with urgency. This was not because of genuine hardship, however: a great kingdom must be, at least in appearance, self-sufficient and not in need of wealth from the outside world. Instead, kings availed themselves of formalized pretexts of specific, personal exigencies, typically the construction of a new palace or monument, a "work" into which the gift—gold, for example—would be made. (Whether the giver fulfilled a specific request was a different matter.) Such a context brings to mind the so-called Tod treasure. This early Twelfth Dynasty temple foundation deposit or cache consists of precious metal ingots and objects, predominantly silver, as well as lapis lazuli, almost all of foreign origin, although what channels brought these things to Egypt—as gift, tribute, trade, or plunder—remain unknown. Gifts were also given in the context of diplomatic marriages, and kings were expected to dispatch envoys with suitable presents to festivities hosted by their "brothers." Failure to do so was criticized, but so was the failure to issue invitations. Correspondingly, as with envoys, a king expected his allies to reject gifts from his foes. It was also unseemly to accept gifts from another king's vassals.

Beyond the mere fact of a gift were its quality and quantity. Gifts included commodities (e.g., gold, silver, semiprecious stones, timber, ivory), finished luxury items, animals, the services of skilled professionals, and visits by cult images. Sometimes the goods sent were not local productions or material but rather something obtained elsewhere, a demonstration that geographical territory did not limit the giver's resources. Inventories that accompanied gifts describe the objects and enumerate their quantity as well as, often, the amount of precious metal that went into making them, to assure the recipient of their high value.

Presenting valuable gifts enhanced the giver's prestige. A recipient could, to an extent, neutralize this with a backhanded compliment: "Gold in your land is dirt," Ashur-uballit of Assyria wrote to Akhenaten (Rainey 2015, v. 1, p. 311). Giving what one has in abundance magnifies one's reputation to a lesser degree. Letters commonly complain that gifts are delayed, lacking, imitation, or otherwise inferior.

While the architecture and pageantry of a royal court directly impressed visiting envoys who would convey their perceptions home, material gifts allowed firsthand manifestation of a king's potency abroad. The recipient turned this to his own advantage by displaying his newly received gifts to his domestic audience and any foreign envoys in attendance (pl. 5): here was his newly acquired wealth—behold what he could command from other great kings. Great kings expected their "brothers" to do this. But Amenhotep III went one step further. During a formal presentation, he mingled the gifts of at least one fellow great king, Kadashman-Enlil of Babylon, with the tribute received from Egypt's vassals. Everyone understood the message: even the Babylonian king was just another foreign chieftain. Kadashman-Enlil understood, too, and protested the affront.

He was objecting to a manifestation of the Egyptian perception of anything received from foreign lands. The Egyptians classified incoming (and outgoing) goods however best suited their own internal purposes. Goods obtained patently via trade from Punt were brought home as *bi3w* ("wonders") received after the expedition made a divine offering there to Hathor. Subjugated foreign locales rendered *b3kw* ("that which is produced"), which was obligatory. Another important classification was *inw* ("what is brought" or "supply"), a term perhaps best broadly defined as "payments made under duress and trade goods, as well as voluntary gifts" (Warburton 1997, p. 236). *Inw* could include *b3kw*. Conceptual and/or physical amalgamation of goods sent freely as gifts by other great kings and those sent under obligation by vassals is typically pharaonic. In the same spirit, Egyptian monuments make no display of the gifts sent out of Egypt to foreign courts. That aspect of diplomacy was not intended for a domestic audience.

DIPLOMATIC EXCHANGES OF WOMEN AND OFFSPRING

Like the diplomatic exchange of gifts, the very ancient practice of intermarriage between royal families of different kingdoms vastly expanded in the Late Bronze Age. Through the exchange of female relatives, kings made literal the familial bonds that they expressed toward one another in correspondence. Egypt and its neighbors perceived and implemented these exchanges through different, even mutually exclusive, points of view.

In contexts of non-parity, diplomatic marriages served as an avenue of domination. Vassals included women among the tribute they sent to the pharaoh; three royal wives with West Semitic names buried at Thebes may have resulted from Thutmose III's campaigns in the region. However, in the Near East the sending of a bride did not signal subjugation. Rather, a great king sent a female relative to impose his will and bloodline upon a vassal: she would become not merely a second-rank wife but rather queen in her new land, where she would give birth to the heir whose lineage would "forever" rule the vassal state. Even when this did not happen—some treaties acknowledged this possibility and provided an alternate line of succession—the eventual heir might be called the Hittite-born queen's "son." (The traditional curses that conclude Hittite treaties spare a vassal's Hittite queen and her children.) This was intended to create a web of royal families centered upon, and loyal to, the great kingdom. Thus when a great king sent a daughter to Egypt, he expected her to become the pharaoh's principle queen, who would give birth to the son who would inherit the Egyptian throne. They were all disappointed. Only Ramesses II's first Hittite wife, a daughter of Hattusili III, seems to have obtained the desired rank of "great royal wife," and the name she received in Egypt, Maathorneferure, was always qualified with an epithet noting her foreign father (fig. 5.1).

To manipulate the ruling families of subjugated states, pharaohs instead imposed Egyptian culture and social ties (or other forms of coercion) directly through a vassal's male line of succession. Beginning no later than the Old Kingdom, Egyptian military expeditions returned from foreign campaigns with captive offspring and other relatives of defeated foes. Textual and iconographic sources indicate that sons of Nubian and Asiatic vassals also arrived in Egypt as tribute. These individuals need not have been children in the strictest sense, as some had chariots or wives. Upon the death of a local ruler, the pharaoh would assign one of these presumably Egyptianized sons to assume the late father's place.

An institution called the *k3p*, the innermost domain of the palace, is thought to have played an important role in this aspect of pharaonic foreign policy. The *k3p* seems to have had among its functions the education of non-royal children alongside those of the king. These children are commonly assumed to have included those of vassals, but most individuals who bore the title *ḥrd n k3p* "child of the *k3p*" were evidently Egyptian. Of the few known foreign "children of the *k3p*," only a late Eighteenth Dynasty Nubian named Hekanefer can be traced with any degree of confidence to a local ruling family. Whether many other such children were held in or fostered through the *k3p* remains an open question.

The children of vassals served as obligatory pledges, if not guarantors, of loyalty. The Egyptians evidently saw a foreign wife largely from this same perspective, even when her father was a fellow great king and the marriage had been achieved only through intense negotiations. Consequently, unlike exchanges of material gifts, royal women flowed only one way: into Egypt. This violation of reciprocity was noteworthy even at the time. Egyptian princesses were so highly prized that counterfeits might be acceptable, but only if they were beautiful and if both sending and receiving parties mutually winked and nudged. The fragmentary "Marriage Vase" found at Ugarit has been interpreted as depicting an Egyptian princess as a foreign king's wife. But the iconography is too ambiguous to preclude the interpretation of its female subject as a non-Egyptian woman in Egyptianizing costume, either à la mode or, perhaps, as a mock pharaoh's daughter—if the piece even presents any historical particularity at all beyond an Ugaritic king's appreciation for the Egyptian artistic style. Hattusili III wanted his granddaughter, born to Ramesses II's great royal wife Maathorneferure, brought to Hatti so that she could participate in yet another diplomatic marriage to secure an alliance between Hatti, Egypt, and a third country. The girl's fate is unknown. Only if the Egyptians considered her Hittite—as they evidently did her mother—would she have been expendable for the sake of diplomacy.

Through all these instruments—diplomatic marriages, material gifts, the language of treaties and diplomatic correspondence—Egypt carefully sought to achieve a balance that mitigated the tensions existing within its parity relationships without compromising the fundamental ideology of its domestic audience, that Egypt was the state without peer.

6 }

The Armies of Re

Anthony Spalinger

The Military in the Old Kingdom

The immutability of pharaonic Egypt is, upon close examination, a false truism. The subject of this disquisition, "Armies of Re," also reveals changes, all owing to the adoption of new weaponry and methods of warfare. Indeed, the ancient Egyptian military system developed over time and differed considerably from one period of strength to the next. Egyptologists are wont to deprecate the earlier phases of civilization during which there appears to have been no large and organized army enabling the rulers to expand successfully south into Nubia or north, far up into central Syria. And it has been said that during the Old and Middle Kingdoms we witness the establishment of a regular military force, one that enabled the Egyptians to move quickly across water. By and large, however, our knowledge of the third millennium system of warfare, not to mention the Egyptian military corporation upholding it, still remains a murky field of research. This is particularly vexatious when one considers the little-known foreign wars undertaken by the Old Kingdom pharaohs. Recent evidence has shown that the Egyptian flotilla must have played a very important role with regard to the sea routes of the eastern Mediterranean. Still the Egyptians seem not to have annexed the heartland of Nubia; the major impetus southwards being mining rather than imperialism in the region between the first and second cataracts. Despite their abilities in utilizing the Nile as a conduit for infantry troops on transport ships, the technological level of the Egyptian army was hardly superior to that of its neighbors. Industry was not based on bronze. Weapons were relatively light, and protective elements such as greaves and helmets were not worn. True, we read of at least one major foray into southern Palestine, an expedition recorded in the famous autobiography of Weni. There is a second account, described in the tomb of Iny, that clearly indicates Egyptian movements into the Levant, if not beyond into Syria. Yet there was no ability to seize and hold foreign territories.

The system of warfare was relatively straightforward, even primitive. Unlike the New Kingdom, the Old Kingdom armies were not regularized. If there was some type of a military corporation, it had not achieved significant influence within the archaic state of Egypt. Lacking bronze as well as horses and chariots, the Old Kingdom army was composed of an archer elite along with infantry who fought with spears, daggers, and sometimes axes. The few extant scenes of contemporary warfare reveal close hand-to-hand fighting. Troops of marching men, depicted running at a regular pace, clearly demonstrate Egyptian military preparedness. It is hard to determine how a battalion—or whatever might have been the division—operated and who led it. Weni's biography indicates that he was put in charge of a host of troops and that there was some form to the structure of the infantry. Of course, the stage of development shown in his account was already far removed from that of the archaic Egyptian state. Nevertheless, there were some basic parameters that we can describe. The most important—and most enlightening—fact is that the pharaoh did not fight in person. None of the scenes from Old Kingdom pyramid complexes sheds light on the personal leadership qualities of the monarch. Indeed, the literature never portrays the king as a generalissimo. Instead, Egyptian armies appear to have been organized independently of him. For this reason many scholars still deny the existence of a state military at this early date.

One difficulty that we face is a simple one and dependent upon the extended use of an official term: the "commander of a host." From earliest times, long-distance donkey caravans had marched westward through the oasis caravan routes of the western Libyan Plateau. By the Third and Fourth Dynasties, the man running the quarrying expeditions and other long-distance expeditions was a natural leader and organizer. He knew his territory because, in pre-horse times, he traversed it slowly on foot. He learned, for example, where to find water and how to provide other necessities for his company. Were he to be put in charge of a host of infantry, such a man could fulfill the duties of a general even if his troops were not finely ranked at this point in military development. Thus one can argue that prior foreign travel provided the wherewithal of the Old Kingdom's military structure. Likewise, I feel, a nascent corporation of military men was already part of the country's bureaucracy, although to what extent remains *sub judice*.

Weni's biography emphasizes the land's division into Upper and Lower Egypt. Moreover, he specifically mentions that all sorts of Nubians as well as Libyans were part of his army. Weni himself was a court official, to be sure, but also a leader of a quarrying expedition. Hence, he could conduct a large number of men into inhospitable regions. In his narrative we also read of other high-ranking infantry leaders. For example, there were "chief district officials" in charge of their men. From this short text it is evident that the army was not continuously deployed, neither was it convened by the king. The presence of foreigners among the troops indicates, to be sure, that mercenaries were part and parcel of Weni's military machine.

No expansion was undertaken as a result of his campaign into southern Palestine; there was no extension of the boundaries of Egypt. After ravaging the countryside and overpowering the alien strongholds, with the added incentive of capturing enemy troops, the Egyptian army did not remain abroad in order to establish a region under permanent Egyptian control.

The Old Kingdom mortuary complexes were decorated in the topoi of military success. Libyan warfare was noteworthy in the key visual depictions in the pyramid temples. The well-known "Libyan family" scene continued to be repeated elsewhere after its introduction in Sahure's mortuary temple, embellished in four registers including donkeys, bulls, goats, sheep, and the like. Evidently, the campaigns westward were aimed at territorial depredation and the capture of booty in the form of animals. Indeed, that relief is reminiscent in attitude of the account of Weni with regard to the presumed success of the Egyptian army.

Yet nowhere in these scenes is there any evidence of a military organization. Even on the causeway blocks from the Old Kingdom mortuary complexes it is impossible to determine any specific details except for the clear-cut evidence of archers standing apart from close-fighting infantry men.

The Military in the First Intermediate Period

The Old Kingdom system of warfare presented in the summary above continued virtually unchanged through the later period of social disintegration and unrest, commonly called the First Intermediate Period, but with one key difference. Evidence comes from the local quasi-independent nomarchs, the "dynasty" of Assiut in Middle Egypt, and from early autobiographic texts predating the Theban hegemony in the Head of the South. The leaders of these political zones fought at the head of their own armies, or at least they were running the Egyptian military in a far more direct fashion than previously. In addition, the Eleventh Dynasty Theban rulers, Intef II, but notably the later Nebhepetre Mentuhotep (II), most certainly took charge of their soldiers. The account of Tefibi in Assiut tomb no. 3, for example, boasts of his leadership abilities. Note especially his use of the possessive in "my soldiers," a phrase that no Old Kingdom ruler would ever have uttered. Indeed, this narrative, replete with warfare, reflects regional military and political self-determination. Likewise in Thebes, the kings of the Eleventh Dynasty personally led their troops and, as did Tefibi, considered their army as much a personal possession as their kingdom.

The very lengthy account of Nebhepetre found at Ballas provides excellent material. The text includes direct speeches of the pharaoh and his personal assessment on his warfare in Lower Nubia and in southern Libya. Finally, Ankhtifi, who lived in the early First Intermediate Period, equally saw himself as the "big man" and "chief" of Mo'alla and as someone who fought for his nome and adjacent territories as a supreme general of generals.

Although *The Teaching to Merikare* has been redated to the Eighteenth Dynasty, it reflects the shift in military values that are noticeable in its purported milieu, the northern Heracleopolitan domain of the Ninth and Tenth Dynasties. The protagonist, Merikare's father King Khety, boasts of his personal role in raising his own troops and leading them upstream. He was an expansionist. Old Kingdom monarchs, by contrast, felt an all-encompassing separation from their people. They had no duty to defend the state and no desire to enlarge it. The only difficulty in using this literary source is that it was written down in the New Kingdom, when the pharaoh was accustomed to being a generalissimo.

Manfred Bietak has studied the three-dimensional models, made during the Eleventh Dynasty and early Twelfth Dynasty, that portray Egyptian soldiers in conjunction with Nubian mercenaries. The armies appear as well coordinated as previously, the Egyptians more so than the Nubians. The troops are typical of the bygone age of the Old Kingdom; that is to say, they are archers as well as lightly protected foot soldiers.

The Military in the Middle Kingdom

The military system of the Middle Kingdom appears to have been very similar to that of the smaller regional units of the First Intermediate Period. Although our knowledge of the social hierarchy within the war machine is incomplete, some points of comparison can be made. First and foremost, the elite troops were those of the marine organization. Two major historical accounts, one of the pharaoh Amenemhat II and the other of the nomarch Khnumhotep III, strikingly reveal the importance of the royal flotilla and the navy in the Twelfth Dynasty. While the Old Kingdom had an overseas policy, during the Middle Kingdom the king led his troops or sent his eldest son upstream against Nubia. From various Twelfth Dynasty tombs at Beni Hassan in the 16th Upper Egyptian nome, we learn of the royal armada and its use by expansionist rulers. By and large, the pharaohs of the Twelfth Dynasty continued their bellicose activities in the same way as Nebhepetre Mentuhotep had operated during the Eleventh Dynasty. The later pharaohs secured Lower Nubia, called Wawat. Amenemhat I and Senwosret I pacified this region between the first and second cataracts. They constructed a barrier composed of fortifications and boundary posts, defended by regular police and military patrols, at the second cataract. From this staging point the Egyptian kings could advance, sometimes in person, into the heartland of Kush and beyond.

The development of this imperialistic policy can be viewed through a series of soldiers' graffiti, biographical inscriptions, and royal stelae. Hence, it is fairly easy to analyze the focus of Egyptian military strength over a relatively long period of time. Inside the second cataract forts, living quarters were set up for the semi-permanent members of the Egyptian army, and a substantial number of food storage silos were built. The garrisons were suited for both administration and offensive warfare. They were excellently situated to observe the local Nubians and to control their passage to and from Egypt. Moreover, the food reservoirs were sufficient for large campaigns into the far south.

The concept of the king as leader of his army seems to have been less overt in the Middle Kingdom than it would become during the New Kingdom, yet significant in a way that it had never been during the Old Kingdom. From the Twelfth Dynasty onward, many rulers emphasized their abilities in war preparation and military leadership, qualities that went considerably beyond the practice of their Old Kingdom predecessors. *The Tale of Sinuhe* begins with the successful return of an army led by the king's son after a Libyan campaign.

If the nomarch Amenemhat of Beni Hassan took autobiographical credit for two major expeditions into Nubia, he was accompanied on one occasion by the king and on the other by the king's son. Amenemhat added that he was the general-in-chief of his own troops from the Oryx nome, but it was the king who overthrew the vile enemies of Kush. During the second flotilla campaign upstream against Kush, the nomarch was interested in the acquisition of gold. This time he accompanied the royal son and the future pharaoh Amenemhat II. It should not surprise us that here, and elsewhere, the leader was engaged in quarrying.

Our real difficulty arises in the later phase of the Middle Kingdom, especially during the Thirteenth Dynasty, because the data are too slim. However, extant sources indicate that despite their weakened control of the Egyptian polity, the pharaohs of this period were as decidedly nationalistic in outlook as their predecessors had been during the epoch of the Theban domination of the south after the fall of the Old Kingdom. While the Thirteenth Dynasty was subject to serious military threats from the Nubians in the south and the Asiatic Hyksos in the north, it revived the intimate capital-oriented chauvinistic behavior that was characteristic of the mid-Eleventh Dynasty. There was an increase in nationalistic fervor in which the city of Thebes, the Twelfth Dynasty seat of government, was reaffirmed as the premier city, with its godhead Amun now conceived to be the central deity of the Egyptian state.

The Military in the Second Intermediate Period

During the Second Intermediate Period, Thebes, although beset from two sides, nevertheless managed to acquire and use the new military technologies that had entered Africa from the northeast. The two key improvements were the horse and chariot. It is difficult to put a timeframe to their wholesale use. There are no horse skeletons or firmly dated archaeological evidence of the first chariots. However, there was a perceptible chariotry elite within the Egyptian army by the close of the Second Intermediate Period. Horse breeding was practiced during Hyksos rule, and it was under their influence that the Egyptians adopted the new composite bow and quiver sometime around the mid-Twelfth to late Thirteenth Dynasties. The Hyksos controlled all of the north of Egypt: the entire Delta plus a sizeable portion of Middle Egypt if not beyond. Thebes was briefly part of their domain. The duration of their domination in the south remains unknown.

Most certainly, the adoption of the horse did not mean that the native rulers of the Seventeenth Dynasty in Upper Egypt were able to resist the Hyksos immediately. Kamose's famous royal account places little emphasis on his chariotry. However, the Egyptian army system was undergoing rapid alteration. Theban influence quickly expanded both upstream to the second cataract at Buhen and downstream past Memphis. Questions remain as to how this was accomplished. It is assumed that the effective nationalistic impulse of the Thebans can partly explain Kamose's remarkable success in moving into Hyksos territory in the northeast Delta. Then, too, he was even more of a generalissimo than any Middle Kingdom warrior pharaoh. Commencing with his father Seqenenre II, the next line of Theban dynasts engaged in a new manner of warfare. They were constant generals and not merely rulers who fought with their troops from time to time. They were actual representatives of a war machine that moved with increasing velocity to the forefront of the state.

These pharaohs desired to represent themselves as chariot warriors par excellence. This image was soon to be utilized in public temple wall reliefs of warfare and conquest as well as in written accounts. The kings of the late Seventeenth Dynasty and those of the Eighteenth Dynasty continued to expand their role as conquerors. Such images and practices were dependent upon the incipient Seventeenth Dynasty's commitment to a military strategy dependent upon the horse and chariot. Unfortunately, the details of campaigning are not described in the earliest historical accounts, *The Story of Apophis and Seqenenre* and Kamose's two Hyksos war stelae. Within a short time, by the end of the reign of Ahmose, the Middle Kingdom marine-based system of the Egyptian army had largely been replaced by a land-oriented one.

The Military in the New Kingdom: Establishing Empire

The incursion of the nascent Eighteenth Dynasty into Asia required a different basis for the Egyptian military even if the Nubian campaigning followed the older practice of sending the army by royal navy. Technological advances enabled the Egyptians to strike hard against the south. The private biography of Ahmose son of Ebana dwelled specifically upon forays far beyond the second cataract by the various kings he served. We can explain the seemingly rapid success of Egyptian arms by their perfection of a superior system of attack. By now Egypt had transformed itself to a full Bronze Age culture. Thus the new "mechanized" division of the pharaoh's army overwhelmed their southern foes, who, moreover, did not possess horses. The Egyptian monarchs could not and did not dispense with their armada, which took their lengthy campaigns beyond the fourth cataract, to their geographic and logistic limits, far outdistancing the Middle Kingdom war machine. The fervor for domination over the Nile Valley was evidence of the ideologically nationalistic and technologically driven unified state that had arisen in the course of the Seventeenth and Eighteenth Dynasties.

In Asia one had to traverse, and then control, all of Sinai as a first step to secure control over the southern littoral of Palestine. Under Ahmose the kingdom of Sharuhen was absorbed. Then came the more arduous task of establishing frontier garrisons connecting the old eastern Delta capital of Avaris, via the border post of Sile, to Gaza, the first major city in southern Palestine. Archaeological data and scholarly textual analyses document the construction of a military infrastructure. By the reign of Hatshepsut, a major highway facilitated advances north. The ultimate stage in war tactics and equipment was in place for Thutmose III to use. Henceforth, the army was an effective presence. Egypt no longer had to worry about incursions from Sinai or neighboring zones. The chariotry could lead the army northward into western Asia with impunity.

The Eighteenth Dynasty army was an overland system. Troops advanced on foot. Horses, donkeys, and oxen carried supplies. The animals could graze outside of the walled cities of Palestine. The host need not always enter. Sometimes all that was necessary was to assemble at the gates of a city-state with a large enough force of troops. The locals could then choose either to resist or to support the advancing Egyptian army. If resistance were offered, there would be a battle close to the citadel, where there was no chance of outside support coming to the aid of the defenders. Thus the Egyptians were able to propel themselves northward in a methodical fashion, without encountering major opposition from either a local kingdom or a regional superpower until Thutmose III was sole pharaoh in his 23rd regnal year.

We can now summarize the basic structure of the pharaohs' armies for most of the Eighteenth Dynasty. The chariot division was the elite one. These vehicles were lightweight, and the two horses who drew them were small by today's standards. Chariot wheels had only four spokes until later on in the dynasty. As time went on, chariots became heavier and horses were bred for their task. Foot soldiers and archers fought at close quarters. The king was in the first division when on campaign, but he would have been protected by an elite group called "followers." No warrior pharaoh ever stood alone at the very front of his army.

The ideal weapon was considered to be the sickle-shaped sword, but this military implement was not used in battle. The chariot warrior—and of course the king—stood in the cab of his vehicle and fired arrows. Hence, the image of a warrior king fighting alone in a chariot quickly became the visual and literary trope of the New Kingdom. The archaic scene of smiting with a mace was relegated to monumental representations of the victorious pharaoh. Instead, the concept of "extending the boundaries of Egypt" became the standard, embodied in theory although not in practice, by the mighty self-engrossed warrior leader at the head of his army.

The king departed for war and led his army. Surrounding the marching foot soldiers were his chariots. Light-armed archers may be seen in various depictions providing distant support for the basic infantrymen. The chariots contained two men, one of whom was the driver (and spear thrower) while the other acted as the archer. By the close of the Eighteenth Dynasty, pharaohs' armies had grown in size as well as in complexity. Shield bearers were introduced as assistants to the charioteers.

The type of military encounter seems to have become regularized as well. For example, in the mid-Eighteenth Dynasty, Thutmose III campaigned almost annually from his 29th regnal year. The basic tactical situation remained the same:

(a) advance on foot and proceed from city to city;
(b) accept the surrender of a recalcitrant city or invest it;
(c) fight outside of the same locality, usually on the open plain;
(d) win.

This type of warfare can be likened to a ratchet, the teeth of which move regularly but in an abrupt manner. In order for the advance to proceed without resistance, the Asiatic city must automatically acquiesce to Egyptian control, either before or soon after the appearance of the pharaoh.

By the beginning of the Eighteenth Dynasty, Gaza had been developed and there were a few Egyptian garrisons in western Asia. Megiddo was the nexus in central Palestine connecting the inland road from Gaza on the southwest to Kumidi in Syria in the central north. Beth Shan, close to the eastern edge of central Palestine, was not used until later. From the Amarna Letters we can see just how precarious Egyptian involvement could be when there was no major force in the field. The development of the Eighteenth Dynasty empire in the north was the result of continual warfare.

Thutmose III effectively put an end to the Palestinian resistance, which had been supported by Kadesh on the Orontes River in Syria. Having secured control over Megiddo, Egypt at the mid-Eighteenth Dynasty faced the inland kingdom of Mittani in Syria. Thutmose III and his son fought there without being able to conquer any major portion of that area. Because of difficult logistics, both adversaries thereafter avoided war. Mittani was very distant from Egypt. The limits of control were stronger than the desires of the pharaoh.

The Egyptian sphere of influence was crossed by major highways such as the Via Maris on the coast of the eastern Mediterranean or the inland route of the King's Highway. A third major route led from Megiddo eastward across to the Transjordan. North of Megiddo the inland highway reached into the Syrian province of Amurru with its capital of Kadesh forming yet another nexus in Syria. In addition, the harbors of the Lebanon were secured and became staging points for military advances eastward from the sea. Thereby, the Levant was controlled.

At the same time in Nubia the Egyptians expanded existing garrison-fortresses and set up new temple-towns to control the zone south of the first cataract. Owing to easy accessibility by water—the Nile—the Egyptian military requirements in Nubia were far different from those in the north.

The Military in the New Kingdom: Logistics, Tactics, Ethos

Likewise the Egyptians could easily transport the army and its supplies on ships to Lebanese seaport cities. The strategy was then to deploy men and materiel by two routes to reach the Euphrates River: either directly eastward or else northeast across central Syria, passing through Kadesh. The inherent division of troop allocation and war materiel can best be seen in Thutmose III's accounts and in the famous campaign of Ramesses II against Kadesh in his 5th regnal year. No other Egyptian monarchs have provided us with so much detail.

There were many stops where the king would halt his advance, provide fodder for his horses and oxen, and replenish victuals and water for his soldiers. The battle reliefs of the Kadesh campaign show quite a number of non-combatants among Ramesses's army at rest. There are rows of horses released from their chariots being tended and watered by grooms and boys. Cooks worked in the open. An Egyptian army in Asia brought along its own equipment in order to encamp outside of a major city.

The method of fighting is rarely discussed in the scholarly literature. Regarding actual combat, our source material—the inscriptions and the visual tableaux—are overwhelming pharaoh-centric. Yet we may note the protective stance of the advance guard, called "followers," at the front of the first division housing the king. Depicted as well are the lightly armored foot soldiers who, with daggers and shields, were ideally suited for quick movement and close one-on-one combat. So far as we know, the chariots were not used to mop up the enemy troops. The bowmen in the cabs of those war vehicles performed a role similar to that of the archer elite on foot during earlier times. No battering rams are known from this epoch. Instead, we have illustrations of attacks upon wooden citadel gates by infantrymen wielding axes. There are mercenaries, or at least non-Egyptians, present in those scenes of warfare. Libyans and Nubians can be identified. In some cases, typically in the Nineteenth Dynasty, the elite mercenaries were the Sherden, a group from among the "Peoples of the Sea." Hence, to claim that the Egyptian army was purely composed of natives is inaccurate, at least during the Ramesside Period (Nineteenth to Twentieth Dynasties).

We are familiar with the nomenclature of the New Kingdom chariot corps. The first title, in Egyptian *snnj* or charioteer, referred to all occupants of the vehicle. The word was common in the early Eighteenth Dynasty but disappeared from practical use by the end of the reign of Amenhotep III. Thereafter the language became more specific. From the Nineteenth Dynasty through the second half of the Twentieth Dynasty, *kr῾w* referred to the shield bearers, who were rather like cadets. Another term also applicable to soldiers in chariots was *kdn*, first attested during the reign of Thutmose III. It has been determined that this person was not a fighter but merely a chariot driver. Nevertheless, the *kdn* of "his majesty," the king's driver, was a very important man. This word was borrowed from western Asia, as was the earlier term *snnj*, which was of Hurrian, though ultimately Semitic, origin. Such usage may betoken the importance of the Hurrians during the period of Egyptian weakness during the Second Intermediate Period.

Until the shield-bearer class was created, there were only two men per chariot to perform three tasks in battle: drive the horses and vehicle, shoot arrows or throw a javelin-lance, and protect themselves with a shield against the enemy. While the army was marching, the driver fulfilled only that role whereas the second man assumed the duty of shield bearer, thereby reverting to the traditional role of a foot soldier. These *kr῾w* served in the lowest sector of the chariotry. All of the men were commanded by superiors (*ḥry snnjw*) who had the rank of a standard bearer. The chariot division was subdivided into groups, each of which had specific insignia for identification.

The Sherden came to a significant force within the Egyptian army by the middle of the Nineteenth Dynasty. They acted as guards in the Egyptian monarch's camp. In Egyptian reliefs they are shown as a unit attacking fortresses, especially by scaling the walls or cutting through or down the city gates. They were lightly armed with rather long daggers and small round shields appropriate for close hand-to-hand combat. The contemporary larger, almost trapezoidal Egyptian shield was considerably bulkier and thus better suited for protection. It derived from the even larger leather or hide shields of the Old and Middle Kingdoms. Shields most often protected infantrymen from enemy archers, but also from axes and spears at close range.

In the contemporary accounts of the important battles of the Eighteenth and Nineteenth Dynasties, chariots play a major role when the king is present. This we must take with a few grains of salt. Such narratives are of a literary nature and, not unsurprisingly, often use archaizing terms for the subdivisions within the army. The major campaigns, nonetheless, seem to follow a scenario relatively close to that of the pictorial accounts. Not all of the individual elements, or visual snapshots, need be included every time:

(a) King in chariot departing to war and on the road.
(b) King in chariot alone before outside a city-fortress and shooting his arrows at the besieged enemy (fig. 6.1).
(c) King in chariot presented as a solitary hero, but in text not infrequently as a wise commander-in-chief.
(d) King smites enemy or receives prisoners; the official count of the slain and the captives.
(e) King in chariot ready to go home; his foot is in the cab and the horses are about to depart from the field.
(f) King in chariot travels home. (This is very rare.)

Often based upon the official war diaries, the lengthy literary records and the monuments always tell the same story. The pharaoh reaches a defended fortress. Either he takes it after a show of strength on the battlefield or else the city acquiesces, recognizing the power of the mighty warrior. Then follow a list of the booty and an accounting of the slain or captured.

Thutmose III's version of his assault on Megiddo was published at Karnak. The battle actually took place outside of the city. Both sides marshaled their troops—and especially the chariots—on open ground in sight of each other. The official narrative has the familiarity of a reworked scenario. The Egyptian account is, unfortunately, the only one we possess. The orientation has to be

FIGURE 6.1 Pharaoh Sety I against Yenoam (east Canaan). Northern exterior wall of the hypostyle hall at Karnak; east side, second register.

taken into consideration just as, many years later, we have to rely almost totally upon Ramesses II for what happened at Kadesh.

The kingly records are thus reflective of the military ethos of the New Kingdom. Because they sought to showcase the elite chariotry along with themselves, their combined efforts are highlighted sufficiently for a reconstruction of battle strategy and tactics. For example, Thutmose III's son Amenhotep II claims to have carried out lone activities that, in truth, he would never have been able to accomplish in the unlikely event that he would have been allowed to attempt them. But in his case, as with Thutmose III and Ramesses II, on the record the generalissimo pharaoh fought in the guise of a hero and with the accouterments of war. (The one reported time when Ramesses II rushed boldly to the fight without any armor can be factual only if he was caught off guard.) Never did a pharaoh storm a city or engage in potentially fatal direct combat. Only in pictorial propaganda did the Egyptian monarch encounter an enemy chief almost (pharaoh is drawn larger) face-to-face, where it was a foregone conclusion that the foe would soon be dispatched by means of the king's javelin-spear or sickle-shaped sword. In one very interesting such record, that of Sety I attacking Hittite troops outside of the city of Kadesh, we see the pharaoh moving against the enemy general or leader. The purpose of that image was not to record an event for posterity but to create visually publicity for Sety in the standard role of the "king in battle," a constant pictorial theme in New Kingdom Egyptian history.

Chariot Tactics at Kadesh and the Presence of the King

Under Ramesses II, the son of Sety I, the famous account of the Kadesh "Poem" further demonstrates the chariot obsession. In this case the objective was to surprise the Hittite chariot corps across the Orontes River. Almost under siege, Ramesses with his own chariot support sped out of camp to engage the Hittite adversaries, not once but six times. Naturally, all of this may be read with some degree of skepticism, and not only because of the emphasis upon the personal valor of the Egyptian king. We may also wonder how effective one group of chariots was against the attack of another. (Note that the combat on the first day involved only the Hittite chariotry attacking the Egyptians.) In the Kadesh Poem the infantry is mentioned only once, at the very beginning of the battle when the enemies sliced through the marching second division of the Egyptian army. Elsewhere, the written narrative persistently fixates upon the king's ideal role as the highest elite warrior performing his miraculous counterattack via chariot.

Yet chariots were not tanks. They were not used to scythe through enemy foot soldiers. Moreover, they were not very fast and they were dependent upon flat terrain. Reliefs show javelins piercing the bodies of enemy horses, and

Egyptian teams must have been vulnerable as well. Certainly, the mobile plat-
forms were not well suited to aiming, whether against enemy horses or soldiers.
Encircling movements, which many scholars still wish to believe was the pre-
ferred modus, were not reported by Ramesses at Kadesh, save possibly by the
Hittite enemy in their first chariot-based attack. Thutmose III did not employ
this tactic at Megiddo. Likewise, the small proportion of historical data of the
New Kingdom pharaohs maintains silence concerning the actual deployment
of the chariots.

Even more perturbing, from the point of view of historical inquiry, is the
written account of second day of battle between Ramesses II and the Hittites
outside of Kadesh. The exact location remains speculative. We do not know
how the confrontation came to pass. Was it another formal show of force in
which the great monarchs of the ancient Near East engaged, à la Huizinga's
homo ludens? It has been argued in the scholarly literature that this method
of military combat was advocated by the great leaders of the empires, be they
Hittites, Egyptians, or Mittanians. This interpretation applies here, if only
because both powers on that fateful second day would have been aware of the
terrain, the approximate strength of each army, and the odds of success. I sus-
pect that there was a formalized, chariot-based encounter supported by much
infantry.

The later years of Ramesses II witnessed repeated campaigns. In the north
he reached into Syria and in his apparent attempt to take over and secure
for eternity the southern border region of Amurru (fig. 6.2). The pictorial

FIGURE 6.2 Pharaoh Ramesses II in Syria fighting the fortress-citadel of Dapur. Ramesseum.

evidence for these military ventures is ample, even if the scenes are standard for the most part—king in chariot, on foot, on the attack—and specificity is infrequent.

The same may be said with respect to Merenptah's Canaanite war, which he may not have continuously led in person. Almost all of the Karnak reliefs of the campaign use only the commonplace visual topoi. In addition, the physically large presence of one of the king's sons lends support to the hypothesis that in at least some of the military clashes Merenptah was absent. Here then is a second crucial point, one that may be seen as a conundrum. Did every scene of king versus enemy actually indicate that the pharaoh was present? Owing to political and social ideology, the superhuman image of the pharaoh exists in every Egyptian account. But persistence does not prove that he was, in truth, "there." After all, the Egyptian monarch is known to have employed battle-hardened generals, especially his sons, in war.

If this argument sounds too daring, let me draw attention to one of the early Twentieth Dynasty Medinet Habu reliefs of Ramesses III. In regnal year 8, he fought against the Sea Peoples, an amalgam of various northern invaders such as the Peleshet (who give us the name of Palestine). By land and by sea they came, in two separate waves, or so the records inform us. Both were definitely considered to be planned and coordinated if, of course, the Egyptian point of view is followed. The pictorial accounts purposely separate the two attacks. The presumed second, by sea, appears to have been a naval battle at the extreme north of the Delta, probably at one of the Nile mouths on the eastern Mediterranean coast. The depiction is unique owing to its remarkable interpretation of a naval encounter between the Egyptian flotilla and the enemy armada. For our purposes it is necessary to focus upon the king once more. Ramesses III is shown standing outside of his chariot. As Egyptian monarchs do, he shoots his arrows at the enemy. This topos is figurative. It merely represents the eternal image of the Egyptian ruler defeating a foe. Created by means of this picture is the expectation that Ramesses was physically present. This, after all, is what the designers and the ruler wanted. Was this true? Or did the actual encounter involve only the Egyptian fleet—and not the chariots of the army—against enemy ships? Indeed, how did the two naval forces meet? I have a strong feeling that Ramesses III was never present, and the scene certainly indicates that he was not in charge of any sea vessel. Thus there remains an ever-present sense of skepticism with regard to the personal military involvement of the pharaoh.

The Military at the End of the Bronze Age

The Egyptian army was faced by new threats at this time. Merenptah had to utilize his heavily armed soldiers in order to confront a major threat from the west, a Libyan invasion. The lengthy written record of this war establishes that the Libyans did not have chariots; yet the Egyptian victory was dependent not only upon their possession of battle vehicles but also upon their superior numbers. Furthermore, the account is clear that the Libyans were attempting to settle in the western Delta. They sought domination over Egypt's peripheral zone of control in the northwest. Noteworthy is the evidence that the Libyans acquired better weaponry from their supporters, the Sea Peoples.

To link this war with the ever-increasing threat of outside naval activity in the Mediterranean is not speculative. The Sea Peoples acted as pirates as well as traders, and they were able to move effectively around the littorals of the eastern Mediterranean. Despite the fearful tone of the Egyptian texts and reliefs, the newcomers' population was not large in comparison to that of the settled countries. They were most successful on the coasts, especially against Palestine and the Delta. Later they struck again the important city-state of Ugarit, a major maritime kingdom farther north. They reached Cyprus. The strength of the Sea Peoples was in the number of their ships.

The Sherden were a Sea People who, after an initial encounter with Ramesses II in his 2nd regnal year, became mercenaries for the Egyptians. Scholars have related the victory at Kadesh three years later to the assistance of the Sherden. Afterwards they formed an important part of the Egyptian army and settled on small plots of land in the north. At least some of them were deployed to strongholds, thereby becoming a separate distinguishable military entity in the Ramesside age (second half of the Nineteenth Dynasty— Twentieth Dynasty). One can surmise that for close fighting and efficacy of movement, these foot soldiers made a new and important contribution to the Egyptian army. The native infantry with their bulkier shields may have become the less favored component, although they comprised the vast majority of men. The Egyptian chariot sector and its support system still remained on a higher level than any of the infantry because, regardless of the immense threat from the west and from the eastern Mediterranean, the Egyptian army did not significantly alter its technical and technological methods. Despite three subsequent invasion attempts by the Libyans and the Sea Peoples during the reign of Ramesses III, no particular changes were made—at least officially—in the system of the Egyptian army.

Egypt, threatened, was successfully maintained under Merenptah and Ramesses III. The great trial of strength that took place in the time of Ramesses III often renders his war reliefs more striking than those of Merenptah and, excluding the visual narration of the battle of Kadesh, even of Ramesses II.

Nevertheless, those representations—the famous Medinet Habu scenes of Ramesses III—reveal many new facets of the Egyptian military. The depictions of the naval battle with the Sea Peoples in combination with the scenes of their land attack in Palestine provide much that is useful for our understanding of late Ramesside war society. Other foreigners besides the Sherden had evidently entered the ranks of the Egyptian army. For the first time we have pictorial evidence of the Egyptian fortresses in the northwest, but the pharaoh is no longer depicted attacking a citadel. The new type of enemy was on the move, not settled: Libyans were coming east and Sea People were coming south over land and sea.

The three major wars that Ramesses III faced within the first eleven years of his reign have rarely been discussed from the aspect of real danger. It is uncertain how severe was the land-based Sea Peoples "invasion" of regnal year 8. Then, too, it is questionable whether the seaborne assault on the Nile Delta was as thoroughly coordinated as the Egyptians believed. The incoming troop ships were intent upon attack but not conquest. They offered no logistic support for the far slower land advance of the Sea Peoples' coalition, which included families with their supplies in carts and heavy wagons. On the other hand, it still seems reasonable to view the ominously steady encroachment down the coast of Syria-Palestine, if that is the historical reconstruction, as a major threat to Egyptian control over Palestine, though not over the Delta. As it turned out, the Sea Peoples ended up taking the port cities of the southern Levant. The Egyptians pulled out of their territories in western Asia within thirty years or so after their defeat in Ramesses III's 8th regnal year.

The Libyan threat was but a continuation of population pressures impinging upon the northwest of the Egyptian nation ever since the time of Sety I. Part of the army was stationed in a series of fortresses close to the coast of the Mediterranean, at the westernmost agricultural tract of the Delta. Merenptah was the last fully successful pharaoh to keep the Libyans at bay. The threat reemerged, or so says one written source, owing to the Egyptian attempt to tamper with the kingship of the Libyans, now called Libu or Meshwesh. (The two are often hard to distinguish.) Ramesses III won his two conflicts with them, but we do not know precisely how his army did so. But the repercussions were by no means positive. The Libyans, for example, continued to settle in the northwestern Delta, and the Peleshet, for example, settled on the coast of Palestine and so became, in effect, the "police" of that region. Unfortunately, such details are never revealed in the texts and scenes at Medinet Habu. One advantage that he possessed was his chariots, but it is probable that the sheer numbers of Egyptian defenders stopped the Libyans.

Nevertheless, by the beginning of the Twenty-second Dynasty, many Libyans families were living in clans in the western Delta. Just like the Sherden, they retained more than a smattering of their military lifestyle, which was primitive in comparison to Iron Age societies. It can be surmised that they joined the Egyptian military and the Egyptian populace.

Synthesis

In broad terms these remarks have followed the history of Egypt. I have emphasized the army in its corporate nature. Certainly, by the middle of the Eighteenth
Dynasty it had become a major component of the national identity. With the
scribal administration and the priestly clergy, the war machine of the empire
achieved the place that it surely desired. In fact, its importance had impacts on
the other important corporate entities. This had not been the situation earlier. In
the Old Kingdom the army played an ancillary role in the ethos of state, kingship, religion, and economy of that era. The internecine warfare of the First
Intermediate Period changed that aspect forever. The military system of this
epoch continued through the Twelfth Dynasty. Once Egypt was unified in the
middle of the Eleventh Dynasty, the Theban state was able to commence a series
of expansionistic policies—and not merely raids—upstream into Nubia. The
major campaign of that era was southern and marine-based in contrast to the
expansionism of the early New Kingdom in Palestine and later Syria.

That the army and the navy worked together can be seen from the patchy
records of the Old and Middle Kingdoms. By the Eighteenth Dynasty the
Egyptian fleet was used to transport war materiel and some troops for the push
into central and eastern Syria. Bietak has argued that the Old Kingdom marine
was often composed of Asiatics, especially from the ports of the Levant. This
is difficult to accept owing to the paucity of early data and the liabilities of
making assumptions. The prosopography of data concerning Egypt's seamen
is meager in comparison to that for the Egyptian army. This difference may,
perhaps, be used to argue for the presence of a large number of non-Egyptians
on military vessels during the New Kingdom, but that conclusion must remain
speculative.

It is difficult to identify a transition point between the Middle Kingdom
naval policy and the subsequent reliance upon foot soldiers and charioteers.
The methods and tactics of New Kingdom warfare evolved to suit the geographic zone of western Asia. Essentially, the elite charioteer division followed the same course of development and status as did their counterparts
in the Hurrian kingdom of Mittani in northern Syria and the kingdom of the
Hittites. However, the Egyptian military was not segmented into various client-
based nations as the Hittite forces were. Notwithstanding the presence of foreign mercenaries, the majority of the army remained Egyptian.

Therefore the tricky question of total size challenges historians, who have
not been able to provide any definite answer. We do not know the total number
or percentage of troops on active service, in the reserves, staffing the garrisons,
or performing administrative duties.

But there is one major and striking vector that courses through the historical
survey presented here—namely the role of pharaoh. Excluding the origin of the

unified Egyptian state and the wars that must have preceded it, the early kings "wear no plumes in their helmets." Their bellicose representations are really just standard ones, topoi that could be added at will to a relief or not. Pharaoh did not lead his troops. The armed forces were not geared for continual warfare. It was the local war leaders of the First Intermediate Period who provided the model for Twelfth Dynasty monarchs to command their armies in person when a major conflict was desired.

The accepted scholarly argument is that the Theban State of the Seventeenth Dynasty formed a strong nucleus of nationalistic fervor owing to its virulent opposition to the domination of the Hyksos. Furthermore, it is assumed that the rise of the state god Amun is directly linked with the martial and spiritual ethos of that domain. Yet the army was enlarged during the Eighteenth Dynasty because of a conscious desire to move northward by land and because the latest weapon, the new chariot and horse combination, had to be accommodated. This process took time. Only when effective logistic control was achieved over Sinai could a thrust be made into Palestine. Furthermore, evidence of sentiment for a strong centralized state pre-dates the Eighteenth Dynasty. We can signal the Theban kingdom of the Eleventh Dynasty as well as the defense of Thebes at the close of the Thirteenth Dynasty. As much as an army needs superior military technology, it also requires an effective centralized leadership willing to engage in a long-range plan. Hence, it is not surprising that the imperial pharaohs of the New Kingdom continued the Middle Kingdom practice of personal involvement on the battlefield.

The "Armies of Re" (to repeat the title of this chapter) were not altogether financed by the country. Men served in the military when they were not otherwise engaged elsewhere in agriculture or administration. Soldiers returned to their own plots of land after a campaign. Because the New Kingdom army was not a standing one, it is not possible to make a full, accurate calculation of its total economic impact. True, horses especially, but also chariots and other manufactured war materiel (e.g., shields) became a part of the New Kingdom's centralized economy. Witness, for example, the armament technology at Piramesse (located at the old site of Avaris) in the northwest Delta during the Nineteenth and Twentieth Dynasties.

Sometimes it is further argued that the state became controlled by the army, especially after the series of setbacks that Egypt received at the close of the Eighteenth Dynasty. The religious reformation (or revolution) of Akhenaton is perceived to have weakened Egyptian control in Asia to such a degree that one high-ranking military man, the general Horemheb, had to take power. Such an interpretation runs counter to the extant data of the New Kingdom. A review of the careers of many princes of the empire indicates that these royals started as warriors. The army of the New Kingdom was yet another pyramid at the top of which was pharaoh, but below were his young adult male children. The Egyptian leader remained in charge of the entire military corporation just as he was nominally the highest prelate of the various cults of Egypt, particularly that of Thebes. As well, pharaoh was at the apex of the civil administration. However, within the Egyptian military corporation there was no individual second-in-command, equivalent to the vizier for civil administration. Pharaoh made military strategy. When he was not present to lead his army, various generals, perhaps a son, did so. In the religious sphere there was a degree of difference in that high priests were always fulfilling his role in any cultic setting when he was absent, neither was there one great high priest who controlled all the temples of Egypt. Thus significant change occurred during the New Kingdom whereby the monarch's full time role became that of permanent army commander-in-chief. Perhaps instead of the title "Armies of Re" we should use the designation, at least for the New Kingdom, "Armies of Pharaoh."

Objects

7

The Long Arm of Merchantry

TRADE INTERACTIONS

Samuel Mark

Long before the first king sat on the throne of a unified Egypt, a well-developed trade network moved goods not only throughout Egypt but also into Egypt from foreign lands. Trade goods from the south came from and through Lower Nubia, while goods from Palestine and as far away as Afghanistan and southern Mesopotamia were brought across the northern Sinai by caravans; some possibly came by sea to ports in the Nile Delta. The desire by chieftains in Upper Egypt, who differentiated their status and rank by ornate clothing, jewelry, and other symbols, to control this northern trade may have led to the unification of Egypt. Domination of these and other resources and judicious redistribution of wealth to loyal followers allowed them to maintain and advance their positions: the most powerful were those who controlled and redistributed the most exotic materials. Through its growth and prosperity Egyptian society became more stratified, eventually evolving into a state-level kingship. Once established, this social order required an increasing amount of exotic materials for an increasing number of elite individuals and institutions, such as temples and funerary monuments, especially for the kings through whom all of this wealth flowed.

Ancient Egypt's own considerable wealth in natural resources provided the foundation for its international trade, which was, like its domestic economy, based on barter, a system of direct exchange of goods and services that persisted until the end of the New Kingdom (fig. 7.1). The annual flooding of the Nile allowed farmers to produce abundant agricultural products, supporting quarrying and mining expeditions that brought stones (for construction and ornamentation) and metals, such as gold and copper, from the Eastern Desert and elsewhere. The extant evidence suggests that most foreign imports continued to be exotica for the Egyptian elite and that for much of dynastic history

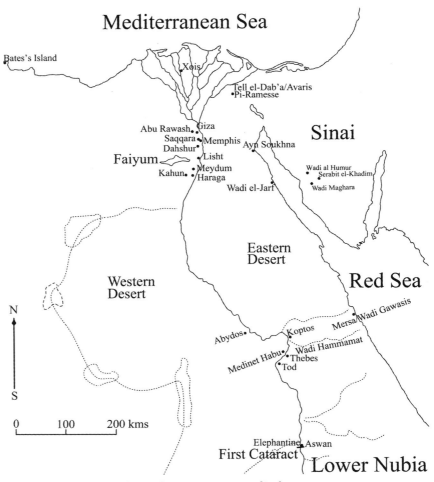

FIGURE 7.1 Map of Egypt and Sinai, showing sites mentioned in the text.

international trade was carried out by the state. This is not to say private merchants did not participate, only that little or no evidence exists for them. Some trading ventures, such as those on the Red Sea, required resources beyond the means of private individuals, who could, however, operate small ships on the Mediterranean or lead donkey caravans to Asia, to Nubia, or even throughout Egypt. The Middle Kingdom *Tale of the Eloquent Peasant* recounts a trip by Khunanup, a private trader from the Wadi Natrun attempting to take his goods to Heracleopolis. He loaded natron, salt, reeds, wooden sticks and staffs, animal skins, stones, and agricultural products on his donkeys, and then traveled south on a system of narrow paths. Such family-level traders were probably common throughout Egyptian history, becoming more important during periods of government decentralization. These small traders are largely invisible because the evidence for most trade comes from royal documents, funerary reliefs, and inscriptions, and imports found in tombs, all of which were meant to celebrate the accomplishments of high-ranking individuals.

Furthermore, most of this trade was in raw materials or in finished goods made from high-value and easily recyclable materials. Those finished goods most likely to survive, such as pottery and stone palettes, were typically copied by those importing them, making it difficult to differentiate between imported objects and local imitations. Some high-quality items, such as Egyptian stone vessels, became either heirlooms or trade items, making it difficult to determine their significance when recovered archaeologically. Thus caution must be taken when reconstructing trade patterns and trade partners or using these latter objects for dating.

Early Dynastic Period (First–Second Dynasties)

Under Aha, first king of the First Dynasty, the Nile was already an efficient highway on which boats moved goods between the Mediterranean and Egypt's southernmost border at Elephantine, a distance of about 1,200 km. Donkey caravans transported wine and olive oil via the Ways of Horus, a road in the northern Sinai that ran between Egypt and its administrative centers at Tell es-Sakan and En Besor and possibly Tel Ma'ahaz and Lod in southern Palestine (fig. 7.2). The evidence for such products comes from tombs, and wine appears to be especially important in the afterlife, but these commodities were also consumed by the living. Additionally, caravans brought turquoise, malachite, and copper obtained through trade with local Sinai populations, and copper might have also come from the Wadi Feinan (southern Jordan). All three of these commodities were imported in quantity no later than the Naqada IIc period. They were used for personal ornamentation (including eye paint) and to adorn other objects, but copper (into which malachite could also be processed) became increasingly important for utilitarian items, especially tools.

Sea trade with Byblos probably began in Predynastic times when this port city was primarily an entrepôt for exotic products (e.g., lapis lazuli from Afghanistan, an import that disappears for a time starting in the First Dynasty) and possibly other raw materials, such as silver and lead, from southwest Anatolia. It became increasingly important at this time as a source for quality timber (cedar), as suggested by the discovery of Early Dynastic Egyptian stone vessels at Byblos. Additional Egyptian exports included some prestige objects in the form of, among other things, palettes, beads, and pottery, but Egypt likely exported goods that left little trace in the archaeological record, including gold, linen, faience, high-quality raw stones, furniture, ointments, and grain.

FIGURE 7.2 Map of the eastern Mediterranean, showing sites mentioned in the text.

Concurrently, in the south, trade moved between Egypt and the so-called Terminal A-Group culture in Lower Nubia (fig. 7.3). Grave goods consisting of pottery from Egypt and Syria/Palestine, copper, and cosmetic palettes of amethyst and quartz suggest considerable wealth among the A-Group elite, who may have flourished as middlemen between Egypt and regions farther to the south. Differentiating Egyptian finished goods from locally produced copies can be difficult, especially when considering that Egyptians, too, may have been living south of the first cataract. Such trade, however, was obviously important, as both groups appear to have experienced a growth of wealth. From Egypt, the Nubians probably acquired not only many of the goods found in their graves but also as bulk cargoes of beer, wine, oils, cheese, cereals, and honey. From the south came ivory, incense, vegetable oils, wild-cat skins, ebony or African blackwood (*Dalbergia melanoxylon*), and obsidian from Ethiopia or Yemen. As Egypt evolved into a state-level society greater quantities of these exotic materials were needed to satisfy the needs of not only a greater number of elite but also an increasing number of temples and royal funerary establishments, suggested by increasingly larger tombs at Abydos. The importance of

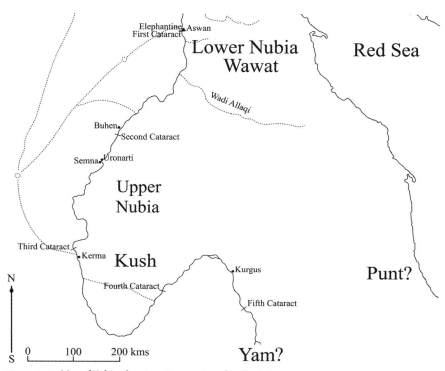

FIGURE 7.3 Map of Nubia, showing sites mentioned in the text.

this southern trade to Egypt may be reflected in the ancient name of the town at modern Aswan, "Swenet," derived from the Egyptian word for "trade."

During the First Dynasty, Egyptian military forays into Lower Nubia (Wawat) drove out the A-Group, and an ebony plaque from the tomb of Aha celebrates such a victory. It seems unlikely that military incursions were instituted to control trade, as it is not until the Sixth Dynasty that the volume of trade in the region seems to have merited such attention. With the disappearance of the A-Group, Lower Nubia remained sparsely populated until later in the Old Kingdom, when the so-called C-Group moved in. During this time, Egypt may have developed the logistical capabilities to move ships across the Eastern Desert for voyages southward along the Red Sea coast to the origin point of some of its most desired exotics, a land called Punt. (The location of the region the Egyptians knew as "Punt" is disputed. Typically, scholars place it somewhere between northern Eritrea and Somalia, and its location probably changed over time.) Alternatively, seagoing rafts from Punt perhaps brought goods to Egypt, as may be depicted much later, in a New Kingdom Theban tomb (TT 143).

Under Aha's successor, Djer, administrative centers in southern Palestine disappeared, but donkey caravans that traveled on the Ways of Horus brought oil and wine from other trading partners farther to the north, Tel Yarmuth and Ai, while copper from Wadi Feinan was obtained through Arad. During the reign of Den, Egyptians themselves were mining copper at Wadi el Humur in Sinai.

Sea trade expanded: ships transported increasing amounts of goods from Byblos, while imports also increased from northern Palestine, where Egyptian officials were stationed at Beth Yerah. This trade coincides with the appearance in Egypt of "Abydos wares," a diverse group of imported Levantine pottery first found in tombs at Abydos. They are typically identified by non-Egyptian traits, such as high and thin handles and globular bodies, as well as a wide variety of decorative techniques, slips, and patterns, including a highly burnished metallic ware. Some were import containers for liquids or resins used in funerary and other ritual contexts. The entrance ramp to the tomb of Semerkhet received a coating of an aromatic oil up to a meter thick, an indication of the abundance of this import. The richness of such First Dynasty tombs indicates that foreign luxury goods were imported in considerable quantities. As these goods are found only in funerary contexts, how widely they were distributed for daily consumption is unknown, but it seems unlikely that they were imported only to be interred, and—although this is speculative—these burial goods are probably a small percentage of what was imported.

Data for trade during the Second Dynasty is scarce. If, however, the tomb of Khasekhemwy at Abydos is any indication, it continued to expand; this king's tomb could hold more goods than all First Dynasty tombs at that site combined.

Old Kingdom (Third–Sixth Dynasties)

Inscriptions indicate that Egyptians were mining at Wadi Maghara (Sinai) by the reign of Djoser, first king of the Third Dynasty, while during that of Sanakht, Egypt seems to control Sinai resources. Stone vessels found at Ai and Tel Yarmuth suggest that trade continued between Egypt and southern Palestine, but, as in the Second Dynasty, little other evidence survives. Regardless, commerce both with the cities of Palestine and with Byblos probably continued to grow.

This included the timber trade. Early Dynastic boat burials at Abydos and Abu Rawash contain hulls that seem to be built only of local timber, while for tomb 3506 at Saqqara wood was at such a premium that its subsidiary graves featured either wood coffins or wood-lined pits, but not both. By the reign of Sneferu, first ruler of the Fourth Dynasty, this had changed: in one year, forty of this king's ships returned to Egypt filled with cedar. The primary entrepôt for this timber was Byblos, but other cities, such as at Tell Arqa and Sidon, may likewise have supplied it.

With this increase in trade must have come a corresponding increase in the acquisition of raw materials (such as through mining) and finished goods for export. Large, state-supported expeditions to the Eastern Desert were needed to obtain the former, and more craftsmen were required to produce the latter. More timber from Byblos and Nubia would have been needed to build an increasing number of riverboats to transport imports, exports, building materials, and workers (such as miners), throughout Egypt. All of this required additional support personnel with more training, suggesting that the Egyptian economy must have undergone considerable expansion and improvement in infrastructure. Organization and management of these increasingly complex operations called for an expanding bureaucracy. Such development is reflected in increasingly larger construction projects, especially royal tombs and temples. Although few imports survive from these tombs, their increasing capacity for grave goods must reflect a ceaseless expansion of trade from the First into the Fourth Dynasties.

From the Levant, larger combed-ware jars replaced Abydos wares and facilitated the importation of greater quantities of liquids, oils, and coniferous resins. Elemental analysis indicates that some came from Byblos, while others probably came from the region of Mount Hermon in Palestine. These larger containers are better suited to be carried aboard ships rather than on donkeys. Any pottery container will add additional weight to a commodity without adding value and can thus actually reduce the value carried by each donkey; using a lighter, leather container would allow an animal to carry additional weight of the commodity of interest to one's trading partners. In contrast, large imported pottery containers or large numbers of small pottery containers suggest transport by ship, which can carry greater volumes over longer distances in a shorter time with less risk of breakage than an overland caravan. In addition to bulk cargoes of oil and timber, Byblos continued to supply exotica found in royal tombs built at Meydum, Dahshur, and Giza.

Lapis lazuli reappeared in Egypt at this time. Ebla may have controlled its import from the east, along with silver from southern Anatolia and possibly animals: a relief, dating to Sahure's reign, shows bears and large cats brought from Syria. Egyptian stone vessels, two of which bear royal names (Khafre; Pepy I), found at Ebla might indicate this city's importance, but they are the only evidence of contact between Ebla and Egypt. They appear to have been crafted over an extended period of time (Fourth Dynasty; Sixth Dynasty) and could indicate a trading relationship that spanned much of the Old Kingdom. Both were found together in the Palace G complex; if they were heirlooms, they could still support this interpretation. They may also have been of considerable value, especially since they were too shallow for commodities. It is equally likely based on current evidence that they could have been acquired more or less contemporaneously as booty or in trade from Egyptians or middlemen dealing in looted items. Like so many exceptional pieces that appear to establish contacts between cultures, the complete story is unknown. That is, whether trade was direct, indirect, or a combination of both; the last is the most likely. The Egyptians desired lapis lazuli, and Ebla was positioned to control this trade along with silver from Anatolia. The Egyptian stone containers are consistent with other recorded diplomatic gifts to ensure a constant supply of these valuable resources in the quantities needed.

Trade caravans from southern Palestine and Sinai continued to enter Egypt via the Ways of Horus. During the Fourth Dynasty, until the reign of Khufu, the Egyptians used a harbor on the Gulf of Suez, at Wadi el-Jarf, to bring ores from the mines at Serabit el-Khadim (southern Sinai). Considering the size and complexity of this site, it may also have been the point of departure for ships bound for Punt. After the abandonment of Wadi el-Jarf, Ayn Soukhna became the new transshipment center between Serabit el-Khadim and Memphis, the capital.

During Khufu's reign a small Egyptian settlement was established at Buhen, near the second cataract, for copper processing and possibly trade, but considering the small size of the site and paucity of evidence of exotic goods, the latter was probably minimal. Evidence of direct trade with Punt dates to only slightly later, the Fifth Dynasty king Sahure, with voyages probably sailing from Mersa/Wadi Gawasis, a harbor far south of Ayn Soukhna. The Palermo Stone states he imported 80,000 measures of myrrh, 6,000 (?) of electrum, and 2,600 staves (possibly ebony) from Punt. A relief depicting relatively small and lightly built ships also shows monkeys (including baboons), dogs, and even Puntite families, while Sahure himself is depicted tending to a myrrh tree.

Even these small seagoing ships could transport volumes of goods far greater than could be obtained via trade along the Nile. Additionally, by sailing to the source of myrrh and cutting out the middlemen in Nubia, the Egyptians could get better value when bartering. The disassembly and storage of ship timbers and equipment in rock-cut galleys at Mersa/Wadi Gawasis suggests that such trading voyages were relatively common and demonstrate considerable time and resources that the Egyptian state invested in each voyage. The undertaking of these risky ventures underscores the need, demanded by state and temple institutions of increasing size and number, for large volumes of exotica, especially myrrh. The depiction of the Sahure Punt ship illustrates another point: an import might not be recognizable as such even when it is rather common in tombs, such as dogs and monkeys. These—for example—are believed to have been interred because they were either a beloved pet or for religious reasons but never because they were valued by their owners as an exotic import that bestowed a degree of status. Taking this into account, virtually none of the goods from Punt cited above in this high-volume trade would survive (e.g., myrrh and electrum, consumed or used to make Egyptian objects) or, as in the case of dogs and monkeys, be readily recognized as foreign.

International trade may have decreased during the Fifth Dynasty, as the archaeological record has yielded fewer imported containers, but a lack of a representative ceramic sampling may skewed the data, as is likewise possible for the Second and Third Dynasties. Moreover, imported ceramics appear in the provinces, further skewing the data because it is not clear if these were primarily containers for imported commodities—possibly suggesting a decentralized government with fewer elite living at court—or if there was a market in the provinces for empty import containers. Even if imports did decrease, the quantities attributed to Sahure's Punt expedition suggest that a great amount and variety of goods continued to arrive in Egypt. It is thus difficult to reconcile a seeming reduction of trade in the Mediterranean when no evidence exists for a reduction of trade with Punt, because, compared to long-distance Red Sea voyages, reaching the Levant was less costly in terms of effort, material, and time.

The importance of commerce with Byblos and possibly Ebla persisted during the Fifth and Sixth Dynasties, as indicated by the large quantities of Aegyptiaca discovered at both sites. At Byblos it appears to include stone vessels, cylinder seals, statuary, furniture, game boards, faience, and semi-precious stones, while at Ebla it consists of only one of the previously noted stone vessels. Inscriptions mentioning voyages also survive. A high official named Iny returned from the Levant with valuables on missions for several kings of the Sixth Dynasty: silver and other products for Pepy I; lapis lazuli, silver, oils, and other products for Merenre; and silver and people for Pepy II.

Under Pepy I, unrest is described in the Sinai and southern Palestine. Another official, Weni, undertook five military expeditions in the northern Sinai and set sail with troops to southern Palestine to quell another revolt. That these events did not disrupt trade is suggested by the discovery of Sixth Dynasty Meidum bowls along the Ways of Horus. Thus commerce in this region may have persisted until late in the Sixth Dynasty or shortly thereafter, when population centers in southern Palestine were abandoned and replaced with semi-nomadic herders.

Interest in Lower Nubia was renewed in the Sixth Dynasty. For Merenre, Weni cut five channels through the first cataract to allow ships to pass through, and he constructed seven boats of acacia, so timber may have been an important import from this region. The first mentions of caravans through Lower Nubia also appear during this time. Harkhuf made four journeys to the distant southern Nubian country of Yam, the precise location of which is uncertain (possibly also Kush or a land farther south). His route is not known (i.e., the desert roads or via the Nile). During his first expedition, for Merenre, he boasts he was the first to explore and "pacify" these regions. On his third journey he returned with a caravan consisting of three hundred donkeys carrying incense, ebony, grain, panthers, ivory, and throw-sticks. Under Pepy II, Harkhuf brought another caravan of goods, including a dancing Pygmy.

Voyages to Punt continued; Anankhet and his men, building a ship for Punt, were massacred by "Sand-dwellers," possibly at Mersa/Wadi Gawasis. Another official, Khnumhotep, traveled to both Kush and Punt. During this period cargoes from Punt may have been smaller, considering that Sahure had sent a flotilla while Anankhet was constructing only one ship. If so, the land-and-river route through Nubia might have supplemented fewer imports arriving by sea.

Middle Kingdom (Late Eleventh–Thirteenth Dynasties)

After the reign of Pepy II, when the decline of the central state resulted in the First Intermediate Period, no evidence exists for significant trade between Egypt and its foreign neighbors until Mentuhotep II reunified the country. He established a garrison at Elephantine and from here made incursions south of the first cataract. One of his officials, Khety, went to Sinai probably for copper, while his steward, Henenu, traveled to Lebanon for cedar. His successor, Mentuhotep III, sent Henenu to Punt for myrrh.

Amenemhat I moved the capital from Thebes to Itj-tawy in the Fayum region, probably near Lisht. The government became more centralized and the bureaucracy grew. Several jewelry caches from royal tombs reflect a considerable increase in wealth, partly due to resources brought from Sinai and Punt, but exploitation of Nubia's mineral resources became increasingly important. Concurrently, trade with the Levant, especially for cedar, grew: Amenemhat I had fleet of twenty cedar ships that helped him defeat another claimant to the throne.

Amenemhat I was succeeded by Senwosret I, who in turn was succeeded by Amenemhat II. The Mit Rahina annals date to his reign and mention the city of Tunip (possibly at Tell Asharneh on the Orontes River) as a trading partner. The text describes three military expeditions against Asiatics: one probably to Sinai, the other two against unknown walled towns somewhere in the Levant. The army returned with 1,554 prisoners, along with considerable quantities of gold, silver, copper, precious stones, oils, trees, wine, and valuable timbers. These spoils of war exemplify the goods that Egyptians most desired and probably later traded for. Given that little evidence exists for substantial trade along the Ways of Horus during this period, these towns were not likely located in southern Palestine, which was still populated by pastoralists. Later in the Middle Kingdom, people indigenous to southern Palestine re-established their cities, but goods still mainly moved westward to coastal cities, instead of southward overland to Egypt. Thus, Egyptian trade in Palestine and the Levant was predominantly along the coastal sea route, possibly in Egyptian ships with Egyptian crews, even as Egyptian ships and crews sailed on the Red Sea.

Amenemhat II may have pursued a strategy that combined trade with military excursions into the Levant. Even as late as the Thirteenth Dynasty, the ruler of Byblos referred to himself as a servant of Egypt. By the late Twelfth Dynasty, Tell el-Dab'a in the eastern Nile Delta was serving as a seaport for the Levantine trade; its importance was such that the construction of a palace began in the Thirteenth Dynasty, but this was never completed. The northeastern location of Tell el-Dab'a also allowed it to receive goods from the Ways of Horus, increasing its importance.

The peaceful reign of Senwosret II concentrated primarily on trade with the Near East, dealing in the same commodities as earlier periods. Byblos likewise remained Egypt's most important trade partner, with other trade partners probably extending from Ashkelon in the south to at least as far north as Ugarit. Ebla also continued to be an important supplier of lapis lazuli, silver, and possibly animals.

No later than sometime in the Twelfth Dynasty, trade with Minoan Crete began, as indicated by the appearance of Minoan pottery, such as Kamares wares, the popularity of which is reflected by the appearance of Egyptianized imitations. They are difficult to date from their archaeological contexts, as they either came from ancient dumps or were poorly documented during excavation. Probably used domestically, Minoan wares are found at Kahun, Haraga, and Lisht. These concentrations were probably influenced by the close proximity to the capital city of Itj-tawy enjoyed by these sites, but Minoan ceramics were likely more common throughout Egypt than the archaeological record suggests, as they appear as far south as Buhen. Furthermore, in the foundation beneath the floor of the temple of Senwosret I at Tod were discovered remains of four copper chests inscribed with the name of Amenemhat II. In them were a large number of silver containers made either by Minoan craftsmen or by Egyptian craftsmen who borrowed Minoan motifs. Some appear to represent seashells; others have a whorl pattern not seen in Egyptian arts or crafts prior to contact with Minoan Crete. Along with these silver pieces was a considerable amount of lapis lazuli, silver ingots and chains, and gold items.

In exchange, Minoans appear to have received ivory and gold from Egypt, but possibly a wider variety of items as well, since, as previously noted, Egyptian exports rarely survive in the archaeological record. Whether trade between Egypt and Crete was direct or "down the line" is unknown. Given that no evidence exists for a trade monopoly by any one country and that the Egyptians competently sailed on the Red Sea, there is no reason to think that they would not do likewise in the Mediterranean. If Egyptian ships were sailing as far north at Ugarit, making an additional stop in Crete would not pose a hardship: in the *Odyssey* (14.257–8), Homer notes that prevailing winds and currents made the voyage from western Crete to Egypt an easy five days.

Senwosret III had a new channel carved through the first cataract to allow ships better access to and from Nubia, and he built two fortresses at Semna and Uronarti, south of the second cataract, establishing this region as the southern border of Egypt. Between this border and the first cataract, he completed fourteen massive forts begun by Senwosret II, providing protection against Kush, a Nubian kingdom ruled from its capital at Kerma above the third cataract. Some forts were also used for trade with local populations. These installations were expensive not only to build but also to support and maintain, requiring shipments of food and other supplies from Egypt. The fortress at Buhen alone was garrisoned by about 5,000 soldiers and possibly their families. That Egypt would and could go to this considerable expense emphasizes that they allowed Egypt to obtain great wealth through exploitation of Nubian gold and other mineral resources and through trade in exotica from even farther to the south. The latest Middle Kingdom record of a Punt voyage dates to Amenemhat IV, but ceramics found at Mersa/Wadi Gawasis suggest that voyages may have continued into the Thirteenth Dynasty.

Very little is known about the state of trade during the Thirteenth Dynasty. By the fifth king, Hor, Lower Nubia was still under Egyptian control, and the ruler of Byblos, Inten, still referred to himself as the king's servant, but in the Delta independent rulers may have governed from Xois and Avaris. As late as Sobekhotep IV, Egypt seems to maintain control over Lower Nubia, but during his reign there are revolts, and Kerma eventually took control of this region. By the end of this dynasty, domination of the north by a dynasty of foreigners known as the Hyksos forced the Egyptian capital to move from Itj-tawy southward, back to Thebes.

Second Intermediate Period (Fourteenth–Seventeenth Dynasties)

Mediterranean trade patterns appear to have changed little from the Middle Kingdom. The Hyksos capital at Avaris (Tell el-Dab'a) continued to be an important seaport for trade with Levantine cities, like Byblos and Ugarit. The Kamose stela, from late in this period, mentions hundreds of cedar ships carrying lapis lazuli, gold, silver, bronze axes, turquoise, oils, honey, and fine woods in its harbor. Through the Second Intermediate Period, however, trade with Cyprus (probably for copper) increased, even though finds of ceramics, scarabs, and inscriptions at Serabit el-Khadim indicate mining for copper and turquoise continued in Sinai. Curiously, little evidence exists for trade with the Minoans. Considering trade flourished with all other of Egypt's Middle Kingdom trade partners, there is no known reason for cessation of trade with Crete.

By the Fifteenth Dynasty, Hyksos rule included an administrative center at Memphis, allowing them to tax goods transported along the Nile. Meanwhile, the southern border of their Theban contemporaries (Sixteenth and Seventeenth

Dynasties) was at Elephantine, beyond which the Kushite kingdom, centered at Kerma, was growing wealthy from mines and quarries in Lower Nubia and from trade in exotica with groups to the south. Kerma and Avaris traded with each other mainly along desert caravan trails west of the Nile, denying Theban Egypt participation in such exchanges. The fortunes of Thebes finally changed under Kamose, who re-conquered Lower Nubia to the second cataract and sailed to the Delta, ending this "intermediate" period.

New Kingdom (Eighteenth–Twentieth Dynasties)

Ahmose, first king of the Eighteenth Dynasty, conquered the north, taking Avaris and its port, and then continued into southern Palestine, creating an infusion of wealth for the newly reunified country. The new dynasty drew resources from the Sinai mines that the Hyksos had continued to exploit and expanded them, with both caravans and ships bringing malachite, copper, and turquoise to Egypt through Ayn Soukhna or a similar port. Ahmose then turned his attention southward, probably to consolidate his southern border and also to obtain raw materials, especially gold.

Thutmose I conquered Kerma and continued on to Kurgus, midway between the fourth and fifth cataracts. Except for occasional uprisings, these lands remained under Egyptian control until near the end of the New Kingdom, providing enormous wealth from mines, quarries, and trade, possibly including from Punt. Scenes in the tomb of Huy, Viceroy of Kush under Tutankhamen, show Nubians bringing tribute, including a giraffe, long-horned cattle, and both wild and tamed leopards (the latter used for hunting). Also depicted are rings and boxes of electrum, boomerangs, ebony, leopard skins, bows, feathers, and ostrich eggs. Whatever goods came down the Nile from Punt seem not to have met Egyptian demand, because sea-lanes were soon reopened.

After the short reign of Thutmose II, his widowed wife and half-sister Hatshepsut, regent for the young Thutmose III, seized power and went on to rule for fifteen years. Her mortuary temple at Deir el-Bahri commemorates her reopening of the sea trade with Punt. Hatshepsut's fleet of five ships—each larger than any of Sahure's—probably sailed from Mersa/Wadi Gawasis and returned with thirty-one incense trees, large quantities of aromatic resins in pyramidal shapes, great quantities of ebony, boxes and rings of gold and electrum, a heap of boomerangs, cinnamon wood, antimony, dogs, various monkeys, elephant tusks, leopard skins, tamed leopards, a herd of cattle, and four Puntite chiefs with a large number of other men, women, and children. Such goods from Punt would have had a major economic impact, and during the reign of Hatshepsut a political impact, especially if voyages were relatively frequent, as suggested by iconographic and textual evidence. During the Hyksos period temples and palaces in Egypt had fallen into disrepair, and some had been stripped of anything of value. By resuming trade with Punt and importing considerable quantities of exotica needed to repair and supply the temples, Hatshepsut was able to win over the support of the priestly class. These exotic goods were also desired by Mediterranean trade partners, and consistent access to large quantities of high-value items allowed Egypt's international trade to expand more rapidly.

Great quantities of the same goods listed on the earlier Kamose stela continued to pass through the port at Tell el-Dab'a. The primary trade partner was, as in previous centuries, Byblos. Most trade continued to be coastal, and cedar continued to be a prized import, with inscriptions emphasizing the use of "new" cedar. The amounts of Levantine pottery found in Egypt indicate that trade between these regions increased, and connections with Minoan Crete (the "Keftiu" of inscriptions) probably reopened during Hatshepsut's reign. The tomb of her royal steward, Senenmut, contains the earliest known images of emissaries from Keftiu bringing gifts to Egypt.

There is disagreement as to whether this trade was direct or indirect. What evidence survives in Egypt consists of a modest amount of Minoan pottery or local copies showing that Egyptian craftsmen were familiar with this foreign ware, while in Crete there are a number of scarabs, some Early Dynastic stone containers, and amethyst from Egypt, all of which would be consistent with indirect trade. However, a scene in the tomb of Rekhmire, who served Thutmose III and Amenhotep II as vizier, shows imports from Keftiu consisting primarily of various gold and silver containers and large amounts of lapis lazuli, silver, and bronze: all of these are either objects easily recyclable or raw materials. Resource-poor Crete imported expensive raw materials and exported high-quality finished goods and, sometimes, the very same exotic raw materials that it had acquired in trade. Thus, most Egyptian imports by the Minoans probably consisted of exotic and expensive raw materials, especially gold, which would not survive untransformed in the archaeological record. Moreover, the Minoans were known as accomplished seafarers, and it seems unlikely that they would avoid the major international port of Tell el-Dab'a, which their ships could reach in only five days. Tell el-Dab'a became important especially after the conquests of Thutmose III, and this king's palace at the port was decorated with frescoes in a Minoan style.

The conquests of Thutmose III in the Near East also brought great wealth in the form of both tribute and trade. He undertook seventeen campaigns, some by land and others by sea, into the Levant and regions farther east, to intimidate the populations and collect tribute. These efforts resulted in unprecedented wealth flowing into Egypt, and they may have opened new markets or possibly established better trade terms with old partners. Shortly after Thutmose III defeated Mittani in his 33rd regnal year, Babylon, Assyria, the Hittites, Cyprus, and Alalakh sent gifts to the pharaoh. Commerce also benefited from this king's practice of creating and enforcing the allegiance of vassals by the Egyptianization of the heirs apparent of local ruling families. Heirs to ruling families were sent at a young age to the Egyptian court to be educated and forge strong bonds with the heir to the Egyptian throne; upon reaching adulthood they returned home as rulers sympathetic to the Egyptian king. Sea routes never appear to change, and before Thutmose III the Ways of Horus primarily served Sinai and southern Palestine. After his conquests, this route becomes increasingly important as indicated by the discovery of 150 New Kingdom sites farther north along the Mediterranean coast, distributed in ten clusters around Egyptian administrative centers or forts, with increased trade probably coming via terrestrial routes from some of these conquered lands.

Amenhotep II undertook only two campaigns in Syria, both to put down rebellions. From Takhsy, the army carried back to Egypt plunder that included 6,800 *deben* (*c.* 745 kg) of gold, 500,000 *deben* (*c.* 55,000 kg) of copper, 210 horses, 300 chariots, and 550 captives. It is, however, this king's alliance with Mitanni that had the greatest impact on trade, allowing amicable and open access to all countries as far as the Euphrates. This elevated the economic importance of the already valuable Ways of Horus, particularly during the reign of his grandson Amenhotep III. Amenhotep III's peaceful thirty-eight-year reign allowed considerable new construction, which was underwritten by bumper crops of grain, as well as immense imports from the south and the north.

By early in Amenhotep III's reign, if not sooner, Minoan Crete fell to the Mycenaean Greeks, although this did not stop trade between Egypt and the Aegean. The evidence for direct and indirect contact remains the same as for earlier periods, but an inscription, the "Aegean list" from Amenhotep III's memorial temple at Kom el-Hetan, presents an inventory of specific sites on Crete and mainland Greece, indicating an intimate knowledge of the region and supporting the possibility of Egyptian voyages there. Possibly during his reign a resupply station may have been established to the west of Egypt on Bates's Island, Marsa Matruh where Minoan, Mycenaean, and Cypriot artifacts have been found. Foreign traders may have traded there with local Libyans, as suggested by the discovery of ostrich eggshells.

Although wealth continued to flow from Nubia, Punt, the Eastern Desert, and the Sinai mines, starting with the reign of Akhenaten and continuing through the 21st year of Ramesses II, the size of the empire to the east expanded and contracted, usually with Mitanni and then the Hittites as the main antagonists. Mismanagement of foreign affairs and a costly war against the Hittites led to a loss of territory and associated reduction of tribute from the east. Additionally, Egypt may have lost access to these lands and harbors, such as Ugarit, which fell under Hittite rule, with a result in diminished trade.

The enormous diversity of international trade that nonetheless persisted during this uneasy period is represented by the Uluburun shipwreck, a ship—possibly Canaanite—that sank off the Anatolian coast late in the Eighteenth Dynasty, carrying a rich cargo that included 10 tons of Cypriot copper, 1 ton of tin, gold jewelry, Egyptian scarabs (including one in gold with the name of Queen Nefertiti), Nubian or Syrian elephant ivory, Egyptian or southern Palestinian hippopotamus ivory, Canaanite and Cypriot carved ivory, Nubian or Libyan ostrich eggshells, Egyptian glass, and ebony from Punt or elsewhere in Africa. The wealth, particularly in raw and recyclable materials, carried aboard this one ship on one voyage suggests that trade was healthy even during these troubled times and probably far more diverse and of greater extent than typically suspected.

In the 21st year of Ramesses II, he concluded a treaty with the Hittites that once again opened peaceful relations among all countries in the region, allowing trade to return to levels not seen since the reign of Amenhotep III. With this wealth Ramesses II built extensively, including, near Avaris, a city he named Piramesse. Commerce by sea and along the Ways of Horus from Palestine and Syria made Piramesse, like Avaris before it, an international entrepôt.

This new golden age was short lived. In the waning years of his reign and that of his son Merenptah, Mycenaean civilization collapsed, as did parts of the Hittite empire. Concurrent with these events was a disruptive movement of populations known collectively in ancient times as the "Peoples of the Sea." Originating largely from the Aegean and Anatolia, these migrants may have been fleeing political or climatic hardships, and in fact the situation in Anatolia became dire enough that Merenptah sent grain to the Hittites to alleviate a famine.

Egypt's struggle for its own stability succeeded with the rise of the Twentieth Dynasty. Beyond Egypt, however, the Hittite empire collapsed, Tarsus and much of Cilicia was sacked, and Alalakh, Ugarit, and Enkomi (capital of Cyprus) were destroyed as well. In year 8 of Ramesses III's thirty-year reign, the Sea Peoples once again attacked Egypt and were again defeated. He was able to retain Egypt's eastern possessions and send what would be the last recorded voyage to Punt. For most of his reign trade flourished, and he completed a splendid memorial temple along the Theban west bank (Medinet Habu), as well as buildings in Piramesse. There is a pattern in Egyptian history of an increase massive building projects corresponding to an influx of wealth from war and trade, but Ramesses III's reign also witnessed decentralization of the government, large contributions to temples, and soaring grain prices. Even the great harbor at Piramesse began to silt up and disappear.

After the death of Ramses III, the disintegration of the Egyptian empire began and with it a loss of markets for trade. Northern possessions quickly slipped from Egypt's grasp, as did Nubia, resulting in a loss of Nubian resources and exotica from Punt, further reducing access to high-value trade goods and resulting wealth from elsewhere. Ramesses VI was the last recorded king to mine in Sinai, and not long after his reign Egyptian rulers could not send successful expeditions even into the Eastern Desert, leaving them with little wealth to trade. The New Kingdom concluded with the throne occupied by Rameses XI, whose rule of some thirty years ended with his kingdom consisting of merely Lower Egypt, while a number of usurpers ruled Upper Egypt from Thebes, the last being Herihor, whose reign obtained its resources largely through tomb robbery rather than trade.

8

Artisans and Their Products

INTERACTION IN ART AND ARCHITECTURE

Stuart Tyson Smith

Ancient Egyptian art and architectural styles impacted cultures in the Levant, Aegean, and Nubia (pl. 6). Egyptian-style temples beyond Egypt's southern border and Egyptianizing coffins in Syria-Palestine are both examples of the widespread influence of Egyptian art and architectural styles, and very likely the movement of Egyptian artisans beyond Egypt's borders. Egypt's engagement with both of these regions increased over time from the Bronze to Iron Age, forming distinctively blended modes of art and architecture and playing a key role in the development of the International Style that flourished in the second and first millennium BCE. At the same time, Egyptian artisans were influenced by foreign elements in an increasingly cosmopolitan society, although these impacts were subtler. The presence of Aegean-style art and Levantine artistic motifs attest to Egyptian importation of foreign art, and very likely artisans and artists, some of whom may have circulated as a part of the official diplomatic exchanges between royal courts that characterized the Near Eastern Bronze and Iron Age. These influences and interactions vary by individual site, region, and period, following on and conditioned by individual interactions and engagement with material culture obtained through trade and conquest. Egypt is often thought of as more engaged and culturally entangled with the Middle East, but the profoundest impacts lay in another part of Africa, Nubia (southern Egypt and northern Sudan).

Going back a hundred years to the diffusionist models of Petrie and Smith, both foreign influence on Egypt and the transfer of Egyptian cultural features to the areas surrounding Egypt, including art and architecture, are often seen as a unidirectional process, where artistic and architectural styles were adopted wholesale. In particular, a model of Egyptianization has been and to some extent still is applied in the context of Egypt's dominant-subordinate relationships with its Levantine and especially Nubian empires. The concept of Egyptianization, like related models of Romanization and Hellenization, is coming under increasing criticism. Cultural transmission is sometimes, but rarely, perfect, and the adoption of cultural practices, including art and architecture, were more often selective and adaptive and flowed in both directions, even in the context of imperial domination.

Michael Dietler's (2010) model of cultural entanglement provides a robust framework that can capture the complex dynamics of intercultural borrowings and the often unintended consequences that can result from the intercultural consumption of material culture, in our case art and architecture. Entanglement takes into account both sides of the exchange, calling for a nuanced analysis of the intersection of the different social and cultural logics of the parties involved, leading to the adoption, adaptation, indifference to, or rejection of different cultural features in any relationship. Additionally, the idea of cultural entanglement allows us to consider the role of individual action where cultural borrowings flow through a constant dialectic between the constraints of cultural predispositions and the pressure of individual adaptation and innovation that comes to the fore through interaction and exposure to different cultural practices, in our case through the movement of material culture, artists, and artisans to and from Egypt.

Early similarities in art and iconography exist between Egypt and the Nubian A-Group during the late Predynastic and into the Early Dynastic Period. Some items were almost certainly made in Egypt and sent as gifts to the A-Group rulers, but other objects, most notably the Qustul incense burner, were clearly made locally using iconography normally connected with Egyptian kingship, probably reflecting mutual influence. The Egyptian expansion into Lower Nubia during the Middle Kingdom reengaged the two regions after a hiatus during the Old Kingdom. The empire introduced artisans of various kinds and large-scale mud-brick architecture through the establishment of a major series of fortresses over the course of the Twelfth Dynasty. By the end of the dynasty, these fortresses were true colonies, with communities of Egyptian immigrants making Nubia their home. Several sites, including Askut, Buhen, Mirgissa, and Serra East, have produced archaeological evidence for local craft production along Egyptian lines, notably pottery workshops, but also including a variety of other basic activities, including weaving, metallurgy, and lithic production. Although the pottery industry largely mimicked contemporary Egyptian forms and decoration, some Nubian stylistic motifs were adopted. Often referred to as "gilded ware," a new decorative mica-rich slip technique that gave a golden glow to vessels was an innovation of Egyptian potters working in Nubia and was eventually adopted by Nubian potters.

Egyptian architects brought the most elaborate forms of large- and small-scale mud-brick architecture to Nubia, constructing some of the most massive and elaborate fortifications seen in the ancient world, as well as administrative complexes and residences for the elite and commons. Tombs of the elite in associated cemeteries were also constructed in Egyptian style with mud-brick architecture and underground complexes, with simpler tombs and burials for the rest of the colony's inhabitants. A variety of jewelry and other examples of the decorative arts, such as furniture and figurines, have also been found in the Egyptian colonial settlements and cemeteries. It is not clear just how much of this material might have been imported, but it is likely that immigrant artisans made many locally. The same may be said for grave goods, including funerary amulets, statuary, and elaborately decorated coffins.

The presence of Nubian material culture at all of these sites suggests a closer interrelationship between the local population and the fortress communities than the general decline of imports and Egyptian influence at indigenous C-Group sites would suggest. In particular, the presence of Nubian pottery and disproportionate presence of large percentages of cooking pottery at Askut points towards intermarriage, bringing with it some Nubian influence in crafts such as ceramic production, figurines, and lithics. In Egypt itself, the presence of Nubian soldiers at sites such as Deir el-Ballas and Avaris (Tell el-Dab'a) is reflected through ceramics and other material culture. Similarly, the Pan Grave culture, loosely correlated with the historic semi-nomadic Medjay, was a distinct presence in Upper Egypt and parts of Nubia, with a distinctive material culture and ceramic tradition that mixed elements drawn from Egypt and Kerma. Direct Nubian influence on Egyptian artisans is hard to trace but includes the use of fly imagery in jewelry, considered to be an award for military valor, such as those of Queen Ahhotep. Golden flies also appear in the Levant, for example in graves at Tell el-Ajuul in the Gaza Strip, presumably transmitted via Egypt.

The invasion of Lower Nubia and construction and elaboration of the fortress system was motivated by the rise of the first kingdom of Kush, whose capital lay just south of the third cataract at Kerma. Based upon the presence of Egyptian-influenced architecture, statuary, and craft industries, Reisner originally thought that the site was the southernmost Egyptian colony, but even at the time this notion was quickly criticized, for example by Junker, who emphasized Kerma's non-Egyptian nature. Although a few individual pieces may represent royal gifts, Egyptian Middle Kingdom statuary, such as the famous seated monuments of the nomarch of Asyut Djefaihapi and his wife Sennuwy found in the last royal tomb, most likely reached Kerma as booty from razzia like the one described in the autobiography of Sobeknakht. We now know that Kerma was the center of a burgeoning state, increasing in centralization and power over the course of the Middle Kingdom, a real rival to Egypt's interests in the region and key partner in managing trade in key luxury materials, including items that were important to Egyptian artisans, such as gold, ivory, and ebony.

Far from being Egyptianized, Kerman artists and architects adapted Egyptian technologies and styles and integrated them into their own cultural framework, probably aided by Egyptian artisans. The earliest architecture was dominated by typically Nubian round post structures but increasingly over time incorporated rectilinear mud-brick architecture and structural features, sometimes in combination with more traditional forms and/or using a distinctive, non-Egyptian layout. Presumably helped by Egyptians, Kerman architects created three massive mud-brick temple complexes during the Second Intermediate Period, when the civilization dominated Egypt. One of these monuments, called *deffufas* in Nubian, lay at the center of the city, while two others provided a cult focus for royal tombs in the massive cemetery. As D. O'Connor has noted, their overall plan echoes the general shape of Egyptian temples, with a kind of pylon feature in the settlement and cemetery *deffufas*, as well as in the axial plan of the cemetery *deffufas*. Unlike Egyptian temples, however, the settlement *deffufa* has a side entrance with a winding passageway and stair leading to the roof within an otherwise solid mass of masonry. The later cemetery *deffufa*, K-II, included a winged sun disk flanked by uraei on its lintel and Egyptianizing faience inlays in the interior (fig. 8.1). The latter included lions and a cavetto cornice custom-made for the building, as well as reused faience vessels cut into presumably Egyptian-inspired rosette patterns and inlaid into the ceiling. The adjacent massive circular royal burial tumuli reflect local architectural traditions but incorporated a mud-brick internal structure that was likely also adapted from Egyptian mud-brick architectural techniques.

FIGURE 8.1 Kerma cemetery *deffufa* K-II with winged sun disk carved in relief on the fallen granite lintel.

A faience workshop was found associated with the settlement *deffufa*, another example of the transfer of technology from Egypt to Nubia. Objects included the inlays discussed above, but also the production of both Egyptian-inspired pieces, as well as items made in local artistic styles, including faience vessels mimicking basketry. Copper-alloy metallurgy was also influenced by Egyptian technology. For example, daggers found and likely made at Kerma were similar in basic shape and fabrication, but employed distinctively Nubian ivory handles—a style that in turn influenced daggers in Egypt during the Second Intermediate Period and early New Kingdom, reflecting the complex two-way entanglements that ultimately characterized these kinds of cultural transfers. Another important adaptive Kerma borrowing from Egypt was in the production and use of stamp seals. Some of these seals were certainly Egyptian imports, in particular scarabs, but distinctively Nubian geometric motifs reflect an adaptation of the medium to suit local preferences. A locally produced handmade bowl found at Kerma imitated an Egyptian wheel-thrown shape, but with an incised Aegean running spiral motif that presumably came via Egypt or perhaps was inspired by an Aegean import, an example of a complex multi-regional entanglement.

Ivory inlays from Egyptian-style beds with decorated footboards also showed a mix of motifs. In particular, inlays featured an adapted version of the goddess Taweret wearing a leather kilt and wielding knives. Vultures with wings spread could also reflect Egyptian influence. Rosettes were likely inspired by the Egyptian and ultimately Near Eastern motif. Near Eastern influence is reflected in the Mesopotamian trope of goats flanking and nibbling on a tree. Other themes such as lions (resonating with the K-II inlays), ostrich, fox, frog, turtle, or giraffe are more likely indigenous, since all of these animals would have been part of the local milieu. Motifs that overlap with the ivory inlays, including likely examples of Taweret, ostrich, giraffe, leopards, plants, and rosettes, were also found on sheets of mica used to decorated clothing, a distinctively Kerman practice.

Early artistic influence on Egypt from the Near East includes the well-known serpopods on the Narmer palette and the use of cylinder seals and glyptic, but these elements were either quickly abandoned or adapted. Although some Egyptian artistic and architectural influence in the Levant goes back to the Old Kingdom, the most dramatic examples of borrowings from Egyptian art and architecture came during the Middle Bronze Age (MB), roughly contemporary with the Middle Kingdom and Kerma civilization. A number of pieces of often monumental royal and more modest statuary of Egyptian officials distributed around the Levant once suggested to Egyptologists the existence of a widespread Middle Kingdom empire similar to that in Lower Nubia. As with Kerma, this notion has been discarded, and most if not all of the statuary appears to have been imported during the Second Intermediate Period, most likely as gifts distributed by the Hyksos rulers, looted from Egyptian cemeteries and temples. Nevertheless, they provided an important material conduit for Egyptian artistic influence, including motifs such as the sphinx and striding/smiting pose. The Hyksos capital at Avaris provided a conduit for Levantine influence into Egypt. MB architecture was introduced in form of temples, metalwork included weaponry (in particular the sickle or *khopesh*-style sword), and perhaps most importantly the art of making chariotry. MB pottery shape and decoration had a profound effect on Egyptian potters, influencing the development types of carinated bowls and small jars, amphoras of various kinds, and monochrome and bichrome decorative motifs that continued through the New Kingdom.

The most dramatic Egyptian influence on the Levant can be seen at centers for Egypt's flourishing trade network, in particular Byblos during the MB, but also on a smaller scale in cemeteries and settlements scattered throughout Syria-Palestine. Byblos's artisans, perhaps bolstered by expatriate Egyptians, produced works that were sometimes highly imitative and at other times highly adaptive. The Byblian taste for Egyptian things doubtless derived from its close trading relationship, stretching back at least to the Old Kingdom, when "Byblos ships" brought cedar and other products to Egypt. The local rulers styled themselves as "governors," but also adopted the trappings of Egyptian kings, including the use of cartouches and uraei.

Some of these items came as royal gifts, but most were commissioned locally in an Egyptian style. Good examples of the latter are three gold-foil falcon collars from separate royal tombs at Byblos, modeled on but departing somewhat from the Egyptian *wesekh*-style broad collar. As a result, they are usually seen as local products, but the rendering of falcons on the best example is masterful, perhaps pointing to the presence of an Egyptian artisan serving a Byblian ruler. Other pieces of jewelry were decorated with Egyptian themes and sometimes bore the names of local rulers enclosed in cartouches. Local artisans also repurposed Egyptian imports into new settings, as was the case with an amethyst scarab set into a simple gold foil bracelet. Although wood and other organic material had decayed, inlaid eyes indicate that the Byblian rulers were buried in wooden coffins modeled on the Middle Kingdom Egyptian rectangular type. Given the ready availability of high-quality wood, they were presumably made by local artisans. Two uraeus inlays found in the Tomb II burial suggest that at least one of the rulers was also buried in a mummiform coffin and perhaps with a funerary mask, although one wonders if the second uraeus might have come from a crown, as was surely the case for a gold band with apotropaic hieroglyphs surmounted by a uraeus. Egyptianizing elements from wooden furniture were also found, but again departing from contemporary Egypt, such as gilded bronze lotiform elements from the legs of a chair or throne.

The plan of the Temple of the Obelisks at Byblos is similar to the layout of Fifth Dynasty sun temples. The layout was nevertheless adaptive, with a tripartite shrine behind a central platform with open courtyard and large obelisk. Arrays of smaller obelisks were placed around the courtyard, resonating with the longstanding indigenous practice of standing stones at shrines. The temple was embellished with obelisks, some of which had hieroglyphic inscriptions, over a long period of time. The offerings at Byblos's temples also show Egyptian influence, including simple faience statuettes of the hippo goddess Taweret and monkey and feline/lion figurines similar to modest votive offerings from contemporary Egypt. As noted above, Taweret appears on bed inlays at Kerma and is rendered in a similar protective pose with knives on art and glyptic from Levant. The popular household leonine dwarf god Bes also makes an appearance in MB glyptic. The most distinctive votive offerings from the Obelisk Temple are the striding figures wearing short kilts and tall crowns, sometimes with a knob reminiscent of the Egyptian white crown (see fig. 8.5 for a later example). These represent the patron god of Byblos, Reshef, who was eventually brought into the Egyptian pantheon. While influenced by the classic Egyptian pose of the striding/smiting king or god, they are nevertheless in a distinctively local style and thus were clearly locally produced.

Bronze weaponry from the period shows a complex set of entanglements in style, technology, and craftsmanship that reach from Egypt through the Levant and into the Aegean. Egyptian artisans developed a sophisticated technique of contrasting colored metal inlays using a "black bronze" method similar to modern Japanese *sakudo* decorative metalwork. They attained the "black bronze" effect by adding gold into the alloy and treating it with an acid solution that produced a durable blue-black copper oxide layer ideal for inlaying contrasting decorative elements of gold, silver, or electrum. One of the most dramatic examples is Ahhotep's dagger from the end of the Second Intermediate Period, although the technique originated in the Middle Kingdom. The method is found at Byblos in an Egyptianizing sword inlaid with uraei and hieroglyphs for King Ip-shemu-abi. This sickle-shaped sword had a hooked end that marks it as a local product. The shape was adapted for the Egyptian scimitar, which lacked the hook at the end, often referred to as *khopesh* for its similarity to the foreleg of sacrificed cattle.

The use of a decorative strip running down the middle of Ahhotep's blade and the inlaid lotus and locust motifs are Egyptian, but a lion chasing a bull in "flying gallop" originated in the Aegean and spread through the Near East and into Egypt, where it also influenced royal and private decorative and monumental hunting scenes. Daggers from tombs in the contemporary Aegean (Late Helladic I and II) use the same "black bronze" technique with a central strip along the blade. Animals in "flying gallop" and Nilotic lotus motifs appear on blades from Mycenae and other sites, although animals and vegetative elements are rendered as solid inlays rather than using wire outlines as in the Egypt and the Levant. An ax from Ahhotep's tomb reflects similar intercultural entanglements. Its shape and decoration is mainly Egyptian, but the blade includes an image of Montu as a griffon in Aegean style, with distinctively rendered head and plumage. The griffon itself, however, originated in Egypt, including the lithe, panther-like body. A competing style with Egyptian falcon face markings and royal crown spread from Egypt to the Near East and became an important motif in the later International Style. Other elements found in Near Eastern and Aegean art reflect Egyptian influence, including a schematized version of the Egyptian Hathor-style curled wig on depictions of sphinxes. Nilotic motifs also appear on Minoan frescoes, as well as palace paintings at MB sites like Tell Sakka in southern Syria, which also has an Egyptian-inspired royal/divine figure wearing a version of the *atef* crown. Several scholars have argued that Aegean painters and sculptors, who may have travelled to Egypt, employed a version of the Egyptian canon of proportions, but in any case they adapted Egyptian artistic styles and created Egyptian-influenced motifs such as the Nilotic theme with bunches of papyrus and lotuses (pl. 6).

The Egyptian New Kingdom empire reached farther than the Middle Kingdom in both the Levant and Nubia. In the latter, it was accompanied by massive building projects in the form of large temple complexes, for example, the famous rock-cut temple at Abu Simbel (pl. 6). New administrative centers were constructed from the second to third cataract, Amara West as late as the Ramesside Period. Stone temples were also built at most of the old fortresses, as well as in the former indigenous centers of Kerma Dokki Gel, Kawa, and Gebel Barkal. Monuments such as Soleb temple were designed entirely along Egyptian lines, decorated with the highest quality reliefs and laid out on an axial plan moving from more open courtyards/porticos to hypostyle halls and, finally, barque-shrine sanctuaries. Since the workmanship is to such a high standard, Egyptian artisans must either have come especially for the temple construction or settled in the colony, where they could work on these and other projects. The temple of Ramesses II at Abu Simbel is exceptional in its rock-cut design and reflects an entanglement with Nubian religious beliefs, which included the use of cave shrines from an early date and later on the concept of a divine presence within a mountain, most notably at Napata/Gebel Barkal and perhaps symbolically earlier with the Kerma settlement *deffufa*. In both places, a local ram deity was syncretized with the Egyptian god Amun. As a result, ram imagery was borrowed for the Nubian manifestation of Amun and exported to Egypt, a reflection of mutual influence in spite of seemingly overwhelming Egyptian cultural domination. Ram imagery appears even earlier at Kerma, perhaps already influenced by Egyptian iconography, highlighting the complexities and long history of entanglement between the two cultures in the sphere of religion and art.

Although traditional Nubian practices and industries survived to some extent, Egyptian-style material culture, including pottery, grave goods, and funerary architecture, was widely adopted throughout Nubia, but more selectively in some places. Some high-quality objects were doubtless imported, but local communities of artisans must have met demand for everyday objects such as pottery, furnishings, and ornaments. Similarly, Egyptian-style mud-brick housing and tomb structures required the presence of architects familiar with the construction of, for example, large-scale mud-brick enclosure walls, rock-cut tombs, and the small mud-brick pyramid tombs common in the New Kingdom. Remnants of high-quality painted decoration found in the rock-cut tomb of the local prince Djehutyhotep in Lower Nubia and fragments from mud-brick pyramid tombs at Sai and Tombos farther south attest to the presence of skilled artists who produced monuments rivaling their counterparts in Egypt.

Both wooden and ceramic coffins were also likely made locally (fig. 8.2), although some very high-quality coffins might have been imported, for example, those with elaborate inlays. Ceramic coffins appear at sites in Nubia but are common at Tombos. They have a range of more "realistic" to more abstract renderings of the face similar to examples from Egypt and the Levant, but with a regional preference for a two-part lid and single-piece trough rather than the more common two-part "slipper" style—a large round jar with an opening at one end covered by a plate where the face was represented. Ceramic coffins are so large and fragile that they were certainly made locally by specialized potters. Although heavily damaged by termites, the carving of the wooden coffin face from Tombos reflects a skilled hand but is not of a quality that would point to an import; instead more likely it was made in a local workshop that helped to meet the colony's demand for Egyptian grave goods. The conquered Kerma

FIGURE 8.2 Heads from locally made New Kingdom ceramic and wooden coffins at Tombos

culture already had a thriving faience industry, so it is likely that many of the Egyptian-style amulets and beads found in cemeteries and settlements were produced in Nubia.

In spite of the Egyptian temples, the region upstream of the third cataract shows a stronger tendency toward adaptation during the New Kingdom. For example, a round mud-brick temple coexisted with mud-brick and later stone temples at Kerma Dokki Gel, indicating that both Egyptian and indigenous architects coexisted. Remains of an Egyptian-style naos from a Third Intermediate Period deposit suggest a degree of architectural entanglement. Similarly, the New Kingdom through Third Intermediate Period cemetery at Hillat el-Arab, near Napata, has underground shaft and chamber complexes modeled along Egyptian lines, but with painted scenes of humans and boats most closely resembling local rock art, suggesting a selective adaptation of Egyptian features by indigenous artisans. Burials included Egyptian-style amulets, again most probably locally produced, but omitted coffins, which were common at colonies like Tombos even after the end of the New Kingdom. Similarly, Nubian pottery traditions continued to exist during the New Kingdom and enjoyed a revival in the Third Intermediate Period, but sometimes mixing Egyptian and Nubian traditions: for example, wheel-thrown but with Nubian polished blacktopped decoration.

With the emergence of the Kushite Twenty-fifth Dynasty, Nubian art and architecture at first glance appears to be entirely imitative, but a closer examination reveals its adaptive and innovative character. For example, kings are often, although not inevitably, shown with a double uraeus, a feature also found on their shabtis. They also developed a new, distinctive cap-crown that continued in use long after they lost control over Egypt (fig. 8.2). Scholars have assumed that local artisans ceased producing Egyptian-style architecture and objects in favor of a Nubian revival immediately after the New Kingdom, but recent archaeological work suggests that some colonial communities continued to thrive throughout the Third Intermediate Period, providing some continuity in architecture, art, and crafts going into the Twenty-fifth Dynasty. Similarly, László Török points out that Kushite temple building adapted the sacred landscape created during the New Kingdom, focusing on the Nubian ram-headed manifestation of Amun along with deities associated with Nubia like Dedwen, the deified Senwosret III, and ram-headed Khnum, his consort Satet, and their daughter Anukis from Aswan. The pre-Twenty-fifth Dynasty vignette and inscription of Nubian Queen Katimala also points toward a continuity in artistic and scribal traditions from the New Kingdom into the Third Intermediate Period. The Nubian pharaohs, especially Taharqa, expanded and rebuilt existing monuments at sites including Kawa and Gebel Barkal, which continued its role of southern counterpart to the great temple of Karnak at Thebes. Taharqa specifically mentions bringing artisans from Egypt to make sure that the work was done properly. Nevertheless, Egyptian artistic styles were adapted and novel forms created based upon Egyptian styles to suit Nubian sensibilities. This included a continuing elaboration of Amun's ram imagery, including a distinctive ram's head amulet shown on depictions of kings and officials that is also attested archaeologically (fig. 8.3). Criosphinxes, which were installed at the great temple of Amun at Karnak during the New Kingdom, appear flanking processional ways, for example at Taharqa's rebuilt and expanded Amun temple at Gebel Barkal.

The pyramids adopted by Kushite kings, queens, and the Nubian elite during the Twenty-fifth Dynasty would seem to represent the adoption of a quintessentially Egyptian royal monument, borrowed in a new wave of influence from Egypt as a tool to legitimize the new dynasty as successors to pharaonic rule (pl. 6). However, the last royal pyramid was built in Egypt at the beginning of the Eighteenth Dynasty, over six hundred years before the first Napatan royal pyramids (at the earliest *c.* 800 BCE). Many royal pyramids in Egypt were of course still visible and theoretically could have provided a model for a Kushite archaizing revival, but the architecture of the Nubian pyramids is quite different from Egyptian royal tombs. Instead, with their scale, steep sides, and attached chapel, they most closely resemble the private pyramids of the New Kingdom, dozens of which were built at colonial centers like Amara, Sai, Soleb, and Tombos over the course of the empire. These monuments, some of which continued in use (and perhaps were still constructed) during the Third

FIGURE 8.3 Wearing the Kushite cap-crown and amulets of Amun as a ram, Pharaoh Tanutamun is led toward Isis by Imsety, one of the Four Sons of Horus, in a scene from the entrance chamber of the underground burial complex of his pyramid tomb at el-Kurru, near Napata.

Intermediate Period at sites such as Tombos, Soleb, and Amara West, would have provided a more immediate model for the new Kushite rulers. Thus, the Nubian pyramids can be seen as the adaptation in more monumental form of what by this time may have been a local architectural style, albeit with Egyptian ties. Decoration and grave goods largely followed Egyptian prototypes. The Osirion at Abydos inspired Taharqa's underground burial complex at Nuri, opposite Gebel Barkal, and the decorative program of the burial complexes of Tanutamun and his mother Qalhata employed Egyptian-style starry ceilings evoking the Duat and passages and vignettes from the *Book of the Dead* (fig. 8.3). Stone sarcophagi, amulets, shabtis, and other grave goods mirrored contemporary Egypt, with some adaptations (for example, the use of a double uraeus) and preferences for certain amulets (such as the double-sided Pataikos/Isis). The fact that Qalhata's and other queen's tombs mirror those of kings in scale and decorative program marks a difference with Egypt, where queens occupied a more subordinate role.

The use and continuing production of Egyptian-style amulets during the Third Intermediate Period and into the Late Period reflects selective adoption of Egyptian iconography, but with some adaptation. Certain deities were favored, in particular Isis, Hathor, Pataikos, and Bes, as seen in amulets from Tombos (fig. 8.4B–F). The eye of Horus and scarabs were also popular (fig. 8.4A and H). Heart scarabs were provided for both royals and high-ranking members of the elite, for example, one associated with a pyramid tomb at Tombos (fig. 8.4I). Its strong similarity to heart scarabs from the royal cemetery at el Kurru suggests a local workshop that supplied the needs of both elite and royals. The inscription is a very accurate rendering of Spell 30b from the *Book of the Dead*, pointing to the existence of a robust scribal society that assisted with the production of art.

Some individual items may have been imported, but it is likely that local artisans made most. In particular, the Bat-Hathor/lotus amulet from Tombos echoes but nevertheless departs from traditional Egyptian iconography, suggesting an adaptive approach by the artisan (fig. 8.4D). The increasing importance of the god Bes in both amulets and architectural settings provides an example of entanglement stretching back to the New Kingdom. An amulet from Tombos was found still in situ around the neck of a woman buried in Nubian style during the late Eighteenth Dynasty (fig. 8.4G), attesting to the dwarf god's early appeal. By the Twenty-fifth Dynasty, Bes appears not only in amuletic form (fig. 8.4F) but also uncharacteristically for Egypt in monumental form, as the pillars from rock-cut Temple B-300 at Gebel Barkal illustrate (c. 690 BCE, fig. 8.4J). Unusual representations of the masculine and feminine aspects of Bes appear on two large ceramic plaques that would have been attached to the walls of a neighborhood temple at Kawa, again attesting to a thriving community of local artisans adapting Egyptian motifs into novel forms. A similarly scaled statue of Bes, atypical for Egypt, was found in Phoenician Sidon.

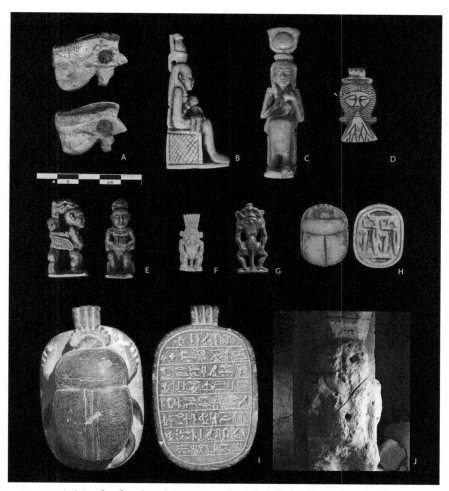

FIGURE 8.4 A–I, Amulets from burials at Tombos, all but G from the Third Intermediate Period; B, C, E, F, and H found together (A, eye of Horus; B, Isis suckling Horus and wearing the crown of Upper and Lower Egypt; C, Isis suckling Horus and wearing a horned crown with sun disk and uraei; D, Bat-Hathor with lotus and uraeus crown; E, Pataikos/Isis; F, Bes from the Third Intermediate Period; G, Bes from the New Kingdom; H, scarab with unusual offering scene; I, heart scarab; and J, a monumental Bes column from Taharqa's rock-cut Temple B-300 at Gebel Barkal.

The Late Bronze Age (LB) saw the emergence of the International Style, blending Egyptian, Levantine, and Aegean motifs, which continued to characterize art and architecture through the Iron Age. The exchange of artists would have contributed to the vibrant interweaving of motifs drawn from Egypt, the Levant, Mesopotamia, Anatolia and the Aegean that characterizes the International Style. As Shaw discusses in this volume, the exchange of artisans was a fundamental part of the ancient Near Eastern palace system, especially moving into the Iron Age. Unlike the heavy investment in colonization to the south, New Kingdom colonies were established at only a few key centers in the Levant, notably at Deir el-Balah in the Gaza Strip, inland at Beth Shean, and farther north along the coast at Tell Dor in northern Israel. Egyptian-style palaces and temples were built at these centers and artisans joined the colonies, leading to lasting influence. In particular, Egyptian-style ceramic coffins appear at Deir el-Balah and Beth Shean, although as noted above unlike at Tombos they were of the "slipper" style. Examples from Egypt and Tombos included elaborate painting along the lines of wooden coffins, but as at Tombos, simpler decoration prevailed in the Levant, ranging from more realistic treatments of the head and arms to very abstract renderings (some very similar to fig. 8.2). As these coffins continued in use, they included features such as the feathered headdress associated with the Philistines, reflecting new entanglements and adaptations. The use and presumably manufacture of Egyptian-style amulets, jewelry, and other decorative objects continued in funerary and settlement contexts into the Iron Age, reflecting the long-term consequences of Egyptian interactions and interventions in the region.

Egyptianizing pieces from the large caches of ivories found in a LB context at Megiddo, probably the palace of an Egyptian administrator, and in the deposits associated with the Iron Age destruction of the Assyrian capital of Nimrud (c. 610 BCE) reflect both the more heavily Egyptianizing Phoenician and less Egyptianizing Syrian ivory-working industries that came to characterize one of the most creative intercultural media. Most of the pieces came from inlays and embellishments on furniture, but Egyptianizing cosmetic vessels also appear at a number of Levantine sites, including Egyptian-inspired ducks with hinged wings as a cover, along with other objects such as mirror handles with Hathor imagery and gaming sets. Egyptian-style sphinxes and both Egyptian- and Aegean-style griffons are among the most common motifs. Anubis and Bes were both represented, and Hathor imagery, often associated with Egyptian-derived lotiform and palmette motifs, was particularly common. Another motif from Nimrud borrowed directly from Egypt shows a lion mauling a Nubian prisoner, a theme that also occurs in Nubia itself, but at Nimrud uncharacteristically on a background of lotuses. Hathor imagery and lotus motifs have also been found in painted palace decoration, famously in the LB palace at Nuzi, where cow-eared Bat-Hathor images alternated with bucrania and palmettes.

Bronze statues of deities continued to be produced with Egyptianizing poses, in particular seated and striding/smiting. Ba'al and Reshep were commonly represented in a smiting pose at sites including Ugarit and Byblos (fig. 8.5), but they often wear a local fringed garment. Egyptian-influenced seated bronze statues representing the Canaanite chief god El commonly wear an Egyptian inspired *atef* crown with uraeus and ram's horns. The use of horns in the Levant would also resonate with Mesopotamian divine iconography. The goddess of

FIGURE 8.5 Figure of Syrian deity, perhaps Ba'al or Reshef, in bronze with gold and silver overlay. New Kingdom.

Byblos was syncretized with Hathor, and locally produced stelae represent her in conventional Egyptian form. The stele of Yehawmilk from Byblos is laid out with winged sun disk above an image of the goddess, but with the owner shown in Persian dress. Gold jewelry also adapted Egyptian divine motifs into a local medium, most commonly in plaques that incorporated Hathor's iconography, but also seen in objects such as a granulated gold falcon pendant and earring from the LB Uluburun shipwreck (late Eighteenth Dynasty). This kind of imagery was found as far north as Syria, including sites like Qatna.

Phoenician artisans also produced bronze, silver, and gold bowls that mixed Egyptian, Near Eastern, and Aegean imagery, commonly including winged sphinxes, griffons (both Egyptian and Aegean style), and royal imagery. The remarkable silver-gilt bowl of King Akestor from Cyprus (c. 725–675 BCE) deploys various Egyptianizing elements in a Phoenician-style layout, including sphinxes, lions dominating prisoners, Hathor cow imagery, and the sacrifice of prisoners by a pharaoh before a falcon-headed god. These were combined with Mesopotamian (Assyrian) tropes, including goats nibbling at palmettes, a king slaying a griffon, and a winged deity slaying a lion, but protected by Egyptian falcons. These remarkable examples of metalwork overlapped iconographically with the equally remarkable fusion of human, animal, and vegetative themes borrowed from Egypt, the Near East, and Aegean found on ivories, suggesting a close connection between the artisans of both media.

The most dramatic direct Aegean influence in Egypt appears in the Minoan-style paintings decorating a palace built around the reign of Thutmose III at the former Hyksos capital of Avaris. Stylistically they conform so closely to Aegean prototypes and techniques that they were surely made by Aegean artisans. The themes most closely resemble those from the queen's throne room at Knossos, including bull-leaping scenes and griffons like those flanking the queen's throne. Aegean style-paintings have also been found in Levantine palaces, suggesting that artisans circulated widely. As noted above, there have long been suggestions of mutual influence, in particular that the Egyptian canon was to some extent applied in early Greek art going back to the Minoans. In the Iron Age, the striding pose of kouroi (c. 615–485 BCE), life-sized mostly male statues, is most often cited as reflecting Egyptian influence. The stance and proportions of the kouroi do show strong similarities to contemporary Egyptian statues, striding with left leg forward, pinched waist and wide shoulders, arms straight to the sides with fists clenched, and gathered hairstyle. The Greek colony of Naukratis was founded during the Saite period (c. 650 BCE), and while the kouroi are clearly the product of Greek artisans, they were likely inspired by Egyptian art either seen during their own visits or acquired through trade. Indirect influence through the spread of the International Style led to lasting Egyptian influence through later Classical art. Ultimately, however, Egypt's impact was more profound in Nubia, still strong at Meroe through the fourth century and at Ballana and Qustul through the sixth century CE.

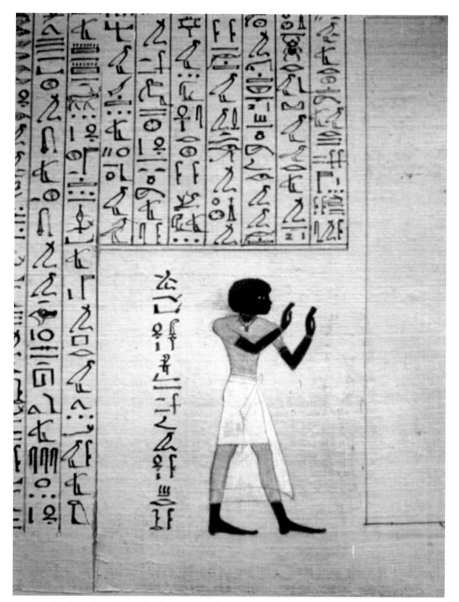

PLATE 1 Maiherpri as depicted in his *Book of the Dead*.

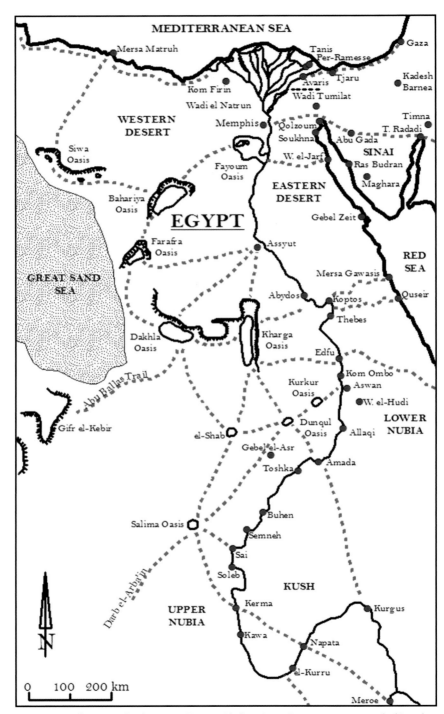

PLATE 2 Map of main overland routes in Egypt, with the primary important routes marked in red.

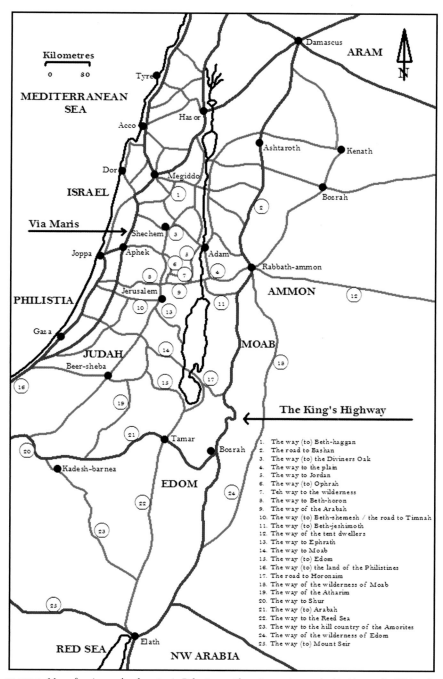

PLATE 3 Map of main overland routes in Palestine, with major routes marked in blue and additional, important through secondary routes, indicated in red.

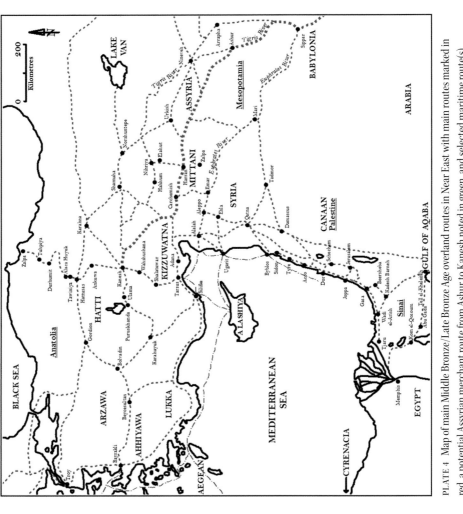

PLATE 4 Map of main Middle Bronze/Late Bronze Age overland routes in Near East with main routes marked in red, a potential Assyrian merchant route from Ashur to Kanesh noted in green, and selected maritime route(s) shown in blue.

PLATE 5 Bowing foreigners watch as the ingots of precious metal they have brought as gifts/tribute to Egypt are weighed. Theban Tomb 39 (Puyemre); Eighteenth Dynasty, reigns of Thutmose III and Hatshepsut.

PLATE 6 Map with images from Thera (Museum of Prehistoric Thera), Byblos, Abu Simbel, and Napata/Gebel Barkal.

PLATE 7 Different visualizations of the finely engraved base design on a Phoenician green jasper scaraboid.

PLATE 8 Left: Hieroglyphic inscription on Khonsu's inner coffin lid. Nineteenth Dynasty, reign of Ramesses II. Right: Hieratic script, a private letter, dated to the beginning of the Middle Kingdom.

PLATE 9   Knot of Isis.

PLATE 10   Cartouche of Hatshepsut offset along a fracture in tomb TT 110 in the Sheikh Abd el-Qurna slump block.

PLATE 11 The Palestrina Mosaic of the Nile showing farmers, farm animals, and wildlife around the islands of the Delta.

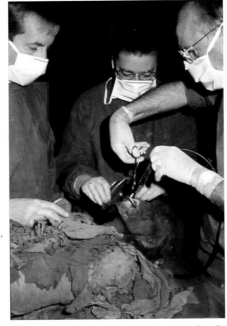

PLATE 12 Immunological and molecular techniques are now being used to identify evidence of epidemic disease in ancient human remains. These processes require tissue samples, which can be obtained from a mummy by using endoscopy (shown here), a virtually non-destructive investigative technique.

9

Traded, Copied, and Kept

THE UBIQUITOUS APPEAL OF SCARABS

Vanessa Boschloos

Prologue

In the early 1990s, a German team discovered in Carthage hundreds of clay sealings impressed by what probably was a scarab-shaped seal bearing the throne name of Sheshi/Maaibra. Sheshi was one of the rulers of the Canaanite dynasty that took over control of the Nile Delta at the end of the Middle Kingdom and ruled it as Egypt's Fifteenth Dynasty. The same second-century BCE context also yielded more than two thousand sealings impressed by seal-amulets with the throne name of Thutmose III, Menkheperre (mid-Eighteenth Dynasty) (fig. 9.1). The name of this famous New Kingdom pharaoh appears on thousands of scarab amulets, dispersed all over the ancient world. It is therefore not impossible that the Carthaginians were familiar with the significance of the name Menkheperre on Egyptian and Egyptianizing seal-amulets, but it is far less likely they remembered a Hyksos king who had ruled a millennium before and whose name is known only from scarabs.

Why use seal-amulets hundreds of years old and bearing the names of long-forgotten kings? Did the owners ignore the meaning of the inscriptions, or did they have a particular significance? Where did they come from, directly from Egypt or through intermediaries? Had the scarabs remained in use since their production period, as heirlooms, or had they been rediscovered in a nearby past? Were these scarabs present in Carthage or were the sealings impressed elsewhere? How and when did they arrive in Carthage...?

Introduction

Generally, scarabs raise more questions than they answer. Small and thus easily transportable, they bear decorative designs or are inscribed with the names of great kings of the past, making them desirable collectibles. Since scarabs

FIGURE 9.1 Clay bulla impressed by a scarab bearing the name of Thutmose III, excavated in Carthage by A. L. Delattre (1850–1932). Digital photograph (above) and four 2D+ models (below) generated by the Portable Light Dome, from left to right: color sharpen, shaded, radiance scaling, and sketch mode.

are extremely popular and widely distributed, they are often used as primary evidence in archaeological and historical studies, in many cases leading to controversial conclusions. A major problem is the lack of securely dated contexts, necessary for establishing reliable typological sequences, and the fact that they can be used for long periods of time and for different purposes. This chapter will address three main issues: distribution, imitation and longevity.

It is not always possible to understand the reasons or the mechanisms behind the distribution of scarabs, or to reconstruct the routes by which scarabs arrived at the site where they were excavated. The available archaeological information does not even allow determining if the sealings or the scarabs of Sheshi and Thutmose III found their way to Carthage together or via the same routes. Given the large numbers found together in the same context, it is not implausible the original scarabs were present in the city. Scarabs with the name of Thutmose III and scarabs of Hyksos kings have been found in Carthage and even farther west, in Spain, distributed along Phoenician, Punic, and Greek trade routes. Unfortunately, analysis of the clay has not yet been conducted to determine whether the sealings were made locally or whether they were made elsewhere and arrived at their destination with the containers they sealed.

It was also suggested that the sealings from Carthage had been made by local copiers, imitating Egyptian models. A scarab's non-Egyptian origin can be indicated by the material, the presence of misrendered hieroglyphs, the use of foreign iconography, the absence of parallels in the Egyptian repertoire.... Of course, semi-finished items and raw materials were also exchanged between regions; people and craftsmen traveled and with them also ideas, know-how, and imagery, making it sometimes difficult to distinguish copies from their Egyptian models. Until the 1980s, the great majority of scarab studies focused on chronology, inscriptions, designs, and classification, but an increasing number of publications contribute to the identification of non-Egyptian types and to understanding how scarabs and Egyptian iconography were perceived, imitated, and transformed in other cultures. Our comprehension of Minoan, Canaanite, Syrian, Phoenician, Israelite, Cypriot, Greek, Sardinian, and Etruscan scarabs has made significant progress by taking into account technical, material, typological, stylistic, archaeological, and iconographical considerations. As for the sealings from Carthage, their compositions have excellent parallels in Egyptian contexts, suggesting they were made by genuine Egyptian scarabs.

A final note on the Menkheperre sealings from Carthage is that they were not made by scarabs produced during the reign of Thutmose III, because parallels for that particular composition are more recent than the Eighteenth Dynasty. His throne name continued to appear on seal-amulets until the Late Period. Since no other pharaoh, not even Ramesses II, is named on scarabs for such a long period and on such a large scale as Thutmose III, it has been argued that the name Menkheperre was popular because the combination of the three signs *mn*, *ḫpr*, and *rˁ* may have been a cryptographic rendering of the name Amun-Re, or that his scarabs were reissued because he was posthumously venerated or divinized.

The Egyptian sealings from Carthage are only one of many similar cases illustrating the problems we are confronted with when interpreting and contextualizing scarabs. This chapter aims to give a glimpse into the complex yet fascinating nature of Egyptian scarabs found outside Egypt and their impact on other cultures, as they are exported, traded, copied ... and kept.

The Omnipresence of Scarabs

As small, easily transportable objects, amulets, seals, and other items of personal adornment traveled vast distances already in antiquity. Scarabs surface in excavations from Sudan to central Europe and from the Atlantic coast to Iran. More Egyptian and Egyptianizing scarabs have been found in the southern than in the northern Levant, few in Mesopotamia and Anatolia: the greater the distance from Egypt, the less scarabs and other Aegyptiaca are encountered. This general rule may, however, be too simplistic a view on the matter. Thus far, southern Mediterranean sites have yielded smaller quantities of scarabs than sites located on the northern shores: few are known from Morocco and Algeria, whereas hundreds of scarabs were found in Spain and Portugal. Although the distance from Egypt and the location on or near important trade routes played an important role, it is also necessary to take into account local excavation policy and history. For instance, the large number of scarabs originating from southern Levantine sites is also partly explained by the fact that controlled excavations have been undertaken for a longer period of time, more intensively, and on a much larger scale in Israel than in Syria.

Their wide geographical distribution makes scarabs important sources for our understanding of ancient cultures, societies, and religions, but especially for the reconstruction and interpretation of intercultural connections and exchange networks in the ancient Near East, in Egypt and Sudan, and throughout the Mediterranean. Egyptian scarabs were exported as trade commodities, were exchanged as gifts, traveled with their owners, and were further redistributed through regional networks.

DIPLOMATIC AND GEOPOLITICAL FACTORS

A fragmentary ivory scarab bearing the name of the Kushite pharaoh Taharqa (Twenty-fifth Dynasty) was discovered in Fort Shalmanasar, a palace in Neo-Assyrian Kalhu/Nimrud. The palace also yielded thousands of ivory plaques carved in Phoenician and Syrian styles, which originally had decorated wooden furniture, boxes, chariots, and horse trappings. Commonly known as the "Nimrud ivories," these Levantine ivories arrived in northern Mesopotamia as diplomatic gifts, tribute, or war booty from the centers along the Mediterranean coast during the period of the expansion of the Assyrian empire (ninth to seventh centuries BCE). If not with the ivories, the Taharqa scarab may have arrived in Nimrud directly from Egypt, as a result of Esarhaddon's and Ashurbanipal's wars on Taharqa and the Assyrian invasion of Egypt.

Diplomatic gift exchange, on the other hand, is often considered to have been the initial incentive for the dispatch to Nubia, the Levant, and the eastern Mediterranean of the so-called historical scarabs of Amenhotep III. These scarabs are much larger than other royal-name scarabs and celebrate particular events in the king's reign, such as marriages or successful hunting parties. Outside Egypt they have turned up in Soleb (Nubia), Sherabit al-Khadim (Sinai), Palaepaphos (Cyprus), and in the Levant at Lachish, Beth Shemesh, Gezer, Jaffa, Beth Shean, and Ugarit. These are primarily places under Egyptian control or in regions strategically important to Egypt for their international relations, suggesting the large commemorative scarabs were sent out as royal gifts to Egyptian officials abroad, to vassal kings, or to foreign rulers. Unfortunately, the few provenanced examples hardly come from precisely dated contexts that are, moreover, generally several centuries younger than the period during which they were produced. Their distribution map therefore does not allow drawing historical or socio-political conclusions, and, as regard to historical sources, the Amarna Letters do not mention this type of object when describing gifts exchanged between rulers. On a more general note, scarabs bearing royal names must be treated with caution: due to their content and the possible historical implications, royal-name scarabs are easily interpreted as historical objects or as evidence for high-level relations with Egypt, or are used for synchronizing chronologies. The scarab impression found on a jar handle in a tomb in Pella (Jordan) was interpreted as referring to the name of a hitherto unknown Hyksos ruler, suggesting elite-level relations between the Hyksos capital Avaris and the Jordan Valley, whereas a recent reinterpretation of the engravings indicated it was made by a Second Intermediate Period design scarab.

Compared to Amenhotep III's large commemorative scarabs, the discovery of a clay sealing impressed by a scarab bearing the throne name of Amenhotep IV/Akhenaten (Neferkheperure Waenre) in a refuse deposit in the Bronze Age palace of Tell Mishrife/Qatna may seem less impressive, but the approximately mid-fourteenth-century BCE context is contemporary with his reign and objects bearing his name are extremely rare in the Levant. The containers sealed by Egyptian and Egyptianizing seals from this refuse may thus have been sent from Egypt to the Levant as part of a larger group of items, perhaps in response to the pleas for help Levantine rulers addressed to the pharaoh in several Amarna Letters. The Egyptian provenance has yet to be confirmed by analysis of the clay. The containers must have reached Qatna via a city on the coast (perhaps Sumur, where an Egyptian garrison was stationed) or via an inland route coming from the southern Levant through the Biqaa Valley (and its Egyptian administrative center, Kamid al-Loz).

TRADE

If not due to Egyptian presence or diplomatic exchanges, the wide spread of Egyptian scarabs and other small amulets in Nubia, the Near East, and Mediterranean is the result of commercial relations. During the second millennium BCE, overland caravans and seaborne routes dispersed Egyptian scarabs to Levantine and eastern Mediterranean centers, where they would then be further distributed along interregional and intraregional networks.

A Middle Kingdom scarab from Middle Bronze Age Tell Mardikh/Ebla (western Syria) must have reached its destination via a route through the Gap of Homs, coming from a center on the coast, most probably Byblos, where about 320 Egyptian Middle Kingdom imports have been found. Scarabs also travel long distances; for example, Canaanite scarabs traveled east via Syrian Desert routes to Tell Ashera/Terqa on the Euphrates, and Egyptian Second

Intermediate Period scarabs (along with a Middle Kingdom scarab amulet) were found in a sixteenth- to fifteenth-century BCE tomb in Assur.

Sea routes, on the other hand, can only be reconstructed when shipwrecks and their cargo are discovered. A golden scarab of Queen Nefertiti was found with glass ingots from Tell el-Amarna, Cypriot copper ingots, Canaanite jars, and other goods from the Uluburun shipwreck, which sunk off the Turkish coast around the late fourteenth century BCE on its way to an Aegean destination. The ship and its crew were probably of Levantine origin, and several hypotheses have been put forward as how such an exceptional scarab would have reached the Levant. Scarabs also traveled as merchandise or accompanied primary trade goods, though this particular scarab may as well have been the property of one of the sailors or passengers aboard the ship.

A much longer journey was made by an identical pair of ninth- to eighth-century BCE Phoenician scarabs found in an early seventh-century BCE tomb in Bisenzio, Etruria. They must have been dispatched together from their place of origin on the Levantine coast (as part of a pair of earrings?), but it is not possible to determine whether their final owner had acquired them in the Levant or after their arrival in Sardinia together with other imports from the East. During the first millennium BCE, scarabs were distributed throughout the Mediterranean by Greek (Euboean), Phoenician, and Cypriot merchants. These networks were already in place at the beginning of the Iron Age; the earliest imports in Italy are found in late tenth- to ninth-centuries BCE burials in Torre Galli, where pottery assemblages reflect relations with Cyprus or the Levant. The first large wave of Aegyptiaca traveling west took place in the eighth to early seventh century BCE; the late seventh century BCE marks the beginning of a second main phase, characterized by the objects assigned to a "faience" workshop at Naukratis (discussed below) and distributed widely along Mediterranean trade routes. The scale of commercial relations with the east is underscored by the quantities of Aegyptiaca found in central and western Mediterranean sites. Some scarabs are even found in contemporary contexts, for example, in a late eighth-century BCE tomb at Pithekoussai (one of the oldest Greek installations in Italy, on the island of Ischia), where a scarab was found bearing the name Wahkare, belonging to the Twenty-fourth Dynasty ruler Bakenrenef/Bocchoris.

SOCIAL AND CULTURAL SIGNIFICANCE OUTSIDE EGYPT

Scarabs that reached the central and western Mediterranean during the first millennium BCE are generally considered to have traveled as trade goods, exotica, or even trinkets with little value. However, in Greece, Italy, and the central Mediterranean islands scarabs surface in burials and temple deposits, indicating that these imports were not just low-valued trade commodities and that the reception culture attributed them with a symbolic meaning. They were part of popular religion and were given a second life as offerings in sanctuaries (especially in the Aegean), as jewelry, or as protective amulets, particularly for women and children.

Outside Egypt, scarabs—like all types of seal-amulets—were additionally appreciated for their engraved decorations and were perceived as foreign objects increasing or reinforcing the social status or prestige of their owner. Understanding the hieroglyphs or Egyptian motifs was not a prerequisite. It is important to acknowledge the fact that accessibility of Egyptian or other imports does not necessarily reflect personal relations with Egyptians. The use of a foreign seal or amulet can also be a means to distinguish oneself from peers or may even reflect personal tastes or beliefs. To this day, scarabs bearing the names of Middle Kingdom Egyptian officials discovered in the Levant are sometimes still being interpreted as evidence for the presence of these individuals in the Levant, but most of these scarabs had been rediscovered or looted from Middle Kingdom tombs in later periods and then found their way to the Levant. Similarly, the presence of Egyptian scarabs in Mesopotamia or their use as sealing devices in Neo-Assyrian and Neo-Babylonian archives (e.g., at Nineveh, Malanate, Nimrud, Assur, Sippar, Babylon, etc.) is not evidence for the presence of an Egyptian individual or for the owner's relations with an Egyptian or Levantine trade network.

The demand for such "exotica" moreover fueled the production of imitations, especially in periods during which Egyptian presence in that region was reduced and the number of imports decreased dramatically.

Non-Egyptian Scarabs: Adoption and Adaptation of the Scarab outside Egypt

The presence of non-Egyptian motifs, misrendered signs, or pseudo-hieroglyphs will hint at the non-Egyptian origin of a scarab, as will their absence on Egyptian prototypes or Egyptian contemporary scarabs. On the other hand, foreign ideas or motifs were also introduced into the Egyptian production. It is therefore necessary to also take into account the number of examples in a region, the geo-chronological distribution pattern, and, most importantly, the oldest stratigraphical context that will establish the first appearance of a type of scarab or design in a particular region. The use of certain materials in the manufacture of scarabs may also point to a non-Egyptian origin, unless the raw material was imported. Current research is therefore increasingly looking at (preferably nondestructive) fabric analysis to further clarify questions pertaining to origin and production centers. Analyses by optical microscopy, X-ray fluorescence, X-ray diffraction, scanning electron microscopy, and Raman spectroscopy determine materials and techniques used in the production of scarabs, but these have thus far been applied to individual scarabs or to a handful of samples. Unless conducted on a representative scale, this may lead to biased and erroneous conclusions about materials and production techniques used in a particular group, region, or period. Fabric analysis can, for example, answer questions regarding the production of Phoenician, Egyptian, Naukratis, and Rhodian scarabs and other "faience" objects spread throughout the Mediterranean. Scarab research additionally benefits from recent developments in imaging and (interactive) visualization techniques allowing in-depth visual examination of technical aspects (engraving techniques, surface characteristics, and workmanship; fig. 9.1, pl. 7).

The following selected cases illustrate how features of Egyptian models are "adopted" and/or "adapted" outside Egypt. In the former case the local craftsman imitates shapes and designs, aiming at replicating or copying the Egyptian model and strongly referring to it; in the latter the model is used as inspiration to create something new, adapted to local traditions and assimilated into the recipient culture.

THE SECOND MILLENNIUM BCE

The earliest copies of Egyptian scarabs appear in Middle Minoan Crete, shortly after the initial arrival of imported scarabs on the island. Early Middle Kingdom scarabs may have reached Crete through direct trade relations with Egypt, dating as far back as the Old Kingdom as indicated by other types of Egyptian imports in Early Minoan contexts. These Middle Minoan adaptations did not appear suddenly but are part of an evolution within the local tradition of animal-shaped seal-amulets. Prepalatial and Early Palatial contexts yielded scarabs imitating Middle Kingdom scarabs in shape, material, and technique: they are manufactured in a local stone resembling Egyptian steatite (though mineralogical analysis still has to be conducted to further identify the differences) and they were probably also glazed. On the other hand, they differ in typological features of the back and sides, in the engraving technique, and in base designs. The scarabs' devices are local and stylistically related to those engraved on Middle Minoan I–II Cretan seals.

Whereas Egyptian Middle Kingdom scarabs were also exported to the Levant and Nubia during this period, they did not engender local imitations—in the Levant, in any case, not before the seventeenth century BCE, at the end of the Middle Kingdom. Contrary to Crete, where only a dozen local copies are attested to date, Egyptian scarabs were imitated on a large scale in Canaan during the Middle Bronze Age IIB–IIC. This was a direct result of the close cultural interactions between Canaanites and Egyptians through the intermediary of the Canaanite population that had settled in the eastern Delta during the Middle Kingdom. These Middle Bronze Age Canaanite scarabs—in older literature referred to as "Hyksos scarabs"— appear in the southern Levant at the end of the Middle Bronze Age IIA and imitate late Middle Kingdom prototypes, both in typological features and in designs (fig. 9.2). Their presence is initially limited to the Levant, but they are exported to Egypt, Crete, inner Syria, and Mesopotamia from the Fifteenth Dynasty onward. Interestingly, certain

FIGURE 9.2 Canaanite Middle Bronze Age scarabs excavated by W. M. F. Petrie at Tell el-Yahudiya.

Canaanite designs subsequently inspired Egyptian seal-cutters, as shown by the introduction of Canaanite motifs and compositions on Second Intermediate Period scarabs. Middle Bronze Age Canaanite scarabs are almost exclusively design scarabs, except for some rare finds, such as a private-name scarab from a seventeenth-century BCE occupation level at Sidon naming ḏd-k̲ȝ-rꜥ lord of Iay. The anthroponym Djedqara is an Egyptian form of a West Semitic name (Sid-Kâr?), and Iay was probably located in the Lebanese part of the Akkar Plain. Canaanite scarabs are predominantly cut from the same greyish white steatite used in the Egyptian production, but Canaanite seal-cutters also used local stones such as dark-colored serpentinite.

It is not always possible to distinguish Egyptian and non-Egyptian scarabs when relations with Egypt were very intense and the local material culture was strongly influenced by the large quantities of Egyptian imports. For the Late Bronze Age Levant, for example, it was thought until recently that all the scarabs found there represent imports because they display designs typical of the Egyptian repertoire. This picture was nuanced by scarabs from Beth Shean, a major urban center in the Jordan Valley. As a result of the Egyptian military presence and direct administrative control in the Levant during the Late Bronze Age, a strong increase in the number of Egyptian imports to the Levant is observed from the mid-Eighteenth Dynasty onward, with a certain decrease at the end of this dynasty and another peak under the Nineteenth and early Twentieth Dynasty. Especially at several southern Levantine centers, mixed Egyptian-Levantine architecture and material culture occurs. At Beth Shean, an Egyptian garrison was stationed, and the growing demand for Egyptian "faience" objects encouraged the emergence of local workshops, importing the raw materials and following the Egyptian recipes and techniques. The Beth Shean "faience" production is characterized by small artifacts, especially beads, pendants, and scarabs (fig. 9.3). At present, two local scarab groups have been identified, one dating to the mid-Eighteenth Dynasty (Thutmose III to Amenhotep III) mainly from stratum IX, and one from stratum VII showing Ramesside-inspired designs.

THE FIRST MILLENNIUM BCE

Current scholarship knows little of what happens in scarab production outside Egypt between the end of the Bronze Age and the first centuries of the Iron Age. One of the largest early Iron Age groups is the so-called late or post-Ramesside mass-produced seal-amulets. This rather heterogeneous group of steatite scarabs and other stamp seals is attested in Egypt and Palestine in contexts dating from the eleventh to tenth centuries BCE onward, and individual examples are also found in Mesopotamia, Cyprus, Crete, Euboea, and Ibiza. Their designs strongly refer to Egyptian Ramesside imagery, with a prevalence of hunting scenes. Their date and origin are much debated issues

FIGURE 9.3 Faience scarab manufactured at Beth Shean (belonging to the so-called Beth Shean Level IX Group), bearing the inscription *s῾nḫ jmn* or *῾nḫ.ś n jmn*.

because of the possible implications for early Iron Age chronology in the (southern) Levant.

In the study of scarabs from the first millennium BCE, research questions pertain mainly to the scarabs' possible historical significance and support for written sources, to the identification of regional groups, to the role they play as evidence for intercultural relations and the circulation of symbolic ideas, and to the degree they reflect the impact of Egyptian(izing) culture in other regions in periods of dwindling Egyptian presence abroad. From the ninth century BCE onward, scarab production was thriving again in the Levant, Syria, and the eastern Mediterranean. Seal cutters used the scarab shape in the production of Syrian, Phoenician, Cypriot, Hebrew, Rhodian, Greek, Etruscan, Persian, and other stamp seals. The current state of research on some major types presented below gives an idea of the outstanding issues and the complexity of the wide range of involved glyptic traditions.

Quite a few Iron Age scarab and scaraboid "groups" are defined principally on stylistic and iconographical grounds; the stratified finds then allow postulation as to their chronology and origin. This is at present the case for several stamp seals attributed to ninth- to seventh-centuries BCE Syrian workshops based on the nature of the designs and the numbers coming from north Syria (such as the so-called Horse Group, the Yunus Cemetery Group, and others). Many of these stylistic groups are not limited to the scarab shape and include other types of stamp seals. Nevertheless, the scarab seems to have witnessed a revival in Syria during that period. Typological classification is hampered by the generally stylized features and the increased popularity of the scaraboid. The same problem arises for scarabs made of poorly preserved soft blue paste, worn to such a degree that—pending archaeometric analysis—only iconography and distribution maps may hint at their region of provenance. This approach allowed recently the identification of one production center for blue paste scarabs in the region of Tell Tayinat, in the Amuq Valley, but more workshops must have been active given the large numbers and wide distribution of such scarabs in the Iron Age Levant. The precise origin of many groups therefore remains subject to discussion.

Though several Levantine and Cypriot seals display Egyptianizing motifs, until three decades ago all Egyptianizing scarabs that could not be classified as proper Egyptian ones were considered to be Phoenician. The early Phoenician scarab production consists of scarabs in steatite and "faience" and is characterized by horizontal register compositions and a well-defined iconographic repertoire (the four-winged beetle, sphinx, etc.) strongly referring to both older and contemporary (Twenty-second Dynasty) Egyptian models. One of these workshops is likely to have been active in the kingdom of Tyre during the Iron Age II. Phoenician seals also served as inspiration for Hebrew, Ammonite, Moabite, and Edomite personal-name scarabs, identified by the script in which the name of their owner is written. For anepigraphic items, the archaeological context (if known) and iconographic elements are used to determine the scarabs' origin. Several are cut from hard stones (cornelian, jasper, quartz) (pl. 7): at least from the eighth century BCE onward, scarabs and scaraboids in hard stones are produced in the Syro-Phoenician region, and glass scarabs also appear.

They prelude the production of hard stone scarabs of the Persian Period, the so-called Classical or Late Phoenician scarabs and Punic scarabs. These were made of green jasper or a stone mineralogically related to it, and manufactured between the sixth and fourth centuries BCE. Even though found in greater numbers in western compared to eastern Mediterranean sites, there are no significant iconographical differences between eastern (Phoenician) and western (Punic) examples. It seems that, at least early in their production, workshops were active both in the east and the west. Many provenanced finds come from Sardinia (especially Tharros, where the first large numbers were discovered, hence they are also called "Tharros gems"), Ibiza, Carthage, Sicily, and to a lesser extent from Phoenicia, where most are known from the antiquities market. They display a different iconographic repertoire than earlier Phoenician scarabs, with both Egyptianizing Phoenician (e.g., Isis, Bes, figures with incense burner or sacred tree) and east Greek (e.g., Heracles, sea deities, warriors) inspiration. Prominent decorative features are a hatched *nb* basket in exergue at the bottom and a hatched border surrounding the design. Examples in a Greek style are sometimes called Greco-Phoenician or Greco-Punic in the literature.

Another Phoenician group of the Persian Period are scarabs in *gemasertem Steatit* (fig. 9.4). This homogenous group shows deep and schematically engraved Phoenician designs and motifs and also looks to contemporary Egyptian developments: the most current themes are the seated sphinx, the

FIGURE 9.4 Phoenician scarab in *gemasertem Steatit* from Dülük Köyü.

FIGURE 9.5 Dark blue paste scarab of the "Naukratis type" found in the Temple of Aphrodite at Miletus.

young sun god Horus with winged Isis, Egyptian names beginning with *Pꜣ-di-*[...], and animals.

Another major player in non-Egyptian scarab production in the first millennium BCE is the Greek world. Possibly under Levantine incentive, Aegean "faience" workshops started producing Egyptianizing scarabs in the late eighth to seventh centuries BCE, imitating Egyptian models. Their coarse material, very limited repertoire of Egyptian signs and motifs (*nfr*, *nb*, ankh, ostrich feather, and uraeus), and their wide distribution in the Mediterranean—especially in the Aegean and on the Greek mainland—indicates they were mass-produced and aimed at the Greek market. Large quantities were found at Perachora (Gulf of Corinth) and Lindos (Rhodes), and Rhodian factories were likely responsible for the production of this type of scarabs.

Other mass-produced scarabs under Greek influence are scarabs of the so-called Naukratis type (seventh to sixth centuries BCE) (fig. 9.5), from the Greek settlement on the Canopic branch of the Nile. Defining the characteristics of the objects associated with "faience" workshops at Naukratis is one of the objectives of the British Museum's Naukratis Project. Traditionally considered a Greek settlement or colony, Naukratis was a multicultural site where Late

Period Egyptian, Greek, and Phoenician objects and influences circulated and interacted. About 5 per cent of artifacts excavated at Naukratis represent amulets or amulet molds. The molds, together with the presence of "faience" wasters, point to the local production of amulets, predominantly scarab shaped. Petrie's "Scarab Factory" in Naukratis did not just appear at the end of the seventh century BCE but built on an Egyptianizing production that already existed in the early seventh century BCE. In addition to the popularity of human-head scaraboids (Black African Heads), the Naukratis scarab production is characterized by the use of "faience" with green, yellow, or light blue glaze on a yellow-grey to light brown soft paste or in dark blue paste. The designs are Egyptian, Egyptianizing (Phoenician), Hellenizing, orientalizing Greek, or a combination thereof. Popular are representations of lions or winged quadrupeds with heads turned back and a sun disk above.

Later developments move even further away from Egyptian traditions. Etruscan and Persian scarabs no longer bear Egyptianizing designs. Scarabs inspired by Greek Late Archaic gems are cut from hard stones (cornelian, agate) in Etruria between the late sixth and second centuries BCE. They probably appeared under the influence of Greek imports and immigrant Greek sealcutters in central Italy. Etruscan scarabs display mythological figures (e.g., Heracles, Achilles) surrounded by a hatched borderline and sometimes accompanied by an Etruscan inscription. They differ from Greek and Phoenician scarabs in the way the base of the scarab is hatched on its sides. Similarly, Persian scarabs do not refer to Egyptian models; they show Greek and Persian subjects, and their scarab shape is taken from Greek and Phoenician hard stone scarabs.

The Longevity of Scarabs: On Archaizing Styles, Heirlooms, Rediscovered, and Reused Scarabs

During nearly two millennia the scarab was the most frequently used shape in the production of Egyptian and Egyptianizing stamp seals and amulets in the ancient Near East and Mediterranean. Owing to their popularity, they also travel in time. As finely decorated objects, sometimes inscribed with a pharaoh's name, they continue to appeal to modern collectors, but this was also the case in antiquity.

This longevity makes scarabs infamous for precise dating purposes: portable objects that could easily be kept and transferred to the next generation. The use of the term "heirloom" is much debated in scarab research because, in the narrow sense, it only covers the circulation of a scarab for at least one generation and its transfer to the next generation(s) (living memory). It has therefore been argued that only valuable items can be heirlooms in younger contexts, such as scarabs in semi-precious stones or exceptional pieces. Some of the large commemorative scarabs of Amenhotep III found in first millennium BCE contexts may indeed have been passed on from generation to generation, but assigning the existence of heirlooms solely to the expensiveness of their material, to the content of the inscription they bear, and to their unusual dimensions or shape does not take into account motives beyond the merely materialistic or functional, such as the foreign, "exotic" nature of the object, its magical power or religious meaning, the sentimental values attached to the property of an ancestor, and so forth. When a minority of somewhat older types is found in an assemblage of scarabs contemporary with their archaeological context, we are dealing with heirlooms, especially when their production period is only slightly older than or partly contemporary with the date of their deposit. A small number of First Intermediate Period scarabs were found among about one hundred early Middle Kingdom scarabs in the Montet Jar in Byblos, a cultic deposit belonging to the Middle Bronze Age phase of the temple of the Ba'alat Gubal. The presence of heirlooms is not confined to religious contexts. They also occur in royal/elite and domestic contexts, as the transfer within a family or social group will have carried value and prestige. Middle Bronze Age Canaanite scarabs used to impress Late Bronze Age jar handles and bullae found at Kamid al-Loz (Lebanon), for example, are likely heirlooms from the preceding period that remained in use.

The material value of an object or the temporal distance between its production period and the period of its deposit does not determine whether or not it could be considered an heirloom. Some authors therefore prefer to speak more generally of "survivals," a term that does not imply deliberate transfer and covers a wide range of older objects found in younger contexts.

One category is scarabs that were rediscovered—more or less accidentally—at a certain moment and reused. Tombs could be re-opened for the interment of other family members or later generations, and such an event provided the opportunity for scarabs to resurface and to be used for the same purpose or for one other than their original function. Many inscribed Middle Kingdom objects found in the Levant were not dispatched during the reign of the pharaoh whose name they bear but rather had been looted from Middle Kingdom tombs in antiquity, probably as early as the Second Intermediate Period. For example, in one of the Middle Assyrian tombs at Mari (contemporary with the Ramesside Period and with a date post quem provided by the presence of a scarab of Sethnakhte, first ruler of the Twentieth Dynasty), the deceased was buried with six Egyptian scarabs; five of them display designs common on Ramesside scarabs, whereas one late Middle Kingdom import is about five or six centuries older. Similarly, whether or not rediscovered fortuitously, the presence of Bronze Age scarabs in Roman, Byzantine, or medieval contexts cannot be attributed to their continued use through the centuries; the Sheshi scarab used for the Carthage sealings was probably also such a rediscovered scarab.

Evidently, throughout its existence, a scarab could have been subject to any combination of the aforementioned scenarios. Whether deliberately handed down as ancestral or professional heirlooms or rediscovered, reused scarabs could receive a different function. This is obvious in the case of the aforementioned Egyptian personal-name scarabs of the Middle Kingdom, of which the formulae accompanying the name of the owner indicate they originally served a funerary purpose, whereas several surfaced in non-funerary contexts both in Egypt and abroad. Some scarabs were even re-cut and adapted to their new function or to the personal taste of their new owner. This is demonstrated by some amethyst scarabs found in Canaan and Minoan Crete, which originally had been undecorated Egyptian scarab amulets but show traces of secondary carving on their base: the material and morphology of the scarab are Egyptian, but the face design is not.

Similar to the continued occurrence of the throne name of Thutmose III until the Late Period, as discussed above, certain motifs and designs remained popular or came back in vogue after a lapse of time. The accompanying motifs, composition, morphology of the scarab and sometimes the style of engraving allow the dating of a scarab, but the reuse of older imagery and archaizing styles further complicate things. During the Ramesside Period, for example, a number of scarabs display designs and features strongly reminiscent of Canaanite Middle Bronze Age scarabs. Whether these archaizing scarabs are to be assigned an Egyptian origin or were produced in the Levant is still debated among scarab specialists. An archaeological approach to these issues, cataloging provenanced scarabs from securely dated contexts to identify the earliest examples, and not limited to their presence in a particular region, may resolve the question regarding their Egyptian and/or non-Egyptian origin. More anecdotic are the references to Bronze Age scarabs observed on several Phoenician scarabs of the ninth to fourth centuries BCE, named "Neo-" or "Pseudo-Hyksos" in the literature. Typologically and stylistically heterogeneous, these Phoenician archaizing scarabs are assigned to different regional groups or workshops. The prevalence of older imagery may therefore be an expression of regional cultural identity in a period of political instability and successive (Assyrian, Egyptian, Babylonian, Persian, and so on) foreign supremacy over the Levantine coast. A renewed interest in the past can also express a desire to match or surpass the glorious past or be a propagandistic means to gain political legitimacy from an association with that past. This was for example a driving force behind the Saite archaizing phenomenon, when probably all known scarabs bearing the names of Old Kingdom pharaohs were manufactured.

Ideas

10 }

Technology in Transit

THE BORROWING OF IDEAS IN SCIENCE AND CRAFTWORK

Ian Shaw

The Theoretical Context

The study of the processes by which different social or ethnic groups of humans develop distinctive forms of material culture has been a core element of archaeology since the early days of the subject. Indeed, at a time when the antiquarian precursors of archaeologists were beginning to form theories regarding observable evidence for technological change in the past, one of the most important tenets of the Enlightenment was the view that progress derived essentially from the use of rational thought to improve the human condition. As archaeology began to emerge as a discipline in the nineteenth century, most scholars still primarily viewed cultural change in terms of evolutionary stages from primitive to advanced forms of culture and technology. At this date, however, studies of technological change were also heavily dominated by diffusionism. Thus Gustav Oscar Montelius argued that European civilization developed in the way that it did because innovation tended to occur in certain areas (in his view, the Near East) and then diffuse outward from these cores toward their peripheries (i.e., northern Europe). The idea of "borrowing" of ideas in science and technology therefore became a persistent—sometimes beneficial and sometimes deeply damaging—theme in the study of ancient cultures, including that of the Nile Valley.

Diffusion differs from migration in that it does not imply the physical movement (or replacement of) peoples. Together with migration, cultural diffusion was the favored mechanism of change for many cultural historians writing about prehistoric peoples before the advent of processual archaeology. This was particularly true from the later nineteenth century, when ethnologists such as Friedrich Ratzel began to argue that independent invention of significant technological advances was highly unlikely to have happened more than once, implying that diffusion or migration would have to be disproved by archaeologists if they wanted to convincingly substantiate the independent origin or evolution of an (already known) idea in any given region.

It was in this scholarly context that the so-called "hyper-diffusionists" argued that there must have been a single point of origin for all cultural innovations. W. J. Perry and Grafton Elliot Smith, for instance, promoted the idea that ancient Egypt was the ultimate source of human civilization. Since then, archaeological theory has passed through many different phases, from cultural historical, through functional and processual, to post-processual and beyond, but disputes concerning the emergence and transfer of different types of technology remain key areas of discussion. John Ray (1986, pp. 307–8) has argued, for instance, that:

> Egypt's role was that of perfecter of ideas, rather than an inventor; most of the innovations in the Ancient Near East come from outside Egypt, but Egypt, once it adopts a new idea, produces a form of it which is often more effective than it was in its original home.

What Contribution Did Ancient Egyptians Make to the Emergence of Scientific Thought?

Before we begin to consider the question of Egyptian technology and innovation (and the degree to which significant developments in material culture derived wholly or partly from other cultures through the borrowing and dissemination of ideas, techniques, and materials), we should consider the extent to which craft was underpinned by more abstract scientific thoughts. Did such a thing as ancient Egyptian science exist? If so, where did it come from and to what extent did it exert influences on the thoughts and practices of other cultural groupings in the three geographical regions within which it was variously embedded: the Near East, the eastern Mediterranean, and northeast Africa.

The ancient Egyptian language did not include a word that is equivalent to the modern concept of scientific enquiry, but then it also had no words for other notions that clearly existed and were practiced, such as art and religion; therefore a linguistic lacuna is by no means an indication of an actual cultural gap. On the other hand there seems to be little evidence for individuals who can be directly identified as practitioners of science in pharaonic Egypt. Early Greek modes of thought and enquiry seem to have centered on the idea of individual thinkers, such as Archimedes, Crates, or Pythagoras, each credited with crucial intellectual, scientific, or technological advances, but such specific individual "proto-scientists" are not really visible in the monuments or texts of pharaonic Egypt. It is not that examples of the unusually lauded thinkers were absent from Egyptian historical sources—such key individuals as Imhotep and Amenhotep son of Hapu were recognized particularly for architectural and engineering feats during their own lifetimes and long afterwards (eventually as the subjects of divine cults). However, as Barry Kemp (2006, p. 159) has pointed out in relation to Imhotep: "he achieved fame as a great official, and it was as a great official, with the inevitable attribute of being 'wise', that he was remembered. It was the fact of his success that counted, not the means—architectural genius—by which he acquired it." In Egypt and the Near East in the third and second millennia BCE, during the era preceding the emergence of early Greek science, the emphasis was on crafts and technologies themselves—the equivalent of the *techne* of classical Athens—rather than the craftsmen or thinkers who were responsible for their introduction or development. This automatically increases the difficulty involved in examining the scientific framework within which Egyptian technology developed.

The best-documented aspects of Egyptian investigation and speculation are in the areas that would now be described as mathematics, structural engineering, medicine, and astronomy. However, Egyptian medicine and astronomy are both particularly intertwined with other areas of culture that would now be regarded as entirely separate: magic and religion. One of the major difficulties in attempting to explore and analyze currents of scientific and technical thought in ancient Egypt is their tendency to be deeply embedded within specific Egyptian cultural and social contexts. The texts, and occasional artifacts, that give us some sense of the ancient Egyptian tendency toward abstract thoughts are also of course specific genres of text, and it can often be difficult to know the extent to which they can actually be regarded as essentially "scientific," as opposed to "descriptive" or "anecdotal"—the two latter terms could easily be applied to many of the texts that are now confidently described as explicitly mathematical or medical.

The earliest surviving texts presenting mathematical problems and their solutions date to the Middle Kingdom (e.g., the Mathematical Leather Roll, BM EA 10250), but earlier depictions of scribes as accountants indicate that a fairly sophisticated system of mathematics was already in use, primarily for accounting and architectural purposes, from at least the beginning of the Old Kingdom. The first known medical texts also date to the Middle Kingdom, although the titles held by individuals such as the Third Dynasty physician and dentist Hesira clearly indicate that the practice of Egyptian medicine also extends back to a much earlier date. As far as the practical contexts and origins of these texts are concerned, there is a distinct lack of evidence for the Egyptians' utilization of methods that might be described in modern terms as experimentation or analytical research. In fact, many Egyptian textual sources tend to indicate the reverse: that knowledge was to be found not by experimentation but by the discovery of magical sources such as the so-called *Book of Thoth* (usually thought to contain everything that was known about the physical world, the divine system of laws, magic, and the nature of the afterlife), which is an important element of such Ptolemaic narrative cycles as the tales of Neferkaptah and Setne Khaemwas. What we also know little about, particularly for the third millennium BCE, is the degree to which developing scientific knowledge in Egypt was shaped and affected by ideas emanating from beyond its borders.

Conservative or Innovative? Writing as a Catalyst for Technology Transfer

Although it is frequently argued that ancient Egypt was an inherently conservative and inflexible civilization, many recent studies of the dynamics of material culture change in the Nile Valley have demonstrated the Egyptians' repeated ability to adapt to new modes of production, adopt and develop innovative techniques, and make use of new materials. The apparent rigidity and permanence of the pharaonic political and social systems from the third to first millennia BCE should not be glibly and automatically transposed onto the materials and technologies of these three millennia.

The propensity of ancient Egyptian culture to absorb and assimilate ideas, people, materials, and artifacts from elsewhere in Africa, the Near East, and the Mediterranean world can be demonstrated below by a number of case studies focusing on different technologies and materials. The first of these—the hieroglyphic writing system itself—is an appropriate one to begin with because of the fact that, as well as being a crucial development within Egyptian culture itself, it was also one of the principal means by which technologies and ideas of various types were transferred into and out of Egypt, via international scribal interconnections and diplomacy.

During the emergence of Egyptian civilization in the late fourth millennium BCE, the emergence of the hieroglyphic writing system was in many ways the first really distinctive ancient Egyptian technological development, not only because of its subsequent impact in such crucial areas as bureaucracy, administration, and social control, but because of its undoubted role, as in many other early cultures, as a kind of "enabling" technology in itself, providing both records of intellectual developments and flexible means of communication that facilitated innovations and technological adaptations.

Writing can also be recognized as one of the most vital stages in the process by which Egyptians exchanged ideas with other cultures in western Asia and the east Mediterranean, particularly at the beginning of the Late Bronze Age, when technologies and craftsmen were spreading more widely across Asia, Africa, and Europe. As Moorey (2001, p. 6) points out, language and writing clearly reflect this process in the lexicography of technology: "The impact of the technology of one region on that of another is likely to be most vividly indicated by the technical terms of foreign origin."

Even before language survives in written form, it can be a crucial element of cultural packages associated with the spread of certain types of material culture or subsistence. As an example of such pre-literate spread of technology, archaeologists working on precocious occurrences of pottery at early Holocene sites in the Nabta Playa-Kiseiba region of southwestern Egypt argue that "the terminology associated with cattle raising in the northern Sudanic division of the Nilo-Saharan languages was established before 8500 BCE, perhaps around the same time that the first pottery-making registered in the lexical data" (Jórdeczka et al., 2011, p. 112). However, it is only with the emergence of much more significant quantities of textual evidence in the Late Bronze Age that texts begin to make a crucial contribution to technology transfer and mobility of craftworkers in northeast Africa and the eastern Mediterranean.

The international situation within which Egyptian scientific and technological ideas developed in the Late Bronze Age and Early Iron Age was characterized by the emergence of ever more complex diplomatic contacts between the royal courts of the ancient Near East. It has frequently been suggested that royal courts and diplomatic systems in Bronze Age were deeply instrumental in widespread processes of technological contact and exchange. After all, it was likely to have been only the royal courts that possessed sufficient resources in terms of labor, materials, sophisticated artifacts, and workshops that could operate at an appropriate scale.

The network of international correspondence across the Late Bronze Age Near East, which primarily used the Akkadian cuneiform script, was clearly part of a process by which scribes and their physical texts fundamentally facilitated links between different elite groupings, including the associated professional craftsmen. There is increasing evidence for the fact that certain types of skilled craftsmen, such as doctors and sculptors, were moving between the elite centers of the Near East and the Aegean. From the Late Bronze Age onward, there is an increasing amount of archaeological and textual evidence for communities of scribes embedded in foreign courts. More than thirty "scholarly tablets" that formed part of the Amarna archive of cuneiform tablets provide particularly good indications that there was a group of "cuneiform scribes" based in the central city at Amarna in the late Eighteenth Dynasty. The tablets include such genres as lexical lists, syllabaries, vocabularies, myths, and historical or literary narratives. The scribes responsible for these texts may perhaps have been Egyptian scribes trained in cuneiform, but they could perhaps also have been resident non-Egyptian scribes sent to Amarna by their respective royal employers. Izre'el has pointed out that several blank, uninscribed clay tablets (now at the Ashmolean and the British Museum) were found at Amarna, perhaps reinforcing the possibility that an Akkadian-speaking foreign scribal community was located there, rather than just an archive created by locals.

Several finds from the New Kingdom northern capital at Qantir (Piramesse), suggest that Bronze Age diplomatic activity and technology transfer across the

Near East and east Mediterranean might have been closely linked. Not only have stone Hittite-style shield molds been found at Qantir, but the excavations have also yielded a worked boar's tusk that may have been part of a cheek-piece from a Mycenaean-style helmet. In addition, in the area of the city designated QVII, part of a cuneiform tablet was unearthed, raising the possibility that a Ramesside diplomatic archive like that at Amarna might have existed in the vicinity. Even if this tablet turns out to be an isolated find, it hints at the possibility that the population of Piramesse included not only Hittite or Mycenaean craftsmen but also perhaps a relatively permanent staff of Near Eastern "embassy" officials. The finds of shield-molds and tablet are given intriguing context by EA 22, a letter in the Amarna archive that was sent by Tushratta, ruler of Mitanni, to Amenhotep III, in which a list of prestigious items sent as gifts to Egypt includes "one leather shield with *urukmannu* of silver weighing ten shekels" (*urukmannu* being the Hurrian term for the outer metal parts of a shield).

This kind of technology transfer and cultural adaptability that began to take place as New Kingdom Egypt became fully integrated into the cosmopolitan world of the Near East was undoubtedly already much more a part of the routine of Near Eastern scribes, considering the more heterogeneous nature of western Asiatic cultures and empires; by the Assyrian period it became common to see depictions of pairs of scribes, one writing cuneiform script on a tablet or board and the other writing Aramaic on a sheet of papyrus, and the Aramaic word *sepiru* was used in Babylon at this date to refer to bilingual administrators. Intriguingly, there is also some evidence for the adoption of a set of exotic symbols incorporated into some Assyrian inscriptions dating to the reigns of Sargon II and Esarhaddon (e.g., British Museum WA 91027: "Lord Aberdeen's Black Stone," from the time of Esarhaddon), which may be an attempt by the Assyrian scribes and elite to imitate hieroglyphic writing. The reverse scenario can be observed in the Nineteenth Dynasty London Medical Papyrus, where six incantations are written in northwest Semitic languages, as well as two invocations that may be some variant of Minoan writing transcribed into a syllabic form of Egyptian hieroglyphs. It is clear that these non-Egyptian interpolations were understood by the writer of the London Medical Papyrus and fully incorporated into the meaning of the text, not least because it includes Egyptian sentences in the middle of the Semitic text. The syncretism of Egyptian and non-Egyptian religious systems is also suggested by the fact that one of the spells describes the god Amun as *rabunna* ("our lord") associated with "my mother Ishtar." It has been argued that this papyrus's fusion of Egyptian and Asiatic text was perhaps a deliberate prophylactic choice, given that the disease in question, identified with the Semitic term *hemektu* (translating as "strangulation"), might have actually been encountered in Asia rather than Egypt and might therefore have only been considered resolvable through the use of Asiatic rituals.

In the early Iron Age, there were Egyptian scribes resident in the Assyrian court from the eighth to sixth centuries BCE, as we can tell most vividly via a set of cuneiform texts from Nimrud listing wine rations from the reign of Adad-Nirari III to that of Shalmaneser IV (around the turn of the eighth century BCE), including references to many Egyptian craftworkers as recipients of the wine, long before Egypt had been conquered by Ashurbanipal. Although it has been suggested that these Egyptian professionals were prisoners of war captured during Assyrian campaigns in Syria-Palestine, it seems more likely that there was some deliberate personal mobility involved, with individual Egyptian artisans, including scribes, perhaps moving from their original workplaces in search of better employment abroad. Indeed Zaccagnini has suggested that the situation in terms of mobility of artisans and professionals may have constituted a state of transition in the first millennium, with new forms of organization and employment of labor emerging in the first millennium BCE, across the Near East. This certainly seems to be the case very soon after Esarhaddon's defeat of Egypt in 671 BCE, given that an Assyrian text dating to some time in the 660s BCE comprises a list of specialized scholars resident at the Assyrian court, including astrologers, physicians, exorcists, diviners, and lamenters, who represent the five traditional branches of Mesopotamian scholarship. These scholars include three Egyptian scribes and three *ḥarṭibe* (an Assyrian term for Egyptian ritual experts of some kind), who appear at the Assyrian court after Esarhaddon's conquest of Egypt. On the basis of several surviving lists of this type, it seems that the Egyptian specialisms that were most appreciated and exploited in Assyria were dream interpretation and magico-medical expertise. This well-attested exchange of documents and scribes across the Near East would surely have not only formed part of the process of technology transfer in the late second and first millennia BCE, but would presumably also have been the means by which a great deal of technical knowledge and practices were communicated and disseminated, i.e., via texts and highly educated scholars rather than simply by the physical import and export of skilled craftworkers, as was probably the case in the second millennium BCE.

Innovation in Egyptian Magic and Medicine, and the Role of the "Exotic"

One of the most important debates concerning ancient Egyptian science and technology centers on the question of ancient attitudes to innovation and "progress." Were ancient Egyptian doctors open to innovation, or were their methods quintessentially rooted in tradition and previous convention? At least two of the surviving medical papyri, much like some *Book of the Dead* papyri, specifically refer to their venerable status as documents written by much earlier scribes. This is part of the evidence suggesting that magico-medical texts tended to be evaluated on the basis of their longevity and links with the past, perhaps ultimately accentuating the sense that spells actually worked by drawing on the primordial magic associated with the deities Heka, Hu, and Sia, the three aspects of divine magic. Some of the surviving medical texts, such as the Edwin Smith Papyrus, actually do seem to have been copied from much earlier antecedents. Despite the survival of only fourteen medical texts from a period of two thousand years, the whole genre seems to be based on a large number of lost texts that were much more ancient, or at the very least that was what the reader was intended to believe.

It can also be argued, however, that Egyptian magico-medical texts, while stressing links with longstanding traditions, may also sometimes contain evidence suggesting that some kinds of innovation were allowed. For instance, such phrases as "another book says" suggest deliberate comparisons between different medical ideas, and some choices being made between a variety of techniques and spells. Foreign terms and spells might also be deliberately introduced to improve remedies (e.g., in the London Medical Papyrus). New medical ideas might have emanated from Assyrian and Persian royal courts, as in the case of the demotic Crocodilopolis medical book (Papyrus Vienna 6257; second century CE). The latter includes a large number of plant and mineral ingredients that are not previously mentioned in earlier medical texts, and Robert Ritner has suggested that these pharmaceutical developments might derive from Achaemenid international trade. Similarly, but on a more practical, visual note, the depiction of surgical instruments in the Roman temple at Kom Ombo includes some artifacts that are clearly Roman rather than Egyptian (e.g., scalpels and a sponge). Thus, even within the archaizing and highly traditional world of Egyptian magic and medicine, there are clear signs that innovation was valued.

Chariots, Composite Bows, and Glass: An Influx of Technologies in the Early New Kingdom

The tendency in the past has been to discuss the origins of various innovations in Egyptian technology in the late Second Intermediate Period and early New Kingdom in terms of contact between different cultural groups resulting in the transmission of ideas, new materials, craftsmen, and products. Scholars have therefore focused primarily on issues concerning the dates when materials and technologies first appeared in Egypt (or at least the earliest survivals in the archaeological record), as well as their possible origins. The process of innovation, however, is usually considerably more complicated, owing as much to the socio-economic context as to the emergence of technological "packages." We should also bear in mind that technologies do not exist in isolation but can in themselves directly impact other technologies, or at least affect the social contexts within which other technologies are emerging. This phenomenon is discussed by Donald Mackenzie and Judy Wajcman in their introductory essay to *The Social Shaping of Technology* (1985), when they discuss the tendency for technology to be shaped not so much by science as by other technology: "existing technology is more than just a precondition of new technology, but is an active shaping force in its development" (p. 9). This certainly seems to be the case with the two case studies discussed below: Late Bronze Age weaponry and glass production.

CHARIOTS AND COMPOSITE BOWS

The chariot is perhaps the most prominent form of technology that is widely accepted as an introduction into Egypt from the Near East. The first Egyptian text to even mention chariotry is on the second Kamose stela, which makes passing reference to the chariots used by the Hyksos. It is around this time that the earliest Egyptian examples of spoked wheels occur, in the form of a small model carriage in the tomb of Ahhotep, mother of King Ahmose (Cairo, Egyptian Museum, JE 4681). The general dearth of any previous depictions of wheeled vehicles in Egypt suggests strongly that the chariot was not invented in Egypt but introduced from the outside world, almost certainly from the Levant.

The chariot was undoubtedly among the most complex artifacts being produced in the ancient world; therefore the workshops producing chariots must have been extremely complex in terms of the diversity of materials involved and the wide range of technological skills required of the individual craftsmen, such as carpenters, joiners, weavers, and leather-workers. All of the six tombs containing scenes of chariot production between the reigns of Hatshepsut and Thutmose IV show these activities as taking place in the workshops of the temple of Amun at Karnak, perhaps because New Kingdom temples—as regular recipients of foreign booty and prisoners of war—might have had more ready access to exotic timber and Asiatic skilled craftsmen.

It can be difficult to determine the extent to which changes and innovations that occurred in the aftermath of the "Hyksos period" are genuinely linked. Probably the most significant development in military technology, apart from chariots, was the appearance of the composite bow. The method of attaching strips of horn and sinew to a wooden self bow produced a considerably more elastic weapon that was generally shorter in length but had a much greater range than its predecessor. If scholars are correct in suggesting that Egyptian chariots served above all as highly mobile bases from which archers could fire at their adversaries from a distance, then the adoption of chariots and composite bows must have been very closely linked. The emergence of the composite bow would have also fueled a demand for new types of wood, other than the acacia that had been primarily used for self bows. Although presumably most horn used in Egypt was derived from African species, there is some evidence to suggest that the horns of the Cretan wild goat (agrimi) might have been imported for making Egyptian composite bows. The introduction of the composite bow clearly also directly influenced changes in the form of arm guards and quivers. New types of arm guards were introduced in the early New Kingdom; the depictions of colored arm guards in tomb paintings seem to indicate that they were tied at both wrist and elbow. Unlike earlier guards, they cover much of the lower arm, but no actual examples seem to have survived, perhaps because they were made of textiles.

As part of this wholesale change in military technology, the typical Middle Kingdom tubular types of arrow quiver were replaced by tapered, round-bottomed quivers. In the Egyptian Museum, Cairo, one of a pair of quivers from the Eighteenth Dynasty tomb of Maiherpri in the Valley of the Kings (KV36) is extremely well preserved and is decorated with designs in raised relief (perhaps block-stamped). Another example of a New Kingdom quiver in the Neues Museum, Berlin, is decorated with openwork appliqués and panels of superimposed colored strips in red, white, green, and black. The new style and high quality of these quivers were almost certainly the result of significant change in the status of bowman, as well as the practical need for both archers and their equipment to be incorporated into the design of the chariot. The arrow and javelin quivers were attached to the side panel of the chariot in such a way and at such a precise angle that the charioteer could easily remove an arrow or javelin from the quivers when needed.

GLASS: EGYPTIAN, NEAR EASTERN, OR BOTH?

The other major technological introduction that appears to have taken place at around the time of the adoption of such military items as chariots and composite bows was glass. Generally speaking, the first significant glass items appearing in Egypt, in the early Eighteenth Dynasty, show all the signs of deriving from technology introduced from the Near East. There is considerable agreement on what constitutes ancient glass, which is based on a soda-lime composition with minor concentrations of potash and magnesia. The major debates in ancient Egyptian glassworking therefore tend to focus on the definition of production processes, and when it is that Egyptians can be said to be producing glass from the basic raw materials, as opposed to melting and re-working imported cullet or ingots of glass. On the one hand, scientists such as Roy Newton (1980, p. 176) argue that:

> the Egyptians could only melt other people's glass even though they could fabricate the most exquisite items from it ... the Egyptian court depended for their basic raw material, or for an essential ingredient thereof, on imports from Asia.

On the other hand, there is the undeniable fact that Egypt has a long history of production of two other important vitreous products: faience and frit. In the context of early Egypt, the best-known form of frit is "Egyptian blue," which is both similar to glass and also a material apparently first produced by the Egyptians. This evidence for Egypt's long experience of production and experimentation with two other kinds of vitreous product might thus be taken to argue that they had the capability to develop early glass roughly simultaneously with other Late Bronze Age cultures in the Near East, such as the kingdom of Mitanni, or that, at the very least, they were capable of quickly assimilating and adapting to this new technology, on the basis that they had been producing similar substances since the Predynastic period.

So what do the archaeological data suggest? The first glass artifacts in Egypt initially appear as exotic products primarily in elite funerary assemblages, such as the tomb of Thutmose I and the tomb of the foreign wives of Thutmose III in Wadi Qubbanet el-Qirud at Thebes, in the early Eighteenth Dynasty. It is argued that the sheer technical accomplishment of these earliest examples of glass in Egypt makes it likely that the technology must have been introduced from outside rather than being the result of a long-term evolution of technology. A few New Kingdom archaeological sites (Amarna, Qantir, and perhaps Malkata) incorporate the remains of areas of production and debris relating to glass working and/or glass making. At Amarna, the late nineteenth-century discoveries of glass manufacture by Flinders Petrie eventually led to excavations conducted by Paul Nicholson in the 1990s, focusing on site O45.1, where the presence of kilns, glass ingot molds, and traces of fritted glass suggest that glass may have been produced from raw materials. In addition, the shipwreck excavated at Uluburun included 100 kg of cobalt blue glass ingots, and ingot molds excavated by Petrie at Amarna correspond closely to the shape and dimensions of the Uluburun ingots. At Qantir (Piramesse), Edgar Pusch's excavations have revealed melting crucibles and frits, specifically connected with red glass, but not yet any kilns or signs of glass working.

As for linguistic and visual evidence, the frequent use of two foreign words for glass (the Hurrian term *ehlipakku* and the Akkadian term *mekku*), alongside some homegrown terms, tends to suggest strongly that New Kingdom glass was a foreign import rather than an indigenous invention. The same general scenario is suggested by the listing and depiction of glass items on the walls of Karnak temple as booty in Thutmose III's *Annals* concerning his Near Eastern military exploits. Glass vessels imported from western Asia are also shown in the tombs of early Eighteenth Dynasty high officials Rekhmire and Kenamun in western Thebes. Finally in the late Eighteenth Dynasty, seven of the Amarna Letters (EA 25, 148, 235, 314, 323, 327, and 331) mention glass as an import, although one (EA 14) lists it among gifts sent by the Egyptian king to the king of Babylon.

The chemical analysis of samples of glass deriving from sites across the eastern Mediterranean and Near East suggests that there were three basic forms of glass being produced in the mid- to late second millennium BCE: (1) a light-blue/turquoise form that was made in Mesopotamia from a plant-ash alkali and copper colorant, and (2) a dark-blue plant-ash alkali glass, with higher quantities of copper, giving it a color resembling lapis lazuli, and (3) a dark-blue cobalt-natron glass made in Egypt. Nicholson and Henderson (2000, p. 220) point out that there is some variety in the composition of Egyptian glasses of different periods:

> although from an early period Egyptian glass displays signs of being a conservative technology ... , and to some extent this is also true of Amarna glass, there is nevertheless some compositional variation, with some relatively high alumina levels occurring in translucent non-cobalt glasses as early as the reign of Thutmose III.

Although it is clear that glass was deliberately manufactured in the Near East from at least as early as the sixteenth century BCE, no Mesopotamian or Egyptian evidence has yet been found for the fritting of glass from primary raw materials in the second millennium BCE. It is still the case that the earliest known glass has been found in Mesopotamia, but it is not yet possible to discount the possibility that it was also fused from primary raw materials in Egypt (albeit possibly at a later date). It has been suggested that the emergence of glass production in the Near East (and perhaps also in Egypt) by the mid-second millennium might have related to new Late Bronze Age economics and working practices, i.e., the emergence of large-scale craft production controlled by royal courts and temples. This theory is perhaps reinforced by the evidence found at Qantir suggesting a close link between glassworking and copper-working areas. Ultimately it is possible that a solution lies in chemical analysis primarily—newly available analytical methods such as laser ablation ICP-MS may well help to clarify the situation further, with regard to the chemical compositions and origins of Egyptian, Near Eastern, and Aegean glass artifacts.

Conclusions and Discussion

Many significant developments in Egyptian technology seem to have emerged directly from migrations of people (whether spontaneous or forced), the exchange of ideas between different ethnic and cultural groups, and major processes of social change brought on by large-scale environmental and political influences. These kinds of innovations in craftwork can be seen to have had important impacts on the social and political contacts between Egypt and the Levant, and between Egypt and the rest of northeastern Africa. The chronology of all this, however, suggests that the turning point for the Egyptians was probably the expulsion of the Hyksos, who may have represented a significant barrier between the Egyptians and access to more sophisticated weaponry such as chariots, composite bows, and body armor, as well as other, non-military materials and crafts.

Certainly it was only in the early Eighteenth Dynasty that the Egyptians were able to gain access both to some of the necessary imported materials and probably also, initially at least, foreign craftsmen, so that they could begin to produce and/or fashion new materials, and produce new kinds of artifacts. Many of the materials needed for chariot manufacture (such as acacia-wood, copper alloy, bone, stone, faience, and rawhide) and much of the technological ability (such as steam-bending, lathe-turning, and drilling) had already been available for some time within Egypt itself, but the crucial changes were the social and political ones, whereby Egyptians gained ready access to the resources of western Asia. Once they were able to import materials and artifacts (such as captured chariots or glass ingots) and craftsmen they could begin to develop their own versions of the technology. This happened primarily through war, trade, and diplomacy.

How then does the knowledge economy of materials and artifacts in use across the Near East and east Mediterranean appear in Egyptian iconography and texts? Do the images, texts, and artifacts overlap and/or correspond with one another? How are commodities (e.g., weapons), ideas, and people (e.g., mercenaries and prisoners of war) moving around the east Mediterranean in the Late Bronze Age? What do we know from Anatolian sources; what do we glean from Egyptian texts and images; and how well do these two bodies of source material correlate? All of these questions will still require more research, and particularly more analysis of individual artifacts, in the future. One crucial concept, however, that already seems to have emerged in relation to technology transfer in the east Mediterranean and Near Eastern is "convergence"—the technologies for stone vessel making, for instance, were gradually becoming relatively homogeneous throughout the region during the Bronze Age. Research into vitreous materials in the Eastern Mediterranean also suggests that there was an extremely complex conjunction of materials and techniques in this area of technology:

> the main body of Aegean Bronze Age faience, as well as Egyptian blue frit and glass fits into the general Aegean iconography and is thus considered as a characteristic Aegean product. There are, however, technical, compositional and even stylistic similarities with both the Near East and Egypt. (Panagiotaki et al. 2004, p. 150)

There are numerous mechanisms by which war, trade, migration and other forms of cultural contact directly affect technology. But to what degree do these social and economic processes actually promote (or even discourage) innovation? Joel Mokyr (1990, p. 183) raises the question of cause and effect: "Whether in fact innovations in military technology provided substantial benefits in the production of peacetime goods and services so that war can be thought of as an agent of technical progress is far from easy to determine." In the context of the development of Late Bronze Age east Mediterranean and Near Eastern technology, there is no doubt that, as in other places and times, the web of social, economic, and technological factors is highly complex, but worth our while to disentangle.

11

The Flow of Words

INTERACTION IN WRITING AND LITERATURE DURING
THE BRONZE AGE

I }

Writing Systems

CUNEIFORM AND HIEROGLYPHS IN THE BRONZE AGE— SCRIPT CONTACT AND THE CREATION OF NEW SCRIPTS

Orly Goldwasser

From Mesopotamia to Egypt? The Invention of Writing in the Late Fourth Millennium

It is difficult to determine if the invention of script systems in the ancient Near East occurred independently in both Egypt and Mesopotamia or if it is rather a case of cultural interference—borrowing or influence. It is reasonable to reconstruct it as a case of adoption of a new cultural "option"—in this case the option of transforming spoken utterances into material signs. Based on the evidence at hand, it seems most likely that writing was born in Mesopotamia, through a long process, and then very early in this script's history, it inspired the production of an independent writing system in Egypt.

The Mesopotamian Proto-literate Period was a time of lively contact between Egypt and Mesopotamia, as can be seen from various archaeological finds, as well as the shared architectural and artistic motifs of the era. During this period, Egyptians and users of the Proto-cuneiform script may have come into contact, whether in Egypt or Mesopotamia. The next step would have been the domestication of the idea of "writing" to serve the specific needs of the nascent Egyptian state and its language, and this endeavor appears to have been independent of Mesopotamian influence. The two writing systems share several semiotic attributes that support this reconstruction. Both started as pictorial systems, both use logograms and at a later stage phonograms, and both feature classifiers (determinatives). Yet the classifiers (signs carrying no phonetic information, only semantic information about the word) generally appear in cuneiform writing before the word, whereas in Egyptian they always appear at the end of the word.

Some early Egyptian hieroglyphs clearly have their roots in the Mesopotamian sphere. A good example is the important *serekh* 𓍶 hieroglyph. This symbol of a royal building façade was the essential signature of the earliest royal names in Egypt, and a very similar icon was common on Mesopotamian cylinder seals from this period (fig. 11.1).

It seems that the "flow of signs" towards the end of the fourth millennium was influenced not only by the existence of the challenging "option" presented by Proto-cuneiform script but also, at least partially, by the system of symbols operating on Mesopotamian cylinder seals and other finds of the period that were available in Egypt.

The Egyptian and Mesopotamian script systems also reveal in their early stage the primary condition that sharply marks script from pictorial representation. In a script system, all referents are represented on the *same scale*, whatever their relative sizes in the real world. This procedure instructs the mind of the potential reader to see the given pictures as *something else*, viz., script. This feature is clearly present in both Egyptian and Mesopotamian materials from the earliest extant examples (fig. 11.2).

FIGURE 11.1 Left: An early Egyptian serekh of an unknown king, possibly *Horus *N.j-N.jt*, incised on a jar from Helwan. Right: A Proto-literate seal from Sin Temple, Khafajah (Mesopotamia).

FIGURE 11.2 Examples of early writing. Left: An early Sumerian clay tablet. The bull's head and the other signs are of the same size. Right: Proto-dynastic Egyptian bone tag from tomb U-J at Abydos. The mountain ridge and the snake are of the same size.

Egyptian Hieroglyphs

Hieroglyphs were used mainly in monumental writing—on stelae, the walls of temples and tombs, and the surfaces of various hard objects (pl. 8), including cylinder seals and scarabs. The miniature iconic signs reflected the universe coded by Egyptian eyes. All hieroglyphs obey the strict representation rules of Egyptian art and many are indelibly imbued with an "Egyptian quality." These include hieroglyphs such as "king," "god," and "man," all of which unquestionably reflect Egyptian pictorial prototypes. In this way, hieroglyphs are not "free markers" of words but are strongly intertwined with the Egyptian cultural sphere.

Naturally, the highly pictorial nature of hieroglyphs was a burden on everyday production of texts. The Egyptians therefore developed very early on various cursive variations of the hieroglyphs for administrative writing and later for literature. The most abstract cursive script—dubbed "hieratic" by the Greeks—was used mainly for writing on papyri and ostraca (pl. 8). The level of iconicity in hieratic and other variations of cursive Egyptian scripts was greatly reduced.

Throughout its history, the Egyptian script was used only to transmit the Egyptian language itself and never to systematically represent any other language.

Cuneiform

In sharp contrast to Egyptian hieroglyphs, the cuneiform script lost its iconicity very early in its history, probably due to the technical limitations of writing on clay tablets. Cuneiform signs are thus "free markers" and do not refer to or iconically evoke visual referents of early Mesopotamian culture (fig. 11.3). Cuneiform almost always functioned strictly as an instrument for conveying linguistic messages.

The cuneiform script was invented and developed by the early Mesopotamians settlers, probably Sumerians, to transcribe their own non-Semitic language. Yet, being a system of non-iconic, wedge-like signs, the cuneiform script enjoyed great success on the cultural market. Once the signs were endowed with logographic and phonetic readings, their low iconicity made them an ideal tool for borrowing. The first languages we can identify as using the cuneiform script are Sumerian and Akkadian during the mid-third millennium. Another important Semitic language, as Akkadian, that used cuneiform in the midst of the third millennium is Eblaite, recorded on thousands of clay tablets found in the palace of Ebla.

The adaptation of cuneiform for different Semitic languages and dialects continued during the second millennium (Mari, Canaan). In addition, an

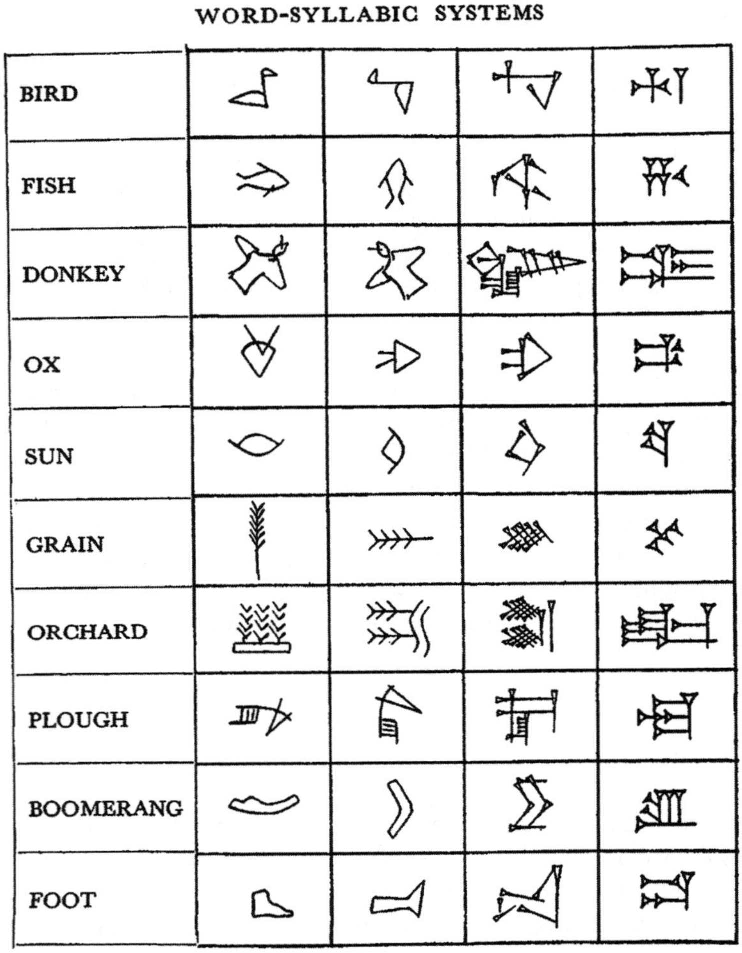

WORD-SYLLABIC SYSTEMS

BIRD				
FISH				
DONKEY				
OX				
SUN				
GRAIN				
ORCHARD				
PLOUGH				
BOOMERANG				
FOOT				

FIGURE 11.3 The reduction of iconicity: the cuneiform script.

important transmission of the script to non-Semitic languages occurred in the midst of the second millennium, when the Hittites used cuneiform to record not only (Indo-European) Hittite texts, but also additional non-Semitic languages, such as Hurrian.

Hieroglyphs in the Levant—"Travelling Symbols"

The quality of "high iconicity," which was rigorously developed and maintained by the Egyptians (e.g., pl. 8), made it possible for a selected group of hieroglyphs to become "travelling symbols" and active agents of the Egyptian culture in the Levant and beyond. Wherever they travelled, they carried along with them a strong additional prestige value—"Egyptian."

The iconic nature of Egyptian, which facilitated the conveying of abstract concepts in a single, very specific, and pictorially recognized icon, made Egyptian script an attractive source of symbols. Moreover, this iconicity enabled hieroglyphs to "return to the icon" and become active players in various pictorial scenes.

The most widely distributed hieroglyph to appear in the Levant is the *ankh* ☥ "life" sign. It lent itself during the seventeenth century BCE to be loaned as a written symbol, probably carrying with it its semantic meaning—"life"—if not its Egyptian phonological content (fig. 11.4).

Parallel to its straightforward use as written signifier for the meaning "life," and due to its specific pictorial qualities, e.g., "being held" or "being given," the *ankh* hieroglyph appears in various pictorial scenes throughout the ancient Levant, mostly when a god is represented as "giving life," i.e., handing the icon to the king. In Egypt, this type of scene is well attested from the earliest periods, and it is found on a wide variety of media.

In their Levantine incarnations, hieroglyphs, mainly on seals, may take a non-Egyptian form or may be inscribed in the "wrong" position (fig. 11.4). Besides the *ankh*, "hieroglyphic koine" on Levantine seals of the Middle Bronze Age includes a few additional signs that carry positive abstract meanings, such as ⚚ "dominion" or 𒀭 "stability." They appear in the Levant alongside images of gods (local or Egyptianized), together with many other Egyptian symbols, such as the winged sun, imitations of Egyptian cartouches, or scenes reflecting Egyptian royal attitudes.

A larger repertoire of hieroglyphs makes it appearance mainly on scarabs in Canaan during the Second Intermediate Period, when Canaanites, later known as Hyksos, settled in the eastern Delta and came to rule Egypt. Canaanite versions of various hieroglyphs imitating Egyptian hieroglyphs

FIGURE 11.4 Left: Old Syrian Dynastic seals depicting king receiving *ankh* from goddess or god. Right: Syrian seal depicting Canaanite goddesses holding an *ankh* sign in the wrong way, upside-down.

appear on scarabs that were produced locally in Canaan. This larger repertoire of hieroglyphs comes into use together with a strong presence of Egyptianized gods, crowns, and other Egyptian symbols. Again, it is difficult to determine if the Canaanite addressee regarded these gods and symbols as Egyptian or "translated" them into his own pantheon. Royal cartouches, correctly or incorrectly written, are also widespread. In this case too, it is difficult to assess which hieroglyphs were carriers of names, and which were activated only as *Neferzeichen*.

Another widely popular Canaanite variation that appears on scarabs during this period was a repetitive group of flat hieroglyphs (known as *anra* in the literature) that makes no sense in Egyptian. This group repeats itself again and again on many Canaanite scarabs and in many variations. It is hard to say if these are only gibberish imitations of "hieroglyphs" that were somehow standardized or if they are a combination of Egyptian hieroglyphs that were given some new local meaning through "Canaanite reading." For instance, signs may have been read iconically, i.e., as ᘛᘚᘛᘚ "water," ᐊ___ᴅ "giving gift," ᴖ "offering", and so forth—not referring to the original Egyptian reading of the signs.

More than "Travelling Symbols"—Hieroglyphs as Catalysts for the Invention of New Scripts

CRETAN AND ANATOLIAN HIEROGLYPHS

During the second millennium, at least two scripts were born probably due to some influence of Egyptian hieroglyphs. The first is a Cretan pictographic script, and the second is Anatolian hieroglyphic. (fig. 11.5).

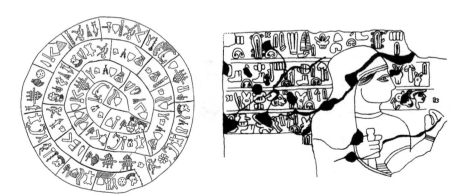

FIGURE 11.5 Left: The Phaistos Disk, a unique find showing highly iconic Cretan hieroglyphs. All hieroglyphs are in the same direction and of the same scale. Right: Anatolian hieroglyphs from Karkemish.

The two new scripts exhibit again the basic semiotic rules that transform a collection of pictures into a script system. Both are made up of a consistent repertoire of hundreds of signs. The signs, as a rule, do not relate to or "touch" each other to create meaning. All pictures undergo scaling to fit a single grid, for example—a human head is of the same size of a full human representation. Like in the Egyptian hieroglyphic system, there is no strict rule for a single direction of writing, but all signs maintain the same direction on a single line. However, Anatolian hieroglyphs are always written in boustrophedon. The large number of signs points immediately to a complex logographic-syllabic writing system, such as the hieroglyphic system or cuneiform.

The inventors of these new scripts completely domesticated the idea of pictorial writing into their own respective cultures and languages. The new scripts did not borrow Egyptian hieroglyphs, but rather each inventor created a whole new culture-specific repertoire of "pictorial signifiers," reflecting their own selected referents in the world, and their own forms of representation.

The Cretan pictorial script was born sometime in the first half of the second millennium BCE. It was short lived and is attested only in central and northeastern Crete. It has no known offspring. The texts are not yet fully deciphered.

Anatolian hieroglyphs, on the other hand, were a much more widespread phenomenon. The inscriptions written in the new pictorial script have been securely deciphered and their language safely identified today as Luwian. Appearing on the stage of history later than the Cretan script, it is not impossible that the Cretan script served as an influence. The inner semiotic structure of the Anatolian hieroglyphs must have been influenced by the cuneiform system. Besides various phonological matters, the script makes use of classifiers (determinatives) that appear regularly before the word but rarely also after the word, as in Sumerian and Akkadian. In Egyptian, the classifiers appear always at the end of the word, as noted above.

Anatolian hieroglyphs, like Egyptian hieroglyphs, according to the material that survived, were used mainly for public display and many are inscribed on seals of officials in the Hittite empire in Anatolia as well as in Syria. Through their iconicity they could function as an instrument for enhancing local images. At the very same time, the Hittite rulers used a parallel writing system made up of borrowed Mesopotamian cuneiform signs to record texts in Hittite and other languages. This Hittite cuneiform script was used for writing all administrative matters as well as myths, annals, and treaties. However, its non-iconic character, and the fact that it was used by many other peoples in the Levant, could not allow it to function as a marker of national identity. The unique pictorial Anatolian hieroglyphic script, on the other hand, constantly enhanced chosen visual referents of the Hittite culture and state, which were repeatedly activated by the script as agents of "Hittite identity."

EGYPTIAN HIEROGLYPHS AS CATALYSTS FOR THE INVENTION
OF THE ALPHABET

The high iconicity of the hieroglyphic script again played a key role on the stage of intellectual history at another crossroad of Egyptian and Levantine cultures. This meeting, and the interference process initiated by it, led to the creation of one of the most influential and long-lasting inventions in the history of western civilization.

Egyptian hieroglyphs served as both catalyst and raw material for the Canaanite invention of the alphabet. This ancient script developed into the Hebrew, Arabic, Greek, and Latin scripts. Of all ancient Near Eastern scripts, the alphabet met with the greatest success on the cultural market of civilization.

Unlike the case of the Minoan and Anatolian scripts, the invention of the alphabet was not born in the environment of erudite scribes, but was apparently created as a non-institutional cultural product by illiterate Canaanite miners. Though they were experts in their professional field of mining, the inventors of the alphabet were far removed from the circles of professional writing in cuneiform and Egyptian. It is precisely this naïveté that allowed them to invent something completely new, as they were unencumbered by the scripts of their day. They were able to think outside the box, inventing a novel writing system—an alphabetic script made of fewer than thirty signs.

In Serabit el-Khadem in Sinai, during the second part of the Twelfth Dynasty, large Egyptian expeditions were engaged by the order of the kings to deliver turquoise from the mines in the area. The expeditions included hundreds of Egyptians, comprising scribes, treasurers, administrators, and various other officials. The expeditions were also charged to build a large temple to the goddess Hathor, the goddess of turquoise, on the plateau near the mines, thus securing the success of the mining efforts. Hundreds of official and private inscriptions dating to the Middle Kingdom were found on the site of the temple. In the meantime, groups of Canaanite expert miners were probably engaged in the mining efforts themselves in the mines around the temple. These Canaanites were surrounded by numerous Egyptian inscriptions, all made of the little pictorial hieroglyphs.

Like the inventors of the Cretan and Anatolian hieroglyphs, the Canaanites borrowed the Egyptian idea of *turning pictures into script*. Yet, not being professional scribes and not working in the service of any official ideology or institution, they did not bother to invent a whole set of new icons. They adopted roughly two dozen icons from the hieroglyphs around them—those that they found useful for their own purposes—and added a few new signs of their own.

Like the Hittites and the Cretans, the inventors of the alphabet adopted the rule of *scaling* used in the Egyptian hieroglyphic system. All new alphabetic signs were written in more or less the same scale in the corpus of inscriptions (around thirty) known from Sinai (fig. 11.6).

An Evolving Alphabet

Hieroglyphic from Sinai	Proto-Sinaitic	Phoenician & Paleo-Hebrew	Early Greek	Greek	Latin	Modern Hebrew
𐤀	𐤀	ⱡ	𐌀	A	A	א
▱	▯	𝟿	ⵥ	B	B	ב
𝉠	𝉠	ⱻ	ⱻ	E	E	ה
	ѱ	𐤊	Ɣ	K	K	כ
∾∾∾	∿∿∿	"𐤌	𝑀	M	M	מ
⸜	⸜	𐤍	𐤍	N	N	נ
◅◉▻	◁◉▷	o	o	O	O	ע
𐀯	𐀯	ⴹ	𐌓	P	R	ר
	ω	w	ⱹ	Ƨ	S	ש
+	+	×	T	T	T	ת

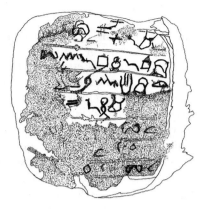

Table illustrating the alphabet's evolution from Egyptian hieroglyphs.

Bottom-left: Egyptian depiction of a contemporary Canaanite warrior with his bow. This type of bow may have served as the prototype for the letter shin. The warrior sports the Canaanite "mushroom" hairdo. (O. Goldwasser)

In the second line one could read, from right to left, the Semitic word r-b "chief"

FIGURE 11.6 Left: The development of Hebrew, Greek, and Latin letters from the Proto-Sinaitic letters. Right: A Proto-Sinaitic inscription from Serabit el-Khadim, Sinai. The inscription is to be read in the "wrong" direction according to Egyptian reading rules.

It seems that the inventors wished to write their names and short prayers to their gods in their own language and in their own way. Their inscriptions are identified today as written in a Semitic dialect. They refer to the Egyptian goddess Hathor by the name of a Canaanite goddess that was probably identified with her—Ba'alat.

Due to their illiteracy, the Canaanite inventors made use of the hieroglyphs only as a source for *pictorial* models, to which they gave their own *pictorial interpretation*, and a name in their Canaanite dialect. Their readings may coincide with the original *iconic meaning* of the sign in the Egyptian system (such as the cases of the hieroglyphs ∿∿∿ "water", ◁◉▷ "eye," or 𐀯 "head"), but in other cases they gave the hieroglyphs their own idiosyncratic Canaanite readings (as in the case of "house," below). Not familiar with the Egyptian script system, they were free to think anew and were not bound by the complex semiotic use of icons in the source hieroglyphic script system—i.e., logograms (with their redundant "phonetic complements"), phonograms, and classifiers.

The illiteracy hypothesis explains why some letters clearly diverge from the Egyptian prototypes. To take but one example, the Proto-Sinaitic exemplars of the letter *bet* (ב) that should represent a "house" (בית), are conceived from a naïve reading of different pictorial icons, none of which are the correct hieroglyph for "house" in the Egyptian source system. The hieroglyph ▯ was probably used primarily as a model for the "house" letter in the early alphabet in Sinai, e.g., ▯ ▱. In the hieroglyphic script system, the original pictorial referent of ▯ is a stool, and it is used in the Egyptian system mainly as the phonogram /p/, which has nothing to do with a house. At the same time, other hieroglyphs and even real-world models were probably involved in the invention of the letter *bet*, as different versions of the letter—as ⊟ and 🏠 (house with an entrance) clearly demonstrate. Such representations of houses are not known in the hieroglyphic record, including the cursive and hieratic variants. Moreover, never was the correct and very common Egyptian "house" hieroglyph ⊏⊐ used by the Canaanite inventors.

Another type of letter exists in the new Canaanite system—a direct borrowing from concrete referents in the world, and not from the hieroglyphic script. Such is the letter *kap* = 🖐 "open palm." Here no pictorial model in available in the hieroglyphic script, and the letter came directly into the script, most probably without the intervention of Egyptian hieroglyphs.

From this point on, the alphabet's creator(s) began to progress alone. They chose to apply only a single reading rule. Here the idea of taking out only the first "sound" of every picture came into play—a process that is known today in linguistic jargon as "acrophony." Every picture in the new script stood only for the "first sound" of the picture, *read in their own language*. The small pictures of bull, eye, water, hand, palm, house, monkey, head, etc., were well known to the inventors and were easily identified. Every icon of the newly invented Canaanite script stood for a single sound, a single consonant. Here iconicity served only as the first step—a reminder of the *name* of the letter. From this name only the first sound should be kept, the meaning of the icon should be discarded. In this way, free individual *letters* were born, i.e. pictorial signifiers that refer directly to sounds alone (fig. 11.6).

During the Late Bronze Age, the alphabet—being a non-institutional invention not backed by scribes or schools—traveled in non-literate circles in Canaan and Egypt (e.g. Wadi el-Hol). It was maintained and likely disseminated by Canaanite professionals on the move, such as soldiers or miners. An early linearization process that should be dated to circa the thirteenth century BCE in Canaan may have resulted from interference processes of such carriers with Egyptian scribes residing in this period in southern Canaan. This linear version of the early iconic alphabet invented in Sinai would develop in the Iron Age to become the national script of the various new identities in Canaan and the Levant—the Hebrews, Moabites, Phoenicians, Arameans, and others.

THE UGARITIC ALPHABET—THE INDIRECT LINK
BETWEEN CUNEIFORM AND HIEROGLYPHS

It seems that sometime during the thirteenth century BCE, the sophisticated scribes of Ugarit on the northern coast of Lebanon came into touch with carriers of the Canaanite alphabet, which had been invented a few centuries earlier in Sinai. It is difficult to assess if they encountered the script in some early iconic version or in its more linear variations that may have already existed in southern Canaan.

As speakers of a Semitic language, they would have immediately recognized the genius of the invention. Yet the letters themselves must have looked too unstable and non-standardized to them, perhaps even as a bad imitation of Egyptian hieroglyphs. They therefore "converted" them into what they doubtless regarded as their better, professional cuneiform sign system. They invented thirty new cuneiform signs—each referring to a single sound. The signs may however be based on the alphabetic sign forms, although because incised in clay they look different. From the similar names that they gave to the letters in their new system, it is very clear that they mastered the earlier pictographic alphabet and its acrophonic principle. To the letters that they adopted from the Proto-Sinaitic or Proto-Canaanite script, they added three letters of their own, of which two functioned as a sort of proto-vowel letter. It is to this script that we owe some of the greatest works of Canaanite literature known today.

Yet the success of the new cuneiform alphabet was only partial. It indeed spread into Canaan, but being a typical institutional product, it came to an end when Ugarit was destroyed around the beginning of the twelfth century BCE. The destruction of the Bronze Age Canaanite town system followed shortly thereafter. The cuneiform alphabet disappeared alongside its urban carriers: scribes in Ugarit and scribes in the urban centers of Canaan.

It is unknown who established the "alphabet" orders. For the first letter in the sequence of the alphabet order we use today, the ʾālep ✶, the icon of the religiously loaded word "bull" was chosen. The bull was the sacred animal of the storm god, the champion Canaanite god. It might have been fitting to be the first in the alphabet. This ʾālep ✶ will later become the Greek *alpha* and Latin **A**, which preserves in a more abstract way the original bull icon "turned on his horns."

II }

Literature

EGYPTIAN AND LEVANTINE *BELLES-LETTRES*—LINKS
AND INFLUENCES DURING THE BRONZE AGE

Noga Ayali-Darshan

While the influence of Egyptian hieroglyphs and visual art upon the Late
Bronze Levant is clearly evident, literature is a very different case. As evidenced by the identification of Egyptian with local gods on the basis of similar
features, some Egyptian oral traditions were assimilated into Levantine literature. Ugaritic literature, for example, locates the dwelling of the craftsman god
Koṯar-waḪasis in Memphis (Ugaritic *Ḫkpt*)—the city of Ptah, his Egyptian
counterpart. Several examples in the biblical literature, composed centuries
later, similarly attest to Israelite familiarity with Late Egyptian literature. In
comparison to the visual arts, however, Egyptian literary influence upon the
Levant seems very limited.

One of the primary reasons for this lies in the random nature of the literary texts that have survived. To date, the only extant Late Bronze (or earlier)
Levantine literature written in the local language is the Ugaritic corpus. Some
traces also exist in the Hurro-Hittite literature found at Boğazköi (Ḫattuša),
which reflects the traditions prevalent in the upper Levant. We do not know,
however, what the local literature of the cities of Phoenicia, Canaan, or the
kingdom of Amurru contained. Similarly, the principal literary genre in the
Ugaritic literature is mythological narrative. While several prayers, hymns, and
spells have survived, no Ugaritic wisdom texts have been found (for the scribal
school texts, see below). Rather than indicating that this genre (and others)
did not exist in the Levant, this fact simply reflects the chance nature of the
findings. Unfortunately, the genres absent from Ugaritic literature are precisely
those most popular in Egypt from a very early date. On the other hand, the
mythological tales so common in Ugaritic and Hurro-Hittite literature only
began to flourish in Egypt during the New Kingdom. It is thus very difficult

195

to prove Egyptian influence on Late Bronze Levantine literature. In fact, the reverse direction is far more conspicuous.

In light of the absence of evidence for Egyptian influence on the Levant during the Late Bronze Age and earlier, scholars have focused their attention on Egyptian influence upon biblical literature (which contains more genres)—the younger representative of the Levantine literature. Even here, however, a close analysis suggests diverse directions of influence. Let us look at five genres.

The Story of the Storm God's Combat with the Sea and Other Mythological Tales

Both Egyptian and Israelite scribes were acquainted with the story of the storm god's combat with the Sea. In Egypt, the principal protagonist was Seth, in Israel ᴙʜᴡʜ, the antagonist being known in both literatures by the West Semitic name Yamm (*p3 ym* in Egyptian, םי in Hebrew). Additional versions and witnesses of this story exist not only in Ugaritic and Hurro-Hittite texts but also in Mari and Mesopotamia. The Egyptian version being one of the earliest, the myth might have been assumed to have originated in the land of the Nile. All the witnesses of the Egyptian version—including the Astarte Papyrus from the reign of Amenhotep II, three spells (Papyrus Hearst 11, 12–15; Papyrus Berlin 3038 XX 9–XXI 3; Papyrus Leiden I 343 + I 345 IV 9–VI 2), and a stich of a Hymn to Ramses III from Deir el Medina (Ostracon Deir el-Medina 1222)—point to a Levantine provenance, however.

In brief, the Astarte Papyrus recounts how *Ym* opposed the gods, covering the whole earth with his waters. Under the leadership of Renenutet, the harvest goddess, the gods pay a tribute to *Ym* that fails to appease him. One offering is brought by Astarte, who sings and laughs before him. Finally, Seth confronts him and delivers the gods from his threats. While the papyrus is broken off before this point, its opening statement, which relates to Seth—". . . that he did for the Ennead in order to fight *Ym*"—indicates that he defeated the Sea and saved the gods from his waters. The above three spells and the *Hymn to Ramses III*, which describe Seth's overpowering of the Sea, confirm not only the end of the plot but also its dissemination in Egypt.

The main protagonists in the papyrus are *Ym* and Seth, Renenutet and Astarte. The other Egyptian gods—Ptah as head of the pantheon and Nut and Geb who bring the offering—play only a secondary role. The Egyptian names and features of *Ym* and Astarte clearly point to their Levantine origin. Despite their Egyptian names, however, Seth and Renenutet are also depicted as Levantine rather than Egyptian figures. Seth is customarily regarded as Osiris's adversary, not yet being revered as a dynastic god. The fact that he serves as the principal protagonist in this story, delivering the gods from *Ym*, demonstrates that the features of the Levantine storm god were attached to him. Renenutet, on the other hand, was a minor harvest goddess before being transformed into one of the main characters and given responsibility for sending the tribute to *Ym*. Like Seth, her role thus appears to have been influenced by that of her counterpart—a far more important figure. In the Hurro-Hittite literature (composed by north Syrian Hurrians) her equivalent in a similar plot (*Hethiter.net* no. 346.9) is in fact Kumarbi, the head of the pantheon and a grain god. This literature (*Hethiter.net* nos. 345; 348) also refers to Astarte's counterpart—Šaušga, the sister of the Hurrian storm god—as going to the Sea in order to entice the creatures within it.

The striking parallels between the Astarte Papyrus and Hurro-Hittite plots, the West Semitic names and features of *Ym* and Astarte, and the discrepancy between the negative and marginal role of Seth and Renenutet (respectively) in the Egyptian pantheon and their positive and central role in the Astarte Papyrus—they all evince that the Egyptian plot originated in a Levantine milieu. Other details in the papyrus strengthen this claim. The story opens with a doxology—"Let me praise" (*dw3.i t3* ...)—an element unknown in Egyptian tales of the period but common in Ugaritic, Hurro-Hittite, and Mesopotamian texts. This is followed by a cosmogony that depicts the earth (*iwtn*) as a female who gives birth—another widely known feature in western Asian cultures but not in Egypt (where the earth god is masculine).

The Astarte Papyrus is both amongst the first literary texts written in the Late Egyptian literary register known to us and one of the first Egyptian compositions to recount a mythological tale in which all the characters are personified gods (for papyrus UCL 32158 and related fragments—which may reflect an earlier mythological narrative—see below). The flourishing of mythological tales during a later era may thus be inspired by the penetration of such foreign elements—whether during the Hyksos period or in the wake of Thutmose III's conquest of the southern Levant. Indirect evidence for this may lie in the inclusion of Levantine gods and their features in mythological tales and historiolas composed in the subsequent Ramesside Period.

One such work is *The Contendings of Horus and Seth*, which may be already be attested in some small Middle Kingdom fragments (in particularly papyrus UCL 32158). This story is set within a mythological Egyptian landscape, in which, in customary fashion, Horus overpowers Seth. According to the New Kingdom account, when Seth is ultimately adduced in a favorable light, however, he is offered "Levantine gifts"—the goddesses Anat and Astarte and the status of storm god. Both these features undoubtedly derive from Seth's amalgamation with the Levantine storm god.

Among the historiolas (mythological tales found within the spells), that in Papyrus Chester Beatty VIII vs. 1.5–2.4 (and its parallels) is most noteworthy. This recounts how Anat came to the rescue of the ailing Seth after he had raped the Seed(-goddess) (*t3 mtwt*) on the beach (the word being written in its Semitic form—*ḥp*). This role accords with Anat's customary function in Egyptian as the healing goddess (like most of the Levantine gods in Egypt). Anat's designation there, however, is associated with another of her aspects—namely her militaristic features: "Anat, the victorious goddess, the woman who acts as a warrior, who wears a skirt like men and a sash like women" (van Dijk 1986, p. 33). This aspect is borrowed *in toto* from Levantine literature, being entirely unrelated to her benign role in the plot. Some of the descriptions of the Seed(-goddess) that bathed on the beach and entered Seth's body after he coupled with her as an ox may also have been borrowed from the Levantine Anat. The spell being against poison (a secondary meaning of *t3 mtwt*), her features are transferred to the object of the spell.

In one of the historialas in Papyrus Leiden I 343 + I 345, Anat is said to bring "*seven* jugs of silver and *eight* jugs of bronze" (rt. III 13) in accordance with the Levantine graded numerical pattern x//x+1. This pattern held no meaning in Egyptian literature but was prevalent in Levantine epics and the biblical texts (cf., e.g., Dietrich et al. 2013, no. 1.3 V: 26–27; *Hethiter.net* no. 342.1.1:38; Micah 5:4). Papyrus Leiden being replete with the names of Levantine gods—Baal, Resheph, Anat, Astarte, Qudšu, Nikkal, Šala, Ušḫara, and Hammarig, and their unique features—it is not surprising that it also contains a stylistic borrowing typical of the Levant, despite the latter possessing no sense in Egyptian.

The openness New Kingdom Egypt displays to the myths prevalent in the Levant may well also be reflected in the fantastical tales composed during this period. Several studies have examined the question of why these were composed precisely during the New Kingdom, addressing the issue of why the protagonists—kings, gods, or significant cosmic ideas—are depicted in such a ludicrous and vulgar fashion. The answers proposed relate primarily to the changes taking place in Egyptian politics, thought, ethics, recreational life, and so forth. It is more accurate to speak, however, of the Egyptian openness to non-Egyptian literature that characterized this era, the motifs found in these tales not being unique to New Kingdom Egypt but forming part of the ancient Near Eastern milieu as a whole.

Thus, for example, the allegorical tale *Truth and Falsehood* is the first example of its genre in Egypt, dating to the Ramesside Period. Although traditionally understood as an allegorical version of the *Contendings*, it also forms a closely contemporary counterpart to the Hurro-Hittite *Apu and His Sons*

Right and Wrong. Some scholars have drawn attention to the striking singularity of the feminine divine name *ma'at* (Truth)—possessed of vast cosmic significance in Egypt—given to the weaker male protagonist in *Truth and Falsehood.* Matching neither the plot nor the gender, this irregularity may indicate its foreign roots rather than a literary device (cf. the analogous case of the goddess Renenutet). Additional examples of this type are found in the *Tale of Two Brothers* and the *Tale of the Doomed Prince,* as demonstrated by several scholars.

Although very few studies have examined this issue to date, the parallels with non-Egyptian literature on the one hand and the foreign nature of motifs within them on the other must be noted in any discussion of the way in which the mythological tales took shape during the New Kingdom.

Wisdom Literature

This is the earliest and most prominent genre of the Egyptian *belles lettres* literature. Since it is not found in Ugarit, it can only be compared with the biblical wisdom corpus. In addition to the many affinities between these two sets of literatures, similarities also exist between the biblical and Mesopotamian wisdom texts. It is thus better to examine the most striking example (according to scholarly consensus)—namely, the influence of the *Instruction of Amenemope* upon the book of Proverbs. This takes the form not only of closely related ideas but also of borrowed Egyptian sapiential terminology. Thus, for example, the phrase "chambers of the belly" (Proverbs 18:8 = 26:22, 20:27, 30) to describe a person's innermost being appears to be an Israelite adaptation of the Egyptian expression "casket of the belly." The term "hot-tempered man" (איש/אמות חמה) (cf. Proverbs 15:18, 22:24) to describe a negative person appears to be the semantic, etymological, and phonetic equivalent of the Egyptian *šmm/ḥmm.* The designation of YHWH as he "who measures the hearts" (Proverbs 21:2, 24:12, cf. 16:2) has its roots in Thoth's weighing of the heart of the deceased in the scales during the judgment of the dead. All these terms are found only in wisdom literature—Proverbs in particular—and possess different Hebrew equivalents in other biblical genres.

The closest parallelism between the *Instruction of Amenemope* and the book of Proverbs occurs in the third collection of Proverbs (22:17–24:22), in particular the first section (22:17–23:11), as the following examples demonstrate. (The English translations of all the Egyptian works cited here follow Simpson 2003; translations of the biblical texts follow the New Jewish Publication Society of America.)

PROVERBS	AMENEMOPE
22:17–19 Incline your ear and hear the words of the sages, and give your heart to my wisdom. For it is good that you store them in your belly, that all of them be constantly on your lips.	3:9–14 Give your ears and hear the sayings, give your heart to understand them; it is profitable to put them on your heart, but woe to him who neglects them. Let them rest in the casket of your belly that they may act as a lock in your heart.
22:24–25 Do not befriend an irascible man, nor go with a hot-tempered man, lest you learn his ways and find yourself ensnared.	11:13–18 Do not befriend the hot-tempered man nor approach him for conversation . . . Do not allow him to cast words only to lasso you.
23:4–5 Do not toil to gain riches, have the sense to desist. When your eyes light upon them, they are gone. They grow wings like an eagle and fly up to the sky. 23:29 See a man skilled (מהיר) in his work— he shall attend to kings.	9:14–10:5 Do not exert yourself to seek out excess; what you have, your own property, is good enough for you. If riches come to you by thievery . . . as soon as day breaks they will not be in your household . . . They will make themselves wings like geese and fly up to the sky. 27:15–16 The scribe who is skilled (*mhr*) in his position, he is found worthy to be a courtier.
23: 1–3 When you sit down to dine with a ruler, observe carefully who is before you. And put a knife into your gullet if you have a large appetite. Do not crave for his dainties, for they are counterfeit food.	23:13–18 Do not eat a meal in the presence of a magistrate, nor set to speaking first. If you are sated, pretend to chew; enjoy yourself with your saliva, look at the bowl in front of you and let it suffice your needs.

Rather than a common abstract thought-pattern, Proverbs and the *Instruction of Amenemope* thus share a chain of motifs of Egyptian provenance. The earliest occurrence of the *Instruction* is upon an ostracon from the Twentieth or Twenty-first Dynasty, the latest from the Twenty-sixth Dynasty. The borrowed Egyptian idioms in Proverbs suggest that rather than representing a lengthy Canaanite legacy, the seventh-century (or later) Israelite scribes were familiar with these maxims, either due to their knowledge of Egyptian wisdom literature or—more probably—via contemporary Aramaic mediation, as attested by the Aramaic words prevalent in Proverbs, in particular the third collection.

Hymnodic Literature

Although some hymns in praise of the gods have been found in Ugaritic literature, they evince no trace of Egyptian influence. Nor does such evidence
exist in the biblical texts—with a single exception. Scholars have long noted the
strikingly close parallel between the *Great Hymn to Aten* found on Ay's tomb
in Amarna and Psalm 104:20–30 (the first verses of this psalm belonging to an
Israelite cosmogonic tradition). As the comparison below demonstrates, the
identical content and order indicate that these texts share the same origin:

PSALM 104: 20–30

[20] You bring on darkness, and it is
night,

when all the beasts of the forest do
creep forth. [21] The lions roar for
prey, seeking their food from God.
[22] The sun arises, they come home,
and crouch in their dens. [23] Man
goes out to his work, to his labor
until the evening.
[25] There is the sea, vast and wide, with
its creatures beyond number, living
things, small and great. [26] There go
the ships, and Leviathan, that you
formed to sport with.
[24] How many are your deeds, O *YHWH*!
You have made them all in your
wisdom; the earth is full of your
creatures. [Note: The order of vss.
25–26 and 24 in Psalm 104 appears
secondary in relation to their
equivalents in the *Great Hymn.*]
[27] All of them wait for you, to give them
their food when it is due. [28] Give it to
them, they gather it up; open your
hand, they are well satisfied.
[29] Hide your face, they are terrified;
take away their breath, they
perish and return to their dust.
[30] Send back your breath, they are
creating, and you renew the face
of the earth.

GREAT HYMN TO ATEN

[3] Whenever you set on the western
horizon, the land is in darkness in
the manner of death . . .
[4] Every lion comes out of its cave and
all the serpents bite, for darkness
is a blanket.
When day breaks you are risen upon
the horizon, and you shine in
the Aten in the daytime . . . [5] The
entire land performs its work . . .
[6] The barges sail upstream and
downstream too, for every way
is open at your rising. The fishes
in the river leap before your face.
Your rays are inside the sea . . .
[7] How many are your deeds, though
hidden from sight. [8] O sole God,
beside whom there is none! You
create the earth as you wish, you
alone, all peoples, herds, and
flocks . . .

You set every man in his place, you
supply their needs, everyone of
them, according to his diet . . .

[12] The earth comes forth into
existence by your hand, and you
make it. When you rise, they live;
when you set, they die . . . All work
ceases when you rest in the west.

In contrast to Egyptian wisdom literature in general and the *Instruction of Amenemope* in particular, no evidence exists that the *Great Hymn to Aten* became a canonical text in post-Amarna Egypt. It is thus likely to have been transmitted to the Levant as early as the Amarna Period itself, the Israelites probably receiving it via a Canaanite agent.

Love Songs

This genre is a relatively new field of literature in Egypt, making its first appearance during the New Kingdom. While these songs may be assumed to have a long oral stage in Egypt, their Late Egyptian literary register and novel content suggest that they were penned during this period. The presence of their themes—desire, love, and lovemaking—in narrative literature and visual artifacts from the New Kingdom onward strengthens this suggestion.

The speakers in the Egyptian love songs, as well as in their equivalent—the biblical book of Canticles—are young human males and females who address one another employing sibling appellatives. The characteristic motifs include admiration of the lover's physical attributes (in the Arabic *waṣf* form), love as an ailment and antidote, the locked door, the garden as a place and image, etc. The heading *šḥmḫ ib*—"diversion of the heart" (i.e., entertainment)—that appears at the beginning of three Egyptian love-song collections, suggest that they were sung at banquets and festivals. The affinities between the biblical and Egyptian examples make it likely that the former also formed part of various festivities.

The earlier dating of the Egyptian love songs in relation to their biblical equivalents have led scholars to assume that here, too, Egyptian influence on the Levant is at work. This is not the only possibility, however. In contrast to Egypt, where this genre (including its reflections in art and narrative) only occurs during the New Kingdom, cultic and mythic love songs are found in Mesopotamia (Sumerian and Akkadian) literature from at least the end of the third millennium BCE, also being reflected in art forms. The same is found in Ugarit. The building blocks that compose these love songs closely correspond to their counterparts in Egypt and Israel. For example:

> SUMERIAN: My sister, I would go with you to my garden ... My sister
> I would go with you to my pomegranate tree ... (Šulgi Z; *Electronic Corpus of Sumerian Literature* 2.4.2.26; Seg B.:10–19)
> AKKADIAN: As I [went down] into the garden of your love ...
> Zarpānitum will go down to the garden. (Tablet British Museum 21005 obv. ii 9; Lambert 1975, pp. 104–5)
> UGARITIC: I will make her field like a vineyard, the field of her love like an orchard. (Dietrich et al. 2013, no. 1.24:22–23; Marcus 1997)

BIBLICAL: I have come to my garden, my sister bride, I have plucked my
myrrh and spice . . . (Canticles 5:1)
EGYPTIAN: How intoxicating are the plants of my garden, [the lips] of
my sister are a lotus. (Papyrus Harris 500, No. 3)

While modern westerners may regard the motifs of the garden and brother/
sister images as self-evident or universal, this reflects the fact that the roots of
western civilization lie in the ancient Near East.

The *Sitz im Leben* of the Mesopotamian and Ugaritic love songs differs from
that of their Egyptian and Israelite counterparts. In Mesopotamia and Ugarit
the songs primarily served in cultic and mythic contexts, the speakers rarely
being human beings. In Egypt and the Hebrew Bible, on the other hand, they
are all spoken by human figures. Numerous additional stylistic comparisons
can nonetheless be adduced that demonstrate the external affinities between
the various collections. The striking similarities and the fact that the genre is
embedded within Mesopotamian literature suggest that its abrupt appearance
in Egypt was due to its penetration into Egypt—in similar fashion to the way
in which the land of the Nile came into contact with Levantine mythological
tales during this period. After its introduction into Egypt, local poets accommodated it to the Egyptian milieu.

The fact that divine love songs are reflected in Ugaritic literature, several
examples of human love lyrics also existing among the Mesopotamian findings, indicates that Levantine literature may have served as the channel through
which this genre was transmitted to Egypt. The question of whether the love
songs in Canticles attest to the existence of repeated, boomerang-like, Egyptian
influence on ancient Israelite culture or the prevalence of love songs from the
Bronze Age onward in western Asia thus remains open.

The *Carpe Diem* Motif in the Harpers' Songs

Orchestra and harpers' songs were engraved on tomb walls from the Middle
Kingdom onward in order to proclaim the deceased's favorable circumstances.
In line with conventional Egyptian thought, the tomb that remains forever is
glorious, as also is the sustenance at its owner's disposal—which, in contrast to
that which he ate while he was still alive, will never run dry. The deceased is thus
happy, his joyful relatives accompanying him to his new abode. In this context,
it is surprising to find—for the first time in an Amarna Period tomb (from
Saqqara)—harpers' songs exhibiting reservations regarding the world of the
dead and the ceremonies that accompany the deceased on his journey thither.

The first—and most extreme—of these is the *Antef Song*, named after the
king adduced in the opening lines. *Contra* all we know of the Egyptian view of
the dead, this depicts the tomb as a temporary place destined to disappear, no

joy thus being present in it. No one ever having returned from the land of the dead (another belief contravening conventional Egyptian thought) to tell of its goodness, it is thus better to seek to be happy in this life rather than in death.

The full text of the *Antef Song* occurs in Papyrus Harris 500, dated to the Ramesside Period. Here it is sandwiched between two love-song collections, also occurring in close proximity to the tales of the *Doomed Prince* and the *Capture of Joppa*. On the basis of the classical language it exhibits, most scholars date it to the reign of an Egyptian king called Antef from the Eleventh Dynasty. The fact that it only appears to have been known to Egyptian scribes from the post-Amarna age onward, however, is incommensurate with this earlier date. Some of the other themes in it—such as the long life of the sages' words—also occur in New Kingdom texts (cf. Papyrus Chester Beatty IV), and traces of later grammar and syntax may strengthen this argument.

The prominent affinities between the *carpe diem* motif in the *Antef Song* and Ecclesiastes is evident in the following verses:

ECCLESIASTES 9:7–8	*ANTEF SONG* 5:26–29
Go, eat your bread in gladness, and drink your wine in joy.	Follow your heart as long as you live. Put myrrh on your head,
Let your clothes be always white;	Dress yourself in fine linen,
and let your head lack no oil.	Anoint yourself with the exquisite oils that are only for the gods.

With this motif in Egypt predating Ecclesiastes, the *Antef Song* may be presumed to have influenced the biblical text. Compositions of this type, however, were prevalent in Mesopotamia (from at least the Old Babylonian period) and the scribal schools of Ugarit, Emar, and Ḫattuša (from the Middle Babylonian period). Mesopotamian literature contains such texts as *Everything is Worthless* and Siduri's speech in the *Gilgamesh Epic*, the Levantine schools the *Ballad of the Early Rulers, Enlil and Namzitara*, and the *Instructions of Šupe-Ameli*. Some of these only refer to the motif of vanity and skepticism, others combine these with the derivative *carpe diem* motif. Although all these texts are Babylonian in origin, written in Sumerian or Akkadian, scholars are divided over whether the *carpe diem* and vanity motifs in the Levantine versions derive from Babylonia or represent Levantine additions. Whatever the case may be in this regard, these compositions were clearly very popular in the Levantine scribal schools during the Late Bronze Age. The closest parallels to Ecclesiastes and the *Antef Song* are Siduri's speech in the *Gilgamesh Epic* and the *Ballad of the Early Rulers*:

> When the gods created mankind, for mankind they established death, life they kept for themselves ... You keep enjoying yourself, day and night. Every day make merry, dance and play day and night. Let your clothes be

clean! Let your head be washed, may you be bathed in water. Let a wife enjoy your repeated embrace. (George 2003, pp. 272–86)

Those came after those, and others came after others .... All life is but a swivel of an eye. The life of mankind cannot last forever. Where is Alulu...? Where is Etana...? Where is Gilgames...? Where is Huwawa...? .... Where are the great kings? ... Repel, drive away your sorrow, scorn silence! ... May Siraš (the Wine Goddess) rejoice over you as if over (her) son! (Cohen 2013, pp. 133–41)

The popularity of the *carpe diem* motif in the Levant and its rarity in Egypt suggests that here, too, the Egyptians borrowed a western Asian model, most probably via the Levant, where it was so celebrated. The speech of Ecclesiastes may thus reflect the Levantine propensity for this genre (originating in Mesopotamia) rather than Egyptian influence.

Conclusions

In conclusion, the five Late Egyptian genres, compositions, and motifs discussed above suggest a familiarity with Levantine and western Asian literature: (1) the Astarte Papyrus and mythical narrative, (2) the *Instruction of Amenemope* and wisdom literature, (3) the *Great Hymn to Aten*, (4) the love songs, and (5) the *carpe diem* motif in the harpers' songs. We have found that the early date of a manuscript does not prove the early origin of the genre, just as a late date does not indicate the sources that influenced it. The wisdom and hymnodic literatures exhibit striking evidence of Egyptian influence on specific biblical texts. The absence of these genres in Ugarit, however, makes it impossible to know how much we can infer from this fact regarding Egyptian influence on the Levant during the Late Bronze Age. In contrast, while traces of the mythological tales, love songs, and the *carpe diem* motif exist in the biblical texts, the influence in this case may be in the opposite direction. The presence of the story of the storm god's combat with the Sea in Egypt demonstrates that Levantine literature reached Egypt and influenced this country's literary output in various ways. In light of this, additional motifs from the mythological tales, love songs, and *carpe diem* literature composed in Egypt during the New Kingdom may have been influenced by the conventional models of these genres long prevalent in western Asia.

12

All Gods Are Our Gods

RELIGIOUS INTERACTION

I }

"From Bes to Baal"

RELIGIOUS INTERCONNECTIONS BETWEEN
EGYPT AND THE EAST

Izak Cornelius

Introduction

Although the region of Egypt was relatively isolated by the Mediterranean in the north, the Nile cataracts in the south, and deserts in the east and the west, it maintained strong contact with its neighbors, including the cultures to the east. These contacts go back to the very early periods, but later contacts should not be neglected. They took the form, on the one hand, of peaceful trade relations going back to the earliest phases of history, and also diplomatic contacts, as reflected in international correspondence such as the Amarna Letters between the pharaohs and the rulers of western Asia. On the other hand, there were more violent contacts through war and conquest, with the Asiatic Hyksos invading and ruling over parts of Egypt, and the conquest of Egypt by the Assyrians, Babylonians, and Persians. The New Kingdom pharaohs conquered and ruled over large parts of the Levant (Syria and Palestine). It is especially in the field of religion that the interconnections might have been the strongest. The Egyptians worshiped "other deities, the deities of the other" (Zivie-Coche 1994).

According to ancient Egyptian thought, Egypt was the *axis mundi* (center of the world), god's land, while foreign lands and the foreigner ("the other") were on the periphery and inferior. But in spite of a seemingly strong "xenophobic" tendency, the relationship between Egypt and other countries—including their respective deities and religions—was not a one-sided influence; there was also influence from "the other" on Egypt, with foreign deities entering Egypt and being accepted in its religion. Because Egypt had a polytheistic system, worshipping a multitude of deities in many forms and never being exclusive or laying claim to the absolute truth, new deities could be incorporated. Similarly, Egyptian deities were "exported" to the east.

The strongest influence in the east was into the Levant and to a lesser, but not insignificant, extent Anatolia, Mesopotamia, and Persia. The reason for the limited influence in the last two cases might have been the geographical distances, and when there was influence it was sometimes more indirect and occurred through intermediaries such as the cultures of the Levant or Anatolia, or in the case of Persia via the Assyrians. Influence in the southern Levant (Palestine/Israel) was naturally stronger because of the close proximity to Egypt and direct Egyptian control and administration of this region under the New Kingdom for nearly four hundred years, although contacts go back much earlier.

The sources informing us on the exchange of religious ideas, symbols, and deities are not only texts but also artifacts and, as far as deities are concerned, the iconography of the deities. In the first case a lot has been written on the influence of Egyptian literature and especially cosmogonies (creation myths) on, for example, the Hebrew Bible (creation by word of mouth as with Ptah of Memphis and Genesis 1). The same is true of the religion of Amarna: the influence on later monotheism and the Aten hymn on Psalm 104. In addition, Yahwism has solar elements of Egyptian origin. But the biblical texts are from a much later period. Copies of Mesopotamian myths such as *Adapa and the Southwind* and *Nergal and Ereshkigal* were found at Amarna (EA 356–357), but these were scholarly texts and do not indicate any direct influence. Other instances of eastern influences on Egyptian religious literature might be found in Levantine mythology mentioning deities such as Baal, Astarte, and Anat, as in the Astarte papyrus, *The Contendings of Horus and Seth*, and the *Tale of the Two Brothers*.

On the other hand, however, there is hardly any influence concerning death and the afterlife, as the views in western Asia were of a totally different nature (a very gloomy underworld and no real afterlife, or no belief in resurrection). According to O. Kaelin, there are a number of cultural innovations that were introduced into Mesopotamia during the third millennium BCE, such as the "worshipper statues," votive plaques, and even the deification of Akkadian kings. But this is disputable, as the religion was totally different, as was the concept of divine kingship. Whether the idea of monumental religious architecture is another example of influence (from which direction: Egypt to Mesopotamia or Mesopotamia to Egypt?) is debatable. Nevertheless, there is a big difference between the pyramid as a tomb and the Mesopotamian ziggurat as a temple.

An issue is the *ways* in which deities were exchanged or entered a certain region. Merchants carried not only goods but also ideas, and in both directions. Along with invaders such as the Hyksos came their deities. There were slaves and prisoners of war from the Levant who, taken to Egypt, brought along their deities. Egyptian deities were carried by their armies marching into the Levant, but soldiers also brought back foreign deities, a case unique to the New Kingdom. It does not seem that the Assyrians, Babylonians, and Persians from the east who invaded and conquered Egypt had that much influence as far as religion is concerned.

Consideration should be given to the question why and how religious ideas and deities are transferred between cultures. Various theoretical approaches have been followed in recent scholarship to explain the phenomenon of religious exchange, from "translating religions" (Smith 2008) to "translative adaptation theory" (Tazawa 2009) to "acculturation" and others (Schneider 2010). These approaches attempt to explain why and how deities were able to migrate to other regions. It seems that a combination of approaches is more appropriate.

Egyptian Deities in the East

Specific named Egyptian deities entered the Levantine and other eastern regions, as did religious symbols. The imagery of many Levantine deities is very much Egyptian in nature, and in this regard a few examples must suffice. The only properly identified god from the Levant is Baal-Zaphon; the name appears on a stela from north Syrian Ugarit with hieroglyphic texts. He is shown in Egyptian form with a high crown, holding a *was*-scepter but with a streamer, which is a non-Egyptian adaptation. In a similar fashion, the only identifiable goddess from the Levant is Anat, who appears on a stela from Beth-Shean and looks very Egyptian. Even the famous Baal stela from Ugarit shows a figure in a style very reminiscent of Egypt, the so-called "smiting god" developed from the iconography of the "smiting pharaoh," but this figure is rather a "menacing god" as there is no enemy shown and hence the gesture as such is of great importance. It has been surmised that Egyptian temples were built in the province of Canaan (e.g., in Beth Shean), but this is only the case in Gaza (Amun temple) as provincial capital, and in Byblos (Hathor).

In Syrian glyptic, Egyptian symbols such as the ankh are used. B. Teissier studied Egyptian iconography, viz. motifs (some religious), on Middle Bronze Age seals (fig. 12.1). Regarding symbols from Egyptian religion, the foremost is the winged disk, which is definitely of Egyptian origin and it spread from there to the Levant, Anatolia, Mesopotamia, and finally Persia. The symbol was linked to the sun god (Re or Horus Behdety), but was adapted and newly interpreted for local circumstances. As in Egypt, it was closely linked with kingship. In some cases the uraei were left out and streams of water were added, linking it more with rain. An even more novel adaptation was adding a man in a circle with flames/fire, in some cases carrying a bow, making it a war god (Shamash or Aššur in Assyria); in Persia he was shown holding a ring. Whether the figure in the last case is the Persian god Ahura Mazda is debatable.

There are many Egyptian or Egyptianizing motifs on the Levantine ivories. There is the goddess Maat on papyrus stalks and the winged uraeus cobra. Other ivories show *ba*-birds and the deities Bastet, Bes, Hathor, Heh, Horus,

FIGURE 12.1 Egyptianizing cylinder seal from north Syrian Alalakh eighteenth/seventeenth centuries BCE. Local ruler with Egyptian deities (Montu and Khnum) and *ankh* signs and two crowned falcons.

Horus-the-child, Isis, Kheper, Khnum, Maat, Nephthys, Sekhmet, Taweret, and Thoth. The Nimrud ivories also have Egyptian or Egyptianizing motifs such as a sphinx and even Egyptian deities. These might have been made in Egypt. Various amulets of Egyptian deities and demons are known and include Isis, Bes, and Patakos. There are also amulets with animals linked to Egyptian deities, such as the cat and the falcon, and object amulets, especially the *wedjat*-eye.

In some instances, specific Egyptian deities are present in western Asian cultures. Hathor and Isis were especially popular in Byblos in the second and first millennia BCE. Egyptian deities were popular in the Levant during the Persian period. Hathor was called "lady of Byblos" (fig. 12.2), and her link with that city goes back to the third millennium BCE, perhaps because of her association with boats and navigation. Like the myth of Osiris, Isis also has a link with Byblos. The craftsman deity of Ugarit, Kothar-wa-khasis, came from Hikuptah, Memphis in Egypt, and can be identified with the Egyptian Ptah.

Seal amulets from the southern Levant depict the pharaoh presenting effigies of the goddess Maat, especially to the god Ptah. A large bronze feather (14 cm tall) found at Late Bronze Age Lachish might come from a *c.*70–80 cm statue of the goddess. The concept of *maat* was known in the southern Levant, and influence on Hebrew concepts of world order and justice is possible but should not be overemphasized; in some cases it is, to use the phrase of M. V. Fox (1995), a "crooked parallel."

The Egyptian household demon/deity Bes, who protected women and children, was represented as a bow-legged dwarf with a protruding tongue and a feathered headdress. Although his origin might be sought in the east or in the enigmatic land of Punt, he is the only Egyptian deity that was widespread in the broader region of western Asia, from Anatolia to Iran. Representations

FIGURE 12.2 Limestone stela from Byblos, height 1.13 m., fifth cent. BCE (Louvre). King Yehawmilk of Byblos and the "lady of Byblos" on an Egyptian throne with papyrus scepter and headdress of Hathor (sun disk and horns); above is a winged sun disk

of Bes are found in the Levant: on early cylinder seals in the north; on ivories (fig. 12.3) and very prominently on amulets in the south. A famous drawing on a Kuntillet Ajrud pithos shows two figures that have been identified as Bes, or maybe Bes and his female counterpart Beset. Bes also occurs on later Persian-period coins from Samaria. There are also Bes vases and statuettes, and he is also found on the Karatepe reliefs in Anatolia. In Mesopotamia Bes is not mentioned in the cuneiform texts (he might have been known under another name), but he is depicted in visual form. There are amulets, figurines on an ivory, and even a copper figurine from Nimrud in the eighth/seventh century BCE. Bes has been linked with the demon Humbaba, serving an apotropaic role. His image is seen on a wide variety of artifacts from the Persian Achaemenid period, e.g., shown as a master of the animals on an earring. K. Abdi argued these might have been brought by Egyptians, but some were appropriated because of some cultural connection and even associated with local deities like the Iranian Mithra, an example of the "Iranization" of Bes.

Although Egyptian beliefs in the afterlife presumably did not influence western Asia or the Levant, anthropoid coffins of terracotta have been found in the southern Levant, and these might be imitations linked to Egyptian prototypes. However, they are not the coffins of Egyptian officials, nor have they anything

FIGURE 12.3 Ivory from Megiddo, Late Bronze Age (Chicago A 22214): Bes with feather crown.

to do with the Sea Peoples. Such coffins have been found at burial sites at Deir el-Balah, Tell el-Farah (South), and Beth Shean and were produced locally. The coffins are in the form of the Egyptian god Osiris. One coffin from Lachisch, dating to the Late Bronze Age, has a crude drawing of the wailing goddesses Isis and Nephthys and a crude hieroglyphic inscription.

Eastern Deities in Egypt

Little information is available as far as the role and influence of deities from the early civilizations of Mesopotamia in Egypt are concerned. One unique case is Ishtar; according to one of the Amarna Letters, the goddess Shauskagawa of Nineveh (Ishtar) visited Egypt. In treaties between Egypt and the Hittites, Egyptian deities were identified with their Hittite counterparts, such as Re with the Hittite sun god and Seth with the storm god Teshub. The Near Eastern demon Sāmānu—who was dangerous to infants, young men and women, and prostitutes (described as having a lion's mouth, dragon's teeth, eagle's claws, and the tail of a scorpion)—was known as Akhu in Egypt.

As far as the Levant is concerned, the situation was unique. Precisely which deities the Hyksos, who came from the Levant, brought with them is still a matter of dispute. The Hyksos of Avaris worshipped Seth, but no available texts mention that this was the case with Baal. From Avaris hails a locally made cylinder seal (dated to the eighteenth century BCE) showing a menacing god in typical Levantine style. It has been identified as Baal or, better, Baal-Zaphon, who was linked with the sea. A personal name mentions Anat.

In later periods the situation changed drastically. There is much better information available on Levantine deities entering Egypt, especially in the time of the New Kingdom. These deities are (in alphabetical order): Anat, Astarte, Baal, Hauron, Qedeshet, and Reshef. Egyptian texts mention these deities. Papyrus Sallier IV refers to Baalat, Qedeshet, Anat, Baal-Zaphon; and a vessel mentions Astarte, Anat, Reshef, and Qedeshet; and a magical spell invokes Reshef, Anat, and Hauron. On the other hand, it is interesting that Egyptian officials in the Levant worshipped the local deities such as Mami or Ugarit Baal-Zaphon (identified with the Egyptian Seth), and a cylinder seal from Beth-Shean even shows Ramesses II with the god Reshef.

The goddesses Anat and Astarte were the daughters of Re, the consorts of Seth (who again was identified with Baal in Egypt), and close to Hathor. Astarte is mentioned for the first time together with Reshef in a text that acknowledges that they are pleased with the horsemanship of Amenhotep II. The link with chariots and horses—Astarte is depicted on a horse—might explain why she became popular. Many Levantine deities were introduced because of their martial traits, giving further support to the military prowess of the pharaoh. The Levantine deities Anat, Astarte, and Reshef are shown armed (fig. 12.4). Anat became important in Egypt somewhat later. She was very popular with Ramesses II, as was the case with Astarte. The Levantine storm god Baal is unique insofar as this god was identified with the Egyptian Seth to such an extent that one can speak of Seth-Baal. There is no Egyptian visual image associated with the name Baal, but stelae with the name Seth show a hybrid god not with the typical Seth head, but rather a figure with Asiatic attributes such as a headdress with horns, as on the famous 400-Year Stela. Baal was worshipped from the time of Thutmose III/Amenhotep II at Perunefer and is often mentioned by pharaohs such as Ramesses II to describe military power. The god Hauron/Horon was also of Levantine origin. He is already mentioned in the execration texts; he was introduced by Amnehotep II and was also popular with Ramesses II. Hauron, assimilated with Horus (Hauron-Harmachis) and depicted as a falcon, was especially popular in the Giza region and linked with the god Shed. Most of these Levantine deities are depicted in human form: Seth-Baal as a hybrid, but Hauron in animal form. Whereas all the deities mentioned so far function in the important religious texts from Ugarit, Qedeshet ("holy one") does not. She is called the daughter of Re, linked to Hathor, and is invoked in magical spells. She is depicted as a naked woman

FIGURE 12.4 Limestone stela from Deir el-Medina, height 75 cm. Nineteenth Dynasty (BM EA 191). Naked Levantine goddess Qedeshet on lion flanked by Egyptian god Min and Levantine god Reshef, below worshippers with armed Levantine goddess Anat.

wearing a Hathor headdress and standing on a lion on a whole series of stelae, sometimes flanked by the Egyptian Min and the Levantine Reshef (fig. 12.4). Whereas Baal was more popular with the pharaohs, Qedeshet was more part of popular religion, e.g., at Deir el-Medinah. In the Levant Reshef is a god of pestilence. He was identified with Montu but not Seth. In Egypt he was worshipped from the time of Amenhotep II. Reshef was linked both with royalty and the common people, related to horses, and depicted as a warrior with a shield and a quiver. Most of these deities remained popular until much later, up to Roman times.

In later periods came new deities like Atargatis—an amalgamation of Anat and Astarte—and Mithras from Persia. Although they never had any influence on the Egyptians themselves, the Jewish colony at Elephantine (sixth century BCE) worshipped Yahu (YHWH, also in forms like Anat-Yahu) and had a temple. Later came Christianity and Manichaeism, both oriental religions. Important Gnostic texts come from the sands of Egypt.

Conclusions

Strong contact between Egypt and western Asia existed, especially as far as religious connections are concerned. Egyptian religious symbolism is found in western Asian iconography. Deities were exchanged—out of Egypt, but also into Egypt. Goddesses like Hathor and Maat were exported to the Levant; the household deity Bes was popular from Anatolia to Iran. A unique case occurs in the New Kingdom, when Levantine deities became popular in Egypt, not only with the pharaohs but also among the common people. In later periods, other deities came to Egypt.

Egypt and Nubia

Kathryn Howley

The Qustul incense burner was discovered in the early 1960s by the Oriental Institute Expedition at the cemetery of Qustul, a site situated near the first cataract of the Nile in a border region that, both anciently and in more modern times, has played host to a rich array of interactions between Egypt and its southern neighbors. The incense burner, though discovered in Nubia, is decorated with a wide array of sunk-relief figures familiar from contemporaneous Egyptian Early Dynastic artifacts. A figure wearing the conical crown of Upper Egypt sits upon a sacred boat, the shape of which exactly matches numerous examples depicted on Egyptian pottery of this period. To his left, a falcon perches on a platform supported by three pillars; the falcon throughout Egyptian history represented Horus, the god of Egyptian kingship, while the platform and pillars correspond to the *serekh*, the ornamental outline that surrounded gods' and kings' names at this period. To the right, a series of concentric rectangles representing a palace façade looms imposingly, echoing the same iconography used in many Early Dynastic religious contexts, including the tombs of Egypt's first kings. Though modest in size and material, measuring only 15 cm in diameter and made of clay, the Qustul incense burner's significance as one of the earliest pieces of evidence for Nubian-Egyptian interaction is great. In fact, it serves as a model for much of the religious interaction that was to follow between Nubian populations in modern-day northern Sudan and their Egyptian neighbors on the Nile.

Despite the close resemblance of the decoration to other Egyptian objects, the true meaning of the Qustul incense burner has eluded scholars: while the religious imagery that it bears seems to belong in an entirely Egyptian context, the form of the object on which the Egyptian king and his god proclaim themselves so confidently—a small, flaring cylindrical incense burner made of clay—appears only in Nubia. Did the imagery on this incense burner have religious significance to the Nubian population in the area, and was it used in

Nubian religious ritual? Could it even be the case that the Nubian kings at this time were presenting themselves as Egyptian pharaohs, with all the office's religious connotations? Or was this object sent from the Egyptian Early Dynastic kings to their counterparts in Nubia, Egyptian religious propaganda wrapped in Nubian clothing?

Though the character and meaning of the religious interaction represented by the Qustul incense burner cannot be reconstructed, this early evidence demonstrates the most important characteristics that govern religious interaction between Nubia and Egypt throughout pharaonic history. Firstly, much of the evidence for religious interaction takes the form of royal monuments, both due to the simple fact that this (often stone) material survives better than the more ephemeral traces of the religious practice of daily life, and also because the use of Egyptian objects and religious ideas seems to have been mostly restricted to the highest sections of Nubian society. Secondly, many of the religious objects and imagery that traveled from Egypt to Nubia gained new forms and functions in order to become meaningful in their new cultural context. Finally, previous scholarly narratives have stressed the one-way movement of Egyptian religious iconography to Nubia and the "Egyptianization" of Nubian religion. A distinct lack of archaeological evidence for native Nubian religious practices, demonstrated by our lack of understanding of the cultural context of the Qustul incense burner, exacerbates the impression of Nubia as a passive receptor of Egyptian ideas. Careful analysis of the roles Egyptian material culture played in Nubian society, as well as a reconsideration of changes in religious practice in Egypt during periods of high political interaction between Egypt and Nubia, can help to illuminate the true richness of Egypto-Nubian religious interaction during the pharaonic period.

* * *

The Nubian civilization of Kerma (contemporary with the late Old Kingdom through the mid-eighteenth Dynasty) offers a case study for the ways in which Egyptian religious imagery was fully adapted by Nubians to its new cultural context. Kerma, its center situated farther south into Nubia than Qustul, near the third cataract of the Nile, appears in Egyptian textual sources as a formidable enemy to the Egyptians; the military ability of Kerma to make incursions into Egyptian territory is also archaeologically attested by the occasional presence of looted Egyptian statuary in Kerman tombs. Overwhelmingly, despite this evidence of the relatively high level of interaction between the two cultures, the vast cemetery and town site at Kerma demonstrate that Kerman religious practices were not rooted in Egyptian belief. This is most strikingly shown in the monumental mud-brick mass of the *deffufas* (temples) and in the immense tumuli and hundreds of human sacrifices that accompanied the burials of the Kerman kings. The site of Kerma provides perhaps our best evidence for native Nubian religious practice, though its interpretation is still elusive: ranks of often winged wild animals such as giraffes, elephants, and rhinoceroses decorate funerary chapel walls and the distinctive Nubian burial beds, while common elite grave goods include ostrich feather fans and distinctive tulip-shaped red-and-black ceramic beakers. While Egyptian goods including scarabs, mirrors, stone vessels, and amulets do occur in small quantities in Kerman graves, the underlying Nubian funerary practices represented by the treatment of the body (laid out on a bed rather than enclosed in an Egyptian coffin) and accompanying grave goods and human sacrifices remain the same. The concentration of Egyptian goods in the highest elite graves instead suggests that possession of foreign material culture was a way of negotiating status in Kerman society, rather than an example of Kermans adopting Egyptian religious beliefs or practices.

In two major examples at Kerma do Egyptian religious beliefs and iconography appear to have been incorporated into Kerman practice rather than appended to traditional Nubian customs as a marker of status. Firstly, the Egyptian motif of the winged sun disk appears prominently in the decoration of the funerary chapel and associated tumulus of one of the Classic Kerma period kings. Secondly, the motif of the Egyptian goddess Taweret, who is generally depicted as a standing hippopotamus, was a popular one for appliqués and inlays on the funerary equipment of elite Kerman women. Taweret undergoes specific transformations in her journey from the Egyptian to Nubian cultural sphere: she often acquires wings and wears a skirt that resembles the costume of Kerman women. As mentioned above, wings were an important attribute of many of the ranks of animals that decorated funerary chapel walls and burial beds at Kerma. It is likely that the winged sun disk was one of the few elements of Egyptian religion appropriated by Kermans because wings were in some way religiously significant to Nubians. Likewise, Taweret may have been adopted by the Kermans because her form as a hippopotamus was appropriate to the importance of wild savannah animals in Nubian religion, perhaps even reflecting the existence of a native hippopotamus deity. In any case, it is important to stress that these were isolated examples that were integrated fully into Nubian religious practice: the Egyptian elements that were adopted appear to have been so because of their relevance to already existing Kerman religious beliefs, and, as in the case of Taweret, are in fact given added Kerman elements to further integrate them into a Nubian belief system. In other words, the existence of Egyptian iconography within a Kerman religious context is not evidence of the "Egyptianization" of Nubian religion at this time; rather, Egyptian iconography was carefully selected and Nubianized in order to serve the purpose of a wholly Nubian cultural system.

* * *

The most monumental representation of Egyptian religious practice in Nubia comes from the series of temples that were built in Lower Nubia by the New

Kingdom pharaohs, which both represents royal control over Nubian-Egyptian religious interaction and highlights our ignorance of native Nubian religious practices. Many of these temples—Semna, Kumma, Buhen, Gebel Barkal, Soleb, Sedeinga, and Kawa—were freestanding stone constructions, built according to the traditional Egyptian plan of peristyle court and hypostyle hall, leading back to a sanctuary. Still more were rock-cut structures, religious spaces carved out of solid rock, including el-Lessiya and Abu Simbel. The gods worshiped at these temples follow a fairly predictable pattern, with the cataract gods Satet, Anuket, and Khnum being especially popular. Dedwen is common, as are forms of Horus linked to the vicinity of the temple (including "Horus, Lord of Nubia" and "Horus of Buhen"). Most strikingly, the deified Egyptian pharaoh often appears, including Amenhotep III at Soleb and Ramesses II at Abu Simbel, as well as at Amara, Gerf Hussein, Wadi es-Sebua, Ed-Derr, and Aksha. The deification of these pharaohs occurs only at their Nubian, and not Egyptian, temples.

The use of "Nubian" gods such as Dedwen, Satet, and Anuket in these temples, as well as their rock-cut architecture, has often been cited as evidence for Nubian influence on the expression of Egyptian religion in Nubia. However, upon closer examination, Dedwen (who is depicted with the same anthropomorphic appearance as many other Egyptian gods) is known as a "Nubian" god through purely Egyptian sources: there is no evidence for his worship in Nubia before these New Kingdom temples. In fact, his first attestation is from the Egyptian Pyramid Texts of Pepi I (Sixth Dynasty), where his epithet proclaims him as Nubian. Moreover, Satet, Anuket, and Khnum are rooted firmly within the Egyptian rather than Nubian tradition, despite their geographical correlation in Egyptian sources with the first cataract area. The idea that native Nubian worship favored rock-cut structures over freestanding buildings has more evidence, with some Nubian cave shrines known at, for example, Sayala. The difficulties of building stone temples in the natural environment of Nubia may also have played a part: the much narrower Nile valley and poor-quality sandstone available for building may have encouraged Egyptian builders to take advantage of natural features of the landscape just as much as any religious influence.

Ironically, the worship of Hathor, a goddess with no geographical connections to Nubia, at Gebel Barkal was perhaps more "Nubian" than the veneration of Dedwen and Anuket: just as Taweret was appropriated by the Kermans, other Egyptian female goddesses seem to have been more likely to be adopted by the Nubians, perhaps because of the prominent role of women in Nubian society. Amun was another Egyptian deity worshipped at Gebel Barkal whose choice and form may have been influenced by native Nubian beliefs. Amun in Nubia generally takes the form of a ram, as opposed to his anthropomorphic representation in Egypt: the discovery in queens' tombs at Kerma of golden headdresses in the shape of rams' horns curling around the ears suggests the existence of a native Nubian ram deity and may explain the ongoing importance of Amun and Gebel Barkal in Nubian religion after the New Kingdom.

Despite their monumentality and corresponding impact on the Nubian landscape, the degree of influence that these Egyptian temples had on Nubian religious practice is exceedingly unclear. Many of the temples, such as Abu Simbel or Soleb, were not located near population centers, and entry to the greater part of Egyptian temples was in any case restricted to properly purified priestly personnel. After the withdrawal of New Kingdom pharaohs from Nubia, the use of these temples appears to have ceased, with the temple complex at Gebel Barkal showing a clear abandonment level. It is therefore doubtful if the majesty of structures such as Abu Simbel had any religious effect on the Nubian population: the prominence of the deified pharaoh, as well as the small degree to which Egyptian religious ideas were adapted to native Nubian practice, may instead suggest that these buildings were intended to influence the local population through propagandistic more than religious methods.

* * *

The advent of a new Nubian dynasty at Napata in the eighth century BCE was to revive the role of Egyptian religion in Nubian society and inaugurated the most intense period of Egypto-Nubian religious interaction in pharaonic history. Much of our evidence for this period comes from the royal Nubian burial sites of el-Kurru and Nuri, located near the fourth cataract of the Nile. The earliest rulers of this dynasty, though burying themselves in Nubian-style tumulus tombs, showed an interest in Egyptian affairs, writing their names in cartouches and, as shown by a stela of King Kashta at Elephantine, perhaps even exercising some territorial control over the southern reaches of Egypt. Both Kashta and his predecessor Alara reintroduced building at the originally New Kingdom Egyptian temples at Kawa and Gebel Barkal. With the full-scale invasion of Egypt by King Piankhy, the Egyptian Twenty-fifth Dynasty was inaugurated and the practice of Egyptian religion in Nubia was fully reintroduced, including the construction of pyramidal royal tombs (fig. 12.5). Previous discussions of this period have characterized this interaction as a total "Egyptianization" of Nubian practice. However, as with previous episodes of religious interaction, we can see that the use of Egyptian religion in the Nubian sphere was overwhelmingly concentrated in the highest levels of society; that many Egyptian religious objects and iconography were adapted in Nubia to function within a Nubian cultural context; and in addition, that many of the changes Egyptian religion underwent in Egypt at this time may have done so under the influence of the Nubian rulers.

The devotion of the Napatan kings to the gods of the Egyptian pantheon was sincere and is preserved for us in Piankhy's Victory Stela, in which he berates the local rulers of Egypt for their impious ways against Amun (in particular eating fish and being uncircumcised) and caps his conquest of Egypt

FIGURE 12.5 The remains of the Twenty-fifth Dynasty royal pyramid tombs at Kurru, Sudan.

by touring the Egyptian Amun temples. Other ways in which religious interaction manifested itself at this period was through the building and repair of Egyptian-style temples in Nubia such as Sanam, Kawa, and Gebel Barkal; for their construction we have textual evidence that King Taharqa brought in craftsmen from Egypt (in the stela from year 6 of Taharqa at Kawa). The kings of the Napatan period also had themselves buried under pyramids rather than tumuli (fig. 12.5), first at el-Kurru and then at Nuri, with walls decorated with traditional Egyptian funerary texts and accompanied by the equipment of an Egyptian burial including shabtis, mummification equipment, and coffins.

Despite the superficially Egyptian appearance of these royal tombs, as at Kerma a closer analysis of the objects' archaeological context demonstrates that many Egyptian objects were used in a non-Egyptian way. This indicates that objects of Egyptian appearance were taking on new meanings in order to function in a Nubian context. Menat amulets and alabaster vessels, both Egyptian object classes in origin, were very prominent in Napatan royal burials: menat amulets in particular seem to have played a crucial role in the funerary ritual, with two placed on each step of the staircase descending to the burial chamber. Yet neither menat amulets nor alabaster vessels were present in Egyptian burials of the same time period, showing that the Nubian use of Egyptian material was not emulating Egyptian models, but rather taking Egyptian source material and molding it for use in distinctively Nubian

FIGURE 12.6 A winged Egyptian goddess depicted on a golden "cylinder sheath" of King Aspelta, buried at Nuri in Sudan *c.*580 BCE.

practices. Notably, winged female Egyptian goddesses remain an important part of the Napatan pantheon, continuing the trend already seen in the Kerma Period and New Kingdom (fig. 12.6).

While this change in royal religious practice in Nubia was going on, funerary religion in Egypt was likewise undergoing transformation. The era of the Twenty-fifth and Twenty-sixth Dynasties is renowned amongst Egyptologists for its archaism, with items of burial equipment that had not been in use for several centuries reintroduced into Egyptian tombs. One of the most notable of these reintroductions was offering tables, intended to serve as a place for libation that would sustain the soul of the deceased in the afterlife. Offering tables are known from royal Nubian tombs at el-Kurru that pre-date Piankhy's invasion of Egypt, therefore representing one of the earliest forms of Egyptian funerary practice to be adopted at el-Kurru. Tellingly, offering tables also appear to be adopted in Nubia before they are reintroduced in Egypt. Offering tables are not attested in Third Intermediate Period tombs, are known only from Twenty-fifth Dynasty tombs in Egypt that belong to Nubian individuals, and do not become widespread in Egypt until the Twenty-sixth Dynasty. The reason for the popularity of the Egyptian offering table in Nubia may well be because of its meaningfulness within native Nubian practice: libation to the dead is an archaeologically well-attested phenomenon in Nubia, with upturned bowls above hardened soil a common occurrence at Kerma graves. The earlier appearance of the tables in Nubia than in Egypt, and the pattern of distribution in Egypt only in tombs with owners of Nubian origin during the Twenty-fifth Dynasty before a wider adoption amongst Egyptians in the Twenty-sixth Dynasty, also suggests that the traditional Nubian practice of libation to the dead could account for offering tables' reintroduction into the Egyptian funerary record, despite the tables' Egyptian appearance.

Many typological features of Egyptian objects in the later Napatan graves at Nuri suggest that the two-way religious interaction shown by items such as offering tables continued even after the Nubian kings left Egypt in the seventh century BCE. The iconographic details of commonly occurring items in the royal Nubian tombs such as shabtis, and the textual choice for certain objects such as heart scarabs, change and develop in exact correspondence to the same items in Egyptian tombs. The dynamic development of royal Napatan funerary goods, keeping up with the "latest styles" in Egypt, shows the importance to the Nubian kings of not relying on fossilized practices, but instead demonstrating their continued contact with craftsmen and priests in Egypt.

Finally, the extensive non-royal cemetery evidence available to us from Nubia in the mid-first millennium BCE shows that, again, religious interaction between Egypt and Nubia was playing out mostly on a royal stage. This was likely because of the role Egyptian material culture had in negotiating status in Napatan society, just as it had in Kerma. The large non-royal cemetery at Sanam shows that the degree of Egyptian material in non-royal tombs was far less than in the royal graves and was restricted mostly to small, portable items such as scarabs. Offering tables were also common, though non-royal examples lacked explicit markers of Egyptianization found on royal specimens, such as hieroglyphic inscriptions. Multiple types of tomb structures and burial positions were found in the graves at Sanam, of which only a small percentage—extended bodies covered in bead nets—could be considered "Egyptianizing." The range of burial practices likely reflects the range of native religious practices that were followed by non-royal Nubians and demonstrates the lack of religious interaction with Egypt at a less elite level in Nubia. Those items we think of as "Egyptian" in non-elite tombs, such as offering tables, were items that already fitted into native Nubian religious practice.

* * *

Interaction takes place not because of the cultural superiority of one civilization over another but often in specific instances where two religious traditions have commonalities. The sphere of religious interaction between Egypt and Nubia is heavily concentrated on the royal domain in Nubia, perhaps because of the ongoing role in status expression that foreign material culture had throughout Nubian history. Conversely, Nubian influence on Egyptian religion has generally been assumed to be minimal, and restricted to deities and forms of the Egyptian New Kingdom temples that were adapted for a local, Nubian audience. While the lack of textual evidence and poor archaeological preservation hampers our knowledge of native Nubian practices and their relation to Egyptian activity in Nubia, emerging understandings of changes in Twenty-fifth and Twenty-sixth Dynasty funerary religion in Egypt suggest that the practices of Nubian kings may have been responsible for more of the period's "archaism" than has previously been admitted. In any case, the ways in which Egyptian material culture and iconography came to take on new meanings and functions in Nubian contexts show that our traditional view of this religious interaction as "Egyptianization" of Nubian practices is inaccurate. Instead we should reframe the exchange as a "Nubianizing" of Egyptian material, in which religious items of Egyptian appearance were repurposed to fit into a distinctly Nubian system of belief and practice.

III }

Religious Interaction between Egypt and the Aegean in the Second Millennium BCE

Nanno Marinatos

It is well-accepted fact that Egypt was the dominant high culture in the eastern Mediterranean for almost three thousand years and that her influence reached the Aegean already during the third millennium BCE. However, the Egyptian impact was not equally strong during all periods of history. It depended on various factors, of which the level of political unity within Egypt, the stability of institutions in Crete, and the compatibility of religious ideas as conceived by the ruling dynasties are important. If these factors are taken into consideration, it is no great wonder that the peak of Egypto-Minoan contacts coincided with two powerful dynasties in Egypt, the twelfth and the eighteenth; the corresponding periods are important also for the palace at Knossos, since they mark its foundation and expansion: there is thus a correlation between Egyptianizing features in Cretan art and religion and strong kingship in both lands.

What conclusions may we draw from this? It will be suggested that a visual and religious vocabulary that included features common to both cultures was created early on; and that such a visual vocabulary would have been a useful tool for inter-state diplomacy. A "club of great powers," as one scholar has put it, needs a language of communication even on the religious level (van de Mieroop 2003, pp. 121–40).

That religion was used for international diplomacy is made clear in the Amarna correspondence where we learn that statuettes of gods were transferred from one royal court to the next. The Mitanni king Tushratta sent his daughter as a bride to pharaoh Amenhotep IV together with an image of the Hurrian-Hittite goddess Shauska. It is reported in the letter that the goddess said: "I wish to go to Egypt, a country that I love, and then return" (EA 23; Moran 1987, p. 61). Conversely, we learn from another letter that Aman (that is, Amun) was asked to bless Tushratta with good fortune (EA 20; Moran 1987,

p. 48). It is clear that the gods of Mitanni were perceived as having the power to bless the people of Egypt and vice versa.

Of course, a foreign religious element may also be an impediment to state policy, in which case a king may choose to isolate himself from the cult practices and symbols of his neighbors and to claim divine support for his decision. In the *Book of Kings*, God warns his favorite king Solomon *not* to accept other gods. "The Lord was angry with Solomon because he not only married many foreign wives but followed their gods" (1 Kings 11:5–9; Graf 2004, pp. 3–16 at 6). Religious osmosis, then, is not to be taken for granted but depends on the tone of the political climate, on the one hand, and personal contacts between royal houses, on the other.

The question may arise: do we have any evidence regarding the relation of Egyptian pharaohs and Cretan kings? Indeed, we do. A statuette of an Egyptian official inscribed with the name "User" (Twelfth or early Thirteenth Dynasty, Middle Minoan II B stratum) was found by Arthur Evans at Knossos. User may have visited the Knossian king and may have left his likeness as a gift and a remembrance of his visit. If this is indeed what happened, it is almost certain that User brought with him other precious objects, among which may have been amulets and symbols of protective divinities.

Another royal contact between Egypt and Crete occurred when the Hyksos pharaoh Khayan (Khyan) of the Second Intermediate Period (equivalent to Middle Minoan III) was in power. Note that he was a powerful king who successfully reunited Egypt, and for this reason it is reasonable to suppose that he sought relations with allies abroad, especially a naval power such as Knossos. Khayan sent his Knossian colleague a stone vase inscribed with his cartouche, a personal gift that no doubt represents an act of good will and possibly cemented an agreement between the two royal houses. Did Khayan send many other gifts besides, including religious objects? This is, of course, pure speculation. And yet there is very strong evidence that the island was receptive to Egyptian religious ideas during the First as well as the Second Palace Periods, and we shall return to this topic shortly.

But first we must note that ideas are not likely to travel through the mere exchange of objects, or trade. Religious syncretism becomes most easily embedded in a tradition when there is official recognition of foreign deities. We may imagine various acts of performance encouraged and organized by the palaces: song, dance, processions, and recitals of mythical texts. Many of these would have been carried out in the courts, and as I have argued elsewhere, the Minoan king and his queen would have performed the role of high priests, a role that is well paralleled in Hittite and Egyptian societies.

This is a useful frame to problematize Cretan religion and its relation to Egyptian but what is the actual evidence? The most striking proof that foreign ideas were accepted on the level of official religion is the incorporation of Egyptian ideograms and pictograms in the hieroglyphic script of the First

FIGURE 12.7 Sacral Knot.

Palace Period. Consider first the Egyptian ankh. We know that it signifies "life" in Egypt, but its form is too abstract to be comprehended without explication. It is therefore more than likely that the meaning of the sign was transferred along with its form. During the Second Palace period, a fetish of religious significance was developed by the Minoans, the so-called sacral knot (fig. 12.7). It is a folded piece of cloth that forms a loop at the top and either stands on its own or constitutes an adornment of royal and priestly garments. It also bears a resemblance to the Egyptian fetish known as "knot of Isis" or "blood of Isis" (pl. 9); on the basis of this, it seems quite certain that Egyptian and Minoan ideas converged both during the Twelfth and during the Eighteenth Dynasties.

Another Minoan hieroglyph of the First Palace Period is likely to have derived from Egypt: the sign of the horizon, the *akhet* (fig. 12.8). Oddly enough, Evans did not recognize the Minoan sign as such and interpreted it instead as the horns of a bull. This explanation has prevailed in the literature and has sent many researchers in the wrong direction to look for concepts of bull-worship or sacrifice. And yet, the similarity between the Minoan and Egyptian sign is too striking for coincidence. Besides, if the so-called sacral horns represent the twin peaks of the horizon, this might explain why the Minoan objects (made

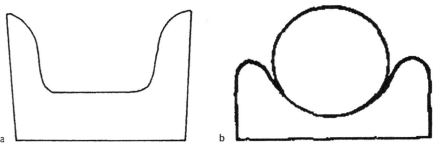

FIGURE 12.8 The sign of the two mountains of the horizon: a. Minoan; b. Egyptian.

FIGURE 12.9 Vase from Pseira, Crete.

of stone or clay) were consistently placed high up, on top of buildings. As in Egypt, Minoan sacred buildings represent aspects of the cosmos, and what is high up is considered to be close to the sky. The point cannot be belabored here any further, but suffice it to say that it is not just the similarity of form between the Minoan and Egyptian signs that is suggestive but also their location.

Having just argued that the so-called sacred horns in Minoan art and religion represent the Egyptian idea of the horizon akhet, I will admit that Evans had also seen something very important when he spoke of sacral horns, because although the twin peaks are not horns (for reasons delineated above), it is nevertheless true that the U-shape of the Egyptian akhet resembles the horns of an ox. It is also true that the head of the ox plays a role in Minoan religious symbolism. Its Egyptian origins will become evident, but first we must look at some examples of animal heads in Minoan art and reflect on their meaning.

On a vase from Pseira, dating to Late Minoan I (early Eighteenth Dynasty), the main scene shows a series of bovine heads among olive sprays (fig. 12.9). In between the horns of each animal head is a double ax, the emblem of the Minoan divinity. That this scene is symbolic, rather than naturalistic, cannot be doubted. Its most stunning feature is the dual identity of the double ax as an object and a lily plant simultaneously. But also the ox head deserves attention, since it is obvious that it could *not* represent the head of a sacrificed animal in the above scene: its eyes are wide open and it bears the double ax and lily between its horns. A clue as to its significance is supplied by a scene on a gold ring of Cretan origin found in the Peloponnese, at Vapheio. A ritual takes place near a sacred tree; in the center is a dancing woman performing a twirl, and, above her, we see the ox head. Whatever our interpretation of the ritual by the tree (this author has suggested an ecstatic dance leading to prophetic visions), the animal head above the dancing female requires some explanation. And there is no way to escape the conclusion that the ox head is a divine sign in heaven, since next to it we see a shooting star (or comet) as well as the sacral knot/ankh. It will be argued next that the ox head has Egyptian origins and refers to the divine cow or bull in heaven.

Since the Pyramid Age, the Egyptians believed that a cow goddess of the flood, Mehet-Weret, gave birth to the sun god and carried the disk as a crown between her horns. She eventually assimilated with Neith, Hathor, and Isis during the Eighteenth Dynasty. Hathor bears the solar disk between her horns, and so does the bull of Re. Is this iconographical scheme not reminiscent of the Minoan ox head bearing the divine emblem of the double ax on the Pseira vase (fig. 12.9)? If so, this motif bears the ineluctable stamp of Egyptian religion.

Consider next a glyptic scene on a seal impression from Zakros where a ram's head is flanked by two birds (a sign of the heavenly realm); above the head is a sacred object that looks like a budding pair of horns; above the latter is a solar disk that constitutes the center of the composition (fig. 12.10). Because of its cryptic nature, this strange iconography cannot be read without decipherment. Behind its conception is Egyptian astral theology because the ram and the sun disk are associated in Egyptian religious iconography where a ram deity carries the solar disk between his horns and embodies the nocturnal manifestation of

FIGURE 12.10 Seal impression from Zakros.

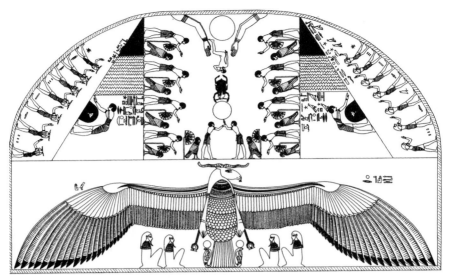

FIGURE 12.11   Ram-headed deity from KV 14, W. Thebes.

Re as Osiris. One example of this ram deity is furnished by tomb KV 14 (originally built for the last ruler of the Nineteenth Dynasty, Queen Tausret); it takes
the form of a creature, a bird with spread wings and a ram's head (fig. 12.11).
The demon gives rise to the sun disk, the birth of which is represented above
its horns taking several guises as a child, a scarab, and as a disk. The association of the ram's head with the sun disk cannot be a coincidence in both the
religions of Crete and Egypt; we can best explain it by applying Egyptian solar
ideas to the Minoan visual vocabulary.

Indeed, a lot more becomes understandable in this fashion. We may better understand why two lions, or possibly dogs, flank and guard the sun disk
on a seal from Knossos (Corpus der minoischen und mykenischen Siegel II
8, 326); the composition mirrors the Egyptian lions that guard the akhet in
Egyptian art.

Consider also the Minoan hybrid creature commonly known as "the
Minoan genius" in Minoan iconography. It is clearly inspired by the Egyptian
goddess Taweret and was introduced in this form to Crete already during the
First Palace period, at about the time of the Twelfth Dynasty. At first, this
Cretan demon had an Egyptian form but later it changed, as the work of Judith
Weingarten has shown. During the era of the New Palaces, corresponding to
the early Eighteenth Dynasty, it becomes transformed into a lion, and greater
emphasis is placed on his (or her) predatorial aspect. Still, Egyptian ideas linger behind the imagery. And yet, there is also convergence of ideas during the
Eighteenth Dynasty. A striking example is Taweret as Isis or *rrt* on the ceilings
of Theban tombs (Tharwas [TT 232], Senenmut [TT 71], and Sety I [KV 17]).

Her role there is to control the Sethian foreleg of a bull, the constellation of the Big Dipper. The foreleg of Seth in the northern sky is tied by a chain to two mooring posts of flint, and Taweret/Isis holds the chain, ensuring that the universe remains in good order. The imagery persists into Ptolemaic times (fig. 12.12a). We find precisely the same astral context of the Minoan genius on a seal from Knossos contemporary to the Eighteenth Dynasty (fig. 12.12b). He is carrying a convoluted deer on his shoulders, a form that may be a reference to a constellation because its contorted position is artificial. Be that as it may, the

FIGURE 12.12a Taweret controlling the leg of Seth. Ceiling of the temple of Isis at Philae; Ptolemaic Period.

FIGURE 12.12b Minoan seal now in Berlin.

important point is that the genius is depicted among the stars and is therefore certainly a reference to the nocturnal sky.

A further insight into Egypto-Minoan relations has been brought about by the excavations of Manfred Bietak at Tell el-Dab'a in the Egyptian Nile Delta, where a palace of the time of Thutmose III or Hatshepsut has been brought to light. The big surprise of this excavation was that parts of the palace were decorated with Minoan murals. Skepticism regarding the style of the frescoes as products of local or Levantine artists has been expressed but is not justified: their technique (string impressions on the still wet plaster, for example) and the semantic value of their motifs (such as a Minoan seal worn around the wrist of a bull-grappler) betray the genuinely Minoan pedigree of the painters. Some of the fragments depict processions, acrobats within a palm grove, bull-leaping, and predatory chase (leopards and lions hunting bulls and deer). But there is also a purely Minoan symbol among the murals that merits our attention because it reveals how a religious motif was internationally recognizable. I am referring to a frieze of half rosettes painted below the bull-leaping and -grappling scene at Tell el-Dab'a. Some viewers may have known that the frieze of half rosettes replicated the stone frieze of the west façade of the palace of Knossos; others may have recognized that the rosette is not unique to Knossos but an international emblem shared by Egyptian, Anatolian, and Syrian iconography. Here is one example from Egypt: a rosette, representing the sun, is shown between the horns of a Hathor cow head in a ceiling painting of Amenhotep III at Malkata. Thus, the half-rosette frieze of the Tell el-Dab'a taureador painting illustrates the commonality of symbols and supports the hypothesis that the palaces played a vital role in the dissemination of religious ideas.

Conclusion: The Impact of Egyptian Solar Theology on Minoan Crete

Egyptian pictograms and ideograms are of great importance for a new appreciation of Minoan religious concepts. It has been argued here, first, that the transmission happened on the level of literate elites and the palace and not on the popular level; second, that the affinities between Minoan and Egyptian religion were based on concepts of solar mythology and imagery. The ankh, the akhet (twin mountain of the horizon), the ox head bearing the solar disk or double ax, the ram's head, the twin lions or dogs as guardians of the sun disk, the Minoan genius/Taweret, and the Minoan half rosette have been considered as part of this vocabulary. Most of these signs appear in Minoan Crete already during the era of the First Palaces, some taking the form of hieroglyphs.

For lack of space, the rest of the Minoan motifs with obvious Egyptian origins will receive only a short mention. The list is nevertheless impressive: griffin, cat, monkey, cow and calf, palm, papyrus, reeds, rosette, wadj plant. Interestingly enough all these motifs have some connection with solar religion.

The same phenomenon, the spread of Egyptian solar cult, is attested in Syria on seals dating to the period of the Twelfth Dynasty (corresponding to the Middle Bronze Age in Syria). They attest to a rich visual vocabulary of Egyptianizing religious motifs, and the list is long: winged sun disk, rosette, ankh, Hathor- or Isis-type goddess, Horus-type falcon god, lions, griffins, sphinxes, palm trees topped with rosette. Also demonic creatures, similar to Bes or Taweret, make their appearance at that time. Is it a coincidence that the aforementioned motifs penetrate Crete at about the same time? Or is it rather the case that Egyptian influences were disseminated from one royal house to the next especially during the Twelfth Dynasty? In any case the religious influence of Egypt in the entire region cannot be doubted.

SECTION V }

Events

13 }

Violence in Earth, Water, and Sky

GEOLOGICAL HAZARDS

James A. Harrell

Ancient Egypt was a land affected by several geological hazards. Chief among these were earthquakes and Nile floods, while wadi flash floods and landslides were secondary threats. Two other hazards, volcanic eruptions and meteorite impacts, only rarely touched Egypt. The Egyptians were not just passive observers or victims of these natural forces, but at times were proactive in mitigating their effects by either building to withstand them or locating their structures out of harm's way. Surviving inscriptions and ruins provide testimony to the destructive power of these forces and also to the ancient Egyptians' attempts to cope with them. A further understanding of what they experienced is gained by studying the effects of geological hazards on modern Egypt.

Earthquakes

Egypt is located in a seismically active part of the world. For over a century, since instrumental readings have been made, hardly a year has passed without an earthquake being felt somewhere in the country, and about once every decade on average one of these earthquakes did serious damage. It was probably no different in ancient Egypt.

Earthquakes are caused by sudden slippage along faults within the lithosphere—that part of the Earth consisting of the crust and uppermost mantle. These movements are ultimately the result of plate tectonic processes. Tectonic plates are vast slabs of lithosphere that encapsulate the Earth with each plate moving in a different direction and at a different rate as dictated by the convection currents in the deeper mantle beneath it. The plates interact along their boundaries with any two adjoining plates either pulling apart with new oceanic crust created between them (the rift zones), colliding with one plate subducted under (overridden by) the other, or sliding past each other along transform faults. Intense seismicity and volcanism are associated with the first two boundary types, and seismicity alone characterizes the third.

Egypt sits atop the African plate at its northeast corner, and here it is bordered by two tectonic boundaries. To the east there is the Red Sea rift pushing the African and Arabian plates apart and thereby creating the Red Sea along with its two northern extensions, the Gulf of Suez to the west and the Gulf of Aqaba to the east. The latter rift branch continues into the Dead Sea rift valley between Israel and Jordan. To the north of Egypt, along a front spanning the entire east–west breadth of the Mediterranean Sea, the African plate is colliding with and being subducted by the Eurasian plate. The most active part of this collision zone nearest to Egypt is the so-called Hellenic (Island) Arc in the southern Aegean Sea between Greece and Turkey.

Earthquakes that strike Egypt and cause significant damage usually measure 5 or more on the logarithmic magnitude scale. Although this scale is open ended, magnitudes over 9 are rare. The stronger seismic events can have an epicenter—the place on the Earth's surface above the earthquake's focus or point of origin—either outside the country or within it. In general, the farther the epicenter or the greater the focal depth, the more powerful an earthquake needs to be in order for it to cause the same amount of damage as a closer or shallower earthquake of lesser magnitude. Outside of Egypt most earthquakes originate in three regions: the northern Red Sea-southern Gulf of Suez, the Gulf of Aqaba-Dead Sea Valley, and the Aegean Sea's Hellenic Arc, with the largest earthquakes (over magnitude 7) coming from the latter region. The majority of earthquakes with an epicenter inside Egypt occur in the northeast corner of the country, a zone roughly centered on Cairo that includes the Nile Delta, the Eastern Desert between the Delta and Gulf of Suez, and the Fayum Depression. These seisms and others with epicenters farther south in Egypt occur along shallow crustal faults within the African plate that are activated by this plate's movement. Such intraplate earthquakes are typically less powerful than those associated with plate boundaries, and in Egypt they rarely have magnitudes exceeding 5.5. One such earthquake, with a 5.2 magnitude, occurred on October 12, 1992 and had an epicenter about 15 km south of central Cairo. It was felt as far north as Alexandria and Port Said and as far south as Assiut, with the serious damage (collapsed and broken buildings) in a region bounded by Zigazig to the north, Beni Suef to the south, and El Fayum to the west. In Cairo, where the destruction was greatest, 350 buildings collapsed and another 9,000 were irreparably broken, and 545 people were killed with 6,512 more injured. Although of lower magnitude, such intraplate earthquakes can be as much or even more damaging within Egypt than the stronger but more distant plate-boundary earthquakes.

Damage from earthquakes comes from ground shaking, but the intensity of this phenomenon depends on the nature of the ground with the shaking much greater in unconsolidated sediment than in solid bedrock. Shaking brings down rigid structures directly and also triggers other destructive processes—landslides from destabilization of sloping ground, liquefaction from fluidization of water-saturated sediment, and differential ground settling from uneven sediment compaction. Less commonly, fault rupture breaks and offsets the ground surface. Seismic sea waves or tsunamis are associated with earthquakes that originate along submarine faults where the seafloor (and hence also the overlying water column) is vertically displaced along the fault. Truly destructive tsunamis require especially large displacements and these are typically accompanied by earthquakes with magnitudes over 7.5. For Egypt, such massive seismic events are limited to the Hellenic Arc, and so it is only the Mediterranean coast that is threatened by tsunamis. Egypt's north coast is also exposed to the smaller tsunamis produced by earthquake-induced submarine landslides.

Many temples and other built structures throughout Egypt were probably damaged by earthquakes during the Dynastic Period, but so far this has been documented only for Dahshur and Thebes. The evidence at Dahshur includes a mud-brick wall in the Senwosret III complex that was sheared off 1.7 m above the courtyard level, limestone casing walls in the mastabas of Khnumhotep and Nebit that were toppled en masse, and the collapsed underground chambers in the Amenemhat III pyramid. This damage may have occurred during the reign of Amenemhat III, as suggested by the extensive small-scale patch-up work found in Twelfth Dynasty monuments at both Dahshur and el-Lisht. The Qasr el-Sagha temple in the northern Fayum desert, an unfinished Twelfth Dynasty structure, shows earthquake damage (block rotation) that is perhaps contemporaneous with the destruction at Dahshur 55 km to the northeast (fig. 13.1). At Thebes the evidence for earthquakes is even more compelling: through-cutting fractures in colossal statues, large stone blocks, and adjoining smaller blocks; colossal statues and large stelae falling in the same direction; rotation of stone blocks in the same direction; wave-like bends in formerly straight masonry walls; and sediment layers deformed by liquefaction beneath stone monuments. One or more of these indicators have been observed in mortuary temples of the Eighteenth through Twentieth Dynasties, including those of Thutmose III (valley temple), Thutmose IV, Amenhotep III (Kom el-Hetan; fig. 13.2), Sety I, Ramesses II (Ramesseum), and Ramesses III (Medinet Habu). The same kind of damage is seen on the east bank in the Luxor and Karnak temples. Those monuments suffering extensive collapse became quarries for stone used in new building projects. This damage was caused either by a single earthquake sometime after the reign of Ramesses III (Twentieth Dynasty) or possibly by both this earthquake and an earlier one during the reign of Merenptah (Nineteenth Dynasty). The source of the earthquake(s) is unknown, but it has been plausibly suggested that it is the fault just east of the Theban escarpment (Gebel

FIGURE 13.1 Rotated block probably caused by an earthquake in the unfinished Twelfth Dynasty sandstone temple of Qasr el-Sagha in the northern Fayum Desert.

Qurna) that extends northeastward from el-Rizeiqat through the Luxor area to Qena. This fault is certainly seismically active and did produce a minor earthquake in October 1926.

Ancient Egyptians attributed earthquakes to the laughter of Geb, the Earth god, as for example in Utterance 511 from a late Fifth Dynasty Pyramid Text (§ 1150), where the word for earthquake is *nhnh3*. Earthquakes were also referred to by other names, including *nwr-t3* and *mnmn*. The earliest ancient text describing the effects of an earthquake in Egypt is that of Strabo (*Geography* 17.1.46), who reported that the northern of the two Memnon Colossi in Thebes (the colossal statues of Amenhotep III flanking the entrance to his mortuary temple, Kom el-Hetan) partially collapsed during an earthquake sometime prior to his arrival in Egypt about 25 BCE. It is commonly claimed, but without supporting evidence, that this event occurred in 27 BCE. It is more likely the damage was done by the same earthquake that brought down much of the rest of Kom el-Hetan sometime during or shortly after the New Kingdom. The broken colossus was repaired during the Roman period and this is conventionally thought to have occurred during the reign of Septimius Severus (fig. 13.2).

Late classical writers describe a massive tsunami that occurred on July 21, 365 CE. This was spawned by an earthquake in the Hellenic Arc and struck coastlines around the eastern Mediterranean, including Egypt. The earliest of these writers, Ammianus Marcellinus (325/330 to after 391 CE) either witnessed this event or heard about it from people who did. In his historical work *Events* (26.10.15–18), Marcellinus provides a remarkably detailed and accurate

FIGURE 13.2 The northern Memnon Colossus at Kom el-Hetan, showing the Roman repair of earthquake damage (the cut and fitted blocks in the torso) to the originally monolithic silicified sandstone (quartzite) statue of Amenhotep III.

account of the tsunami as it approached the shore, surged over it, and then continued inland. In Alexandria, Egypt, he says the tsunami deposited boats on top of buildings. Another, slightly later account of this same event and its effects on the Nile Delta is given by John Cassian (360–435 CE; *Conferences* 11.3.1), who reports the wave destroyed many villages and turned once fertile lands into salt marshes. Other large earthquake-generated tsunamis must have struck Egypt's Mediterranean coast during the Dynastic Period, although in comparison to 365 CE there would have been fewer settlements and people at risk.

The ancient Egyptians understood the dangers posed by earthquakes and so often re-enforced their stone structures with clamps (or cramps) and other measures. Dovetail clamps were widely used throughout the Dynastic Period but even more extensively during Greco-Roman times. The clamps were made of wood or occasionally bronze, and placed in sunken recesses (mortises) carved into the tops of adjoining blocks (fig. 13.3). Less commonly, and apparently only during the Old Kingdom, blocks were also connected vertically with stone dowels set in mortises cut into the blocks' tops and bottoms. Also during the Old Kingdom, stone blocks were sometimes held in place by gypsum mortar or mortise-and-tenon cuts where the blocks joined. Such practices also helped to stabilize walls during differential settling of the foundations, a problem affecting structures built on compactible ground. It is not known if the use

FIGURE 13.3 Wooden dovetail clamp joining two sandstone blocks in the Eighteenth Dynasty Montu temple at Karnak. Length of the exposed part of the clamp is 24 cm.

of block connectors arose primarily from a concern with such settling or with earthquakes, although the latter were certainly the greater threat to structural integrity. Dovetail clamps were also sometimes used to repair earthquake damage, as seen in one of the colossal statues of Ramesses II in front of the first pylon at Luxor temple. Here clamps (now missing) were placed across through-cutting fractures in order to hold the statue together.

Nile Floods

It is normal for a river to flood during the rainy season in its headwaters region. In the case of the Nile River in Egypt, floodwaters reach their highest levels in August and September in response to monsoonal rains in the Ethiopian Highlands. The annual flood was of enormous benefit to ancient Egypt in that it kept the Nile floodplain fertile with new deposits of clay and silt, and it supplied the water that allowed crops to flourish. Whenever the Nile flood rose above its normal range, however, it became more detrimental than beneficial. At such times rampant floodwaters washed away field canals and dikes, drowned livestock, and inundated settlements along with their food stores and seed stocks. The additional water left standing on the fields delayed planting and so reduced harvests. Exceptionally low Nile flood levels were also disastrous, with the croplands left dry or insufficiently wetted and the resulting crop failures leading to widespread starvation.

Another aspect of the Nile flood is avulsion, the large-scale shifting of a river course during flooding. As floodwaters rise above a river's channel banks and spread out across the adjoining floodplain, the main body of the flow will seek the steepest gradient—the path providing the greatest elevation drop per unit of distance traveled. Along stretches where the Nile follows a meandering course, avulsion causes the river to cut across the neck of a meander loop because of the gradient advantage provided by this shorter, more direct course. As a consequence, a potentially large tract of land along one bank of the river either becomes an island or is joined to the opposite bank once the old and now abandoned channel dries up and fills in with sediment.

The effects of avulsion are more spectacular (and disastrous) in the Nile Delta. This great alluvial deposit was created by the Nile River dumping its sediment load into the Mediterranean Sea. The Delta's fan-like shape is the byproduct of the constant lateral shifting of the river's distributary channels. Two characteristics of the delta plain promote such channel movements: first, the nearly flat seaward-sloping topography; and second, the continual but uneven subsidence of the surface, especially along the delta's seaward sector, due to both isostatic depression of the underlying crust and sediment compaction. Compaction has the greater effect on surface elevations and results from the weight of the upper sediment layers compressing and simultaneously expelling pore water from the lower layers in a process referred to as autocompaction. Ground shaking during earthquakes can cause additional compaction. Surface gradients are constantly changing as a result of delta subsidence, and so floodwaters periodically find new, more advantageous courses. In this way, avulsion causes old distributary channels to be abandoned and new ones to be formed. Today the Nile Delta has only two active channels, the Rosetta to the west and the Damietta to the east, but in past there were more channels flowing across other parts of the Delta. Classical writers (Herodotus, *History* 2.17; Strabo, *Geography* 17.1.4; and Pliny the Elder, *Natural History* 5.11.64) mention up to seven active distributaries, with the Canopic and Pelusiac the most important ones. Many ancient cities in the Nile Delta were originally built along active channels that were later left dry by the Nile River. For example, two of the greatest of these cities, the Ramesside Piramesse (near modern Qantir) and the adjoining Hyksos Avaris (modern Tell el-Dab'a) are located on the now defunct Pelusiac branch of the Nile.

Flow velocities in a river are highest along the outside edge of a channel bend and become more erosive as they increase during floods. It is thus at these times that river channels migrate laterally by eroding floodplain sediments at the outside of bends and then redepositing them on the inside, where flow velocities are at a minimum. The Kom Ombo temple of Ptolemaic and Roman age is located on a high bluff on the outside of a large bend in the Nile. As a consequence, undercutting by the river removed a portion of this temple's forecourt along with possibly other parts of the temple complex. Another Ptolemaic-Roman temple near Qau el-Kebir (ancient Antaeopolis), also located on the outside of a former river bend, was completely swept away during a flood in 1821. It is likely that other temples were similarly damaged or destroyed by flood erosion during the Dynastic Period.

The Egyptians tried to protect at least some of their temples from inundation and erosion accompanying high floods. For example, two ancient texts refer to a flood wall or embankment that was built around Luxor temple during the reign of Thutmose III (Eighteenth Dynasty). The earliest of these texts is the now-destroyed stela of Smendes (Twenty-first Dynasty) in the el-Dibabiya limestone quarry across the Nile from el-Gebelein. It says the king quarried limestone to repair this barrier after, apparently, it had sustained flood damage. Further repairs, again after a flood, are reported in an inscription in Luxor temple from the reign of Osorkon III (Twenty-second Dynasty; not Osorkon II as commonly stated in earlier literature). The level of the same flood event referred to in Osorkon III's text was marked on Karnak temple's west-side quay (a stone river wall with stairways and boat ramps), where it is the second highest of the forty-five flood levels recorded during the Twenty-second to Twenty-sixth Dynasties. As high as it was, this flood was still below the floor of

FIGURE 13.4 Multiple mortises for dovetail clamps in sandstone blocks of the Late Period quay on the west side of Karnak temple. Scale is 30 cm long.

Karnak temple but would have easily swamped the much lower Luxor temple. The sandstone blocks in the Karnak quay are held in place by dovetail clamps along their adjoining sides (fig. 13.4), and although this offered protection from earthquakes, the main purpose of the clamps was probably to reinforce the quay against river erosion.

Wadi Flash Floods

Egypt is an arid land where it rains infrequently. When it does rain, it usually comes as torrential downpours of short duration. This precipitation has essentially no effect on the level of the Nile River, but it can cause flash floods in the dry desert valleys (wadis) leading to the Nile. Such flooding results from rainwater coming down faster than it can infiltrate into the ground, and so much of it is converted to runoff. Floodwaters gather quickly and arrive at the end of a wadi with little or no warning. These storms are typically local in extent, but occasionally affect large regions. A storm of the latter type occurred during November 1–2, 1994, and it struck most of Egypt north of Aswan and progressed across the Sinai Peninsula into Israel. It produced heavy rains and strong winds, and locally hail and sandstorms. Destructive flash floods were unleashed with most of the reported damage in wadis entering the Nile Valley between Luxor and Assiut. At Luxor, for example, a flood coming down Wadi el-Muluk (Valley of the Kings) was up to 2 m deep. It invaded many of the royal tombs and swept away much of the mud brick wall around the Sety I temple along with over one hundred houses in its path. Such storms would have occurred occasionally in ancient Egypt, and it is probably one of these that is referred to in the so-called Tempest Stela of Ahmose. This stela was erected in Thebes during Ahmose's reign sometime before his 22nd year. Its broken pieces were found by excavators among the rubble fill in the third pylon at Karnak temple. The stela's text mentions a rainstorm accompanied by a dark, thunderous sky and a flood that swept away houses and people. It says this event occurred across the "Two Lands," meaning both Upper and Lower Egypt, although this could be an exaggeration of the sort found in many royal proclamations. In a later part of the text, the king promises to repair tombs and temples, but it is not clear whether this is a reference to flood damage or decay from years of neglect. This ancient tempest with its flash flooding sounds very much like the 1994 storm in Egypt. This was a purely meteorological phenomenon, and yet some scholars have interpreted the stela as describing a storm that was the byproduct of a volcanic eruption in the southern Aegean Sea (see below).

In at least one instance ancient Egyptians tried to protect themselves from wadi flash floods. This is a flood-control dam of the Third or Fourth Dynasty in Wadi Garawi, about 10 km southeast of Helwan, and known today by its Arabic name, Sadd el-Kafara. It is not known what the dam was protecting farther down the wadi. Only the two ends of this wadi-spanning barrier remain, but originally it was about 113 m long and up to 14 m high. Its sediment-fill core was faced on both sides with well-cut blocks of limestone (fig. 13.5). The fact that its central portion has been washed away indicates that at some point the dam failed due to floodwaters either overtopping it or, more likely, seeping through it and internally eroding the fill. Conceivably, the dam was first

FIGURE 13.5 The north end of Sadd el-Kafara, an early Old Kingdom flood-control dam in Wadi Garawi, near Helwan. The view is down the wadi, looking at the upstream side of the dam.

weakened by an earthquake, with this leading to failure when the next major flood came.

Landslides

The Nile Valley is bordered by cliffs of sandstone between the second cataract in northern Sudan and Esna in southern Egypt and then by limestone cliffs from Esna north to Cairo. Such steep slopes are inherently unstable and so prone to rock falls, a type of landslide involving the free fall of loose rock fragments. To the extent that the Egyptians built their homes and temples at the foot of cliffs, they were exposed to this kind of hazard. Such is the case for the three temples at Deir el-Bahri in Thebes (those of Mentuhotep II, Thutmose III, and Hatshepsut), which are located at the foot of a 100 m-high limestone cliff and consequently have suffered from rock falls. No graffiti or votive objects in the Thutmose III temple post-date the late Twentieth Dynasty, and after this dynasty there is evidence—abandoned tools and recut blocks— of the Mentuhotep II temple being quarried for its stone. Taken together, these observations suggest that both monuments were destroyed by a rock fall at the end of the Ramesside period.

Along the Nile between Esna and Qena, the limestone forming the valley walls is underlain by a thick rock formation known as the Esna Shale. This rock is a structurally weak material, and this is largely because of its high clay mineral content. As a consequence, the overlying limestone cliffs have failed in many places in another kind of landslide known as a slump or rotational slide, where the rock moves downslope as a massive block that rotates in the opposite direction in which it slides. The outstanding example of this phenomenon is again at Thebes. Here there is a series of low hills just east of the Theban escarpment, with the most prominent of these being Qurnet Murai and Sheikh Abd el-Qurna, both of which host numerous non-royal tombs. These hills are huge, prehistoric slump blocks that slid off the escarpment to the west (fig. 13.6). Although pre-dating the tombs and temples in the area, these slumps have continued their slow, intermittent downslope movement during the Dynastic Period and later, as indicated by displacements along fractures within some of the tombs (pl. 10).

Rock falls, slumps, and other kinds of landslides can occur without any obvious triggering event, but most are the result of some destabilizing incident. Ground shaking during earthquakes always produces landslides and especially rock falls. The Theban slumps, however, were probably caused by heavy rainfall. The sudden addition of large amounts of water to the limestone and especially the underlying shale weakened slopes through the added weight of the infiltrated water, the increased pore water pressure along fractures, and the loss of cohesion in the clay (a hydrophilic mineral that readily absorbs water).

FIGURE 13.6 The Sheikh Abd el-Qurna slump block with the Theban escarpment, from which it slid, at left.

Volcanic Eruptions

There are no volcanoes in Egypt. There are, however, many volcanic deposits, but the most recent of these, lava flows from fissure eruptions, date to about 15 million years ago. Active volcanism (eruptions during the last 10,000 years) does occur in the regions surrounding Egypt: the Aegean's Hellenic Arc between Greece and Turkey, western and central Turkey, northwestern and southwestern Syria, the west side of the Arabian Peninsula in Saudi Arabia and Yemen, the southern Red Sea, Eritrea, eastern Ethiopia, western and northeastern Sudan, and south-central Libya. Ancient Egyptians were probably aware of volcanic eruptions, and those involved in maritime trade may have witnessed them on their voyages through the southern Red Sea to Punt, or to Greece and Crete on the Aegean Sea.

Given the prevailing wind directions in the Middle East, the only volcanic eruptions with the potential of directly affecting Egypt, and then only peripherally, are those in the Hellenic Arc. The largest known eruption in this region and the only eruption anywhere with a documented effect on Dynastic Egypt occurred on the Greek island of Thera (modern Santorini) sometime in the middle of the second millennium BCE. Geological evidence supports a date in the early part of this interval (corresponding to Egypt's early Second Intermediate Period), whereas archaeological evidence favors the later dating (during the early Eighteenth Dynasty). This event is commonly referred to as the "Minoan eruption" because of its supposed catastrophic effects on Crete's Minoan civilization. Its adverse regional effects were limited to two phenomena: air-borne volcanic ash and coastal tsunami waves. At the time of the eruption, prevailing westerly winds carried the ash plume toward Turkey, but its southern edge passed over northern Egypt, where up to 0.5 cm of ash fell to the ground. This was probably not a disaster for people living in Lower Egypt, merely a gritty inconvenience. It would have been harmful, however, to grazing livestock if they ingested the ash, which consists of fine shards of glass. Egyptians initially would have observed a slight darkening of the sky due to the suspended ash blocking some of the incoming sunlight. Over a period of days the sky would have cleared as the ash settled to the ground. As noted in the section on wadi flash floods, it has been suggested by some scholars that the early Eighteenth Dynasty Tempest Stela describes a great storm caused by the Minoan eruption. While it is true that a volcanic eruption can produce a strong enough updraft to generate a convective storm, and also that the expelled aerosols (ash particles and gas molecules) promote cloud seeding, it seems unlikely that the Minoan eruption could have had a significant effect on the weather in Egypt, which was far to the south of Thera (1,300 km at Thebes) and its eastward-moving eruption plume. In any case, a resolution of the debate over the Tempest Stela will have to await a more conclusive dating of this eruption event.

In the initial stages of the Minoan eruption, a massive column of ash and coarser pyroclastic material was blasted many kilometers into the atmosphere. At some point when the eruption intensity slackened, this column was no longer supported by the explosive rise of volcanic gases and so collapsed onto the volcano and surrounding sea. The sudden addition of such a great mass of material to the sea produced a tsunami. Many such waves were probably created as the intensity of the eruption alternately waxed and waned. Toward the end of the eruption cycle an even larger and more far-reaching tsunami was generated when the volcano collapsed into its underlying, now-emptied magma chamber. The tsunamis directed toward Egypt were largely blocked by the island of Crete, and although they still reached the Egyptian coast, it was in a much-diminished state. The height of the largest tsunami wave as it came on shore in Egypt was a fraction of the maximum 10-m wave height recorded on the north coast of Crete, 110 km south of Thera. Pumice found in an early Eighteenth Dynasty stratum at the aforementioned Tell el-Dab'a (ancient Avaris) has been cited as evidence of the Minoan eruption. Although pieces of this glassy, porous volcanic rock float on water, they could not be carried by a tsunami up the Pelusiac branch to Avaris. The pumice may not even come from Thera because there are many potential pumice sources in the surrounding regions and this rock, which was used as a depilatory, was a popular trade item.

Meteorite Impacts

In antiquity, as now, the night sky in Egypt was marked by the fiery streaks of meteors. Ancient Egyptians understood what happened when meteors became impacting meteorites. For example, in the early Middle Kingdom fable of the shipwrecked sailor, the giant serpent who shares an island with the eponymous sailor tells him that all its fellow serpents were killed by a "falling star." Egyptians additionally understood what meteorites, the metallic ones at least, were composed of as indicated by their earliest name for metallic iron, which was *bi3 n pt* or "iron from heaven." This name pre-dates the period when iron smelting became commonplace in Egypt, beginning in the Twenty-sixth Dynasty, and derives from the occasional use of meteoritic iron as far back as the Predynastic Period.

Ancient Egyptians must have seen one or more meteorite impacts or, at least, learned of them from people in the surrounding regions. There is only one known impact site in Egypt that might date to the Dynastic Period, and this is the so-called Kamil Crater in the country's southwest corner, about 100 km east of Gebel Uweinat. This crater has a diameter of 45 m and an average depth of 16 m. It is estimated that it was created by an iron meteorite with a diameter of about 1.3 m. This site is in a remote part of the desert, and so it is unlikely the impact was witnessed by anyone, although the meteorite's passage across the sky would have been seen by people in the Nile Valley. Beyond this, the impact was too small to have had an effect outside the local area. The date of this event is not well established but is thought to be sometime within the last 5,000 years. If other meteorite impacts left craters during the Dynastic Period, these have either disappeared or gone unrecognized. Small craters would tend to be rapidly buried by sediments or destroyed by erosion. Only where these processes operate slowly, such as at Kamil Crater, does the evidence of meteorite impacts survive.

14 }

The Fickle Nile

EFFECTS OF DROUGHTS AND FLOODS

Judith Bunbury

Herodotus described Egypt as the "gift of the Nile" since it was, and still is, the rich Nile alluvium, gleaned from the basalts of the Ethiopian Highlands, that created the fertile silt of the Nile Valley on which the majority of the Egyptian population is dependent. Since most Egyptians live on and are dependent upon the river floodplain of the Nile, they are also at the mercy of its floods. It follows that much of Egyptian history has been preoccupied with the management of the Nile, from the placation of the Nile gods to the more mundane construction of embankments and canals to provide flood relief and irrigation. By the twentieth century the desire for control led to the creation of a large reservoir, Lake Nasser, which required the evacuation of the inhabitants of Nubia to increase food security for Egypt as a whole.

In its native state the level of the Nile is determined by the contributions from its two main sources: the White Nile and the Blue Nile. While the former, which rises in lakes of the East African Rift, has a relatively steady flow, the latter rises dramatically during the summer months as a result of the monsoon in the Ethiopian Highlands. The rise begins in July and continues until early October and thus became a key event in the Egyptian calendar with the amount of rise determining whether there would be a low flood and famine, a perfect flood and feast or, in the case of an overwhelming flood, disaster. The flood season (*3ḥt*) was the first and was followed by growth (*prt*) and harvest (*šmw*), calendrical points that persist in the Coptic calendar of today.

On a longer timescale the magnitude of the flood and the behavior of the Nile in its valley and delta fluctuated in response to natural climate change. At times of high global temperature the monsoon was enhanced and local rainfall also fell across the Saharan region, sometimes re-mobilizing ancient river systems in the desert of Egypt that are known as wadis. At other times of global cooling, the monsoon diminished and even failed, and local rainfall, as today, was sparse. Global temperature change also had an effect on sea level in the Mediterranean. During the last ice age much water was locked up in the ice caps and sea level was low. At the end of the ice age, the ice melted and sea level began to rise. The Nile River, which had cut down through its ancient sediments to form a gulley, was reanimated, and the Egyptian Nile became a wet and marshy area subject to intense flooding, the so-called Wild Nile.

In the Holocene (the past 12,500 years since the last ice age) there were times when the Nile became so full that it overflowed the Nile Canyon and spread out to form large lakes such as Lake Qarun in the Fayum depression and another in the area of the Kharga Oasis (fig. 14.1). In both cases the accumulation of silts in the oasis basins laid the foundation of later agricultural activity, since the lake sediments slope gently into the center of the lakebed and are fertile. The Fayum, being closely connected to the Nile and easy to irrigate, would eventually become the "bread-basket" of the eastern Mediterranean, growing cereals for the Roman Empire. Kharga, a little more distant from the Nile, became a source of fruit, particularly dates and vines from which fine wine was produced with the help of wells and *qanats* (underground chains of wells). We know from evidence of carbon dates of hearths both under and on top of the sediments in the Toshka Spillway that feeds the Kharga depression that these

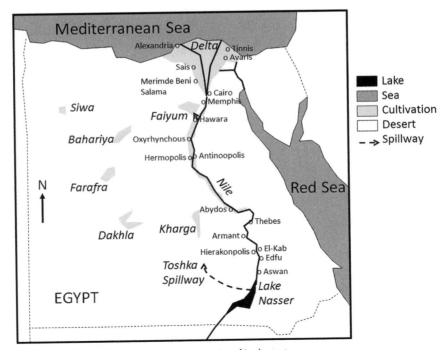

FIGURE 14.1 Map of Egypt showing areas mentioned in the text.

overflows occurred during the early Holocene but had ceased by the Neolithic (*c.*4000 BCE).

Until around 6000 BCE the inhabitants of Egypt treated the valley of the Wild Nile with circumspection, camping and hunting on the terraces that flanked it. At the same time they made good use of the then-abundant network of oases in the Saharan region. Work in the Dakhla Oasis suggests that during the wetter period between *c.*10,000 and 8,000 BCE food was sufficiently abundant that people became increasingly settled in the region, mirroring observations from the Kharga and the Farafra regions. Rock art from this area documents the presence of elephant, crocodiles, hippopotami, ostriches, and giraffes, some of which are associated with standing water, along with many other species that no longer survive in the area. All that started to change around 4000 BCE, when climate change reduced the rainfall in the deserts and the wildness of the Nile in the Nile Valley. The scene was set for the development of agriculture in the Nile Valley and the unification of the Egyptian people, linked by the thread of the Nile, for the first time in history.

Sites like Hierakonpolis in the Nile Valley in Upper Egypt flourished during the late fifth millennium BCE and show that Egypt still had abundant wood to use in architecture and that some animal species associated with wetter climes could still survive there, including elephant and baboon. Other sites up and down Egypt of this period share archaeological features, although the regions were still culturally distinctive. The contemporary site of El-Badari, near Assiut, shows that the inhabitants survived by a mixture of agriculture, fishing, and pastoralism. The period also saw a flourishing of technology, in particular the production of flaked, fire-hardened flint that may correspond to a coalescence of people and technology from the Saharan region as the habitat of the hinterland deteriorated and that of the Nile Valley improved. For the first time, Egyptians were united by close proximity to the Nile, which in turn led to cooperation, conflict, and conquest.

The unification of Upper and Lower Egypt under King Scorpion is recorded on the Narmer palette found at Hierakonpolis by Quibell and Green during their 1897–1898 dig season. The palette, now in the Egyptian Museum in Cairo, is similar in design to those used for preparation of pigment, although it is too large for daily practical use and is interpreted as being a ceremonial object. The palette, the iconography of which emphasizes the power of the king, shows him on one side wearing the white crown of Upper Egypt and on the other wearing the red crown of Lower Egypt—it is one of the earliest evidence for the unification of Egypt. Although Egypt was now unified along the Nile, the distinction between Upper Egypt of the Nile Valley and the Lower Egypt of the Delta persists to this day.

With the unification of Egypt came the beginnings of state enterprise and cooperation, a florescence of writing with lists, labels, accounts, and public property, and in particular the organization of irrigation and agriculture on a large scale. In common with other large rivers, cooperation with neighbors both up and downstream became important to survival. A prerequisite for managing the Nile was to understand its behavior, and a priestly class emerged whose role was to monitor, measure, and record the Nile, as well as petition and placate its gods. An early identity of the flood is the god Hapi, whose origin is shrouded in the mists of time and whose attributes, those of a heavy-breasted and bearded man, are indicative of the importance of the flood to fertility in Egypt. One of Hapi's putative locations was at Elephantine, the site of the first cataract, where an almost continuous Nile floodplain begins. With time other gods associated with irrigation and the control of water emerged, including Sobek, the crocodile god.

The Nile floodplain varies between one to around twenty kilometers wide at its greatest extent. Within it there is limited topography of around 2 m and usually one channel (sometimes more) of the river. Since there are no tributaries within Egypt, the behavior of the Nile and the floodplain remains relatively similar throughout the whole of Upper Egypt. In Lower Egypt the river enters the delta and splits into distributaries where water disperses into canals, marshes, brackish swamps, saltpans, lagoons, and finally the sea. As it flows, it builds up levees that are sandy riverbanks rising above the surrounding silts. In common with most rivers, the Nile also meanders as it flows though its own soft sediment, snaking across the floodplain sideways at an average rate of around 2 km per thousand years. Generally bends move outward and downstream, with islands and sand bars tending to form in the bends. People trying to find a purchase in this dynamic floodplain adopted a number of different solutions at different periods. The main criterion was that the ground should be high, since most architecture was unbaked mud brick, which, when confronted with water, simply melts. Each year the flood rose, deposited silt, and then fell. The village surveyor (*dalal*) then laid out the plots of the village again using landscape features such as levees to delineate agricultural areas (*hod*) and then a measuring stick to sub-divide them into fields.

During the Predynastic Period the wadi mouths and ancient river terraces that flanked the then wilder Nile were popular for habitation, especially as they also provided access to the resources of the surrounding desert-savanna. However, during the Old Kingdom as the climate became dryer and the wadis unstable, settlements were tempted out into the floodplain, particularly to the levees, leading to ribbon developments along the Nile banks. Evidence from excavations at Mit Rahina (site of ancient Memphis near Cairo) show that when flood levels were low, the settlements encroached on the Nile banks but that, at times of high floods, buildings were washed away and settlements were forced to retreat. Accumulation of mud brick at settlement sites to form *kôms* meant that, as the floodplain rose when annual doses of silt were deposited, the sites kept ahead and remained above water. Particularly vibrant sites like Memphis could rise to a considerable height (up to 10 m) above the floodplain and also expand by in-filling marshes and minor channels with rubbish. Islands, another popular site for settlement, offered proximity to water on either side and may have formed the nucleus of many large sites like Karnak and Memphis. Inevitably, as the Nile migrated these islands bonded to the mainland on one side and, often within a century, were islands no more. The same pattern of habitation persisted until the inception of the Aswan Dam in the late nineteenth century.

During the flood season the Nile rose and spread out over the floodplain. The extent of ancient interest in flood levels is demonstrated by the construction of nilometers at Aswan, Thebes, and Cairo, both at ancient Memphis and at Roda, as well as in other cities. The nilometers recorded an annual increase in river level of around 14 m at Aswan (where the valley is narrow), 12 m at Luxor, and 8 m at Cairo. From this rise, the forecast for the success of the coming growing season could be made and the tax rate set accordingly. Too low a flood meant that insufficient land could be irrigated and there would be famine, while too high a flood would sweep away irrigation works and homes leading to disaster. A rise at Cairo of 16 cubits (just over 7 m) was regarded as ensuring abundance without leading to disaster (fig. 14.2). To ensure that water was delivered to the correct places, the river levees were breached in order to liberate the water at the right moment. In many depictions, for example the Scorpion macehead from Hierakonpolis (now in the Ashmolean Museum), the

FIGURE 14.2 Nile god with sixteen *putti*, representing the fertility of a sixteen-cubit rise of the Nile during the flood.

FIGURE 14.3 Sketch after a figure on the Narmer mace head: the king symbolically carrying a hoe.

king is shown ceremonially breaching the levee with a hoe (fig. 14.3), indicating what a key function this was. No doubt, in practice, the authority was generally delegated to local priests while the hoe was the province of the local farmers.

A scattering of nilometer records survive from the Early Dynastic Period, although they are frustratingly not linked to any specific nilometer. They do, however, indicate a general decline in flood level through the Early Dynastic. The declining flood meant that the floodplain became easier to inhabit, and it seems that thickets were cleared and a mixture of hunting, gathering, and agriculture was practiced. Informal agriculture could be supplemented during the rainy season by hunting and herding in the deserts. Fifth Dynasty tomb scenes from Saqqara and Abusir show desert-savanna in the Memphis area with abundant game. Declining monsoon rains were caused by a fall in global temperature, which saw a corresponding reduction in rainfall in the deserts, leading to degradation of the wadi habitat from scrub to desert. Ultimately, the death of the vegetation led to catastrophic collapse of wadi sands, forming tongues of sand that rushed out into the river floodplain. Desertification also led to an increasing reliance on pastoralism in the Nile Valley and near desert. Species that had been present in the area in the Mid-Holocene such as elephant, giraffe, and many others were marginalized southwards perhaps partly as a result of loss of habitat through herding and through hunting. Toward the end of the Old Kingdom, flood levels declined still further and there was an influx of sand that had been released from the Saharan region during desertification. The increased sand in the river was re-deposited as islands and over the flood-plain, raising its level, and collected downstream in the Delta, further consolidating it. The result was famine and disaster, culminating in the collapse of the Old Kingdom and the rule of Egypt as a number of smaller districts during the First Intermediate Period. Oscillations of the flood continued until the present day with much investment in nilometers and records across Egypt. Periods of high floods were devastating in the short term but ultimately lead to an expansion of the floodplain, particularly during the New Kingdom, providing more, fertile land for cultivation in their aftermath. The Roda Nilometer built around 715 CE maintained records through the Islamic Period and provides an exceptional index of Nile behavior.

The scene was set for the management of water in the Nile Valley on a large scale, since floods were lower and therefore more manageable, but sufficient food could not be gleaned without organized irrigation. In this unending task the careful measurement and record keeping of the priests was counterpointed with the role of the pharaoh in maintaining *maat*, the state of balance and order in the face of potential chaos. Maintenance of *maat* involved an increasingly sophisticated network of canals, embankments, and basins nominally under control of the king but locally delegated. The floodplain of the Nile, while generally flat, has natural rises of up to 3 m where levees, abandoned levees, and channels crisscross it. These natural embankments, augmented by dikes, could be used to form basins into which water was released during the flood. When the water returned to the main channel during the recession it left well-watered fields that had been fertilized by fresh silt. By the judicious breaching of embankments and blocking canals, the amount of land irrigated was controlled in accordance with the measured flood level. Equally, embankments were used to store water for later release. This system ensured that the best possible use was made of the agricultural land upon which the country had become dependent. It also required greater cooperation with those upstream and downstream. Too much water taken off upstream could lead to a paucity downstream, while too little water taken could cause catastrophic flooding.

Beyond the Nile floodplain, the large lake floor (around 1,800 km^2) of the Fayum had been exposed by evaporation, since declining flood levels meant water no longer overflowed through a gap at Hawara to refill the lake annually. The only thing required to bring this large lakebed under agriculture was a controlled supply of water. During the Twelfth Dynasty, schemes emerged to refill the lake and to store floodwaters from the Nile's minor channel, the Bahr Yusuf, by diverting it into reservoirs in the Fayum. By the time of Amenemhat III, half the lakebed had been refilled with water, an event that was commemorated by the construction of two colossi at Biahmu. It is perhaps at this Middle Kingdom moment that the relationship between the Nile and the inhabitants of the valley changed from one of response to one of "dialogue." Patterns of land use and the annual cycle of activity remained remarkably stable from this period until the construction of the High Dam at Aswan during the 1960s, which ended the annual flood. Mobilization of public effort at the end of *Shemu*, the harvest season, could prepare embankments and irrigation channels as well as construct ceremonial monuments. Recent work at Memphis has shown that, by the New Kingdom, minor channels of the Nile were sometimes reactivated, while at other times they were blocked to form harbor basins and to protect drained areas for buildings like the Temple of Ptah at Memphis. The god Ptah himself was associated with surveying, since the land appeared new-made each year as the flood receded. Agricultural area names, coined by these surveyors, survive on modern cadastral maps of Egypt and many recall earlier topographies (for example, the time when the plot was formerly an island). While there continued to be some high and low floods, a pattern of Nile management had emerged that, in conjunction with the storage of surpluses, created relative food security in Egypt.

Within the basins of the Nile Valley, natural meandering of the river caused loss of land on one side of the valley, with corresponding gains on the other (fig. 14.4). Settlements that abutted the riverbank tended to find that they were either eroded or left behind by the Nile. Of course, we have no records of towns that were eroded, as these probably did not survive beyond the development of a village. However, settlements that were left behind by the Nile had the benefit that there was new prime land created on the riverbank ripe for development. Moreover, the old town, by now run down and far from the river, could be quarried for mud or stone for buildings, a sustainable way in which towns could move to remain in touch with the river. Other examples of focus on islands include Thebes, where the Middle Kingdom harbor area known as "Tell Karnak" abutted the settlement of the priests. At this settlement there is evidence for baking, brewing, and other practical day-to-day activities close to the water.

In antiquity, myths emerged from observations of the Nile behavior, particularly regarding the colonization of islands: They were the primordial land that had emerged from the waters of chaos. Islands that formed in the Nile had the multiple virtues of being accessible, well supplied with water, and relatively protected from erosion. The adjacent minor channels are biodiverse, attracting waterfowl and large fish, other important resources. There is some evidence that islands were favored as locations for temples, perhaps particularly important if the priests were responsible for monitoring the rise of the Nile (which was expected soon after the rising of the Dog Star) and for directing the irrigation (and later taxation) activities in accordance with the level the flood had reached. Conveniently, the low ground flanking habitable islands was

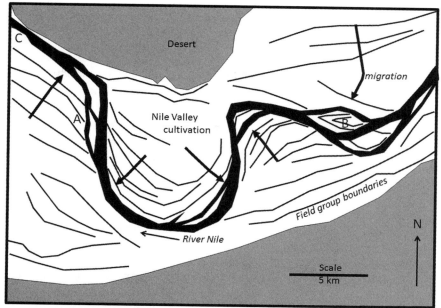

FIGURE 14.4 Plan of meander bends in the Nile Valley near Abydos, showing the constraints of the desert canyon, the meander pattern of the Nile, the thin dark lines that follow roads and *hôd* (field) boundaries that indicate the direction of migration of the Nile (shown with arrows).

ideal for industrial activity, being accessible, spacious, close to a source of water and mud for brick making, and with the added advantage that it was annually cleansed. Evvliya Celebi, the seventeenth-century Ottoman geographer, vividly describes how, as the flood began to recede, there was such a frenzy of activity on the riverbank that one could "find no place to drop a needle."

A modern analogue of this is Crocodile Island, just south of Luxor, where a luxury hotel has been constructed, and its neighbor, Banana Island, a popular objective for felucca tours, which is no longer actually an island. Often, modern-day farms are located on islands adjacent to the minor channel and on the high ground created by the river levee. The advantages still outweigh the disadvantages of having to take a boat to get to the shops. Observations of Badrshein Island near Mit Rahina (Memphis) show that the island formed during the late nineteenth century in the channel near a bend and was subsequently joined to the mainland within a century. In the meantime it had had the advantage of a Nile frontage on one side and a quiet-water channel suitable for a harbor and a brickworks on the other.

Confidence in public construction projects and Nile management grew through the New Kingdom with the creation of embankments and the extensive Ptah Temple at Memphis. Huge basins, known as *birket*, were excavated in the Theban area. Of these, a fine example is part of the complex, constructed by the Eighteenth Dynasty pharaoh Amenhotep III, of Malkata and Birket Habu on the west bank of the Nile at Thebes. Malkata is a palace built on the desert edge, served by a large harbor basin connected to the Nile by a channel. The mounds of earth that were thrown up during the excavations of the basin were sufficiently large that they can still be seen today and are the site of a village, Medinet Habu. Arguably a brief period of wetter climate around this time meant that hunting and travel through the desert became easier. The development of horse-drawn chariots, a novelty imported by the elite and which required prepared roads, increased the use of the broad wadis behind the palace. By dint of a great deal of digging, access by water to the Nile had been assured even for this desert-edge site. Unfortunately this benign period was short-lived, and during the time of Akhenaten the site was abandoned for a move to Amarna and subsequently Thebes.

While the main channel of the Nile remained difficult to manage, the minor channels could easily be controlled and, having less water and lower velocities, meandered on a much smaller scale than the main river. One such narrow channel, the Bahr Yusuf, was an ideal partner to the development of a town, and from the example of Oxyrhynchus a sophisticated pattern of location within the landscape and symbiosis with it emerges. Oxyrhynchus was located on the desert edge, and the Bahr Yusuf was diverted from its normal course to one farther west that abutted the desert for maximum convenience, since residence in the desert edge guarded against flooding and erosion. Rather than following the river, the Ptolemaic and Roman residents had brought the river to themselves. Physical remains of the town are still visible, but more exceptionally its enormous archive of rubbish, dumped in the desert, also survived. So abundant were the records that a hundred years after they were excavated the collation and translation of the documents continues. From these documents we learn of lovers' tiffs, a kind gift of a puppy to a lonely bride now far from home, and many more mundane matters pertinent to the running of the town. The combined record of the archaeology and the documents shows that a channel, taken from the Bahr Yusuf upstream where it joined the desert edge, brought water to a large tank at the upper desert side of the town. From here a grid of channels served the town in all but the lowest part of the river's annual cycle. The channels brought fresh water down from the cistern into the houses and delivered the used water to the river below the town. At times when the water was exhausted, a man was employed to raise water to the town, and we learn from his correspondence that in a particularly long dry season he felt disgruntled that the remuneration did not match the labor required. Embankments also enclosed fishponds, while marshy areas might attract game birds.

Agriculture could be conducted on a grand scale where the Nile floodplain was wide, but, at the same time, cities were vulnerable to loss of access to the migrating channel. In the Edfu region, a relatively wide part of the floodplain, we see an interplay of the various cities in the region, Edfu, El-Kab, and Nekhen as the river wandered across the floodplain, changing the resources available to the towns. Correspondingly in Middle Egypt, the largest part of the floodplain, a complex system of agricultural basins was created, but few towns could persist for long. Exceptions to this include Karnak, where the complex became so large that the river could not re-cross the city and was forced to meander to the west, and Edfu, where the town was located on a rocky eminence invulnerable to erosion. Strategic points emerged where the valley narrowed, such as Aswan, Saqqara, and Armant, where a location on the stable desert edge assured command of the Nile, which was unable to escape from the constricting valley. An excellent example of these processes is the town of Hermopolis, which, according to the foundation myth, developed on an island when the Nile was at the center point of a wide tract of fertile land during the Middle Kingdom. With time the river meandered away to the east, and the papyri tell us that by Roman times land transport was required to take the sailors from the town to its own harbor. Pragmatically, in the second century CE Hadrian re-founded the town at Antinoopolis, where his lover Antinous had drowned. The site also had the strategic advantage of being on the desert edge and therefore impregnable to erosion. Better still, by this time a combination of revetment of the riverbank and diversion of excess water into abandoned channels and flood basins could prevent the Nile from leaving the new city. Meandering continued in the rural hinterland, and the river's changes in location are recorded in land exchange documents through the centuries of the first millennium CE. Since Antinoopolis had originally been founded with little agricultural land, most purchases before the sixth century CE are Antinoopolites obtaining land from Hermopolites. Later, as the river upstream turned and started to migrate towards Hermopolis, the Hermopolites were keen to purchase land from their Antinoopolite neighbors. Arguably, it was the Romans who had finally attained mastery of the Nile.

Meanwhile, downstream the Delta was gradually extending and accumulating sediment. Agricultural practices in use in the Nile Valley could also be deployed in the Delta. Until c. 2000 BCE the Delta had been marshy with abundant papyrus and reeds and many interconnected channels. When channels burst their banks the resulting sediment fans were ideal locations for small-scale agriculture, while the pools and marshes were home to game, waterfowl, and fish. Indeed evidence from Neolithic Merimde Beni-Salame shows that hippopotami were sufficiently abundant that the doorsteps of the houses were made of hippo tibia. The Old Kingdom tomb of Ti at Saqqara has a fine image of a gentleman hunting and fishing in the marshes, accompanied by his wife in her finest wig. The same tomb contains scenes of marsh men with their water-resistant reed kilts delivering cattle to the Saqqara area. This evidence is complemented by observations from Kom el-Hisn in the western Delta where, study of dung reveals, the main animals farmed there were cattle. Contrastingly, the evidence from the bones of animals butchered at the site shows that the main animals eaten were sheep or goats. Archaeologists conclude that the site was a cattle ranch exporting to the Saqqara area. So, the early Delta habitat was rich and diverse, if replete with mosquitos and bilharzia. With time, however, marshes in the Delta started to fill with sediment, and the channel network changed from many interconnected channels to fewer channels that fanned out from a point around Memphis.

By the fifth century BCE, Herodotus records some six main channels remaining. The sparser nutrients of this new environment and the hierarchical structure of the river channels meant that Memphis, through which all ships going from Upper to Lower Egypt had to pass, became pre-eminent in the region. Flooding was extensive during the rise of the Nile, hence settlements of the period were located around the fringes of *gezireh*, raised sandbanks sometimes also known as turtle-backs. The somewhat fanciful Palestrina mosaic (pl. 11) shows arched reed huts perching on top of sandy eminences surrounded by water and populated by farmers, fowl, and cattle, and fringed by fish. People settled farther out in the Delta had to balance access to food, whether from the richer coastal region or the poorer hinterland, with access to fresh water. Unfortunately, considerable sedimentation since the Predynastic Period means that we do not have a clear view of how settlements were distributed at that period. Perhaps sedimentation and the resulting loss of habitat was to some extent the cause of land losses in the Delta to invasions of Hyksos and other hostile forces from the Levant or Libya. However with a return of energy in the New Kingdom and re-conquest of the Delta, trade routes with the eastern Mediterranean were established and ports of the Delta flourished, for example Avaris (Piramesse), Kom Firin, and Sais.

In 331 BCE Alexander the Great recognized the great potential of the site of Alexandria. He located it on a beach ridge with access to the sea to the north and Mareotis to the south. The city also had a secure supply of fresh water underground in ancient beach ridges. By medieval times, construction of drinking water storage cisterns that were filled by water-lifting wheels during the fresh-water flood meant that a city like Tinnis, on an island in a coastal Manzala lagoon, could become an important entrepôt, a "Venice of the East," even if seasonally some water had to be imported to the site from farther upstream by boat. During the Mediterranean sailing season, which coincided approximately with the time of the flood, fresh water was abundant, as was trade. Seagoing ships could be unloaded, reloaded, and provisioned, while shallow draft smaller boats conveyed goods through the Delta canal network. The town also developed a luxury textile industry producing linens.

Since Herodotus' visit, the number of distributary channels in the Nile Delta has continued to reduce until there are only two main branches today: the Rosetta and the Damietta. Silting of the coastal lagoons has also reduced their size considerably. Moreover, the delta head has moved northward from old Memphis to north of Cairo as the Delta has continued to develop and consolidate. Since the late nineteenth century even greater efforts have been made to control the fickle Nile. Muhammad Ali commissioned the Aswan Dam in order to reduce the height of the flood maximum and to increase the amount of water during the dry season. The aim of this and subsequent projects was to impound water during the flood season and to release it during the rest of the year. By this means, the danger of flooding and disaster could be alleviated and the productivity of the floodplain assured. The initial effect of the dam was to spawn a large number of new villages, and the Nile course in Muhammad Ali's late nineteenth century can in places be tracked from these chains of villages. With better control of the flood, settlements could also expand and, as motorcars became widely available, street patterns and plot sizes changed. The patterns created by these historical processes are still visible in Egyptian settlements today (fig. 14.5).

Subsequently, in the 1960s President Gamal Abdel Nasser commissioned the High Dam, which now maintains the Nile at mid-height for the whole year. However, as with many ambitious schemes, there are also downsides. Water is impounded in a huge lake 200 km long, but so is the sediment that for so long built up the floodplain and ensured the fertility of Egypt. The silt that was previously distributed across Egypt is now deposited in Lake Nasser, and a new delta is emerging at the southern end of the lake. In Egypt the cleansing

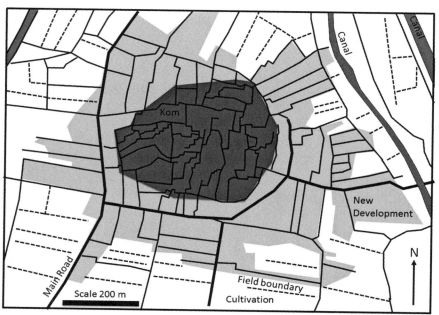

FIGURE 14.5 Diagram of Egyptian village in the Nile floodplain showing the dense irregular street patterns of the old settlement that has formed a *kôm* (dark gray shading), newer development (pale gray), and the remaining cultivation (unshaded). New development tends to following the field plot system and has a straighter more regular road pattern.

effects of the flood have been removed, and the high evaporation rate is leading to an accumulation of salt in the soil. To replace the natural fertility that Herodotus described as the "gift of the Nile," chemical fertilizers are added and, in the absence of the annual flood, excess salt and fertilizer is no longer swept away. Characteristically, Egypt has continued to adapt. Sand is brought from the desert to wick up the salt so that it can be disposed of back in the desert, and additional water is allowed to flow into Lake Qarun and the pools and lagoons of the Delta to prevent the lakes from turning pink with excess chemicals. The Nile continues to represent life and destruction and, in common with the ancient pharaohs, the maintenance of the balance of *maat*, even if we know it by the new name of "productivity," continues to be paramount.

15 }

Illness from Afar

EPIDEMICS AND THEIR AFTERMATH

Rosalie David

Disease, Medical Concepts, and Treatments: Cross-cultural Impact and Transmission

Although deserts and seas provided protection against frequent invasion, Egypt's roles as a great politico-military power and a cultural crossroads ensured continuing contact with neighboring lands. Population transfer, whether via military campaigns or migration, brought Egypt into contact with the peoples of Nubia, Asia Minor, and the Mediterranean, and the two-way transmission of foreign influences, with regard to disease, medical concepts, and treatments, is well documented.

The skills of Egyptian doctors, who gained extensive experience from accompanying military, quarrying, and mining expeditions, were internationally renowned and acknowledged. For instance, the ruler of Ugarit dispatched a letter (EA 49 in the Amarna archive) to the pharaoh, asking him to send a physician, the Hittite king invited Egyptian doctors to attend his court, and later, Egyptian and Greek doctors held prominent positions at the Persian court. After the Persian invasion of Egypt, Udjahorresne, an Egyptian naval officer, was appointed by Cambyses (525–522 BCE) as a courtier and chief physician. In his statue inscription, he relates how Darius I (521–486 BCE), the next Persian ruler of Egypt, commissioned him to restore and re-equip the House of Life at Sais, famed for its role in treating the sick.

Significant migrations to Egypt in the Greco-Roman Period (332 BCE–395 CE) doubtless ensured that some elements of Egyptian medicine were transmitted to the Greek and Roman systems. Graffiti in the temple of Hatshepsut at Deir el-Bahri demonstrate that, during the same period, foreigners travelled to Egypt to seek cures at temple sanatoria. Medical exchanges and transmission are also known from pharaonic times. For example, the Egyptian medical papyri have references to diseases and treatments of foreign origin, and even some native remedies include pharmaceutical and other ingredients imported from outside Egypt.

High-level diplomacy sometimes focused on medical treatment. In one instance, a letter (EA23 in the Amarna archive) mentions that the Mitannian king, Tushratta, sent a statue of the goddess Ishtar of Nineveh to the Egyptian court, possibly in the hope that the deity would cure the ailments of Amenhotep III (Eighteenth Dynasty). A later work of fiction relates how medical assistance was sought from Egypt when the Hittite sister-in-law of Ramesses II (Nineteenth Dynasty) became ill. The skills of an Egyptian physician having failed, the princess's evil spirit was finally exorcised when a healing statue of Khonsu was sent from Egypt.

Paleopathological evidence indicates that contact with foreigners could result in personal injury. The nearly complete body of King Seneb-Kay of the early Second Intermediate Period provides evidence that a massive assault with bladed weapons caused his demise, while the severe wounds visible in the badly damaged, disarticulated mummy of Tao II Seqenenre (Seventeenth Dynasty) may be the result of battlefield conflict or injuries inflicted by assassins. The bodies of some sixty soldiers buried within the funerary complex of Nebhepetre Mentuhotep II (Eleventh Dynasty) at Deir el-Bahri also exhibit severe wounds, probably inflicted by arrows or stones during an onslaught on a fortress.

Epidemic Diseases in Ancient Egypt

In view of the extensive interaction between Egypt and her neighbors, it might be expected that ample evidence of epidemic and pandemic diseases would be preserved in the archaeological and paleopathological records.

The first extant attempt to identify the influence that external and environmental factors had on endemic and epidemic diseases is found in the works of Hippocrates (c.450–370 BCE) and his followers. These sources discuss the impact that climate, winds, water supply, soil, geographical location, and population lifestyle exerts on patterns of disease. Modern studies have confirmed that the spread of disease is facilitated by rising population density and the establishment of cities and towns, with their overcrowded housing, inadequate ventilation, poor sanitation, and unhygienic waste disposal; these conditions were all present in ancient Egypt.

Climatic and environmental factors, combined with unique burial practices, have ensured that a wealth of source material has survived in Egypt. This includes archaeological assemblages, inscribed records, and bodies preserved by natural (unintentional) or artificial (intentional) mummification processes. Biomedical and scientific techniques used to study these human remains have provided new evidence about disease patterns (pl. 12). These sources inform current knowledge about the following types of epidemic disease that may have afflicted the ancient Egyptians.

THE BIBLICAL PLAGUES

The biblical plagues include what is probably the best-known reference to an Egyptian epidemic. According to the Book of Exodus, these ten plagues were divinely inflicted upon Egypt to force the pharaoh to release the Hebrews from slavery. They have been the subject of considerable debate, and historians continue to dispute whether the account is allegorical, a memory-compilation of disconnected natural disasters, or a chain of events that actually happened, set in motion by climatic and environmental changes.

It has been suggested that the sixth plague (Exodus 9:8–12), which brought a festering skin condition (perhaps a symptom of some epidemic disease) to the Egyptians and their livestock, could have resulted from the transmission to humans of the livestock disease mentioned in the fifth plague. The tenth plague—in which the Egyptians' firstborn children were annihilated (Exodus 11:1–12:36)—has also been the subject of much discussion.

According to one hypothesis, the infants' deaths may have been caused by toxins present in their morning meal, perhaps the result of overnight pollution by locusts or black mold. There has also been speculation that the biblical account may be the first extant record of a bubonic plague epidemic, or it may describe conditions attributable to bacillary dysentery or intestinal schistosomiasis.

The discovery of tomb KV 5 in the Valley of the Kings, which contained skeletal remains probably attributable to several of Ramesses II's sons, excited considerable interest and raised questions about whether one of the bodies might belong to the pharaoh's firstborn as mentioned in Exodus and whether this might present an opportunity for diagnostic investigation to identify the nature of the biblical plague. However, Weeks believes that this line of enquiry would lead nowhere. Apart from the difficulty of identifying an epidemic-type disease in ancient human remains, there is no historical evidence that the Exodus ever occurred and no proof that the biblical pharaoh was Ramesses II; additionally, it is unclear whether Amunhirkhopshef was indeed Ramesses II's firstborn son, or if his body is among those found in KV 5.

BUBONIC PLAGUE

Scholars have generally assumed that bubonic plague (*Yersinia pestis*) did not exist in Egypt in pharaonic times, perhaps only arriving there after the Moslem conquest of the country in the seventh century CE. Any evidence of an earlier presence is scanty and controversial. There is no direct allusion to the disease in the medical papyri, although it has been suggested that the "tumors of

Khonsu" mentioned in the Ebers Papyrus (39) may refer to the inflamed and enlarged lymph glands (buboes) that characterize bubonic plague. Other symptoms possibly attributable to bubonic plague, including coal-black spots and blood-red urine, are described in the Hearst Medical Papyrus (H XI 12–15) and the London Medical Papyrus (15: 8–10).

Bubonic plague has only been tentatively identified in one ancient Egyptian body: based on the evidence of a lung lesion, Ruffer suggested that the owner of a mummy dating to the Ptolemaic Period (332–30 BCE) may have suffered from the pneumonic form of this disease. However, a general lack of paleopathological evidence is not surprising since major symptoms of the disease—high fever, tachycardia, headache, and chills—would leave no gross pathological traces in the archaeological record. However, modern genetic techniques, successfully used to identify plague in other contexts, may offer new opportunities for the Egyptian material.

Bubonic plague is a disease of rats, not humans, but it is also a zoonosis (a disease passed between animals and humans). The causative bacillus, *Yersinia pestis*, is transmitted from one rodent to another, and once the disease kills the animal, its fleas (*Xenopsylla cheopis*) move to a human host. The bacillus is then transferred to the human host via the fleas' bites and can subsequently be spread through person-to-person contact.

The bubonic plague is believed to have originated as a disease associated with the black rat (*Rattus rattus*), probably starting in the rodent's homeland of northwestern India, and then moving elsewhere at a later date. However, the archaeological record of a Nile rat at Tell el Dab'a (Thirteenth Dynasty), its depiction in the Tomb of Baket III at Beni Hasan (No. 15) (Eleventh Dynasty), and the discovery of remnants of human and animal fleas in domestic contexts at Amarna (late Eighteenth Dynasty) may indicate a different scenario that would support the suggestion that bubonic plague existed in pharaonic Egypt.

This hypothesis proposes that the disease was originally associated with the Nile rat (*Arvicanthis niloticus*) whose flea (*Xenopsylla cheopis*) then jumped to a new host, the black rat (*Rattus rattus*), accidentally imported into Egypt from India through sea-trade or possibly via Mesopotamia. Once the black rat had established itself as a reservoir for bubonic plague, it then transmitted the bacillus farther afield, and what may have started as a relatively rare disease in humans now became the cause of a series of devastating pandemics. Indeed, rituals and offerings may have been organized on a grand scale in an attempt to curtail such disasters. It has been suggested that over three hundred statues of Sekhmet may have been erected in the Precinct of Mut at Karnak during the reign of Amenhotep III (Eighteenth Dynasty) as a focal point for ceremonies to placate the goddess. The heavy abrasion and wear noted on the legs and left arms of some of these statues have been tentatively attributed to the frequent touch of worshippers.

Earlier, there is evidence that the substantial Thirteenth Dynasty settlement at Tell el-Dab'a was partially abandoned, possibly as the result of an epidemic. Graves in Stratum G appear to have been prepared for emergency burials: bodies were thrown in, and most graves did not contain offerings. Anthropological studies have indicated that the population suffered many health problems, and their consequent lowered resistance would have facilitated the rapid spread of an epidemic (either bubonic plague or the "Asiatic disease" have been suggested as possibilities). However, as yet, there is no firm scientific evidence to confirm the existence of plague in this community.

Aside from these intriguing hypotheses, historians generally acknowledge that the account of the "Plague of Justinian" written by Procopius (died *c.*563 CE) is the first extant record of a bubonic plague epidemic. Originating in Constantinople in 542 CE, this pandemic reputedly killed a quarter of the population of the Roman Empire and may have been responsible for its ultimate collapse. By 547 CE, the disease had reached western Europe where, from the fourteenth century onward, recurrent epidemics of the so-called "Black Death" continued to decimate the population.

MALARIA

The unique nature of the fever associated with malaria is first noted in the *Hippocratic Corpus*, which also mentions splenomegaly (enlarged spleen) as a symptom associated with the disease. However, malarial organisms are known to be much older; as one of the most ancient human parasites, they probably existed from at least Neolithic times.

The infection, which can either be acute or chronic and recurrent, is caused by protozoal parasites of the genus *Plasmodium*. This is composed of a large number of species, four of which, including *P. falciparum*, infect humans; these parasites are usually transmitted to humans through the bite of infected *Anopheles* mosquitoes, which feed on the host's blood. Symptoms associated with this type of malaria are fever, enlargement of the spleen and often of the liver, bilious vomiting and jaundice, and severe anemia.

The disease is characteristically seasonal and will only occur in areas with appropriate climatic and environmental conditions, human hosts, and a population of *Anopheles* mosquitoes infected with malarial parasites. The presence of water, preferably standing or slow running, is necessary in order for the mosquitoes to breed. All these conditions are known to have existed in pharaonic and Greco-Roman Egypt, particularly in the Fayum and possibly in the Delta.

However, the medical papyri make no reference to the characteristic fever associated with malaria, which recurs at three- or four-day intervals, and evidence of the disease has been difficult to identify in human remains. This is not surprising since the disease would not generally produce gross pathological changes, although Ruffer discussed the possibility that the splenomegaly noted in several Coptic Period (early centuries CE) mummies might be indicative of malaria. Because of this lack of evidence, some early researchers, including Henschen and Sigerist, concluded that malaria probably did not exist in pharaonic times.

However, immunological approaches have provided a new perspective. When the *Para*Sight™-F test, developed as a diagnostic tool to detect the antigen produced by *Plasmodium falciparum* in modern populations, was modified and applied to ancient remains, the relevant antigen was detected in seven out of eighteen human remains from all the periods studied. These included a series of naturally desiccated bodies from the Predynastic Period as well as mummies from the New Kingdom, the Twenty-fifth Dynasty, and the Nubian Ballana period (350–550 CE).

Based on these results, the researchers concluded that these people had all been infected with malaria at the time of death. However, Hillson has argued that stronger proof is needed to confirm that malaria was present in ancient Egypt. Other immunological studies have produced interesting, if controversial, results. In one case, Krotoski used immunofluorescence to examine tissue taken from the mummy of Nakht (ROM 1); although this produced positive reactions, the results were insufficient to demonstrate the presence of malaria in the mummy. With the successful design of DNA primers to detect various diseases in antiquity, including malaria, modern genetic techniques are now starting to offer other analytical opportunities. One example is the tentative identification of *P. falciparum* in liver samples obtained from mummies in the Dakhla oasis.

POLIOMYELITIS

When Elliot Smith unwrapped the mummy of Siptah (Nineteenth Dynasty), he noted a shortening of the left leg and gross deformity of the ankle, which he identified as congenital clubfoot (*talipes equino-varus*) (figs. 15.1–2). Some researchers have supported this diagnosis, but radiological studies indicate that the king may have suffered from a neuromuscular disease, possibly poliomyelitis. The unilateral shortening of a femur observed in another mummy (from Deshasha, *c.* 700 BCE) could also be due to poliomyelitis.

A funerary stela of the Eighteenth or Nineteenth Dynasty depicts Roma, a temple doorkeeper, supporting himself on a staff; his severely wasted and shortened leg may have been the result of clubfoot deformity or childhood poliomyelitis. These represent rare, unconfirmed cases, and since the disease does not occur in isolation, and examples of similar deformities in other mummies have not been identified, the evidence for poliomyelitis in Egypt remains inconclusive.

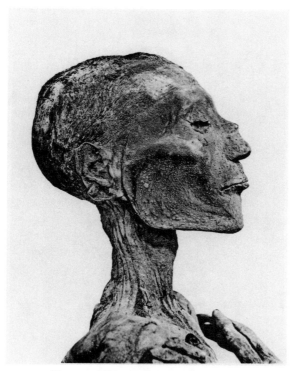

FIGURE 15.1 The mummy of Ramesses V (Twentieth Dynasty), unwrapped in 1905. Immunological techniques have confirmed a tentative diagnosis of smallpox made on the basis of cutaneous vesicles observed on the face (seen here) and elsewhere on the body.

SMALLPOX

Elliot Smith unwrapped the mummy of Ramesses V (Twentieth Dynasty) in 1905 and tentatively identified smallpox as the cause of cutaneous vesicles observed on the face, neck, chest, and lower abdomen (fig. 15.3). In 1971, researchers used minute skin samples from the mummy to test this diagnosis, but attempts to identify the virus using electron microscopy and a radioimmunoassay were inconclusive. However, a more sensitive immunoprecipitation test has since confirmed the presence of smallpox.

Another tentative diagnosis of smallpox, based on a skin lesion observed on a mummy dating to the Twentieth Dynasty, is not universally accepted. On the evidence available, widespread existence of this acute crowd infection cannot be confirmed: the characteristic vesicles are not mentioned in the medical papyri, and evidence for smallpox in human remains in Egypt, reviewed by Sandison, is tenuous. Smallpox is a density-dependent disease requiring a population of at least 200,000: survivors carry immunization against future attacks, and therefore a large population pool is required to provide new human hosts. The size

FIGURE 15.2 The mummy of Siptah (Nineteenth Dynasty), showing a shortening of the left leg and gross deformity of the ankle. Cairo Museum.

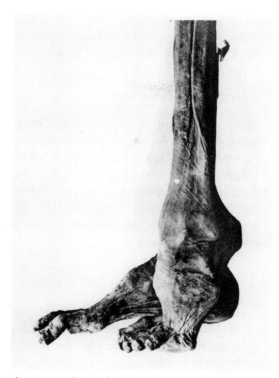

FIGURE 15.3 When the mummy of Siptah (Nineteenth Dynasty) was unwrapped in 1905, the deformity evident in the left leg and foot was identified as a case of congenital clubfoot (*talipes equino-varus*). More recent radiological studies indicate a neuromuscular disease, possibly poliomyelitis. Cairo Museum.

of local populations in Egypt may simply not have been sufficient to support such epidemics.

LEPROSY

No evidence of nodular leprosy has been found in mummified human remains from pharaonic Egypt. A possible explanation for this is that, if the disease was known to be infectious and victims were isolated during life, they may not have had access to mummification. Ebbell translated the term "tumors of Khons" as leprosy in two passages in the Ebers Papyrus (874 and 877). Although this identification has received some support, the translation remains problematic, and the passages may in fact refer to other diseases, including cancer or bubonic plague.

Leprosy has been confirmed in several bodies from the post-pharaonic period. The earliest skeletal evidence comes from two skulls (*c.*200 BCE) from the Dakhla oasis, and the disease has also been noted in some skulls (fourth to seventh centuries CE) from sites near Aswan. Also, a macroscopic and radiological review of the evidence has confirmed the diagnosis of leprosy in a mummy from a sixth century CE Coptic Christian burial at Biga.

SALMONELLA, TYPHUS, AND TYPHOID

The high temperatures periodically experienced in Egypt, together with unhealthy water sources, doubtless gave rise to salmonella, typhus, and typhoid, diseases caused by contaminated food, water, and milk. However, these acute conditions, which resulted in either a patient's early death or complete recovery, leave no record behind in human remains. Literary sources are also inconclusive: although references to fevers—characteristic of such illnesses—do occur in the medical papyri, descriptions of the symptoms are so general that they cannot be attributed to a specific disease.

THE "ASIATIC" OR "CANAANITE" DISEASE

The main source of information about this disease are eight spells in the Edwin Smith Surgical Papyrus (Second Intermediate Period) that are devoted to exorcising an annual epidemic known as "the pest of the year." It was generally believed that epidemics were brought about by malignant deities, demons, the disembodied dead, and the wind. These incantations were addressed to benign gods and spirits so that they would protect and heal the patients, and also to the bringers of disease, especially the goddess Sekhmet, in the hope of placating her (fig. 15.4).

It is remarkable that some of these incantations identify the wind as a carrier of disease agents; this is the earliest extant reference to the idea that pestilence could be transferred in the air. The sixth incantation identifies a fly as a potential disease agent; however, this does not imply that the Egyptians were aware of the biological role of insects in disease transmission—the spell was merely intended to render the fly ineffective by expelling it from the patient's stomach and intestines.

Another incantation exorcises the disease pest from food, bedding, and household articles. Although this recalls modern practices of disinfecting food and other items because they may harbor bacteria and viruses (which modern microbiological techniques have been able to identify), the Egyptians were unaware that these organisms existed: the intention of this spell was simply to utilize magic as an effective means of cleansing the home.

The texts identify the wind, breath, or the arrows of night-demons (Sekhmet's messengers) as agents of hostility who could transmit disease malignancy to mankind. The use of arrows is associated with the belief that diseases without

FIGURE 15.4 Statue of the lioness-headed goddess, Sekhmet, feared as the bringer of plagues and epidemics to Egypt. She was worshipped as a principal deity of medicine, in order to placate her anger. Eighteenth Dynasty. World Museum, Liverpool.

an obvious cause were the result of an external agent invading the body: the arrows transmitted Sekhmet's rage to the victim, who subsequently developed a pathological condition.

The term "Asiatic" or "Canaanite" indicates that the disease was associated in some way with neighboring lands, although it is unclear if this name implies that the pestilence originated in these regions. An alternative speculation is that the name possibly refers to the Asiatic population at Tell el-Dab'a in the Delta who may have been affected by an unconfirmed epidemic in the Thirteenth Dynasty. Later evidence indicates that the disease apparently arrived at the turn of the year, coinciding with the Nile inundation, at a time of mythological chaos and confusion when Sekhmet and her messengers caused destruction, disease, and death. Inscriptions infer that the pestilence occurred regularly but did not always result in death.

None of the texts clearly defines the symptoms associated with this condition, making it impossible to specifically identify the disease. It was obviously a type of epidemic pestilence, and possibilities include the biblical plagues and malaria. However, Győry has suggested that the illnesses mentioned in the Edwin Smith Papyrus can be identified with three diseases found in the Ebers Papyrus and other sources, which may describe different types of well-known endemic febrile diseases such as typhoid and dengue fever. The texts indicate that these illnesses were spread by air or breath and were commonly defined by a fever that caused physical weakness. Győry concludes that the term "pestilence of the year" probably did not apply to one specific disease but embraced a more diverse group of infections that may have included typhoid, typhus, and dengue fever.

THE CYPRIAN PLAGUE

The Cyprian Plague is named after Cyprian, bishop of Carthage in Tunisia, whose writings (*De mortalitate*) provide details of the dreadful symptoms suffered by disease victims prior to death; these, he believed, presaged the end of the world. His account probably describes a series of epidemics that occurred across the Roman world in the third century CE.

Excavations carried out between 1997 and 2012 by the Italian Mission to Luxor in the funerary complex of Harwa (TT 37) and Akhimenru (TT 404) in western Thebes have revealed evidence that may relate to these epidemics. Various findings indicate that, following the burial of Harwa and his successor, Akhimenru, the place was used for body disposal during a period of plague. Discoveries include three kilns where slaked lime (used as a disinfectant) was produced; the remains of a large bonfire containing corpses, vessels, and partially burnt bricks; and an assemblage of human remains covered with a thick layer of lime.

Archaeologists have suggested that the complex was used, at least once, for the disposal of large numbers of corpses during a disease outbreak. These activities can be dated by the associated pottery to a narrow range that coincides with epidemics that weakened the Roman Empire between 250 and 271 CE (generally acknowledged to be the Cyprian Plague). This disease—possibly smallpox or measles—decimated the Roman Empire, perhaps killing more than five thousand people a day, including the emperors Hostilian (251 CE) and Claudius II Gothicus (270 CE). This funerary complex, never used again as a conventional burial site, was rediscovered by tomb robbers in the nineteenth century CE.

The Spread, Severity, and Aftermath of Epidemics in Egypt

Pharaonic Egypt may not have had a population large enough to support the emergence of major epidemics, but otherwise, all climatic, environmental, and domestic conditions conducive to these diseases were present. In addition, there were famines (which may increase the body's vulnerability to disease) and significant population movements. These included not only foreign settlers who entered Egypt during the Greco-Roman Period but also the incursions of the Sea Peoples (reign of Ramesses III, Twentieth Dynasty) and the transfer of prisoners-of-war to Egypt during the campaigns of the New Kingdom. The large armies possessed by Egypt and her enemies also presented considerable opportunities for the transmission of disease.

Evidence clearly indicates that epidemic-type diseases existed in ancient Egypt and neighboring countries. Mesopotamian sources mention a pandemic fever (probably fifth century BCE) and an epidemic that afflicted weavers, craftsmen, and agricultural workers at Mari; also, Babylonian astronomical texts of the first millennium BCE include predictions relating to plagues and epidemics. Bodies discovered at Tell el-Dab'a appear to have been disposed of during an epidemic (Thirteenth Dynasty), and there are references to plagues in the Amarna Letters, including the disease that ravaged the Egyptian base at Sumar. One letter in this archive (EA 35), sent to the pharaoh by the king of Alashiya (possibly Cyprus), states that he has only sent a small amount of copper to Egypt because all his country's copper-workers have been killed by a plague.

The plague prayers of Mursil II describe an epidemic in Khatti that killed King Suppiluliuma and his successor, Arnuwanda II. This disease was apparently transmitted by Egyptian prisoners taken at the battle of Amka in Syria (late Eighteenth Dynasty) and continued to afflict the Hittites for twenty years. One of several foreign incantations in the London Medical Papyrus (late Eighteenth Dynasty) is written in the "language of Keftiu (Crete)," and is designed to counteract the "Canaanite illness."

The Egyptians were sufficiently familiar with the concept of epidemic disease to envisage the need for special divine protection. Sekhmet fulfilled this role: although the so-called Asiatic disease and possibly other epidemics were attributed to this goddess, it was hoped that regular acts of worship would appease her so that she would stop the spread of pestilence. She was doubtless the recipient of special rituals and large-scale offerings made throughout Egypt whenever these periodic threats occurred.

However, despite indications that epidemic-type diseases were present in pharaonic Egypt, there is no conclusive evidence of widespread, devastating plagues in any of the surviving literary, archaeological, or paleopathological records. This perception may be erroneous, perhaps due to the chance of discovery, and would perhaps need to be adjusted if further information was ever forthcoming.

However, this lack of information may actually be due to the intrinsic limitations of the Egyptian evidence. First of all, relatively few human remains have been investigated to confirm or refute the presence of these diseases, and the evidence, obtained mostly from bodies of the elite, provides an unbalanced picture of overall disease patterns. Secondly, most indicators of epidemic disease are not preserved in human remains, and although new immunological and molecular methods of detection offer great opportunities, they also pose considerable technical challenges.

The literary sources are also problematic. The medical papyri provide no clear-cut evidence of epidemic disease: symptoms are simply listed rather than attributed to specific diseases, and many (for example, fever) can be indicative of a wide variety of epidemic illnesses. Notably, some characteristic markers of specific illnesses, such as the fever pattern associated with malaria or the distinctive cutaneous vesicles observed in smallpox, are not mentioned in these sources. In addition, some words and phrases, such as the "tumors of Khonsu," pose considerable translation difficulties.

Egyptian literature provides no extant historical account of a plague. Again, this omission is perhaps not surprising: generally, Egyptian "historical" texts were not intended to recount current events, however momentous, but to praise the pharaoh's domestic and foreign achievements. However, a true folk memory of devastating conditions associated with epidemics may survive in the *Admonitions of Ipuwer*. This text, preserved in Papyrus Leiden 1116B (Eighteenth Dynasty), describes how the disintegration of Egyptian society came about, as the result of widespread chaos, violence, robbery, murder, foreign infiltration, famine, and disease. Scholars have disputed whether this text, and other similar documents that comprise the so-called "Pessimistic Literature," are indeed historical accounts of events that actually happened, perhaps at the end of the Old Kingdom and in the early years of the First Intermediate Period, or whether they are purely rhetorical, a literary device for discussing the concept of order versus chaos.

In contrast, classical writers provide contemporary descriptions of various epidemics and plagues that occurred in Greek and Roman times. These include a "new" disease (possibly bubonic plague, typhus, smallpox, measles, or syphilis) in the fourth century BCE, which is said to have annihilated part of the Athenian army and perhaps over a third of the Athenian population. From the second century CE, a series of epidemics (perhaps including smallpox, measles, or malaria) devastated the Roman Empire. These plagues decimated the population of towns, obliterated villages, disrupted agricultural and social patterns, and may even have contributed to the collapse of the Roman Empire. Surprisingly, there is no evidence that Greco-Roman Egypt experienced epidemics or disruption on a similar scale, although significant immigration at this time from other areas of the Hellenistic and Roman empires would have exposed both the host population and incomers to new diseases.

In summary, the extent of epidemic disease and the role it played in pharaonic and Greco-Roman Egypt remain unclear. In order to produce significant new data, much more extensive examination of human remains, focusing on immunological and molecular techniques, is required. Additionally, reassessment and reinterpretation of some of the medical papyri could provide fresh insight into this challenging area of Egyptology.

REFERENCES AND FURTHER READING

Schneider, Chapter 1—Finding the Beyond . . .

Altenmüller, Hartwig (ed.). 2015. *Zwei Annalenfragmente aus dem frühen Mittleren Reich.* Studien zur altägyptischen Kultur, Beihefte 16.

Assmann, Jan. 1970. *Der König als Sonnenpriester. Ein kosmographischer Begleittext zur kultischen Sonnenhymnik in thebanischen Tempeln und Gräbern.* Abhandlungen des Deutschen Archäologischen Instituts, Abteilung Kairo 7. Glückstadt: Augustin.

Bard, Kathryn A. and Rodolfo Fattovich. 2015. "Mersa/Wadi Gawasis and Ancient Egyptian Trade in the Red Sea." *Near Eastern Archaeology* 78(1): 4–11.

Bates, Oric. 1914. *The Eastern Libyans: An Essay.* London: MacMillan.

Beaux, Nathalie. 1990. *Le cabinet de curiosités de Thoutmosis III: plantes et animaux du "Jardin botanique" de Karnak.* Orientalia Lovaniensia Analecta 36. Leuven: Peeters.

Bietak, Manfred. 1996. *Avaris, the Capital of the Hyksos: Recent Excavations at Tell el-Dab'a.* London: British Museum Press.

Bietak, Manfred, Nannó Marinatos, and Clairy Palivou. 2007. *Taureador Scenes in Tell el-Dab'a (Avaris) and Knossos.* With a contribution by Ann Brysbaer. Denkschriften der Gesamtakademie 43. Untersuchungen der Zweigstelle Kairo des Österreichischen Archäologischen Institutes 27. Wien: Verlag der Österreichischen Akademie der Wissenschaften.

Bourriau, Janine and Jacqueline Sharon Phillips. 2004. *Invention and Innovation: The Social Context of Technological Change. Egypt, the Aegean and the Near East, 1650–1150 BC.* 2 vols. Oxford: Oxbow Books.

Breyer, Francis A. 2010. *Ägypten und Anatolien. Politische, kulturelle und sprachliche Kontakte zwischen dem Niltal und Kleinasien im 2. Jahrtausend v. Chr.* Contributions to the Chronology of the Eastern Mediterranean = Österreichische Akademie der Wissenschaften, Denkschriften der Gesamtakademie, 43. Wien: Österreichische Akademie der Wissenschaften.

Breyer, Francis A. 2014. "Vorlagen zur 'Punthalle' von Dair al-Baḥrī aus dem Alten Reich. Philologisch-epigraphische, textkritische und ikonographische cruces im Zusammenspiel von Darstellungen und Inschriften." *Studien zur altägyptischen Kultur* 43: 47–91.

Breyer, Francis A. In Press. *Punt. Die Suche nach dem Gottesland. Culture and History of the Ancient Near East.* Leiden: Brill.

Cohen, Raymond and Raymond Westbrook (eds.). 2000. *Amarna Diplomacy: The Beginnings of International Relations.* Baltimore: Johns Hopkins University Press.

Cooper, Julien. 2012. "Reconsidering the Location of Yam." *Journal of the Amercian Research Center in Egypt* 48: 1–21.

Cwiek, Andrzej. 2014. "Old and Middle Kingdom Tradition in the Temple of Hatshepsut at Deir el-Bahari." *Études et Travaux* 27: 62–93.

Dobbs, David. 2013. "Restless Genes." *National Geographic*, January 2013. <http://ngm. nationalgeographic.com/2013/01/125-restless-genes/dobbs-text>, retrieved 1 July 2015.

Edel, Elmar and Manfred Görg. 2005 . *Die Ortsnamenlisten im nördlichen Säulenhof des Totentempels Amenophis' III.* Ägypten und Altes Testament 50. Wiesbaden: Harrassowitz.

Eichler, Eckhard. 1992. *Untersuchungen zum Expeditionswesen des ägyptischen Alten Reiches*. Wiesbaden: Harrassowitz.

el-Awady, Tarek. 2009. *Abusir*, Volume 16: *Sahure—The Pyramid Causeway: History and Decoration Program in the Old Kingdom*. Prag: Charles University.

el-Awady, Tarek. 2011. "King Sahura with the Precious Trees from Punt in a Unique Scene!" In *Old Kingdom, New Perspectives: Egyptian Art and Archaeology 2750–2150 BC*, ed. Nigel Strudwick and Helen Strudwick, 37–44. Oxford: Oxbow Books.

Fischer-Elfert, Hans-Werner. 1986. *Die satirische Streitschrift des Papyrus Anastasi I. Übersetzung und Kommentar*. Ägyptologische Abhandlungen 44. Wiesbaden: Harrassowitz.

Förster, Frank. 2007. "With Donkeys, Jars and Water Bags Into the Libyan Desert: The Abu Ballas Trail in the Late Old Kingdom/First Intermediate Period." *British Museum Studies in Ancient Egypt and Sudan* 7: 1–39.

Förster, Frank. 2015. Der Abu Ballas Weg. Eine pharaonische Karawanenroute durch die Libysche Wüste. Africa Praehistorica 28. Köln.

Galán, José M. 1994. "The Stela of Hor in Context." *Studien zur altägyptischen Kultur* 21: 65–79.

Gertzen, Thomas L. 2010. "Der angebliche Bericht über die Umschiffung Afrikas. Eine wissenschaftsgeschichtliche Einordnung." *Zeitschrift für ägyptische Sprache und Altertumskunde* 137: 104–12.

Gnirs, Andrea M. 2013. "Coping With the Army: The Military and the State in the New Kingdom." In *Ancient Egyptian Administration*, ed. Juan Carlos Moreno García, 639–718. Handbook of Oriental Studies I. Leiden: Brill.

Goedicke, Hans. 2002. "The Perimeter of Geographical Awareness in the Fourth Dynasty and the Significance of *ḥȝw-nbwt* in the Pyramid Texts." *Studien zur altägyptischen Kultur* 30: 121–36.

Goldwasser, Orly. 2002. *Prophets, Lovers and Giraffes: Wor(l)d Classification in Ancient Egypt*. Classification and Categorization in Ancient Egypt 3; Göttinger Orientforschungen 4. Reihe Ägypten 38. Wiesbaden: Harrassowitz.

Guyot, Frédéric. 2004. "Structuration sociale et dynamisme des émulations interculturelles: quelques considérations sur les contacts entre l'Égypte et la Mésopotamie au 4e millénaire." *Archéo-Nil* 14: 81–100.

Gundlach, Rolf. 1980. "Mentuhotep IV. und Min. Analyse der Inschriften M 110, M 191 und M 192a aus dem Wâdi Hammâmât." *Studien zur altägyptischen Kultur* 8: 89–114.

Harvey, Stephen P. 2003. "Interpreting Punt: Geographic, Cultural and Artistic Landscapes." In *Mysterious Lands*, ed. David O'Connor and Stephen Quirke, 81–91. London: UCL Press.

Hasan, Ali and Richard Fumerton. 2015. "Knowledge by Acquaintance vs. Description." In *The Stanford Encyclopedia of Philosophy*, spring 2014 edition, ed. Edward N. Zalta. <http://plato.stanford.edu/archives/spr2014/entries/knowledge-acquaindescrip/>, retrieved July 1, 2015.

Hawkins, J. David. 2009. "The Arzawa Letters in Recent Perspective." *British Museum Studies in Ancient Egypt and Sudan* 14: 73–83.

Heggie, Vanessa. 2014. "Why Isn't Exploration a Science?" *Isis* 105: 318–34.

Heinz, Marlies. 2007. "Sargon of Akkad: Rebel and Usurper in Kish." In *Representations of Political Power: Case Histories from Times of Change and Dissolving Order in the Ancient Near East*, ed. Marlies Heinz, 67–86. Winona Lake: Eisenbrauns.

Higginbotham, Carolyn R. 2000. *Egyptianization and Elite Emulation in Ramesside Palestine: Governance and Accommodation on the Imperial Periphery*. Leiden: Brill.

Hirsch, Eileen. 2008. *Die sakrale Legitimation Sesostris' I.: Kontaktphänomene in königsideologischen Texten*. Königtum, Staat und Gesellschaft früher Hochkulturen 6. Wiesbaden: Harrassowitz.

Hrouda, Barthel, Wolfram Nagel, and Eva Strommenger. 2009. *Vorderasiatische Altertums kunde: Forschungsinhalte und Perspektiven seit 1945*. Köln: Böhlau.

Janick, Jules. 2007. "Plant Exploration: From Queen Hatshepsut to Sir Joseph Banks." *HortScience* 42(2): 191–6.

Kaelin, Oskar. 2006. *"Modell Ägypten". Adoption von Innovationen im Mesopotamien des 3. Jahrtausends v. Chr.* Orbis Biblicus et Orientalis, Series Archaeologica 26. Fribourg: Academic Press.

Kennedy, Dane. 2014. "Introduction: Reinterpreting Exploration." In *Reinterpreting Exploration: The West in the World*, ed. D. Kennedy, 1–19. Oxford: Oxford University Press.

Kloth, Nicole. 2002. *Die (auto-) biographischen Inschriften des ägyptischen Alten Reiches. Untersuchungen zu Phraseologie und Entwicklung*, Hamburg: Buske.

Laboury, Dimitri. 2007. "Archaeological and Textual Evidence for the Function of the 'Botanical Garden' of Karnak in the Initiation Ritual." In *Sacred Space and Sacred Function in Ancient Thebes*, ed. Peter F. Dorman and Betsy M. Bryan, 27–34. Studies in Ancient Oriental Civilisation 61. Chicago: Oriental Institute.

Lamar, Howard R. 1988. "Introduction." In *Essays on the History of North American Discovery and Exploration*, ed. Stanley H. Palmer and Dennis Reinhartz, xi. College Station: Texas A&M University Press,

Liszka, Kate. 2015. "Are the Bearers of the Pan-Grave Archaeological Culture Identical to the Medjay-People in the Egyptian Textual Record?" *Journal of Ancient Egyptian Interconnections* 7(2): 42–60.

Loprieno, Antonio. 2003. "Travel and Fiction in Egyptian Literature." In: *Mysterious Lands*, ed. David O'Connor and Stephen Quirke, 31–51. London: UCL Press.

MacDonald, Kevin C. 2003. "Cheikh Anta Diop and Africa." In *Ancient Egypt in Africa*, ed. David O'Connor and Andrew Reid, 93–106 London: UCL Press.

Marcus, Ezra S. 2007. "Amenemhet II and the Sea: Maritime Aspects of the Mit Rahina (Memphis) Inscription." *Ägypten und Levante* 17: 137–90.

Moje, Jan. 2003. "Die angebliche phönizische Umsegelung Afrikas im Auftrag des Pharaos Necho. Der Wahrheitsgehalt der Textstelle Hdt IV, 42." In *Ägypten und Münster. Kulturwissenschaftliche Studien zu Ägypten, dem Vorderen Orient und verwandten Gebieten. Donum natalicium viro doctissimo Erharto Graefe sexagenario ab amicis collegis discipulis ex aedibus Schlaunstraße 2/Rosenstraße 9 oblatum*, ed. Anke Ilona Blöbaum, Jochem Kahl, and Simon D. Schweitzer, 197–211. Wiesbaden: Harrassowitz.

Moran, William L. 1992. *The Amarna Letters.* Baltimore: Johns Hopkins University Press.

Morenz, Ludwig D. 2009. Review of *"Modell Ägypten." Adoption von Innovationen im Mesopotamien des 3. Jahrtausends v. Chr.,* by Oskar Kaelin: *Wiener Zeitschrift für die Kunde des Morgenlandes* 99: 399–403.

Morenz, Siegfried. 1965. "Der Alte Orient. Von Bedeutung und Struktur seiner Geschichte." In *Summa Historica. Die Grundzüge der welthistorischen Epochen,* ed. Solo Mann, Alfred Heuss, und Ernst Wilhelm Graf Lynar, 25–64. Propyläen Weltgeschichte [11]. Berlin: Propyläen Verlag.

Morris, Ellen F. 2005. *The Architecture of Imperialism: Military Bases and the Evolution of Foreign Policy in Egypt's New Kingdom.* Leiden: Brill.

Müller, Ingeborg. 2013. *Die Verwaltung Nubiens im Neuen Reich.* Meroitica, Schriften zur altsudanesischen Geschichte und Archäologie 18 (118). Wiesbaden: Harrassowitz.

Müller, Willi. 1891. *Die Umsegelung Afrikas durch phönizische Schiffe um das Jahr 600 v. Christus.* Rathenow: Max Babenzien.

Northrup, Cynthia Clark (ed.). 2005. *Encyclopedia of World Trade: From Ancient Times to the Present.* Armonk: Sharpe Reference.

O'Connor, David and Stephen Quirke. 2003. "Mapping the Unknown in Ancient Egypt." In *Mysterious Lands,* ed. David O'Connor and Stephen Quirke, 1–21. London: UCL Press.

Pierrat-Bonnefois, Geneviève. 2008. "The Tôd Treasure." In *Beyond Babylon: Art, Trade, and Diplomacy in the Second Millennium B.C.,* ed. J. Aruz, K. Benzel, and J. M. Evans. The Metropolitan Museum of Art, New York/Yale University Press, New Haven/London, 65–7.

Ray, John D. 1998. "The Marquis, the Urchin, and the Labyrinth: Egyptology and the University of Cambridge. The Steven Glanville Lecture for 1995." In *Proceedings of the Seventh International Congress of Egyptologists. Cambridge, 3–9 September 1995,* ed. C. J. Eyre, 1–17. Orientalia Lovaniensia Analecta 82. Leuven: Peeters.

Roth, Silke. 2002. *Gebieterin aller Länder. Die Rolle der königlichen Frauen in der fiktiven und realen Außenpolitik des ägyptischen Neuen Reiches.* Orbis Biblicus et Orientalis 185. Göttingen: Vandenhoeck & Ruprecht.

Schneider, Thomas. 2002. "Sinuhes Notiz über die Könige. Syrisch-anatolische Herrschertitel in ägyptischer Überlieferung." *Ägypten und Levante* 12: 257–72.

Schneider, Thomas. 2003. "Foreign Egypt: Egyptology and the Concept of Cultural Appropriation." *Ägypten und Levante* 13: 155–61.

Schneider, Thomas. 2008. "Fremdwörter in der ägyptischen Militärsprache des Neuen Reiches und ein Bravourstück des Elitesoldaten (Pap. Anastasi I 23, 2–7)." *Journal of the Society for the Study of Egyptian Antiquities* 35: 181–205.

Schneider, Thomas. 2010. "Foreigners in Egypt: Archaeological Evidence and Cultural Context." In *Egyptian Archaeology,* ed. W. Wendrich, 143–63. Blackwell Studies in Global Archaeology. Oxford: Blackwell.

Schneider, Thomas. 2010. "The West Beyond the West: The Mysterious 'Wernes' of the Egyptian Underworld and the Chad Palaeolakes." *Journal of Ancient Egyptian Interconnections* 2(4): 1–14.

Schneider, Thomas. 2011. "Egypt and the Chad: Some Additional Remarks." *Journal of Ancient Egyptian Interconnections* 3(4): 12–15.

Schneider, Thomas. 2015. "The Old Kingdom Abroad: An Epistemological Perspective. With Remarks on the Biography of Iny and the Kingdom of Dugurasu." In *Towards a New History of the Old Kingdom. Perspectives on the Pyramid Age. Proceedings of the Conference at Harvard University, April 26th, 2012*, ed. Peter Der Manuelian and Thomas Schneider, 431–57. Harvard Egyptological Studies 1. Leiden: Brill.

Schneider, Thomas. In press. "'What is the Past but a Once Material Existence Now Silenced?' The First Intermediate Period from an Epistemological Perspective." In *The Early/Middle Bronze Age Transition in the Ancient Near East: Chronology, C14, and Climate Change*, ed. Felix Höflmayer. Chicago: Oriental Institute.

Schrakamp, Ingo. 2013. "Sargon of Akkad and His Dynasty." In *The Encyclopedia of Ancient History*, ed. R. Bagnall, 6045–7. Malden: Wiley-Blackwell.

Sethe, Kurt. 1909. *Urkunden der 18. Dynastie.* Band 4. *Historisch-biographische Urkunden der 18. Dynastie. Heft 13–16. Zeit Thutmosis' III. und seiner Nachfolger.* Leipzig: Hinrichs.

Shaw, Ian. 2012. *Ancient Egyptian Technology and Innovation*. London: Bristol Classical Press.

Shortland, Andrew J. 2001. *The Social Context of Technological Change*. Oxford: Oxbow.

Sievertsen, Uwe. 2003. "Synchronismen zwischen Mesopotamien, der Levante und Ägypten in der 2. Hälfte des 4. Jts. v. Chr.: Das zeitliche Verhältnis der Uruk-Kultur und Protoelams zur Negade-Kultur." In *Altertumswissenschaften im Dialog*, ed. Wolfram Nagel, 467–512. Münster: Ugarit Verlag.

Smith, Stuart Tyson. 2003. *Wretched Kush: Ethnic Identities and Boundaries in Egypt's Nubian Empire*. London: Routledge.

Sommerfeld, Walther. 2009. "Sargon." In *Reallexikon der Assyriologie*, ed. E. Ebeling et al., Band 12, 44–9. Berlin: De Gruyter.

Sowada, Karen N. 2009. *Egypt in the Eastern Mediterranean during the Old Kingdom: An Archaeological Perspective*. With a contribution by Peter Grave. Orbis Biblicus et Orientalis 237. Fribourg: Academic Press.

SPA/Saudi Gazette. n.d. "Saudi Archeologists Discover First-ever Pharaonic Artifact." *Saudi Gazette*, <http://www.saudigazette.com.sa/index.cfm?method=home.regcon&contentID=2010110886980>, retrieved July 21, 2015.

Steel, Louise. 2007. "Egypt and the Mediterranean World." In *The Egyptian World*, ed. Toby Wilkinson, 459–76. London: Routledge.

Störk, Lotar. 1977. *Die Nashörner: Verbreitungs- und kulturgeschichtliche Materialien unter besonderer Berücksichtigung der afrikanischen Arten und des altägyptischen Kulturbereiches*. Hamburg: Born.

Suter, Claudia E. 2007. Review of *"Modell Ägypten". Adoption von Innovationen im Mesopotamien des 3. Jahrtausends v. Chr.*, by Oskar Kaelin. *Journal of the American Oriental Society* 127(3): 384–6.

Tallet, Pierre and Gregory Marouard. 2014. "The Harbor of Khufu on the Red Sea Coast at Wadi al-Jarf, Egypt." *Near Eastern Archaeology* 77(1): 4–14.

Török, László. 2009. *Between Two Worlds: The Frontier Region Between Ancient Nubia and Egypt 3700 BC–500 AD*. Probleme der Ägyptologie. Leiden: Brill.

van Koppen, Frans and Karen Radner. 2009. "Ein Tontafelfragment aus der diplomatischen Korrespondenz der Hyksosherrscher mit Babylonien." *Ägypten und Levante* 19: 115–18.

Wastlhuber, Christian. 2010. *Die Beziehungen zwischen Ägypten und der Levante während der 12. Dynastie. Ökonomie und Prestige in Außenpolitik und Handel*. PhD dissertation, Ludwig-Maximilians-Universität München: Fakultät für Kulturwissenschaften.

Webb, Walter Prescott. 2003. *The Great Frontier*. Reprint. Reno: University of Nevada Press.

Wilkinson, Toby A. H. 2002. "Uruk into Egypt: Imports and Imitations." In: *Artefacts of Complexity: Tracking the Uruk in the Near East*, ed. J. N. Postgate, 237–48. Warminster: British School of Archaeology in Iraq.

Willems, Harco. 1996. *The Coffin of Heqata (Cairo JdE 36418): A Case Study of Egyptian Funerary Culture of the Early Middle Kingdom*. Orientalia Lovaniensia Analecta 70. Leuven: Peeters.

Wright, John K.1947. "Terrae Incognitae: The Place of Imagination in Geography." *Annals of the Association of American Geographers* 37(1): 1–15.

Wollermann, Renate Müller. 2003. "'Zoologische Gärten' als Mittel der Herrschaftslegitimation im Alten Ägypten." *Die Welt des Orients* 33: 31–43.

Zivie, Alain. 2006. "Le messager royal égyptien Pirikhnawa." *British Museum Studies in Ancient Egypt and Sudan* 6: 68–78.

Creasman and Doyle, Chapter 2—Paths in the Deep . . .

Abd el-Raziq, M., G. Castel, P. Tallet, and G. Marouard. 2012. "The Pharaonic Site of Ayn Soukhna in the Gulf of Suez: 2001–2009 Progress Report." In *The Red Sea in Pharaonic Times: Recent Discoveries along the Red Sea Coast: Proceedings of the Colloquium Held in Cairo/Ayn Soukhna 11th–12th January 2009*, ed. P. Tallet and El-S. Mahfouz, 3–20. Le Caire: Institut français d'archéologie orientale.

Bard, K. A. and R. Fattovich. 2010. "Spatial Use of the Twelfth Dynasty Harbor at Mersa/Wadi Gawasis for the Seafaring Expeditions to Punt." *Journal of Ancient Egyptian Interconnections* 2(3): 1–13.

Bard, K. A. and R. Fattovich (eds.). 2007. *Harbor of the Pharaohs to the Land of Punt: Archaeological Investigations at Mersa/Wadi Gawasis, Egypt, 2001–2005*. Napoli: Istituto Universitario Orientale.

Bietak, M. 2005. "The Tuthmoside Stronghold of Perunefer." *Egyptian Archaeology* 26: 13–17.

Bietak, M. 2009. "Perunefer: The Principal New Kingdom Naval Base." *Egyptian Archaeology* 34: 15–17.

Cline, E. H. and S. M. Stannish. 2011. "Sailing the Great Green Sea? Amenhotep III's 'Aegean List' from Kom el-Hetan, Once More." *Journal of Ancient Egyptian Interconnections* 3(2): 6–16.

Creasman, P. P. 2014. "Hatshepsut and the Politics of Punt." *African Archaeological Review* 3(3): 395–405.

Creasman, P. P. and N. Doyle. 2010. "Overland Boat Transportation during the Pharaonic Period: Archaeology and Iconography." *Journal of Ancient Egyptian Interconnections* 2(3): 14–30.

Creasman, P. P. and N. Doyle. Forthcoming. *Fleets of the Pharaohs: A Maritime History of Ancient Egypt*. New York: Oxford University Press.

Darnell, J. C. 1992. "The *Kbn.wt* Vessels of the Late Period." In *Life in a Multi-cultural Society: Egypt from Cambyses to Constantine and Beyond*, ed. J. H. Johnson, 67–89. Chicago: The Oriental Institute of the University of Chicago.

Davies, N. de G. and R. O. Faulkner. 1948. "A Syrian Trading Venture in Egypt." *Journal of Egyptian Archaeology* 33: 40–6.

Day, P. M., P. S. Quinn, J. B. Rutter, and V. Kilikoglou. 2000. "A World of Goods: Transport Jars and Commodity Exchange at the Late Bronze Age Harbor of Kommos, Crete." *Hesperia* 80: 511–58.

Doyle, Noreen. 2013. "Curious Nautical Details from the Eleventh Dynasty Temple at Deir el-Bahri." In *Archaeological Research in the Valley of the Kings and Ancient Thebes: Papers Presented in Honor of Richard H. Wilkinson*, ed. P. P. Creasman, 123–47. Tucson: University of Arizona Egyptian Expedition.

Erskine, A. 2013. "Polybius and Ptolemaic Sea Power." In *The Ptolemies, the Sea and the Nile: Studies in Waterborne Power*, ed. K. Buraseis, M. Stefanou, and D. J. Thompson, 82–96. Cambridge: Cambridge University Press.

Fattovich, R. and K. A. Bard. 2012. "Archaeological Investigations at Wadi/Mersa Gawasis, Egypt: 2006–2007, 2007–2008 and 2009 Field Seasons." In *The Red Sea in Pharaonic Times: Recent Discoveries along the Red Sea Coast: Proceedings of the Colloquium Held in Cairo/Ayn Soukhna 11th–12th January 2009*, ed. P. Tallet, and El-S. Mahfouz, 21–6. Le Caire: Institut français d'archéologie orientale.

Fattovich, R. and K. A. Bard. 2012. "Ships Bound for Punt." In *The Red Sea in Pharaonic Times: Recent Discoveries along the Red Sea Coast: Proceedings of the Colloquium Held in Cairo/Ayn Soukhna 11th–12th January 2009*, ed. P. Tallet, and El-S. Mahfouz, 27–33. Le Caire: Institut français d'archéologie orientale.

Forstner-Müller. 2014. "Avaris, Its Harbours and the Perunefer Problem." *Egyptian Archaeology* 45: 32–5.

Goedicke, H. 1975. *The Report of Wenamun*. Baltimore: The Johns Hopkins University Press.

Goldwasser, O. and E. D. Oren. 2015. "Marine Units on the 'Ways Of Horus' in the Days of Seti I." *Journal of Ancient Egyptian Interconnections* 7(1): 25–38.

Grajetzki, W. 2006. *The Middle Kingdom of Ancient Egypt: History, Archaeology and Society*. London: Duckworth.

Grandet, P. 1994. *Le Papyrus Harris I (BM 9999)*. 2 vols. Le Caire: Institut français d'archéologie orientale.

Habachi, L. 1972. *The Second Stela of Kamose and His Struggle against the Hyksos Ruler and His Capital*. Glückstadt: J. J. Augustin.

Hoffmeier, J. K. (ed.). 2014. *Tell el-Borg I: The "Dwelling of the Lion" on the Ways of Horus*. Winona Lake: Eisenbrauns.

Jeffreys, D. 2006. "Perunefer: At Memphis or Avaris?" *Egyptian Archaeology* 28: 36–7.

Mahfouz, El-S. 2012. "New Epigraphic Material from Wadi Gawasis." In *The Red Sea in Pharaonic Times: Recent Discoveries along the Red Sea Coast: Proceedings of the Colloquium Held in Cairo/Ayn Soukhna 11th–12th January 2009*, ed. P. Tallet, and El-S. Mahfouz, 117–32. Le Caire: Institut français d'archéologie orientale.

Marcus, E. 2002. "Early Seafaring and Maritime Activity in the Southern Levant from Prehistory through the Third Millennium BCE." In *Egypt and the Levant: Interrelations from the 4th through the Early 3rd Millennium BCE*, ed. E. C. M. van den Brink and T. E. Levy, 403–17. London: Leicester University Press.

Marcus, E. 2007. "Amenemhet II and the Sea: Maritime Aspects of the Mit Rahina (Memphis) Inscription." *Ägypten und Levante* 17: 137–90.

Mumford, G. 2006. "Tell Ras Budran (Site 345): Defining Egypt's Eastern Frontier and Mining Operations in South Sinai during the Late Old Kingdom (Early EB IV/MB I)." *Bulletin of the American Schools of Oriental Research* 342: 13–67.

Parcak, S. 2004. "Egypt's Old Kingdom 'Empire' (?): A Case Study Focusing on South Sinai." In *Egypt, Israel, and the Ancient Mediterranean World: Studies in Honor of Donald B. Redford*, ed. G. N. Knoppers and A. Hirsch, 41–60. Leiden: Brill.

Phillips, J. 2008. *Aegyptiaca on the Island of Crete in Their Chronological Context: A Critical Review*. 2 vols. Wien: Verlag der Österreichischen Akademie der Wissenschaften.

Porten, B. 1996. *The Elephantine Papyri in English: Three Millennia of Cross-cultural Continuity and Change*. Leiden: Brill.

Pulak, C. 2008. "The Uluburun Shipwreck and Late Bronze Age Trade." In *Beyond Babylon: Art, Trade, and Diplomacy in the Second Millennium B.C.*, ed. J. Aruz, K. Benzel, and J. M. Evans, 288–310. New York: The Metropolitan Museum of Art.

Quirke, S. 2009. "Sehel and Suez: Canal-cutting and Periodisation in Ancient and Modern History." In *Das Ereignis: Geschichtsschreibung zwischen Vorfall und Befund, Workshop vom 03.10. bis 05.10.08*, ed. M. Fitzenreiter, 223–30. London: Golden House.

Redford, D. B. 1986. "Egypt and Western Asia in the Old Kingdom." *Journal of the American Research Center in Egypt* 23: 125–43.

Roy, J. 2011. *The Politics of Trade: Egypt and Lower Nubia in the 4th Millennium BC*. Leiden: Brill.

Ryholt, K. S. B. 1997. *The Political Situation in Egypt during the Second Intermediate Period c.1800–1550 BC*. Copenhagen: The Carsten Niebuhr Institute of Near Eastern Studies, University of Copenhagen.

Säve-Söderbergh, T. 1946. *The Navy of the Eighteenth Egyptian Dynasty*. Uppsala: Lundequistska Bokhandeln.

Sayed, A. M. A. H. 1977. "Discovery of the Site of the 12th Dynasty Port at Wadi Gawasis on the Red Sea Shore (Preliminary Report on the Excavations of the Faculty of Arts, University of Alexandria, in the Eastern Desert of Egypt—March 1976)." *Revue d'égyptologie* 29: 138–78.

Somaglino, C. and P. Tallet. 2011. "Une mystérieuse route sud-orientale sous le règne de Ramsès III." *Bulletin de l'Institut français d'archéologie orientale* 111: 361–9.

Somaglino, C. and P. Tallet. 2015. "Une campagne en Nubie sous la Ire dynastie: la scène nagadienne du Gebel Sheikh Suleiman comme prototype et modèle." *NeHeT* 1: 1–46.

Sowada, K. N. 2009. *Egypt in the Eastern Mediterranean during the Old Kingdom: An Archaeological Perspective*. Fribourg; Göttingen: Academic Press.

Snape, S. 2013. "A Stroll along the Corniche? Coastal Routes between the Nile Delta and Cyrenaica in the Late Bronze Age." In *Desert Road Archaeology in Ancient Egypt and Beyond*, ed. F. Förster and H. Riemer, 439–59. Köln: Heinrich-Barth-Institut.

Stager, L. E. 2001. "Port Power in the Early and the Middle Bronze Age: The Organization of Maritime Trade and Hinterland Production." In *Studies in the Archaeology of Israel and Neighboring Lands in Memory of Douglas L. Esse*, ed. S. R. Wolff, 625–57. Chicago: Oriental Institute.

Strudwick, N. C. 2005. *Texts from the Pyramid Age*. Atlanta: Society of Biblical Literature; Brill.

Tallet, P. 2012. "Ayn Sukhna and Wadi el-Jarf: Two Newly Discovered Pharaonic Harbours on the Suez Gulf." *British Museum Studies in Ancient Egypt and Sudan* 18: 147–68.

Tallet, P. 2012. "Sur la fondation de la ville de Memphis au début de l'histoire pharaonique de nouvelles données au Oudi 'Ameyra (Sud-Sinaï)." *Comptes rendus de l'Académie des inscriptions et belles-lettres* 2012 (IV): 1649–58.

Tallet, P. 2012. "New Inscriptions from Ayn Soukhna: 2002–2009." In *The Red Sea in Pharaonic Times: Recent Discoveries along the Red Sea Coast: Proceedings of the Colloquium Held in Cairo/Ayn Soukhna 11th–12th January 2009*, ed. P. Tallet and El-S. Mahfouz, 105–15. Le Caire: Institut français d'archéologie orientale.

Tallet, P. 2012. *La zone minière pharaonique du Sud-Sinaï I: Catalogue complémentaire des inscriptions du Sinaï.* 2 vols. Le Caire: Institut français d'archéologie orientale.

Tallet, P. 2013. "The Wadi el-Jarf Site: A Harbor of Khufu on the Red Sea." *Journal of Ancient Egyptian Interconnections* 5(1): 76–84.

Tallet, P. and D. Laisney. 2012. "Iry-Hor et Narmer au Sud-Sinaï (Ouadi 'Ameyra): un complément à la chronologie des expéditions minières égyptiennes." *Bulletin de l'Institut français d'archéologie orientale* 112: 381–98.

Tallet, P. and G. Marouard. 2012. "An Early Pharaonic Harbour on the Red Sea Coast." *Egyptian Archaeology* 40: 40–3.

Tallet, P. and G. Marouard. 2014. "The Harbor of Khufu on the Red Sea Coast at Wadi al-Jarf, Egypt." *Near Eastern Archaeology* 77(1): 4–14.

Török, L. 2009. *Between Two Worlds: The Frontier Region between Ancient Nubia and Egypt 3700 BC–500 AD.* Leiden: Brill.

Tuplin, C. 1991. "Darius's Suez Canal and Persian Imperialism." In *Achaemenid History IV: Asia Minor and Egypt: Old Cultures in a New Empire: Proceedings of the Groningen 1988 Achaemenid History Workshop*, ed. H. Sancisi-Weedenburg and A. Kuhrt, 237–83. Leiden: Nederlands Instituut voor Het Nabijue Oosten.

von Bomhard, A.-S. 2012. *The Decree of Saïs: The Stelae of Thonis-Heracleion and Naukratis.* Oxford: School of Archaeology, University of Oxford.

Wachsmann, S. 1998. *Seagoing Ships and Seamanship in the Bronze Age Levant.* College Station: Texas A&M University Press.

Ward, C. A. 2004. "Boatbuilding in Ancient Egypt." In *The Philosophy of Shipbuilding*, ed. F. M. Hocker and C. A. Ward, 13–24. College Station: Texas A&M University Press.

Ward, W. A. 1969. "The Nomarch Khnumḥotep at Pelusium." *Journal of Egyptian Archaeology* 55: 215–16.

Warren, P. 1995. "Minoan Crete and Pharaonic Egypt." In *Egypt, the Aegean and the Levant: Interconnections in the Second Millennium BC*, ed. W. V. Davies and L. Schofield, 1–18. London: The British Museum Press.

White, Donald (ed.). 2002. *Marsa Matruh: The University of Pennsylvania Museum of Archaeology and Anthropology's Excavations on Bates's Island, Marsa Matruh, Egypt 1985–1989.* 2 vols. Philadelphia: Institute for Aegean Prehistory Press.

Wilkinson, T. A. H. 1999. *Early Dynastic Egypt.* London: Routledge.

Wilkinson, T. A. H. 2000. *Royal Annals of Ancient Egypt: The Palermo Stone and Its Associated Fragments.* London; New York: Kegan Paul International.

Mumford, Chapter 3—Pathways to Distant Kingdoms . . .

Adams, Russell B. (ed.). 2008. *Jordan: An Archaeological Reader.* London: Equinox.

Aharoni, Yohanan. 1979. *The Land of the Bible: A Historical Geography.* Translated by A. F. Rainey. London: Burns and Oates.

Akkermans, P. M. M. G. and G. M. Schwarz. 2003. *The Archaeology of Syria: From Complex Hunter-Gatherers to Early Urban Societies (ca. 16,000–300 BC).* Cambridge: Cambridge University Press.

Arnold, Dieter. 1991. *Building in Egypt: Pharaonic Stone Masonry.* Oxford: Oxford University Press.

Aruz, J., S. B. Graff, and Y. Rakic (eds.). 2013. *Cultures in Contact: From Mesopotamia to the Mediterranean in the Second Millennium B.C.* New York: The Metropolitan Museum of Art.

Bagnell, R., K. Brodersen, C. Champion, A. Erskine, and S. Huebner (eds.). 2013. *Encyclopaedia of Ancient History.* Oxford: Wiley-Blackwell Publishing Ltd.

Baines, J. and J. Malek. 2000. *Atlas of Ancient Egypt.* Revised ed. Oxford: Phaidon Press Ltd.

Bard, K. A. and R. Fattovich (eds.). 2007. *Harbor of the Pharaohs to the Land of Punt: Archaeological Investigations at Mersa/Wadi Gawasis Egypt, 2001–2005.* Napoli: Universita Degli Studi di Napoli "l'Orientale."

Bard, K. and S. Shubert (eds.). 1999. *Encyclopedia of the Archaeology of Ancient Egypt.* London: Routledge.

Barnard, Hans and Kim Duistermaat (eds.). 2012. *The History of the Peoples of the Eastern Desert.* UCLA Cotsen Institute of Archaeology Monograph 73. Los Angeles: Cotsen Institute of Archaeology Press.

Bienkowski, P. and K. Galor (eds.). 2006. *Crossing the Rift: Resources, Routes, Settlement Patterns and Interactions in the Wadi Arabah.* Levant Supplementary Series 3. Oxford: Oxbow Books.

Bryce, Trevor (ed.). 2009. *The Routledge Handbook of the Peoples and Places of Ancient Western Asia: The Near East from the Early Bronze Age to the Fall of the Persian Empire.* London: Routledge.

Cohen, Raymond and Raymond Westbrook (eds.). 2000. *Amarna Diplomacy: The Beginnings of International Relations.* Baltimore: John Hopkins University Press.

Darnell, John Coleman. 2013. *Theban Desert Road Survey II: The Rock Shrine of Pahu, Gebel Akhenaton, and Other Rock Inscriptions from the Western Hinterland of Qamula.* Yale Egyptological Publications 1. New Haven: Yale Egyptological Institute.

Dorsey, David A. 1992. *The Roads and Highways of Ancient Israel.* Baltimore: Johns Hopkins University Press.

Finneran, Niall. 2007. *The Archaeology of Ethiopia.* London: Routledge.

Fisher, Marjorie M., Peter Lacovara, Salilma Ikram, and Sue D'Auria (eds.). 2012. *Ancient Nubia: African Kingdoms of the Nile.* Cairo: The American University in Cairo Press.

Förster, Frank and Heiko Riemer (eds.). 2013. *Desert Road Archaeology in Egypt and Beyond.* Africa Praehistorica 27. Köln: Heinrich-Barth Institut.

Franke, U., J. Gierlichs, S. Vassilopoulou, and L. Wagner (eds.). 2011. *Roads of Arabia: The Archaeological Treasures of Saudi Arabia,* Translated by L. Schilcher and M. Marx. Berlin: Ernst Wasmuth Verlag Tübingen and Staatliche Museen zu Berlin.

Friedman, Renee (ed.). 2002. *Egypt and Nubia: Gifts of the Desert.* London: British Museum Press.

Gardiner, Alan H. 1920. "The Ancient Military Road between Egypt and Palestine." *Journal of Egyptian Archaeology* 6: 99–116.

Gerharz, Rudolf. 1994. *Jebel Moya.* Meroitica: Schriften zur altsudanesischen Geschichte und Archäologie 14. Berlin: Akademie Verlag.

Gunter, A. C. (ed.). 2005. *Caravan Kingdoms: Yemen and the Ancient Incense Trade.* Washington: Arthur M. Sackler Gallery.

Hamblin, W. J. 2006. *Warfare in the Ancient Near East to 1600 BC: Holy Warriors at the Dawn of History.* London: Routledge.

Higginbotham, Carolyn R. 2000. *Egyptianization and Elite Emulation in Ramesside Palestine: Governance and Accommodation on the Imperial Periphery.* Culture and History of the Ancient Near East 2. Leiden: Brill.

Hussein, Hesham and Elsayed, Abdel Alim. 2015. "The Way(s) of Horus in the Saite Period: Tell el-Kedwa and Its Key Location Guarding Egypt's Northeastern Frontier." *Journal of Ancient Egyptian Interconnections* 7(1): 1–13.

Jackson, Robert B. 2002. *At Empire's Edge: Exploring Rome's Egyptian Frontier.* New Haven: Yale University.

Kemp, Barry J. 2006. *Ancient Egypt: Anatomy of a Civilization.* 2nd edition. London: Routledge.

Kendall, Timothy. 1997. *Kerma and the Kingdom of Kush 2500–1500 BC: The Archaeological Discovery of an Ancient Nubian Empire.* Washington: National Museum of African Art.

Klemm, Rosemarie and Dietrich D. Klemm. 2008. *Stones and Quarries in Ancient Egypt.* London: The British Museum Press.

Klemm, Rosemarie and Dietrich Klemm. 2013. *Gold and Gold Mining in Ancient Egypt and Nubia: Geoarchaeology of the Ancient Gold Mining Sites in the Egyptian and Sudanese Eastern Deserts.* Translated by P. Larsen. London: Springer-Verlag.

Klotz, David. 2013. "Administration of the Deserts and Oases: First Millennium B.C.E." In *Ancient Egyptian Administration*, ed. Juan Carlos Moreno-Garcia, 901–9. Handbook of Oriental Studies 104. Leiden: Brill Academic Publishers.

Kousoulis, P. and K. Magliveras (eds.). 2007. *Moving Across Borders: Foreign Relations, Religion and Cultural Interactions in the Ancient Mediterranean.* Orientalia Lovaniensia Analecta 159. Leuven: Uitgeverij Peeters.

Levy, Thomas E. 2007. *Journey to the Copper Age: Archaeology in the Holy Land.* San Diego: San Diego Museum of Man.

Littauer, Mary A. and Joost H. Crouwel. 1979. *Wheeled Vehicles and Ridden Animals in the Ancient Near East.* Handbuch der Orientalistik: Kunst und Archäologie 7. Leiden: Brill.

Lloyd, Alan B. (ed.). 2010. *A Companion to Ancient Egypt.* Malden: Wiley-Blackwell.

Lunde, Paul and Alexandra Porter (eds.). 2004. *Trade and Travel in the Red Sea Region. Proceedings of Red Sea Project I. Held in the British Museum, October 2002.* BAR International Series 1269. Oxford: Archaeopress.

Mallinson, M. D. S., L. M. V. Smith, S. Ikram, C. Le Quesne, and P. Sheehan (eds.). 1996. *Road Archaeology in the Middle Nile*, Volume 1: *The SARS Survey from Bagrawya-Meroe to Atbara 1993.* London: The Sudan Archaeological Research Society.

Martin, Geoffrey T. 1991. *The Hidden Tombs of Memphis: New Discoveries from the Time of Tutankhamun.* London: Thames and Hudson.

Meyers, Eric M. (ed.). 1997. *The Oxford Encyclopedia of Archaeology in the Near East.* 5 vols. New York: Oxford University Press.

Mitchell, Peter. 2005. *African Connections: Archaeological Perspectives on Africa and the Wider World.* Walnut Creek: Alta Mira Press.

Monnier, Franck. 2010. *Les Forteresses égyptiennes du Predynastique au Nouvel Empire.* Connaissance de l'Egypte ancienne 11. Bruxelles: Editions Safran.

Moran, William L. 1992. *The Amarna Letters.* Baltimore: The Johns Hopkins University Press.

Morris, Ellen Fowles. 2005. *The Architecture of Imperialism: Military Bases and the Evolution of Foreign Policy in Egypt's New Kingdom.* Probleme der Agyptologie 22. Leiden: Brill.

Mumford, Gregory. 2007. "Egypto-Asiatic Relations during the Iron Age to Early Persian Periods (Egyptian Dynasties Late 20–26)." In *Egyptian Stories: A British Egyptological Tribute to Alan B. Lloyd on the Occasion of His Retirement,* ed. T. Schneider and K. Szpakowska, 225–88. Alter Orient und Altes Testament Band 347. Münster: Ugarit-Verlag.

Mumford, Gregory. 2012. "Ras Budran and the Old Kingdom Trade in Red Sea Shells and Other Exotica." *British Museum Studies in Ancient Egypt and Sudan* 18: 107–45.

Mumford, Gregory. 2014. "Egypt and the Levant." In *The Oxford Handbook of the Archaeology of the Levant c.8000–332 BCE,* ed. M. Steiner and A. E. Killebrew, 69–89. Oxford: Oxford University Press.

Mumford, Gregory. 2015. "The Sinai Peninsula and Its Environs: Our Changing Perceptions of a Pivotal Land Bridge between Egypt, the Levant, and Arabia." *Journal of Ancient Egyptian Interconnections* 7(1): 1–24.

Mumford, Gregory. 2015. "The Amman Airport Structure: A Re-assessment of Its Date-range, Function and Overall Role in the Levant." In *Walls of the Prince: Egyptian Interactions with Southwest Asia in Antiquity: Essays in Honour of John S. Holladay, Jr.,* ed. Timothy P. Harrison, Edward B. Banning, and Stanley Klassen, 89–198. Culture and History of the Ancient Near East. Leiden: Brill.

Mynářová, Jana (ed.). 2011. *Egypt and the Near East: Proceedings of an International Conference on the Relations of Egypt and the Near East in the Bronze Age, Prague, September 1–3, 2010.* Prague: Charles University in Prague.

Nicholson, Paul T. and Ian Shaw (eds.). 2000. *Ancient Egyptian Materials and Technology.* Cambridge: Cambridge University Press.

O'Connor, David. 2014. *The Old Kingdom Town at Buhen.* EES Excavation Memoir 106. London: Egypt Exploration Society.

O'Connor, David and Andrew Reid (eds.). 2003. *Ancient Egypt in Africa.* Walnut Creek: Left Coast Press.

O'Connor, David and Quirke, Stephan (eds.). 2003. *Mysterious Lands.* London: University College London Press.

Oppenheim, A., Do. Arnold, D. Arnold, and K. Yamamoto (eds.). 2015. *Ancient Egypt Transformed: The Middle Kingdom.* New York: The Metropolitam Museum of Art/Yale University Press.

Partridge, Robert B. 1996. *Transport in Ancient Egypt.* London: The Rubicon Press.

Peden, Alexander J. 2001. *The Graffiti of Pharaonic Egypt: Scope and Roles of Informal Writings (c.3100–332 BC).* Probleme der Ägyptologie 17. Leiden: Brill.

Radner, Karen (ed.). 2014. *State Correspondence in the Ancient World: From New Kingdom Egypt to the Roman Empire.* Oxford: Oxford University Press.

Redford, Donald B. (ed.). 2001. *The Oxford Encyclopedia of Ancient Egypt.* 3 vols. New York: Oxford University Press.

Régen, Isabelle and Georges Soukiassian. 2008. *Gebel el-Zeit II. Le Matérial Inscrit. Moyen Empire—Nouvel Empire.* Fouilles de l'Institut français d'archeologie orientale du Caire 57. Le Caire: l'Institut français d'archeologie orientale du Caire.

Roaf, Michael. 1990. *Cultural Atlas of Mesopotamia and the Ancient Near East.* New York: Facts on File, Inc.

Roy, Jane. 2011. *The Politics of Trade: Egypt and Nubia in the 4th Millennium BC.* Culture and History of the Ancient Near East 47. Leiden: Brill.

Ruzicka, Stephen. 2012. *Trouble in the West: Egypt and the Persian Empire 525–332 BCE.* Oxford: Oxford University Press.

Sasson, Jack M. (ed.). 1995. *Civilizations of the Ancient Near East.* 4 vols. Peabody: Hendrickson Publishers, Inc.

Sidebotham, Steven, Martin Hense, and Hendrikje Nouwens. 2008. *The Red Land: The Illustrated Archaeology of Egypt's Eastern Desert.* Cairo: The American University in Cairo Press.

Simpson, W. K. (ed.). 2003. *The Literature of Ancient Egypt: An Anthology of Stories, Instructions, Stelae, Autobiographies, and Poetry.* Third ed. New Haven: Yale University Press.

Smith, Stuart Tyson. 2003. *Wretched Kush: Ethnic Identities and Boundaries in Egypt's Nubian Empire.* New York: Routledge.

Snape, Steven. 2014. *The Complete Cities of Ancient Egypt.* London: Thames and Hudson.

Sowada, Karin N. 2009. *Egypt in the Eastern Mediterranean during the Old Kingdom: An Archaeological Perspective.* Orbis Biblicus et Orientalis 237. Freiburg: Vandenhoeck & Ruprecht Gottingen.

Spalinger, Anthony J. 2005. *War in Ancient Egypt.* Oxford: Blackwell Publishing.

Starkey, J., P. Starkey, and T. Wilkinson (eds.). 2007. *Natural Resources and Cultural Connections of the Red Sea.* BAR International Series 1661. Oxford: Archaeopress.

Stern, Ephraim. 2001. *Archaeology of the Land of the Bible*, Volume II: *The Assyrian, Babylonian, and Persian Periods (732–332 B.C.E.).* New York: Doubleday.

Stern, E., A. Lewinson-Gilboa, J. Aviram, G. Hillel, and A. Paris (eds.). 1993–2008. *The New Encyclopedia of Archaeological Excavations in the Holy Land.* 5 vols. New York: Simon and Schuster.

Tallet, Pierre et al. 2012. *La Zone Minière Pharaonique du Sud-Sinaï*, Tome I: *Catalogue complémentaire des inscriptions du Sinaï (Texte et Planches).* Memoires de l'Institut francais d'archeologie orientale du Caire 130. Paris: Institut francais d'archeologie orientale.

Teeter, E. (ed.). 2011. *Before the Pyramids: The Origins of Egyptian Civilization.* Oriental Institute Museum Publications 33. Chicago: The Oriental Institute of the University of Chicago.

Török, László. 1997. *The Kingdom of Kush: Handbook of the Napatan-Meroitic Civilization.* Handbuch der Orientalistik 31. Leiden: Brill.

Török, László. 2009. *Between Two Worlds: The Frontier Region Between Ancient Nubia and Egypt 3700 BC–500 AD.* Probleme der Agyptologie 29. Leiden: Brill.

van den Brink, Edwin C. M. and Thomas E. Levy (eds.). 2002. *Egypt and the Levant: Interrelations from the 4th through the Early 3rd Millennium BCE.* London: Leicester University Press.

van Neer, W., O. Lernau, R. Friedman, G. Mumford, J. Poblome, J., and M. Waelkens. 2004. "Fish Remains from Archaeological Sites as Indicators of Former Trade Connections in the Eastern Mediterranean." *Paléorient* 30(1): 101–48.

Vogel, Carola. 2010. *The Fortifications of Ancient Egypt 3000–1780 BC.* Fortress 98. Oxford: Osprey Publishing Ltd.

Wilkinson, Toby (ed.). 2007. *The Egyptian World.* The Routledge Worlds. New York: Routledge.

Zohary, Daniel, Maria Hopf, and Ehud Weiss (eds.). 2012. *Domestication of Plants in the Old World: The Origin and Spread of Domesticated Plants in South-west Asia, Europe, and the Mediterranean Basin.* 4th ed. Oxford: Oxford University Press.

Bader, Chapter 4—Children of Other Gods . . .

Altenmüller, Hartwig. 2015. *Zwei Annalenfragmente aus dem frühen Mittleren Reich.* Beihefte zu Studien der altägyptischen Kultur 16. Hamburg: Helmut Buske.

Bader, Bettina. 2013. "Cultural Mixing in Egyptian Archaeology: The 'Hyksos' as a Case Study." *Archaeological Review from Cambridge Issue* 28(1): 257–86.

Bader, Bettina. 2015. "Egypt and the Bronze Age Mediterranean: The Archaeological Evidence." *Oxford Handbooks Online*, ed. C. Riggs. DOI: 10.1093/oxfordhb/9780199935413.013.35.

Bhabha, Homi K. 1995. *The Location of Culture.* 2nd reprint. London: Routledge.

Bietak, Manfred. 1988. "Zur Marine des Alten Reiches." In *Pyramid Studies and Other Essays Presented to I. E. S. Edwards*, ed. J. Baines, T. G. H. James, A. Leahy, and A. F. Shore, 35–40. London: Egypt Exploration Society.

Bietak, Manfred. 1996. *Avaris: The Capital of the Hyksos: Recent Excavations at Tell el-Dab'a.* London: British Museum Press.

Bietak, Manfred. 2007. "Egypt and the Levant." In *The Egyptian World*, ed. T. Wilkinson, 417–48. London: Routledge.

Cohen, Susan L. 2015. "Interpretative Uses and Abuses of the Beni Hasan Tomb Painting." *Journal of Near Eastern Studies* 74: 19–38.

Czerny, Ernst. 1999. *Tell el-Daba*, Volume IX. *Eine Plansiedlung des frühen Mittleren Reiches.* Untersuchungen der Zweigstelle Kairo 15. Vienna: Austrian Academy of Sciences.

Czerny, Ernst. 2015. *Tell el-Daba*, Volume XXII. *Der Mund der beiden Wege. Die Siedlung und der Tempelbezirk des Mittleren Reiches von Ezbet Ruschdi.* Untersuchungen der Zweigstelle Kairo 38. Vienna: Austrian Academy of Sciences.

David, Arlette. 2014. "Identification in Ancient Egypt from the Old Kingdom to the End of the New Kingdom (2650–1100 BCE)." In *Identifiers and Identification, Methods in the Ancient World*, ed. M. Depauw and S. Coussement, 57–74. Orientalia Lovaniensia Analecta 229. Leuven: Peeters.

de Miroschedji, Pierre. 2002. "The Socio-Political Dynamics of Egyptian-Canaanite Interaction in the Early Bronze Age." In *Egypt and the Levant, Interrelations from the 4th through to the 3rd Millennium BC*, ed. E. C. M. van den Brink and T. E. Levy, 39–57. London: Leicester University Press.

de Souza, Aaron. 2013. "The Egyptianisation of the Pan-grave Culture: A New Look at an Old Idea." *Bulletin of the Australian Centre for Egyptology* 24: 109–26.

Goldwasser, Orly. 2012–2013. "Out of the Mists of the Alphabet—Redrawing the 'Brother of the Ruler of Retenu.'" *Egypt and the Levant* 22/23: 353–74.

Hallmann, Silke. 2006. *Die Tributszenen des Neuen Reiches.* Ägypten und Altes Testament 66. Wiesbaden: Harassowitz.

Hartung, Ulrich. 2001. *Umm el-Qaab*, Volume II. *Importkeramik aus dem Friedhof U in Abydos und die Beziehungen Ägyptens to Vorderasien im 4. Jahrtausend v. Chr.* Archäologische Veröffentlichungen 92. Mainz: Phillip von Zabern.

Hayes, William C. 1955. *A Late Middle Kingdom Papyrus in the Brooklyn Museum.* Brooklyn: Brooklyn Museum.

Hendrickx, Stan and L. Bavay. 2002. "The Relative Chronological Position of Egyptian Predynastic and Early Dynastic Tombs with Objects Imported from the Near East and the Nature of Interregional Contacts." In *Egypt and the Levant, Interrelations from the 4th through to the 3rd Millennium BC*, ed. E. M. C. van den Brink and T. E. Levy, 58–80. London: Leicester University Press.

Kamrin, Janice. 2013. "The Procession of 'Asiatics' at Beni Hasan." In *Cultures in Contact. From Mesopotamia to the Mediterranean in the Second Millennium B.C.*, ed. J. Aruz, S. B. Graff, and Y. Rakic, 156–69. New York: Metropolitan Museum of Art.

Koenig, Yvan. 1990. "Les textes d'envoûtement de Mirgissa." *Revue d'égyptologie* 41: 101–25.

Levy, Thomas E. and E. C. M. van den Brink. 2002. "Interaction Models, Egypt and the Levantine Periphery." In *Egypt and the Levant, Interrelations from the 4th through to the 3rd Millennium BC*, ed. E. C. M. van den Brink and T. E. Levy, 3–38. London: Leicester University Press.

Lichtheim, Miriam. 1976. *Ancient Egyptian Literature*, Volume II. *The New Kingdom.* Berkeley: University of California Press.

Liszka, Kate. 2012. *"We Have Come to Serve Pharaoh": A Study of the Medjay and Pan-Grave as an Ethnic Group as Mercenaries from c.2300 BCE until c.1050 BCE.* PhD dissertation, University of Pennsylvania.

Loprieno, Antonio. 1988. *Topos und Mimesis. Zum Ausländer in der ägyptischen Literatur.* Ägyptologische Abhandlungen 48. Wiesbaden: Harrassowitz.

Loprieno, Antonio. 1992. "Der Sklave." Translated by Asa-Bettina Wuthenow. In *Der Mensch des Alten Ägypten*, ed. S. Donadoni, 222–59. Paris: Campus Verlag/Éditions de la Maison des sciences de l'homme.

Luft, Ulrich. 1993. "Asiatics in Illahun: A Preliminary Report." In *Atti Sesto Congresso Internazionale di Egittologia*, ed. Comitato Organizzativo del Congresso, volume II, 291–7. Societa Italiana per il Gas p. A., Torino: Tipografia Torinese—Stabilimento Poligrafico S.p.A., 1993.

Maczynska, Agnieszka. 2008. "Some Remarks on Egyptian-Southern Levantine Interrelations." In *Egypt at its Origins 2*, ed. B. Midant-Reynes and Y. Tristan, 763–81. Orientalia Lovaniensia Analecta 172. Leuven: Peeters.

MacSweeney, Naoíse. 2009. "Beyond Ethnicity: The Overlooked Diversity of Group Identities." *Journal of Mediterranean Archaeology* 22(1): 101–26.

Moers, Gerald. 2015. "'Egyptian Identity'? Unlikely, and Never National." In *Fuzzy Boundaries: Festschrift for Antonio Loprieno*, ed. H. Amstutz, A. Dorn, M. Müller, M. Ronsdorf, and S. Uljas, volume 2, 693–704. Hamburg: Widmaier Verlag.

Müller, Vera. 2014. "Relations between Egypt and the Near East during the First Egyptian Dynasty as Represented by the Royal Tomb of Den at Umm el-Qaab/Abydos." In *Egypt and the Southern Levant in the Early Bronze Age*, ed. F. Höflmayer, R. Eichmann, 241–58. Rahden/Westf.: Deutsches Archäologisches Institut, Orient-Abteilung Band 31, Verlag Marie Leidorf GmbH.

Porat, Naomi. 1986–1987. "Local Industry of Egyptian Pottery in Southern Palestine During the Early Bronze I Period." *Bulletin of the Egyptological Seminar* 8: 109–29.

Posener, Georges. 1940. *Princes et pays d'Asie et de Nubie. Textes hieratiques sur des figurines d'envoutement du Moyen Empire*. Bruxelles: Fondation égyptologique reine Élisabeth.

Raue, Dietrich. 2008. "Who Was Who in Elephantine in the Third Millennium BC?" *British Museum Studies in Ancient Egypt and Sudan* 9: 1–14.

Reeves, Nicholas and Richard H. Wilkinson. 1996. *The Complete Valley of the Kings*. London: Thames and Hudson.

Sass, Benjamin. 1988. *The Genesis of the Alphabet and Its Development in the Second Millennium B.C.* Ägypten und Altes Testament 13. Wiesbaden: Harassowitz.

Säve-Söderbergh, Torgny. 1975. "Bogenvölker." In *Lexikon der Ägyptologie*, ed. W. Helck, and E. Otto, volume 1, cols. 845–6. Wiesbaden: Harassowitz.

Schneider, Thomas. 2003. *Ausländer in Ägypten während des Mittleren Reiches und der Hyksoszeit. Die ausländische Bevölkerung*. Ägypten und Altes Testament 42/2. Wiesbaden: Harrassowitz.

Smith, Stewart Tyson. 2003. *Wretched Kush: Ethnic Identities and Boundaries in Egypt's Nubian Empire*. London: Routledge.

Smith, Stewart Tyson. 2007. "Ethnicity and Culture." In *The Egyptian World*, ed. T. Wilkinson, 218–41. London; New York: Routledge, 2007.

Sowada, Karin. 2009. *Egypt in the Eastern Mediterranean during the Old Kingdom: An Archaeological Perspective*. Orbis Biblicus et Orientalis 237. Göttingen: Academic Press Fribourg, Vandenhoeck & Ruprecht.

Sparks, Rachael T. 2004. "Canaan in Egypt: Archaeological Evidence for a Social Phenomenon." In *Invention and Innovation, The Social Context of Technological Change 2, Egypt, the Aegean and the Near East, 1650–1150 BC*, ed. J. Bourriau and J. Phillips, 25–54. Oxford: Oxbow.

Stockhammer, Philip W. 2012. "Conceptualizing Cultural Hybridization in Archaeology." In *Conceptualizing Cultural Hybridization: A Transdisciplinary Approach*, ed. P. W. Stockhammer, 43–58. Berlin: Springer.

van den Brink, Edwin C. M. and E. Braun. 2003. "Egyptian Elements and Influence on the Early Bronze Age I of the Southern Levant: Recent Excavations, Research and Publications." *Archéo-Nil* 13, 77–91.

Vittmann, Günter. 2003. *Ägypten und die Fremden im ersten vorchristlichen Jahrtausend*. Mainz: Philipp von Zabern.

Wilkinson and Doyle, Chapter 5—Between Brothers . . .

Abbas, R. A. 2013. "A Survey of the Diplomatic Role of the Charioteers in the Ramesside Period." In *Chasing Chariots: Proceedings of the First International Chariot Conference (Cairo 2012)*, ed. A. J. Veldmeijer and S. Ikram, 17–27. Leiden: Sidestone Press.

Aruz, J., K. Benzel, and J. M. Evans (eds.). 2008. *Beyond Babylon: Art, Trade, and Diplomacy in the Second Millennium B.C.* New York: The Metropolitan Museum of Art.

Bahr, S., D. Kahn, and J. J. Shirley (eds.). 2011. *Egypt, Canaan and Israel: History, Imperialism, Ideology and Literature. Proceedings of Conference at the University of Haifa, 3–7 May, 2009*. Leiden: Brill.

Beckman, G. 1996. *Hittite Diplomatic Texts.* Atlanta: Scholars Press.

Beckman, G. 1999. *Hittite Diplomatic Texts.* 2nd ed. Atlanta: Scholars Press.

Berridge, G. 2000. "Amarna Diplomacy: A Full-fledged Diplomatic System?" In *Amarna Diplomacy: The Beginnings of International Relations,* ed. R. Cohen and R. Westbrook, 212–24. Baltimore: Johns Hopkins University Press.

Bietak, M., N. Math, and V. Müller. 2012. "Report on the Excavations of a Hyksos Palace at Tell el-Dab'a/Avaris (23rd August–15th November 2011)." *Ägypten und Levante* 22: 17–53.

Cochavi-Rainey, Z. 1999. *Royal Gifts in the Late Bronze Age Fourteenth to Thirteenth Centuries B.C.E.: Selected Texts Recording Gifts to Royal Personages.* With Archaeological Contributions by C. Lilyquist. [Beersheba]: Ben-Gurion University of the Negev Press.

Cohen, R. 2000. "Intelligence in the Amarna Letters." In *Amarna Diplomacy: The Beginnings of International Relations,* ed. R. Cohen and R. Westbrook, 85–98. Baltimore: Johns Hopkins University Press.

Cohen, R. and R. Westbrook (eds.). 2000. *Amarna Diplomacy: The Beginnings of International Relations.* Baltimore: Johns Hopkins University Press.

Cowie, P. J. 2008. "Guaranteeing the *Pax Aegyptiaca*? Re-assessing the Role of Elite Offspring as Wards and Hostages within the New Kingdom Egyptian Empire in the Levant." *Bulletin of the Australian Centre for Egyptology* 19: 17–28.

Cumming, B. 1982. *Egyptian Historical Records of the Late Eighteenth Dynasty.* Fascicle 1. Warminster: Aris and Phillips.

El-Saady, H. 1999. "The External Royal Envoys of the Ramessides: A Study on the Egyptian Diplomats." *Mitteilungen des Deutschen Archäologischen Instituts, Abteilung Kairo* 55: 411–26.

Feldman, M. H. 2002. "Ambiguous Identities: The 'Marriage' Vase of Niqmaddu II and the Elusive Egyptian Princess." *Journal of Mediterranean Archaeology* 15(1): 75–99.

Feucht, E. 1990. "Kinder fremder Völker in Ägypten." *Studien zur Altägyptischen Kultur* 17: 177–204.

Fischer, E. 2013. "Niqmaddu of Ugarit and His Consort: A Reassessment of the So-called Marriage Vase." In *SOMA 2012. Identity and Connectivity: Proceedings of the 16th Symposium on Mediterranean Archaeology, Florence, Italy, 1–3 March 2012,* ed. L. Bombardieri, A. D'Agostino, G. Guarducci, S. Valentini, and V. Orsi, volume 1, 165–73. Oxford: Archaeopress.

Fisher, M. 2013. "A Diplomatic Marriage in the Ramesside Period: Maathorneferure, Daughter of the Great Ruler of Hatti." In *Beyond Hatti: A Tribute to Gary Beckman,* ed. B. J. Collins and P. Michalowski, 75–119. Atlanta: Lockwood Press.

Gelb, I. J. 1968. "The Word for Dragoman in the Ancient Near East." *Glossa* 2: 93–104.

Gundlach, R. and U. Rößler-Köhler (eds.). 2003. *Das Königtum der Ramessidenzeit: Akten des 3. Symposions zur ägyptischen Königsideologie.* Wiesbaden: Harrassowitz.

Gundlach, R. and A. Klug. 2004. *Das ägyptische Königtum im Spannungsfeld zwischen Innen- und Außenpolitik im 2. Jahrtausend v. Chr.* KSG 1. Wiesbaden: Harrassowitz.

Hill, J. A., P. Jones, and A. J. Morales (eds.). 2013. *Experiencing Power, Generating Authority: Cosmos, Politics, and the Ideology of Kingship in Ancient Egypt and Mesopotamia.* Philadelphia: University of Pennsylvania Museum of Archaeology and Anthropology.

Jakob, S. 2006. "Pharaoh and His Brothers." *British Museum Studies in Ancient Egypt and Sudan* 6: 12–30.

Jönsson, C. 2000. "Diplomatic Signalling in the Amarna Letters." In *Amarna Diplomacy: The Beginnings of International Relations*, ed. R. Cohen and R. Westbrook, 191–204. Baltimore: Johns Hopkins University Press.

Kitchen, K. 1996. *Ramesside Inscriptions: Translated and Annotated: Translations*, Volume II: *Ramesses II, Royal Inscriptions*. Oxford: Blackwell.

Kontopoulos, G. I. 2014. "The Egyptian Diplomatic System in the Late Bronze Age: Beyond the Terms of 'Brotherhood' and 'Equality': The Egyptian 'Abandonment' of Power and Aspects of Pharaonic Identity and Kingship." *Journal of Ancient Egyptian Interconnections* 6(4): 42–3.

Knoppers, G. N. and A. Girsch (eds.). 2004. *Egypt, Israel and the Ancient Mediterranean World: Studies in Honor of Donald B. Redford*. Leiden: Brill.

Lilyqust, C. 2003. *The Tomb of Three Foreign Wives of Tuthmosis III*. With Contributions by James E. Hoch and A. J. Peden. New York: Metropolitan Museum of Art.

Liverani, M. 1979. *Three Amarna Essays*. Monographs on the Ancient Near East 1(5). Malibu: Undena.

Liverani, M. 1990. *Prestige and Interest: International Relations in the Near East ca. 1600–1100 BC*. Padova: Sargon.

Liverani, M. 2000. "The Great Powers' Club." In *Amarna Diplomacy: The Beginnings of International Relations*, ed. R. Cohen and R. Westbrook, 15–27. Baltimore: Johns Hopkins University Press.

Liverani, M. 2001. *International Relations in the Ancient Near East (1690–1100 BC)*. New York: Palgrave.

Lorton, D. 1974. *Juridical Terminology of International Relations in Egyptian Texts through Dynasty XVIII*. Baltimore: Johns Hopkins University Press.

Marcus, E. 2007. "Amenemhet II and the Sea: Maritime Aspects of the Mit Rahina (Memphis) Inscription." *Ägypten und Levante* 17: 137–90.

Mathieu, B. 2000. "L'énigme du recrutement des 'enfants du kap': un solution?" *Göttinger Miszellen* 177: 41–8.

Meier, S. A. 1988. *The Messenger in the Ancient Semitic World*. Harvard Semitic Monographs 45. Atlanta: Scholars Press.

Meier, S. A. 2000. "Diplomacy and International Marriage." In *Amarna Diplomacy: The Beginnings of International Relations*, ed. R. Cohen and R. Westbrook, 165–73. Baltimore: Johns Hopkins University Press.

Meltzer, E. S. 2001. "Children of the *Kap*—Upwardly Mobile, Talented Youth in Ancient Egypt." *Seshat* 5: 20–6.

Moran, W. L. 1992. *The Amarna Letters*. Baltimore: Johns Hopkins University Press.

Müller, M. 2011. "A View to a Kill: Egypt's Grand Strategy in Her Northern Empire." In *Egypt, Canaan and Israel: History, Imperialism, Ideology and Literature. Proceedings of a Conference at the University of Haifa, 3–7 May 2009*, ed. S. Bar, D. Kahn, and J. J. Shirley, 236–51. Leiden: Brill.

Murnane, W. 2000. "Imperial Egypt and the Limits of Power." In *Amarna Diplomacy: The Beginnings of International Relations*, ed. R. Cohen and R. Westbrook, 101–10. Baltimore: Johns Hopkins University Press.

Mynářová, J. 2014. "Egyptian State Correspondence of the New Kingdom." In *State Correspondence in the Ancient World from New Kingdom Egypt to the Roman Empire*, ed. K. Radner, 10–31. Oxford: Oxford University Press.

Na'aman, N. 2000. "The Egyptian-Canaanite Correspondence." In *Amarna Diplomacy: The Beginnings of International Relations*, ed. R. Cohen and R. Westbrook, 125–38. Baltimore: Johns Hopkins University Press.

Panagiotopoulos, D. 2006. "Foreigners in Egypt in the Time of Hatshepsut and Thutmose III." In *Thutmose III: A New Biography*, ed. E. H. Cline and D. O'Connor, 370–412. Ann Arbor: University of Michigan Press.

Rainey, A. F. 2015. *The El-Amarna Correspondence*. 2 vols. Leiden: Brill.

Redford, D. 1992. *Egypt, Canaan and Israel in Ancient Times*. Princeton: Princeton University Press.

Redford, D. 2003. *The Wars in Syria and Palestine of Thutmose III*. Culture and History of the Ancient Near East 16. Leiden: Brill.

Roth, S. 2002. *Gebieterin aller Länder*. Orbis Biblicus et Orientalis 185. Freiburg: University Press.

Roth, S. 2003. "'Da wurden an diesem Tage die zwei großen Länder zu einem Lande': Zum Verhältnis von Königsodeologie und internationaler Heiratspolitik in der Zeit Ramses' II." In *Das Königtum der Ramessidenzeit: Akten des 3. Symposions zur ägyptischen Königsideologie*, ed. R. Gundlach and U. Rößler-Köhler, 175–95. Wiesbaden: Harrassowitz.

Schneider, T. 2002. "Sinuhes Notiz über die Könige: syrisch-anatolische Herrschertitel in ägyptischer Überlieferung." *Ägypten und Levante* 12: 257–72.

Schulman, A. R. 1979. "Diplomatic Marriage in the Egyptian New Kingdom." *Journal of Near Eastern Studies* 38(3): 177–93.

Shaw, G. 2012. "Treaties, Pharaonic Egypt." In *The Encyclopedia of Ancient History*. Hoboken: Wiley. doi:10.1002/9781444338386.wbeah15403 or http://onlinelibrary.wiley.com/doi/10.1002/9781444338386.wbeah15403/full, retrieved January 15, 2015.

Simpson, W. K. 1963. *Heka-Nefer and the Dynastic Material from Toshka and Arminna*. Publications of the Pennsylvania-Yale expedition to Egypt 1. New Haven: Peabody Museum of Natural History of Yale University.

Singer, I. 2011. *The Calm before the Storm: Selected Writings of Itamar Singer on the Late Bronze Age in Anatolia and the Levant*. Atlanta: Society of Biblical Literature.

Vallogia, M. 1976. *Recherche sur les "messagers" (*wpwtyw*) dans les sources égyptiennes profanes*. Genève: Librairie Droz.

Warburton, D. A. 1997. *State and Economy in Ancient Egypt: Fiscal Vocabulary of the New Kingdom*. Orbis Biblicus et Orientalis 151. Fribourg: Fribourg University Press.

Xekalaki, G. 2007. "Egyptian Royal Women and Diplomatic Activity during the New Kingdom." In *Current Research in Egyptology 2005: Proceedings of the Sixth Annual Symposium, University of Cambridge, 6–8 January 2005*, ed. R. Mairs and A. Stevenson, 163–73. Oxford: Oxbow.

Zaccagnini, C. 1987. "Aspects of Ceremonial Exchange in the Near East during the Late Second Millennium BC." In *Centre and Periphery in the Ancient World*, ed. M. Rowlands, M. Larsen, and K. Kristianesen, 57–65. Cambridge: Cambridge University Press.

Zaccagnini, C. 2000. "The Interdependence of the Great Powers." In *Amarna Diplomacy: The Beginnings of International Relations*, ed. R. Cohen and R. Westbrook, 141–53. Baltimore: Johns Hopkins University Press.

Spalinger, Chapter 6—The Armies of Re

Cavillier, Giacomo. 2001. *Il faraone guerriero: i Sovrani del Nuovo Regno alla Conquista dell'Asia tra Mito, Strategia Bellica e Realtà Archeologica.* Turin: Tirrenia Stampatori.

Darnell, John Coleman. 2004. "The Route of Eleventh Dynasty Expansion into Nubia." *Zeitschrift für ägyptische Sprache* 131: 23–37.

Darnell, John Coleman. 2008. "The Eleventh Dynasty Royal Inscription from Deir el-Ballas." *Revue d'égyptologie* 59: 81–110.

Darnell, John Coleman and Colleen Manassa. 2007. *Tutankhamun's Armies: Battle and Conquest during Ancient Egypt's Late Eighteenth Dynasty.* Hoboken, NJ: John Wiley & Sons.

Fischer, Henry. 1961. "The Nubian Mercenaries of Gebelein During the First Intermediate Period." *Kush* 9: 101–8.

Goedicke, Hans (ed.). 1985. *Perspectives on the Battle of Kadesh.* Baltimore: Halgo.

Gnirs, Andrea. 1996. *Militär und Gesellschaft: ein Beitrag zur Sozialgeschichte des Neuen Reichs.* Heidelberg: Heidelberger Orientverlag.

Kemp, Barry J. 1986. "Large Middle Kingdom Granary Buildings (and the Archaeology of Administration)." *Zeitschrift für ägyptische Sprache* 113: 120–36.

Manassa, Colleen. 2013. *Imagining the Past: Historical Fiction in New Kingdom Egypt.* New York: Oxford University Press.

Oren, Eliezer (ed.). 1997. *The Hyksos: New Historical and Archaeological Perspectives.* Philadelphia: University Museum.

Oren, Eliezer (ed.). 2000. *The Sea Peoples and Their World: A Reassessment.* Philadelphia: University Museum.

Partridge, Robert B. 2002. *Fighting Pharaohs: Weapons and Warfare in Ancient Egypt.* Manchester: Peartree.

Redford, Donald B. 2003. *The Wars in Syria and Palestine of Thutmose III.* Leiden and Boston: Brill.

Schulman, Alan. 1964. *Military Rank, Title, and Organization in the Egyptian New Kingdom.* Berlin: Hessling.

Spalinger, Anthony. 2006. *Warfare in Ancient Egypt: The New Kingdom.* Malden, MA: Blackwell.

Spalinger, Anthony. 2013. "The Organisation of the Pharaonic Army (Old to New Kingdom)." In *Ancient Egyptian Administration*, ed. Juan Carlos Garciá Moreno, 393–478. Leiden and Boston: Brill.

Shaw, Ian. 1991. *Egyptian Warfare and Weapons.* Princes Risborough: Shire.

Stefanovic, Danijela, 2006. *The Holders of Regular Military Titles in the Period of the Middle Kingdom: Dossiers.* London: Golden House.

von der Way, Thomas. 1984. *Die Textüberlieferung Ramses' II. zur Qades-Schlach: Analyse und Struktur.* Hildesheim: Gerstenberg Verlag.

Mark, Chapter 7—The Long Arm of Merchantry . . .

Bard, Kathryn. 2003. "The Emergence of the Egyptian State (*c.*3200–2686 BC)." In *The Oxford History of Ancient Egypt*, ed. Ian Shaw, 57–82. Oxford: Oxford University Press.

Barrett, Caitlín. 2009. "Perceived Value of Minoan and Minoanizing Pottery in Egypt." *Journal of Mediterranean Archaeology* 22(2): 211–34.

Bourriau, Janine. 2003. "The Second Intermediate Period (*c.*1650–1550 BC)." In *The Oxford History of Ancient Egypt*, ed. Ian Shaw, 172–206. Oxford: Oxford University Press.

Bryan, Betsy. 2003. "The 18th Dynasty before the Amarna Period (*c.*1550–1352 BC)." In *The Oxford History of Ancient Egypt*, ed. Ian Shaw, 207–64. Oxford: Oxford University Press.

Callender, Gae. 2003. "The Middle Kingdom Renaissance (*c.*2055–1650 BC)." In *The Oxford History of Ancient Egypt*, ed. Ian Shaw, 137–71. Oxford: Oxford University Press.

Cohen, Susan. 2002. *Canaanites, Chronologies, and Connections*. Winona Lake, IN: Eisenbrauns.

Colburn, Cynthia. 2011. "Egyptian Gold in Prepalatial Crete? A Consideration of the Evidence." *Journal of Ancient Egyptian Interconnections* 3(3): 1–13.

Creasman, Pearce Paul. 2014. "Hatshepsut and the Politics of Punt." *African Archaeological Review* 31(3): 395–405.

Dijk, Jacobus van. 2003. "The Amarna Period and the Late New Kingdom (*c.*1352–1069 BC)." In *The Oxford History of Ancient Egypt*, ed. Ian Shaw, 265–307. Oxford: Oxford University Press.

Espinel, Andres Diego. 2012. "Egypt and the Levant during the Old Kingdom." *Der Alte Orient* 30: 359–67.

Fattovich, Rodolfo and Katheryn Bard. 2012. "Ships Bound for Punt." In *The Red Sea in Pharaonic Times*, ed. Pierre Tallet and El-Sayed Mahfouz, 27–33. Le Caire: Institut français d'archéologie orientale.

Malek, Jaromir. 2003. "The Old Kingdom (*c.*2686–2160 BC)." In *The Oxford History of Ancient Egypt*, ed. Ian Shaw, 83–107. Oxford: Oxford University Press.

Mark, Samuel. 2013. "The Earliest Sailboats in Egypt and Their Influence on the Development of Trade, Seafaring in the Red Sea, and State Development." *Journal of Ancient Egyptian Interconnections* 5(1): 28–37.

Mark, Samuel. 2014. "Notes on the Mediterranean and Red Sea Ships and Ship Construction from Sahure to Hatshepsut." *Journal of Ancient Egyptian Interconnections* 6(2): 34–49.

Mumford, Gregory. 2015. "The Sinai Peninsula and Its Environs: Our Changing Perceptions of a Pivotal Land Bridge Between Egypt, The Levant, and Arabia." *Journal of Ancient Egyptian Interconnections* 7(1): 1–24.

Parkinson, R. B. 1997. *The Tale of Sinuhe and Other Ancient Egyptian Poems 1940–1640 BC*. Oxford: Oxford University Press.

Petrie, William M. Flinders. 1899. *Egyptian Tales: Translated from the Papyri, First Series: IVth to XIIth Dynasty*. London: Methuen and Co.

Sowada, Karin. 2009. *Egypt in the Eastern Mediterranean during the Old Kingdom*. Fribourg: Academic Press.

Tallet, Pierre. 2012. "Ayn Sukhna and Wadi el-Jarf: Two Newly Discovered Pharaonic Harbours on the Suez Gulf." *British Museum Studies in Ancient Egypt and Sudan* 18: 147–68.

Tallet, Pierre. 2013. "The Wadi el-Jarf Site: A Harbor of Khufu on the Red Sea." *Journal of Ancient Egyptian Interconnections* 5(1): 76–84.

White, Donald. 1986. "1985 Excavations on Bates's Island, Marsa Matruh." *Journal of American Research Center in Egypt* 23: 51–84.

S. T. Smith, Chapter 8—Artisans and Their Products . . .

Aruz, Joan, Kim Benzel, and Jean M. Evans. 2009. *Beyond Babylon: Art, Trade, and Diplomacy in the Second Millennium B.C.* New York: Metropolitan Museum of Art.

Bietak, Manfred, Nanno Marinatos, Clairy Palivou, and Ann Brysbaert. 2007. *Taureador Scenes in Tell El-Dab'a (Avaris) and Knossos.* Denkschriften der Gesamtakademie. Wien: Verlag der Osterreichischen Akademie der Wissenschaften.

Bonnet, Charles, and Dominique Valbelle. 2006. *The Nubian Pharaohs: Black Kings on the Nile.* Cairo: American University in Cairo Press.

Cotelle-Michel, Laurence. 2004. *Les sarcophages en terre cuite: en Egypte et en Nubie de l'époque prédynastique à l'époque romaine.* Dijon: Faton.

Darnell, John. 2006. *The Inscription of Queen Katimala at Semna: Textual Evidence for the Origins of the Napatan State.* Yale Egyptological Studies 7. New Haven: Yale University Press.

Dietler, Michael. 2010. *Archaeologies of Colonialism: Consumption, Entanglement, and Violence in Ancient Mediterranean France.* Berkeley: University of California Press.

Feldman, Marian H. 2006. *Diplomacy by Design: Luxury Arts and an "International Style" in the Ancient Near East, 1400–1200 BCE.* Chicago: University of Chicago Press.

Kopetzky, Karin. 2015. "Egyptian Burial Costumes in the Royal Tombs I–III of Byblos." *BAAL Hors-Série* 10: 393–412.

Lacovara, Peter. 1998. "Nubian Faience." In *Gifts of the Nile: Ancient Egyptian Faience*, ed. Florence D. Friedman, Georgina Borromeo, and Mimi Leveque, 46–9. New York: Thames and Hudson.

O'Connor, David. 1984. "Kerma and Egypt: The Significance of the Monumental Buildings Kerma I, II, and XI." *Journal of the American Research Center in Egypt* 21: 65–108.

Ogden, Jack M. 2000. "Metals." In *Ancient Egyptian Materials and Technology*, ed. Paul T. Nicholson and Ian Shaw, 148–76. Cambridge: Cambridge University Press.

Smith, Stuart Tyson. 2003. *Wretched Kush: Ethnic Identities and Boundaries in Egypt's Nubian Empire.* London: Routledge.

Smith, Stuart Tyson. 2013. "The Garrison and Inhabitants: A View from Askut." In *The Power of Walls—Fortifications in Ancient Northeastern Africa*, ed. Friederike Jesse and Carola Vogel, 269–91. Colloquium Africanum 5. Köln: Heinrich-Barth-Institut.

Smith, Stuart Tyson, and Michele R. Buzon. 2014. "Identity, Commemoration and Remembrance in Colonial Encounters: Burials at Tombos during the Egyptian New Kingdom Empire and Its Aftermath." In *Remembering and Commemorating the Dead: Recent Contributions in Bioarchaeology and Mortuary Analysis from the Ancient Near East*, ed. Benjamin Porter and Alex Boutin, 185–215. Boulder: University Press of Colorado.

Török, László. 2009. *Between Two Worlds: The Frontier Region between Ancient Nubia and Egypt, 3700 BC–500 AD*. Leiden: Brill.

Vincentelli, Irene. 2006. *Hillat el-Arab: The Joint Sudanese-Italian Expedition in the Napatan Region, Sudan*. British Archaeological Reports 1570. Oxford: Archaeopress.

Weingarten, Judith. 2000. "Reading the Minoan Body: Proportions and the Palaikastro Kouros." *British School at Athens Studies* 6: 103–11.

Boschloos, Chapter 9—Traded, Copied, and Kept . . .

Ahrens, Alexander. 2012. " 'From a Country Far, Far Away . . .': Remarks on the Middle Bronze Age Scarabs from Tomb Ass. 12949 at Qal'at Šerqat." In *Stories of Long Ago: Festschrift für Michael D. Roaf*, ed. Heather D. Baker, Kai Kaniuth, and Adelheid Otto, 1–9. Münster: Ugarit-Verlag.

Ahrens, Alexander. 2015. "Objects from Afar—The Distribution of Egyptian Imports in the Northern Levant." In *Policies of Exchange: Political Systems and Modes of Interaction in the Aegean and the Near East in the 2nd Millennium BCE*, ed. Birgitta Eder and Regine Pruzsinszky, 141–56. Vienna: Österreichische Akademie der Wissenschaften.

Avigad, Nahman and Benjamin Sass. 1997. *Corpus of West-Semitic Stamp Seals*. Jerusalem: Israel Academy of Sciences and Humanities/Israel Exploration Society/ Hebrew University of Jerusalem.

Ben-Tor, Daphna. 2006. "Chronological and Historical Implications of the Early Egyptian Scarabs on Crete." In *Timelines: Studies in Honour of Manfred Bietak*, ed. Ernst Czerny, Irmgard Hein, Hermann Hunger, Dagmar Melman, and Angela Schwab, volume 2, 77–86. Leuven: Peeters.

Ben-Tor, Daphna. 2007. *Scarabs, Chronology and Interconnections: Egypt and Palestine in the Second Intermediate Period*. Fribourg: Academic Press/Göttingen: Vandenhoeck & Ruprecht.

Ben-Tor, Daphna and Othmar Keel. 2012. "The Beth-Shean Level IX-Group: A Local Scarab Workshop of the Late Bronze Age I." In *All the Wisdom of the East: Studies in Near Eastern Archaeology and History in Honor of Eliezer D. Oren*, ed. Mayer Gruber, Shmuel Ahituv, Gunnar Lehmann, and Zipora Talshir, 87–104. Fribourg: Academic Press/Göttingen: Vandenhoeck & Ruprecht.

Bietak, Manfred and Ernst Czerny (eds.). 2004. *Scarabs of the Second Millennium BC from Egypt, Nubia, Crete and the Levant: Chronological and Historical Implications. Papers of a Symposium, Vienna, 10th–13th of January 2002*. Vienna: Austrian Academy of Sciences Press.

Blankenberg-Van Delden, Catharina. 1969. *The Large Commemorative Scarabs of Amenhotep III*. Leiden: Brill.

Boardman, John. 2003. *Classical Phoenician Scarabs: A Catalogue and Study*. Oxford: Archaeopress.

Boschloos, Vanessa. 2013. "Interregional Contacts in the Biqa'a Valley from a Beetle's Point of View: Egyptian and Egyptianising Scarabs at Bronze Age Kāmid al-Lōz (Kumidi)." *Altorientalische Forschungen* 40(2): 195–219.

Boschloos, Vanessa. 2014. "The Hyksos and the Middle Bronze Age IIB-IIC/III in Jordan: What Imported Egyptian Seals Tell Us." In *"From Gilead to Edom": Studies in the Archaeology and History of Jordan in Honor of Denyse Homès-Fredericq on the Occasion of Her Eightieth Birthday*, ed. Ingrid Swinnen and Eric Gubel, 107–22. Brussels: Cultura.

Boschloos, Vanessa. 2016. "Phoenician Identity through Retro-Glyptic: Egyptian Pseudo-inscriptions and the Neo-'Hyksos' Style on Iron Age II–III Phoenician and Hebrew Seals." In *Transformation and Crisis in the Mediterranean II: "Identity" and Interculturality in the Levant and Phoenician West Between the 8th and 5th Centuries BCE*, ed. Giuseppe Garbati and Tatiana Pedrazzi, 43–57. Roma: Consiglio Nazionale delle Ricerche-Instituto di Studi sul Mediterraneo Antico.

Buchanan, Briggs and Roger Moorey. 1988. *Catalogue of Ancient Near Eastern Seals in the Ashmolean Museum*, Volume III. *The Iron Age Stamp Seals (c.1200–350 B.C.)*. Oxford: Clarendon.

Gubel, Eric. 1993. "The Iconography of Inscribed Phoenician Glyptic." In *Studies in the Iconography of Northwest Semitic Inscribed Seals: Proceedings of a Symposium held in Fribourg on April 17–20, 1991*, ed. Benjamin Sass and Christoph Uehlinger, 101–29. Fribourg: Academic Press/Göttingen: Vandenhoeck & Ruprecht.

Gubel, Eric and Henri Loffet. 2011. "Sidon, Qedem and the Land of Iay." *Archaeology and History in Lebanon* 34–5: 79–92.

Hölbl, Günther. 1979. *Beziehungen der ägyptischen Kultur zu Altitalien*. 2 vols. Leiden: Brill.

Hölbl, Günther. 1986. *Ägyptisches Kulturgut im phönikischen und punischen Sardinien*. 2 vols. Leiden: Brill.

Hölbl, Günther. 1999. "Funde aus Milet, VIII: Die Aegyptiaca vom Aphroditetempel auf dem Zeytintepe." *Archäologischer Anzeiger* 1999: 345–71.

Hölbl, Günther. 2010. "Testimonianze della cultura egizia in Italia meridionale e nella Sicilia greca in Età Arcaica." *Serekh* 5: 93–107.

Jaeger, Bertrand. 1992. *Essai de classification et datation des scarabées Menkhéperrê*. Fribourg: Academic Press/Göttingen: Vandenhoeck & Ruprecht.

Jeffreys, David. 2003. "All in the Family? Heirlooms in Ancient Egypt." In *"Never Had the Like Occurred": Egypt's View of Its Past*, ed. John Tait, 197–211. London: UCL Press.

Keel, Othmar. 1995. *Corpus der Stempelsiegel-Amulette aus Palästina-Israel. Von den Anfang bis zur Perserzeit I Einleitung*. Fribourg: Academic Press/Göttingen: Vandenhoeck & Ruprecht.

Lohwasser, Angelika (ed.). 2014. *Skarabäen des 1. Jahrtausends. Ein Workshop in Münster am 17. Oktober 2012*. Fribourg: Academic Press/Göttingen: Vandenhoeck & Ruprecht.

Meyer, Jan-Waalke. 2008. *Die eisenzeitlichen Stempelsiegel aus dem 'Amuq-Gebiet. Ein Beitrag zur Ikonographie altorientalischer Siegelbilder*. Fribourg: Academic Press/Göttingen: Vandenhoeck & Ruprecht.

Münger, Stefan. 2005. "Stamp-Seal Amulets and Early Iron Age Chronology." In *The Bible and Radiocarbon Dating: Archaeology, Text and Science*, ed. Thomas E. Levy, Thomas Higham, and A. J. Shortland, 381–404. London: Routledge.

Nunn, Astrid and Regine Schulz (eds.). 2004. *Skarabäen ausserhalb Ägyptens: lokale Produktion oder Import?* Oxford: Archaeopress.

Redissi, Taoufik. 1999. "Etude des empreintes de sceaux de Carthage." In *Karthago III. Die Deutschen Ausgrabungen in Karthago*, ed. Friedrich Rakok, 4–92. Mainz: Von Zabern.

Tufnell, Olga, Geoffrey Thorndike Martin, and William A. Ward. 1984. *Studies on Scarab Seals*, Volume Two: *Scarab Seals and Their Contribution to History in the Early Second Millennium B.C.*, 2 vols. Warminster: Aris and Phillips.

Ward, William A. 1978. *Studies on Scarab Seals*, Volume 1: *Pre-12th Dynasty Scarab Amulets*, Warminster: Aris and Phillips.

Ward, William A. and William G. Dever. 1994. *Studies on Scarab Seals*, Volume 3: *Scarab Typology and Archaeological Context. An Essay on Middle Bronze Age Chronology*, San Antonio: Van Siclen.

Shaw, Chapter 10—Technology in Transit . . .

Collier, M. and S. Quirke. 2004. *The UCL Lahun Papyri: Religious, Literary, Legal, Mathematical and Medical*. Oxford: Archaeopress.

Ehret, C. 2006. "Linguistic Stratigraphies and Holocene History in Northeastern Africa." In *Archaeology of Early Northeastern Africa: In Memory of Lech Krzyzaniak*, ed. M. Chlodnicki and K. Kroeper, 1019–55. Poznań: Poznań Archaeological Museum.

Finkel, I. L. and J. E. Reade. 1996. "Assyrian Hieroglyphs." *Zeitschrift für Assyriologie und vorderasiatische Archäologie* 86: 244–68.

Imhausen, A. 2007. "Egyptian Mathematics." In *The Mathematics of Egypt, Mesopotamia, China, India and Islam: A Sourcebook*, ed. V. J. Katz, 7–57. Princeton: Princeton University Press.

Izre'el, S. 1997. *The Amarna Scholarly Tablets*. Groningen: Styx.

Jórdeczka, M., H. Królik, M. Masojć, and R. Schild. 2011. "Early Holocene Pottery in the Western Desert of Egypt: New Data from Nabta Playa." *Antiquity* 85: 99–115.

Kemp, B. 2006. *Ancient Egypt: Anatomy of a Civilization*. 2nd ed. London: Routledge.

Lichtheim, M. 1980. *Ancient Egyptian Literature*, Volume 3: *The Late Period*. Los Angeles: University of California Press.

Mackenzie, D. and J. Wajcman (eds.). 1985. *The Social Shaping of Technology*. Milton Keynes: Open University Press.

Mokyr, J. 1990. *The Lever of Riches: Technological Creativity and Economic Progress*. Oxford: Oxford University Press.

Montelius, G. O. 1899. *Der Orient und Europa*. Stockholm: Kungl. Hofboktryckeriet.

Moorey, P. R. S. 2001. "The Mobility of Artisans and Opportunities for Technology Transfer." In *The Social Context of Technological Change: Egypt and the Near East, 1650–1550 BC*, ed. A. J. Shortland, 1–14. Oxford: Oxbow.

Newton, R. G. 1980. "Recent Views on Ancient Glasses." *Glass Technology* 21(4): 173–83.

Nicholson, P. T. 2007. *Brilliant Things for Akhenaten: The Production of Glass, Vitreous Materials and Pottery at Amarna Site O45.1*. London: Egypt Exploration Society.

Nicholson, P. T. and J. Henderson. 2000. "Glass." In *Ancient Egyptian Materials and Technology*, ed. P. T. Nicholson and I. Shaw, 195–224. Cambridge: Cambridge University Press.

Nicholson, P. T., C. M. Jackson, and K. M. Trott. 1997. "The Ulu Burun Glass Ingots, Cylindrical Vessels and Egyptian Glass." *Journal of Egyptian Archaeology* 83: 143–53.

Panagiotaki, M., Y. Maniatis, D. Kavoussanaki, G. Hatton, and M. Tite. 2004. "The Production Technology of Aegean Bronze Age Vitreous Materials." In *Invention and Innovation: The Social Context of Technological Change 2: Egypt, the Aegean and the Near East 1650–1150 BC*, ed. J. Bourriau and J. Phillips, 149–75. Oxford: Oxbow.

Pearce, L. E. 1999. "Sepiru and luaba: Scribes of the Late First Millennium." In *Languages and Cultures in Contact: At the Crossroads of Civilizations in the Syro-Mesopotamian Realm*, ed. K. van Lerberghe and G. Voet, 355–68. Leuven: Peeters.

Peltenburg, E. J. 1987. "Early Faience: Recent Studies, Origins, and Relations with Glass." In *Early Vitreous Materials*, ed. M. Bimson and I. Freestone, 5–29. London: British Museum.

Perry, W. J. 1923. *The Children of the Sun: A Study in the Early History of Civilization.* London: Methuen.

Pusch, E. 1996. "'Pi-Ramesses-beloved-of-Amun, Headquarters of Thy Chariotry': Egyptians and Hittites in the Delta residence of the Ramessides." In *Pelizaeus Museum Hildesheim: The Egyptian Collection*, ed. A. Eggebrecht, 126–44. Mainz: Verlag Philipp von Zabern.

Pusch, E. and T. Rehren. 2007. *Hochtemperatur-Technologie in der Ramses-Stadt: Rubinglas für den Pharao.* Hildesheim: Gerstenberg.

Quibell, J. E. 1913. *Excavations at Saqqara, 1911–12: The Tomb of Hesy.* Le Caire: Institut français d'archéologie orientale.

Ratzel, F. 1882–1891. *Anthropogeographie.* Stuttgart: J. Engelhorn.

Ray, J. D. 1986. "The Emergence of Writing in Egypt." *World Archaeology* 17(3): 307–16.

Rehren, T. 2014. "Glass Production and Consumption between Egypt, Mesopotamia and the Aegean." In *Contextualizing Grave Inventories in the Ancient Near East*, ed. P. Pfälzner, H. Niehr, E. Pernicka, S. Lange, and T. Köster, 217–23. Wiesbaden: Harrassowitz.

Rehren, T., E. B. Pusch, and A. Herold. 2001. "Qantir-Piramesses and the Organization of the Egyptian Glass Industry." In *The Social Context of Technological Change: Egypt and the Near East, 1650–1550 BC*, ed. A. J. Shortland, 223–38. Oxford: Oxbow.

Ritner, R. K. 2000. "Innovations and Adaptations in Ancient Egyptian Medicine." *Journal of Near Eastern Studies* 59(2): 107–17.

Smith, G. E. 1923. *The Ancient Egyptians and the Origin of Civilization.* London: Harper & Bros.

Smith, G. E. 1933. *The Diffusion of Culture.* London: Watts and Co.

Spalinger, A. J. 2005. *War in Ancient Egypt: The New Kingdom.* Malden: Blackwell.

Zaccagnini, C. 1983. "Patterns of Mobility among Ancient Near Eastern Craftsmen." *Journal of Near Eastern Studies* 42: 245–64.

Goldwasser, Chapter 11, pt. I—Writing Systems . . .

Amiet, Pierre. 1980. *La glyptique Mésopotamienne archaïque.* Paris: Éditions du Centre national de la recherche scientifique.

Baines, John. 2004. "The Earliest Egyptian Writing: Development, Context, Purpose." In *The First Writing: Script Invention as History and Process*, ed. Stephan Houston, 150–89, 354–94. Cambridge: Cambridge University Press.

Baines, John. 2007. *Visual and Written Culture in Ancient Egypt.* New York: Oxford University Press.

Beck, Pirhiya. 2002. *Imagery and Representation: Studies in the Art and Iconography of Ancient Palestine: Collected Articles.* Tel Aviv: Emery and Claire Yass Publications in Archaeology.

Ben-Tor, Daphna. 2007. *Scarabs, Chronology, and Interconnections: Egypt and Palestine in the Second Intermediate Period.* Fribourg: Academic Press.

Cross, Frank Moore, Jr., and Thomas O. Lambdin. 1960. "An Ugaritic Abecedary and the Origins of the Proto-Canaanite Alphabet." *Bulletin of the American Schools of Oriental Research* 160: 21–6.

Darnell, John Coleman, F. W. Dobbs-Allsopp, Marilyn Lundberg, P. Kyle McCarter, and Bruce Zuckerman. 2005. *Two Early Alphabetic Inscriptions from the Wadi el-Hol: New Evidence for the Origin of the Alphabet from the Western Desert of Egypt.* Boston: American Schools of Oriental Research.

Davies, William V. 1987. *Egyptian Hieroglyphs.* London: British Museum Publications.

Dehaene, Stanislas. 2009. *Reading in the Brain: The Science and Evolution of a Human Invention.* New York: Viking.

Depuydt, Leo. 1994. "On the Nature of the Hieroglyphic Script." *Zeitschrift für ägyptische Sprache* 121: 17–36.

Doumet-Serhal, Claude. 2011. "A Decorated Box from Sidon." In *And Canaan Begat Sidon His Firstborn: A Tribute to Dr. John Curtis on His 65th Birthday*, ed. Claudde Doumet-Serhal, Anne Rabate, Andrea Resek, and John Curtis, 93–103. Beirut: Lebanese British Friends of the National Museum.

Dreyer, Günter and Ulrich Hartung 1998. *Umm el-Qaab I. Das prädynastische Königsgrab U-j und seine frühen Schriftzeugnisse.* Mainz: Verlag Philipp von Zabern.

Finkelberg, Margalit. 2014. "Pre-Greek Languages." In *Encyclopedia of Ancient Greek Language and Linguistics*, ed. Georgios K. Giannakis, volume 3, 133–6. Leiden: Brill.

Finkelstein, Israel and Benjamin Sass. 2013. "The West Semitic Alphabetic Inscriptions, Late Bronze II to Iron IIA: Archeological Context, Distribution and Chronology." *Hebrew Bible and Ancient Israel* 2(2): 149–220.

Frost, Ram. 2012. *"Towards a Universal Model of Reading."* *Behavioural and Brain Sciences* 35: 263–80.

Gelb, Ignace J. 1963. *A Study of Writing.* Chicago: University of Chicago Press.

Godart, Louis. 1994. *Il disco di Festo. L'enigma di una scrittura.* Torino: Giulio Einaudi.

Goldwasser, Orly. 1995. *From Icon to Metaphor: Studies in the Semiotics of the Hieroglyphic Script.* Fribourg: Fribourg University Press.

Goldwasser, Orly. 2002. *Lovers, Prophets and Giraffes: Wor[l]d Classification in Ancient Egypt.* Wiesbaden: Otto Harrassowitz.

Goldwasser, Orly. 2006. "Canaanites Reading Hieroglyphs. Part I—Horus is Hathor? Part II—The Invention of the Alphabet in Sinai." *Ägypten und Levante* 16: 121–60.

Goldwasser, Orly. 2010. "How the Alphabet Was Born from Hieroglyphs." *Biblical Archaeology Review* 36(2): 40–53.

Goldwasser, Orly. 2011. "The Advantage of Cultural Periphery: The Invention of the Alphabet in Sinai (circa 1840 B.C.E)." In *Culture Contacts and the Making of Cultures: Papers in Homage to Itamar Even-Zohar*, ed. Rakefet Sela-Sheffy and Gideon Toury, 251–316. Tel Aviv: Tel Aviv University/Unit of Culture Research.

Goldwasser, Orly. 2012. "The Miners that Invented the Alphabet—A Response to Christopher Rollston." *Journal of Ancient Egyptian Interconnections* 4(3): 9–22.

Goldwasser, Orly. 2015. "The Invention of the Alphabet: On 'Lost Papyri' and the 'Egyptian Alphabet.'" In *How Did the Alphabet Come About*, ed. Attuci Claudia and Christophe Rico, 124–41. Newcastle-upon-Tyne: Cambridge Scholars Pub.

Groenewegen-Frankfort, Henriette A. 1972. *Arrest and Movement: An Essay on Space and Time in the Representational Art of the Ancient Near East.* New York: Hacker Art Books.

Hamilton, Gordon J. 2006. *The Origins of the West Semitic Alphabet in Egyptian Scripts.* Washington, DC: Catholic Biblical Association of America.

Harring, Ben. 2015. "*halaḥam* on an Ostracon of the Early New Kingdom?" *Journal of Near Eastern Studies* 74(2): 189–96.

Hawkins, David J. 1979. "The Origin and Dissemination of Writing in Western Asia." In *The Origins of Civilization*, ed. Peter R. S. Moorey, 128–66. Oxford: Clarendon Press.

Hawkins, David J. 1986. "Writing in Anatolia: Imported and Indigenous Systems." *World Archaeology* 17(3): 363–76.

Hoch, James E. 1994. *Semitic Words in Egyptian Texts of the New Kingdom and Third Intermediate Period*. Princeton, NJ: Princeton University Press.

Horowitz, Wayne, Oshima Takayoshi, and Seth Sanders. 2006. *Cuneiform in Canaan: Cuneiform Sources from the Land of Israel in Ancient Times*. Jerusalem: Israel Exploration Society.

Kahl, Jochem. 2003. "Die frühen Schriftzeugnisse aus dem Grab Uj in Umm el-Qaab." *Chronique d'Egypte* 78: 112–35.

Kammerzell, Frank. 2009. "Defining Non-textual Marking Systems, Writing and Other Systems of Graphic Information Processing." In *Non-textual Marking Systems, Writing and Pseudo Script from Prehistory to Present Times*, ed. Petra Andrassy, Julia Budka, and Frank Kammerzell, 277–308. Göttingen: Seminar für Ägyptologie und Koptologie.

Karnava, Artemis 2015. "Phaistos Disc." In *Encyclopedia of Ancient Greek Language and Linguistics*. Brill Online. <http://referenceworks.brillonline.com/entries/encyclopedia-of-ancient-greek-language-and-linguistics/phaistos-disc-SIM_00000510>, retrieved August 2015.

Keel, Othmar. 2010. *Corpus der Stempelsiegel-Amulette aus Palästina/Israel von den Anfängen bis zur Perserzeit*. Fribourg: Academic Press.

Köhler, Christiana E. and Edwin C. M. van den Brink. 2002. "Four Jars with Incised Serekh-Signs from Helwan Recently Retrieved from the Cairo Museum." *Göttinger Miszellen* 187: 59–81.

Kooij, Gerrit van der. 2014. "Archaeological and Palaeographic Aspects of the Deir 'Alla Late Bronze Age Clay Tablets." In *A Pioneer of Arabia: Studies in the Archaeology and Epigraphy of the Levant and the Arabian Peninsula in Honor of Moawiyah Ibrahim*, ed. Zeidan Kafafi and Mohammed Maraqten, 157–77. Rome: La Sapienza.

Morenz, Ludwig D. 2004. *Bild-Buchstaben und symbolische Zeichen: die Herausbildung der Schrift in der hohen Kultur Altägyptens*. Fribourg: Academic Press.

Morenz, Ludwig D. 2014. *Anfänge der ägyptischen Kunst: eine problemgeschichtliche Einführung in ägyptologische Bild-Anthropologie*. Fribourg: Academic Press.

Naveh, Joseph. 1997. *Early History of the Alphabet: An Introduction to West Semitic Epigraphy and Palaeography*. Jerusalem: Magnes Press, Hebrew University.

Nissen, Hans J. 1986. "The Archaic Texts from Uruk." *World Archaeology* 17(3): 317–34.

Nissen, Hans J., Peter Damerow, and Robert K. Englund. 1993. *Archaic Bookkeeping: Writing and Techniques of Economic Administration in the Ancient Near East*. Chicago: University of Chicago Press.

Pardee, Denis. 2007. "The Ugaritic Alphabetic Cuneiform Writing System in the Context of Other Alphabetic Systems." In *Studies in Semitic and Afroasiatic Linguistics Presented to Gene B. Gragg*, ed. Cynthia L. Miller, 181–200. Chicago: Oriental Institute of the University of Chicago.

Pardee, Denis. 2011. *The Ugaritic Texts and the Origins of West-Semitic Literary Composition*. Oxford: Oxford University Press.

Payne, Annick. 2010. *Hieroglyphic Luwian: An Introduction with Original Texts*. Wiesbaden: Harrassowitz.

Ray, John D. 1986. "The Emergence of Writing in Egypt." *World Archaeology* 17(3): 307–16.

Regulski, Ilona. 2008. "The Origin of Writing in Relation to the Emergence of the Egyptian State." In *Egypt at Its Origins 2: Proceedings of the International Conference "Origin of the State, Predynastic and Early Dynastic Egypt", Toulouse (France), 5th–8th September 2005,* ed. Béatrix Midant-Reynes, Yann Tristant, Joanne Rowland, and Stan Hendrickx, 983–1007. Leuven: Peeters.

Regulski, Ilona. 2009. "The Beginning of Hieratic Writing in Egypt." *Studien zur altägyptischen Kultur* 38: 259–74.

Sanders, Seth. 2004. "What Was the Alphabet for? The Rise of Written Vernaculars and the Making of Israelite National Literature." *Maarav* 11: 25–56.

Sass, Benjamin. 1988. *The Genesis of the Alphabet and Its Development in the Second Millennium B.C.* Wiesbaden: Otto Harrassowitz.

Sass, Benjamin. 2005. *The Alphabet at the Turn of the Millennium: The West Semitic Alphabet ca. 1150–850 BCE: The Antiquity of the Arabian, Greek and Phrygian Alphabets.* Tel-Aviv: Emery and Claire Yass Publications in Archaeology.

Schmandt-Besserat, Denise. 1992. *Before Writing*, Volume 1: *From Counting to Cuneiform.* Austin: The University of Texas Press.

Seri, Andrea. 2010. "Adaptation of Cuneiform to Write Akkadian." In *Visible Language: Inventions of Writing in the Ancient Middle East and Beyond*, ed. Christopher Woods, Geoff Emberling, and Emily Teeter, 85–98. Chicago: Oriental Institute of the University of Chicago.

Singer, Itamar. 2000. "Cuneiform, Linear, Alphabetic: The Contest between Writing Systems in the Eastern Mediterranean." In *Mediterranean Cultural Interaction. Howard Gilman International Conference II*, ed. Asher Ovadiah, 23–32. Tel Aviv: Ramot Publ. House, Tel Aviv University.

Sznycer, Maurice. 1994. "Les inscriptions «pseudo-hiéroglyphiques» de Byblos." *In Biblo. Una città e la sua cultura. Atti del colloquio internazionale, Roma, 5–7 dicembre 1990*, ed. Enrico Acquaro et al., 167–78. Collezione di Studi Fenici 34. Roma: Consiglio nazionale delle ricerche.

Teissier, Beatrice. 1996. *Egyptian Iconography on Syro-Palestinian Cylinder Seals of the Middle Bronze Age.* Fribourg: Fribourg University Press.

van der Brink, Edwin C. M. 2001. "The Pottery-Incised Serekh-Signs of Dynasties 0–1. Part 11: Fragments and Additional Complete Vessels." *Archéo Nil* 11: 23–100.

van der Hout, Theo. 2010. "The Rise and Fall of Cuneiform Script in Hittite Anatolia." In *Visible Language: Inventions of Writing in the Ancient Middle East and Beyond*, ed. Christopher Woods, Geoff Emberling, and Emily Teeter, 99–108. Chicago: Oriental Institute of the University of Chicago.

Vernus, Pascal. 2001. "Les premières attestations de l'écriture hiéroglyphique." *Aegyptus* 81: 13–35.

Vernus, Pascal. 2015. "Typologie comparée de l'écriture hiéroglyphique égyptienne et de l'écriture protosinaïtique: acrophonie 'forte' et acrophonie 'faible.'" In *How Did the Alphabet Come About*, ed. Attuci Claudia and Christophe Rico, 142–75. Newcastle-upon-Tyne: Cambridge Scholars Pub.

Wilkinson, Richard H. 1994. *Reading Egyptian Art: A Hieroglyphic Guide to Ancient Egyptian Painting and Sculpture.* London: Thames and Hudson.

Woodard, Roger D. 2000. "Greek-Phoenician Interaction and the Origin of the Alphabet." In *Mediterranean Cultural Interaction: Howard Gilman International Conference II*, ed. Asher Ovadiah, 33–51. Tel Aviv: Ramot Publ. House, Tel Aviv University.

Woods, Christopher. 2010. "Earliest Mesopotamian Writing." In *Visible Language: Inventions of Writing in the Ancient Middle East and Beyond*, ed. Christopher Woods, Geoff Emberling, and Emily Teeter, 33–84. Chicago: Oriental Institute of the University of Chicago.

Woods, Christopher, Geoff Emberling, and Emily Teeter. 2010. *Visible Language: Inventions of Writing in the Ancient Middle East and Beyond*. Chicago: Oriental Institute of the University of Chicago.

Yakubovich, Ilia. 2010. "Anatolian Hieroglyphic Writing." In *Visible Language: Inventions of Writing in the Ancient Middle East and Beyond*, ed. Christopher Woods, Geoff Emberling, and Emily Teeter, 203–14. Chicago: Oriental Institute of the University of Chicago.

Ziffer, Irit. 1990. *At That Time the Canaanites Were in the Land*. Tel-Aviv: Eretz Israel Museum.

Ayali-Darshan, Chapter 11, pt. II—Literature . . .

Allon, N. 2007. "Seth is Baal: Evidence from the Egyptian Script." *Ägypten und Levante* 17: 15–22.

Alster, B. (ed.). 2005. *Wisdom in Ancient Sumer*. Bethesda: CDL Press.

Assman, J. 2005. *Death and Salvation in Ancient Egypt*. Translated by D. Lorton. Ithaca: Cornell University Press.

Ayali-Darshan, N. 2013. "The Cedar Forest's Traditions in the Egyptian *Tale of The Two Brothers* and Genesis 2–3." *Shnaton* 22: 147–64 (in Hebrew).

Ayali-Darshan, N. 2015. "The Earlier Version of the Story of the Storm-god's Combat with the Sea in the Light of Egyptian, Ugaritic, and Hurro-Hittite Texts." *Journal of Ancient Near Eastern Religions* 15: 20–51.

Ayali-Darshan, N. 2015. "The Identification of ḥmrk̠ in Leiden Magical Papyrus I 343 + I 345 in Light of the Eblaite Texts." *Journal of Near Eastern Studies* 74: 87–9.

Beck, S. 2015. *Sāmānu: Ein vorderasiatischer Dämon in Ägypten*. Ägypten und Altes Testament 83. Münster: Ugarit-Verlag.

Breasted, J. H. 1964. *History of Egypt*. New York: Scribner.

Broze, M. 1996. *Les Aventures d'Horus et Seth dans le Papyrus Chester Beatty I*. Leuven: Peeters.

Cohen, Y. 2013. *Wisdom from the Late Bronze Age*. Atlanta: Society of Biblical Literature.

Collier, M and S. Quirke 2004. *The UCL Lahun Papyri: Religious, Literary, Legal, Mathematical and Medical*. BAR International Series 1209. Oxford: BAR

Collombert, P. and L. Coulon. 2000. "Les dieux contre la mer: le début du 'papyrus d'Astarte' (pBN 202)." *Bulletin de l'Institute française d'archéologie orientale* 100: 193–242.

Dietrich, M., O. Loretz, and J. Sanmartin. 2013. *The Cuneiform Alphabetic Texts from Ugarit, Ras Ibn Hani, and Other Places*. 3rd ed. Alter Orient und Altes Testament 360/1. Münster: Ugarit Verlag.

Dijk, J. van. 1986. "Anat, Seth and the Seed of Preʿ." In *Scripta Signa Vocis: Studies about Scripts, Scriptures, Scribes and Languages in the Near East Presented to J. H. Hospers by His Pupils, Colleagues and Friends*, ed. H. L. J. Vanstiphout, 31–51. Groningen: Forsten.

Dijkstra, M. 2011. "Ishtar Seduces the Sea-Serpent." *Ugarit-Forschungen* 43: 53–83.

Dion, P. E. 1991. "YHWH as Storm-god and Sun-god." *Zeitschrift für die alttestamentliche Wissenschaft* 103: 43–71.

Emerton, J. A. 2001. "The Teaching of Amenemope and Proverbs XXII 17 XXIV 22: Further Reflections on a Long-Standing Problem." *Vetus Testamentus* 51: 431–65.

Erman, A. 1924. "Eine ägyptische Quelle der 'Sprüche Salmos.'" *Sitzungsberichte der Preussischen Akademie der Wissenschaften, Phil.-hist.* 15: 86–93.

Fischer, S. 2002. "Qohelet and the 'Heretic' Harpers Songs." *Journal for the Study of the Old Testament* 98: 105–21.

Fischer-Elfert, H.-W. 2003. "Representations of the Past in New Kingdom Literature." In *"Never Had the Like Occurred": Egypt's View of Its Past*, ed. J. Tait, 126–31. London: University College London.

Fox, M. V. 1977. "A Study of Antef." *Orientalia* 46: 393–423.

Fox, M. V. 1982. "The Entertainment Song Genre in Egyptian Literature." *Scripta Hierosolymitana* 28: 268–316.

Fox, M. V. 1985. *The Song of Songs and the Ancient Egyptian Love Songs*. Madison: University of Wisconsin Press.

Fox, M. V. 2009. "The Formation of Proverbs 22:17–23:11." *Die Welt des Orient* 38: 22–37.

Fox, M. V. 2014. "From Amenemope to Proverbs: Editorial Art in Proverbs 22,17–23,11." *Zeitschrift für die alttestamentliche Wissenschaft* 126: 76–91.

Gardiner, A. H. 1932. "The Astarte Papyrus." In *Studies Presented to F. L. Griffith*, ed. S. R. K. Glanville, 74–85. London: Egyptian Exploration Society.

Gaster, T. H. 1952. "The Egyptian 'Story of Astarte' and the Ugaritic Poem of Baal." *Bibliotheca Orientalis* 9: 82–5.

George, A. R. 2003. *The Babylonian Gilgamesh Epic: Introduction, Critical Edition and Cuneiform Texts*. 2 vols. Oxford: Oxford University Press.

Goedicke, H. 1977. "The Date of the 'Antef Song.'" In *Fragen an die altägyptische Literatur: Studien zum Gedenken an Eberhard Otto*, ed. J. Assmann and E. R. Grieshammer, 185–96. Wiesbaden: Harrassowitz.

Gressmann, H. 1924. "Die neugefundene Lehredes Amen-em-ope und die vorexilische Spruchdichtung Israels." *Zeitschrift für die alttestamentliche Wissenschaft* 42: 272–96.

Grottanelli, C. 1978. "Observations sur l'histoire d'Appou." *Revue Hittite et Asianique* 36: 49–57.

Guglielmi, W. 1996. "Die ägyptische Liebespoesie." In *Ancient Egyptian Literature: History and Forms*, ed. A. Loprieno, 335–47. Leiden: Brill.

Helck, W. 1971. *Die Beziehungen Ägyptens zu Vorderasien im 3. Und 2. Jahrtausend vor Chr.* Wiesbaden: Harrassowitz.

Helck, W. 1983. "Zur Herkunft der Erzählung dessog: Astartepapyrus." In *Fontes atque Pontes: Eine Fest-gabe für Hellmut Brunner*, ed. M. Görg, 215–23. Ägypten und Altes Testament 5. Wiesbaden: Harrassowitz.

Herrmann, A. 1959. *Altägytische Liebesdichtung*. Wiesbaden: Harrassowitz.

Houwink ten Cate, P. H. J. 1992. "The Hittite Storm God: His Role and his Rule According to Hittite Cuneiform Sources." In *Natural Phenomena: Their Meaning, Depiction and Description in the Ancient Near East: Proceedings of the Colloquium, Amsterdam, 6–8 July 1989*, ed. D. J. W. Meijer, 83–148. Amsterdam: Royal Netherlands Academy.

Hurovitz, A. V. 2001. "'Thirty(?) of Counsel and Knowledge': Structural and Interpretive Remarks on the 'Words of the Sages' (Prov 22:17–24:22)." In *Homage to Shmuel: Studies in the World of the Bible*, ed. Y. Talshir and S. Talshir, 146–60. Jerusalem: Bialik Institute (in Hebrew).

Kaiser, O. 1962. *Die mythische Bedeutung des Meeres in Ägypten, Ugarit und Israel.* 2nd ed. Beiheft zur Zeitschrift die alttestamentliche Wissenschaft 78. Berlin: Verlag Alfred Töpelmann.

Kákosy, L. and Z. I. Fabian, 1995. "Harper's Song in the Tomb of Djehutimes (TT 32)." *Studien zur Altägyptischen Kultur* 22: 211–25.

Kämmerer, T. R. 1998. *Šimâ milka: Induktion und Reception der mittelbabylonischen Dichtung von Ugarit, Emār und Tell el-'Amārna.* Münster: Ugarit-Verlag.

Laisney, V. P.-M. 2007. *L'enseignement d'Aménémopé.* Rome: Pontifical Biblical Institute.

Lambert, W. G. 1975. "The Problem of the Love Lyrics." In *Unity and Diversity*, ed. H. Goedicke and J. J. M. Roberts, 104–5. Baltimore: John Hopkins University.

Lambert, W. G. 1995. "Some New Babylonian Wisdom Literature." In *Wisdom in Ancient Israel: Essays in Honour of J. A. Emerton*, ed. J. Day, R. P. Gordon, and H. G. M. Williamson, 38–42. Cambridge: Cambridge University Press.

Lesko, L. H. 1986. "Three Late Egyptian Stories Reconsidered." In *Egyptological Studies in Honor of Richard A. Parker Presented on the Occasion of His 78th Birthday December 10, 1983*, ed. L. H. Lesko, 98–103. Hanover: University Press of New England.

Lichtheim, M. 1945. "The Songs of the Harpers." *Journal of Near Eastern Studies* 4: 178–212.

Massart, A. 1954. *The Leiden Magical Papyrus I 343 + I 345.* Oudheidkundige mededelingen uit het Rijksmuseum van Oudheden te Leiden, Nieuwe reeks, Supplement 34. Leiden: Brill.

Mathieu, B. 1996. *La poésie amoureuse de l'Égypte ancienne. Recherches sur un genre littéraire au Nouvel Empire.* Cairo: Institut français d'archéologie orientale.

Marcus, D. 1997. "The Betrothal of Yarikh and Nikkal-Ib." In *Ugaritic Narrative Poetry*, ed. S. B. Parker, 215–18. Atlanta: Scholars Press.

Paul, S. M. 1997. "A Lover's Garden of Verse: Literal and Metaphorical Imagery in Ancient Near Eastern Love Poetry." In *Tehillah Le-Moshe: Biblical and Judaic Studies in Honor of Moshe Greenberg*, ed. M. Cogan et al., 99–110. Winona Lake: Eisenbrauns.

Pehal, M. 2014. *Interpreting Ancient Egyptian Narratives: A Structural Analysis of the Tale of Two Brothers, the Anat Myth, the Osirian Cycle, and the Astarte Papyrus.* Bruxelles: Éditions modulaires européennes.

Posener, G. 1953. "La légende Égyptienne de la mer insatiable." *Annuaire de l'Institut de philologie et d'histoire orientales et slaves* 13: 461–78.

Redford, D. B. 1992. *Egypt, Canaan and Israel in Ancient Times.* Princeton: Princeton University Press.

Quack, J. F. 1994. *Die Lehren des Ani. Ein neuägyptischer Weisheitstext in seinem kulturellen Umfeld.* OBO 141. Freiburg: Universitätsverlag.

Quack, J. F. 2009. Erzählen als Preisen. Vom Astartepapyrus zu den koptischen Märtyrerlegenden. In: *Das Erzählen in frühen Hochkulturen I. Der Fall Ägypten*, ed. H. Roeder, 291–312. Munich: Wilhelm Fink.

Schneider, T. 2003. "Texte über den syrischen Wettergot aus Ägypten." *Ugarit-Forschungen* 35: 605–27.

Schneider, T. 2008. "Innovation in Literature on behalf of Politics: The *Tale of the Two Brothers*, Ugarit, and the 19th Dynasty History." *Ägypten und Levante* 18: 315–26.

Shupak, N. 2005. "The Instruction of Amenemope and Proverbs 22:17–24:22 from the Perspective of Contemporary Research." In *Seeking Out the Wisdom of the Ancients: Essays Offered to Honor Michael V. Fox on the Occasion of His Sixty-fifth Birthday*, ed. R. L. Troxel, K. G. Friebel, and D. R. Magary, 203–17. Winona Lake: Eisenbrauns.

Shupak, N. 2006–2007. "'He Hath Subdued the Water Monster/Crocodile': God's Battle with the Sea in Egyptian Sources." *Jaarbericht van het Vooraziatisch-egyptisch Genootschap Ex Oriente Lux* 40: 77–90.

Shupak, N. 2011. "Ancient Egyptian Literature." In *The Literature of the Hebrew Bible: Introductions and Studies*, ed. Z. Talshir, volume 2, 605–56. Jerusalem: Magnes (in Hebrew).

Siegelová, J. 1971. *Appu-Märchen und Hedammu-Mythus*. Wiesbaden: Harrassowitz.

Simpson W.K. (ed.). 2003. *The Literature of Ancient Egypt*. 3rd ed. New Haven: Yale University Press.

Spalinger, A. J. 2007. "Transformations in Egyptian Folktales: The Royal Influence." *Revue d'égyptologie* 58: 137–56.

Tazawa, K. 2009. *Syro-Palestinian Deities in New Kingdom Egypt: The Hermeneutics of Their Existence*. BAR International Series 1965. Oxford: British Archaeological Reports.

Vandersleyen, C. 1999. *Ouadj our. W3ḏ wr. Un autre aspect de la vallée du Nil*. Brussels: Connaissance de l'Égypte ancienne.

Velde, H. te. 1967. *Seth, God of Confusion: A Study of His Role in Egyptian Mythology and Religion*. Translated by G. E. van Baaren-Pape. Leiden: Brill.

Verhoeven, U. 1996. "Ein historischer 'Sitz im Leben' für die Erzälung von Horus und Seth des Papyrus Chester Beatty I." In *Wege öfnen. Festschrift für Rolf Gundlach zum 65. Geburstag*, ed. M. Schaude-Busch, 343–63. Ägypten und Altes Testaments: Studien zur Geschichte, Kultur und Religion Ägyptens und des Alten Testaments 65. Wiesbaden: Harrassowitz.

Wente, E. F. 1962. "Egyptian 'Make Merry' Songs Reconsidered." *Journal of Near Eastern Studies* 21: 118–28.

Westenholz, J. G. 1992. "Metaphorical Language in the Poetry of Love in the Ancient Near East." In *La circulation de biens, des personnes et des idées dans le Proche-Orient ancient: Actes de la XXXVIIIe Rencontre assyriologique international (Paris, 8–10 juillet 1991)*, ed. D. Charpin and F. Joannès, 381–7. Paris: Editions recherche sur les civilisations.

Westenholz, J. G. and A. Westenholz. 1977. "Help for Rejected Suitors: The Old Akkadian Love Incantation MAD V 8." *Orientalia* 46: 198–219.

Wettengel, W. 2003. *Die Erzählung von den beiden Brüdern: Der Papyrus d'Orbiney und die Königsideologie der Ramesside*. Orbis biblicus et orientalis 195. Göttingen: Vandenhoeck & Ruprecht.

Cornelius, Chapter 12, pt. I—From Bes to Baal . . .

Abdi, K. 1999. "Bes in the Achaemenid Empire." *Ars Orientalis* 29: 111, 113–40.

Abdi, K. 2002. "Notes on the Iranianization of Bes in the Achaemenid Empire." *Ars Orientalis* 32: 133–62.

Ayali-Darshan, N. 2010 "'The Bride of the Sea': The Traditions about Astarte and Yamm in the Ancient Near East." In *A Woman of Valor: Ancient Near Eastern Studies in Honor of Joan Westenholz*, ed. J. G. Westenholz, W. Horowitz, U. Gabbay, and F. Vukosavović, 19–33. Madrid: Consejo Superior de Investigaciones Científicas.

Beck, P. 2012. "The Drawings and Decorative Designs." In *Kuntillet Ajrud (Horvat Teman): An Iron Age II Religious Site on the Judah-Sinai Border*, ed. Z. Meshel, 143–203. Jerusalem: Israel Exploration Society.

Beck, S. 2015. *Sāmānu: Ein vorderasiatische Dämon in Ägypten*. Münster: Ugarit-Verlag.

Bietak, M. 1990. "Zur Herkunft des Seth von Avaris." *Ägypten und Levante* 1: 9–16.

Bietak, M. 2007. "Egypt and the Levant." In *The Egyptian World*, ed. T. A. H. Wilkinson, 417–48. London: Routledge.

Breyer, F. 2010. *Ägypten & Anatolien: Politische, kulturelle und sprachliche Kontakte zwischen dem Niltal und Kleinasien im 2. Jahrtausend v. Chr.* Vienna: Österreichische Akademie der Wissenschaften.

Budin, S. L. 2015. "Qedešet: A Syro-Anatolian Goddess in Egypt." *Journal of Ancient Egyptian Interconnections* 7(4): 1–20.

Cornelius, I. 1994. *The Iconography of the Canaanite Gods Reshef and Ba'al*. Fribourg: Fribourg University Press.

Cornelius, I. 2014. "'Trading Religions' and 'Visible Religion' in the Ancient Near East." In *Religions and Trade*, ed. V. Rabens and P. Wick, 141–65. Leiden: Brill.

Cornelius, I. and H. Niehr. 2004. *Götter und Kulte in Ugarit*. Mainz: Von Zabern.

Fox, M. V. 1995. "World Order and *Maat*: A Crooked Parallel." *Journal of Ancient Near Eastern Society of Columbia University* 23: 31–48.

Görg, M. 2007. *Religionen in der Umwelt des Alten Testaments, Band 3: Ägyptische Religion*. Stuttgart: Kohlhammer.

Helck, W. 1971. *Die Beziehungen Ägyptens zu Vorderasien im 3. und 2. Jahrtausend v. Chr.* Wiesbaden: Harrassowitz.

Herrmann, C. 1994. *Ägyptische Amulette aus Palästina*. Fribourg: Universitätsverlag.

Herrmann, C. et al. 2010. *1001 Amulett*. Stuttgart: Katholisches Bibelwerk.

Hollis, S. T. 2009. "Hathor and Isis in Byblos in the Second and First Millennia BCE." *Journal of Ancient Egyptian Interconnections* 1(2): 1–8.

Izreʿel, S. 1997. *The Amarna Scholarly Tablets*. Groningen: Styx.

Kaelin, O. 2006. *Adoption von Innovationen im Mesopotamien des 3. Jahrtausends v. Chr.* Fribourg: Universitätsverlag.

Kitchen, K. A. and P. J. N. Lawrence. 2012. *Treaty, Law and Covenant in the Ancient Near East*. Wiesbaden: Harrassowitz.

Lahn, M. K. 2014. *Die Göttin Qedeschet: Genese einer Hybridgottheit*. Hamburg: MOSAIKjournal.

Levy, E. 2014. "A Fresh Look at the Baal-Zaphon Stele." *Journal of Egyptian Archaeology* 100: 293–310.

Mark, S. 2006. *From Egypt to Mesopotamia: A Study of Predynastic Trade Routes*. Texas: A&M University Press.

Moran, W. 1992. *The Amarna Letters*. Baltimore: Johns Hopkins University Press.

Mumford, G. D. 2007. "Egypto-Levantine Relations during the Iron Age to Early Persian Periods." In *Egyptian Stories: A British Egyptological Tribute to Alan B. Lloyd on the Occasion of His Retirement*, ed. T. Schneider and K. M. Szpakowska, 225–88. Münster: Ugarit-Verlag.

Mumford, G. D. 2014. "Egypt and the Levant" In *The Oxford Handbook of the Archaeology of the Levant c.8000–332 BCE*, ed. M. Steiner and A. E. Killebrew, 69–89. Oxford: Oxford University Press.

Münnich, M. M. 2013. *The God Resheph in the Ancient Near East*. Tübingen: Mohr Siebeck.

Nagy, A. 2007. "Meaning Behind Motif: Bes in the Ancient Near East." *Göttinger Miszellen* 215: 85–9.

Oates, D. and J. Oates. 2004. *Nimrud: An Assyrian Imperial City Revealed*. London: British School of Archaeology in Iraq.

Orthmann, W. 1971. *Untersuchungen zur späthethitischen Kunst*. Bonn: Habelt.

Schneider, T. 2010. "Foreigners in Egypt." In *Egyptian Archaeology*, ed. W. Wendrich, 141–63. Oxford: Blackwell Publishing.

Smith, M. S. 2008. *God in Translation: Deities in Cross Cultural Discourse in the Biblical World*. Tübingen: Mohr Siebeck.

Suter, C. E. 2007. Review of *"Modell Ägypten": Adoption von Innovationen im Mesopotamien des 3. Jahrtausends v. Chr.* by Oskar Kaelin. *Journal of the American Oriental Society* 127(3): 384–6.

Tallet, G. and C. Zivie-Coche. 2012. "Imported Cults." In *The Oxford Handbook of Roman Egypt*, ed. C. Riggs, 436–56. Oxford: Oxford University Press.

Tazawa, K. 2009. *Syro-Palestinian Deities in New Kingdom Egypt: The Hermeneutics of Their Existence*. Oxford: Archaeopress.

Teissier, B. 1996. *Egyptian Iconography on Syro-Palestinian Cylinder Seals of the Middle Bronze Age*. Fribourg: Fribourg University Press.

Tufnell, O. 1958. *Lachish (Tell el Duweir)*, Volume 4: *The Bronze Age*. Oxford: Oxford University Press.

van den Brink, E. C. M. and T. E. Levy. 2002. *Egypt and the Levant: Interrelations from the 4th through the Early 3rd Millennium B.C.E.* London: Leicester University Press.

de Vartavan, C. 2005. "Bes, the Bow-Legged Dwarf or the Ladies' Companion." *Bulletin of Parthian and Mixed Oriental Studies* 1: 81–95.

de Vartavan, C. 2014. "Leather and Skin as Markers of Early Exchanges Between Western Asia and Egypt?" *Journal of Ancient Egyptian Interconnections* 6(2): 59–61.

Wettengel, W. 2003. *Die Erzählung von den beiden Brüdern: Der Papyrus d'Orbiney und die Königsideologie der Ramessiden*. Fribourg: Fribourg University Press.

Wimmer, S. 1998. "(No) More Egyptian Temples in Canaan and Sinai." In *Jerusalem Studies in Egyptology*, ed. I. Shirun-Grumach, 87–123. Wiesbaden: Harrassowitz.

Wyssmann, P. 2014. "The Coinage Imagery of Samaria and Judah in the Late Persian Period." In *A "Religious Revolution" in Yehûd? The Material Culture of the Persian Period As a Test Case*, ed. C. Frevel, K. Pyschny, and I. Cornelius, 221–66. Fribourg: Fribourg University Press.

Zivie-Coche, C. 1994. "Dieux autres, dieux des autres: Identité culturelle et altérité dans l'Egypte ancienne." In *Concepts of the Other in Near Eastern Religions*, ed. I. Alon et al., 39–80. Leiden: Brill.

Zivie-Coche, C. 2011. "Foreign Deities in Egypt." In *UCLA Encyclopedia of Egyptology*, ed. J. Dieleman and W. Wendrich. Los Angeles: UCLA. <http://escholarship.org/uc/item/7tr1814c>.

Howley, Chapter 12, pt. II—Egypt and Nubia

Aston, David A. 2009. *Burial Assemblages of Dynasty 21–25: Chronology, Typology, Developments*. Wien: Verlag der Österreichischen Akademie der Wissenschaften.

Caminos, Ricardo A. 1974. *The New Kingdom Temples of Buhen*. London: Egypt Exploration Society.

Caminos, Ricardo A. 1998. *Semna-Kumma*, Volume 1: *The Temple of Semna*. London: Egypt Exploration Society.

Caminos, Ricardo A. 1998. *Semna-Kumma*, Volume 2: *The Temple of Kumma*. London: Egypt Exploration Society.

Desroches-Noblecourt, Christiane et al. 1968. *Le spéos d'El-Lessiya*. 2 vols. Le Caire: Centre de documentation et d'études sur l'ancienne Egypte.

Dunham, Dows. 1950. *Royal Cemeteries of Kush*, Volume 1: *El Kurru*. Cambridge, MA: Harvard University Press.

Dunham, Dows. 1955. *Royal Cemeteries of Kush*, Volume 2: *Nuri*. Cambridge, MA: Published for the Museum of Fine Arts by Harvard University Press.

Gauthier, Henri. 1924. "Le dieu nubien Doudoun," *Revue Egyptologique* 2(1–2): 1–41.

Gilbert, Pierre. 1960. "L'adaptation de l'architecture religieuse de l'Egypte aux sites de Basse Nubie," *Chronique d'Egypte* 35: 47–64.

Lohwasser, Angelika. 1997. "Die Götterwelt im Reich von Kusch: Götter aus dem ägyptischen Pantheon," *Mitteilungen der Sudanarchaeologischen Gesellschaft/Der Antiken Sudan* 6: 28–35.

Lohwasser, Angelika. 2010. *The Kushite Cemetery of Sanam: A Non-Royal Burial Ground of the Nubian Capital, c.800–600 BC*. London: Golden House Publications.

Minor, Elizabeth. 2012. *The Use of Egyptian and Egyptianizing Material Culture in Nubian Burials of the Classic Kerma Period*. PhD dissertation. University of California Berkeley.

Reisner, George Andrew. 1923. *Excavations at Kerma*. 2 vols. Cambridge, MA: Peabody Museum of Harvard University.

Schiff Giorgini, Michela. 2002. *Soleb*, Volume 3: *Le temple. Description*. Florenz: Sansoni.

Schiff Giorgini, Michela. 2003. *Soleb*, Volume 4: *Le temple. Plans et photographies*. Florenz: Sansoni.

Schiff Giorgini, Michela. 2005. *Soleb*, Volume 5: *Le temple, bas-reliefs et inscriptions*. Florenz: Sansoni.

Williams, Bruce. 1986. *The A-Group Royal Cemetery at Qustul: Cemetery L*. Chicago: Oriental Institute.

Marinatos, Chapter 12, pt. III—Religious Interaction . . .

Bietak, Manfred. 1994. "Die Wandmalereien aus Tell el-Dab'a / 'EzbetHelmi, Erste Eindrücke." *Ägypten und Levante* 4: 44–81.

Bietak, Manfred, Nanno Marinatos, Clairy Palyvou, et al. 2007. *Taureador Scenes in Tell el Dab'a and Knossos*. Vienna: Verlagder Österreichischen Akademie der Wissenschaften.

Betancourt Philip B and Costis Davaras. 1995. *Pseira*, Volume 1: *The Minoan Building on the West Side of Area A*. Philadelphia: University Museum, University of Pennsylvania.

Blakolmer, Fritz. 2014. "Gottheiten auf Tieren. Zur Transformation Orientalisher Bildmotive in derminoisch-mykenischen Ikonographie." *Ägypten und Levante* 24: 191–209.

Cantor, Helen. 1999. *Plant Ornament in the Ancient Near East*. Chicago: Oriental Institute.

Cline, Eric H. 1995. " 'My Brother, My Son': Rulership and Trade between the LBA Aegean, Egypt and the Near East." In *The Role of the Ruler in the Prehistoric Aegean: Proceedings of a Panel Discussion Presented at the Annual Meeting of the Archaeological Institute of America, New Orleans, Louisiana, 28 December 1992*, ed. Paul Rehak, 143–50. Aegaeum 11. Liège: Université de Liège.

Crowley, Janice L. 1989. *The Aegean and the East: An Investigation into the Transference of Artistic Motifs between the Aegean, Egypt, and the Near East in the Bronze Age*. Gothenburg: Paul Åströms.

Evans, Arthur. 1921–1936. *The Palace of Minos: A Comparative Account of the Successive Stages of the Early Cretan Civilization as Illustrated by the Discoveries at Knossos*. 4 vols. London: Macmillan.

Graf, Fritz. 2004. "What is Ancient Mediterranean Religion?" In *Religions of the Ancient World: A Guide*, ed. Sarah Iles Johnson, 3–16. Cambridge, MA: Belknap Press.

Hägg, Robin. 1987. "On the Reconstruction of the West Façade of the Palace of Knossos." In R. and N. Marinatos (eds.), *The Function of Minoan Palaces. Proceedings of the Fourth International Symposium at the Swedish Institute in Athens, 10–16 June, 1984*, ed. Robin Hägg and Nanno Marinatos, 129–34. Stockholm: Svenska institutet i Athen.

Hornung, Erik. 1982. *Conceptions of God in Ancient Egypt: The One and the Many*. Translated by John Baines. Ithaca: Cornell University Press.

Hornung, Erik. 1990. *The Valley of the Kings: Horizon of Eternity*. Translated by David Warburton. New York: Timken.

MacGillivray, Alexander J. 2012. "The Minoan Double Axe Goddess and Her Astral Realm." In *Athanasia: The Earthly, the Celestial and the Underworld in the Mediterranean from the Late Bronze and the Early Iron Age, International Archaeological Conference, Rhodes, 28–31 May, 2009*, ed. Nicholas Chr. Stampolidis, Athanasia Kanta, and Angeliki Giannikouri, 115–26. Irakleion: University of Crete.

Marinatos, Nanno. 2010. *Minoan Kingship and the Solar Goddess: A Near Eastern Koine*. Urbana: University of Illinois Press.

Marinatos, Nanno. 2010. "Lions from Tell el Dab'a." *Ägypten und Levante* 20: 325–56.

Matz, F., H. Biesantz, and I. Pini (eds.). 1964. *Corpus der minoischen und mykenischen Siegel*, Band 1. *Die minoischen und mykenischen Siegel des Nationalmuseums in Athen*. Berlin: Akademie der Literatur und Wissenschaften.

Matz, F., H. Biesantz, and I. Pini (eds.). 1984. *Corpus der minoischen und mykenischen Siegel*, Band 2. *Iraklion, Archäologisches Museum*. Teil 3. *Die Siegelabdrücke von Kato Zakros: unter Einbeziehung von Funden aus anderen Museen*. Berlin: Akademie der Literatur und Wissenschaften.

Matz, F., H. Biesantz, and I. Pini (eds.). 1988. *Corpus der minoischen und mykenischen Siegel*. Band 11. *Kleinere Europäische Sammlungen*. Berlin: Akademie der Literatur und Wissenschaften.

Matz, F., H. Biesantz, and I. Pini (eds.). 2002. *Corpus der minoischen und mykenischen Siegel*, Band 2. *Iraklion, Archäologisches Museum.* Teil 8. *Die Siegelabdrücke von Knossos: unter Einbeziehung von Funden aus anderen Museen.* Berlin: Akademie der Literatur und Wissenschaften.

Moran, William. N. 1992. *The Amarna Letters.* Baltimore: Johns Hopkins University Press.

Morgan, Lyvia. 2010. "A Pride of Leopards: A Unique Aspect of the Hunt frieze at Tell el Dab'a." *Ägypten und Levante* 20: 263–302.

Nilsson, M. P. 1950. *The Minoan and Mycenaean Religion and Its Survival in Greek Religion.* 2nd ed. Acta Regiae Societatis Humaniorum Litterarum Lundensis 9. Lund: C. W. K. Gleerup.

Phillips, Jacke. 2006. "Why? ... And Why Not? Minoan Reception and Perceptions of Egyptian Influence." In *Timelines: Studies in Honour of Manfred Bietak*, ed. Ernst Czerny, I. Hein, H. Hunger, D. Melman, and A. Schwab, 293–300. Orientalia Lovaniensia Analecta 149. Leuven: Uitgeverij Peeters en Departement Oosterse Studies.

Ritner, Robert. 2008. "Household Religion in Ancient Egypt." In *Household and Family Religion in Antiquity,* ed. John Bodel and Saul M. Olyan, 171–96. Oxford: Blackwell.

Streng, Georg. 1918. *Das Rosettenmotiv in der Kunst und Kulturgeschichte.* München: Müller and Fröhlich.

Shaw, Maria. 2009. "A Bull Leaping Fresco from the Nile Delta and a Search for Patrons and Artists." *American Journal of Archaeology* 113: 471–6.

Tessier, Beatrice. 1996. *Egyptian Iconography on Syro-Palestinian Cylinder Seals of the Middle Bronze Age.* Orbis biblicus et orientalis Series Archaeologica 1. Fribourg: Fribourg University Press.

Van de Mieroop, Marc. 2003. *A History of the Ancient Near East, c.3000–323 BC.* Oxford: Blackwell.

Warren, Peter. 1995. "Minoan Crete and Pharaonic Egypt." In *Egypt, the Aegean and the Levant: Interconnections in the Second Millennium B.C.*, ed. W. Vivian Davies and Louise Schofield, 1–18. London: British Museum.

Warren, Peter. 2005. "A Model of Iconographic Transfer: The Case of Crete and Egypt." In *Κρης Τεχνιτης L'Artisan Crétois: Recueil d'articles en l'honneur de Jean-Claude Poursat I*, Bradfer Burdet, B. Detournay, and R. Laffineur (eds.), 221–8. Liège: Université de Liège.

Watrous, Vance L. 1998. "Egypt and Crete in the Early Middle Bronze Age: A Case of Cultural Diffusion." In *The Aegean and the Orient in the Second Millennium: Proceedings of the 50th Anniversary Symposium, University of Cincinnati, 18–20 April 1997,* ed. E. H. Cline and D. Harris-Cline, 19–28. Aegaeum 18. Liège: Université de Liège.

Weingarten, Judith. 1991. *The Transformation of Taweret into the Minoan Genius: A Study in Cultural Transmission in the Middle Bronze Age.* Partille: P. Åströms.

Wilkinson, Richard H. 1991. "New Kingdom Astronomical Paintings and Methods of Finding and Extending Direction." *Journal of the American Research Center in Egypt* 28: 149–54.

Wilkinson, Richard H. 1992. *Reading Egyptian Art.* London: Thames and Hudson.

Wilkinson, Richard H. 1994. *Symbol and Magic in Egyptian Art.* London: Thames and Hudson.

Wilkinson, Richard H. 2003. *The Complete Gods and Goddesses of Ancient Egypt.* London: Thames and Hudson.

Wilkinson, Richard H. (ed.). 2012. *Tausret: Forgotten Queen and Pharaoh of Egypt.* Oxford: Oxford University Press.

Harrell, Chapter 13—Violence in Earth, Water and Sky . . .

Ambraseys, Nicholas N., Charles P. Melville, and Robin D. Adams. 1994. *The Seismicity of Egypt, Arabia and the Red Sea—A Historical Review.* Cambridge: Cambridge University Press.

Arnold, Dieter. 1991. *Building in Egypt: Pharaonic Stone Masonry.* Oxford: Oxford University Press.

Arnold, Dieter. 2010. "Earthquakes in Egypt in the Pharaonic Period: The Evidence at Dahshur in the Late Middle Kingdom." *Culture and History of the Ancient Near East* 38: 9–15.

Ball, John. 1912. *The Meteorite of El Nakhla El Baharia.* Cairo: Survey Department.

Bietak, Manfred. 1992. "Minoan Wall-Paintings Unearthed at Ancient Avaris." *Egyptian Archaeology* 2: 26–8.

Breasted, James H. 1906. *Ancient Records of Egypt: Historical Documents from the Earliest Times to the Persian Conquest IV: The Twentieth to the Twenty-sixth Dynasties.* Chicago: University of Chicago Press.

Daressy, Georges. 1896. "Une inondation à Thèbes sous le règne d'Osorkon II." *Recueil de travaux relatifs à la philologie et à l'archéologie égyptiennes et assyriennes* 18: 181–6.

Degg, Martin. 1993. "The 1992 Cairo Earthquake: Cause, Effect and Response." *Disasters* 17(3): 226–38.

Dupuis, Christian, Marie-Pierre Aubry, Chris King, Robert W. O. Knox, William A. Berggren, Mostafa Youssef, Wael F. Galal, and Marc Roche. 2011. "Genesis and Geometry of Tilted Blocks in the Theban Hills, near Luxor (Upper Egypt)." *Journal of African Earth Sciences* 61: 245–67.

Faulkner, Raymond O. 1962. *A Concise Dictionary of Middle Egyptian.* Oxford: Griffith Institute.

Faulkner, Raymond O. 1969. *The Ancient Egyptian Pyramid Texts.* Oxford: Clarendon Press.

Folco, Luigi et al. 2011. "Kamil Crater (Egypt): Ground Truth for Small-Scale Meteorite Impacts. *Geology* 39(2): 179–82.

Foster, John L. 1988. "The Shipwrecked Sailor: Prose or Verse?" *Studien zur Altägyptischen Kultur* 15: 69–109.

Garbrecht, Günther. 1999. "Wadi Garawi Dam." In *Encyclopedia of the Archaeology of Ancient Egypt*, ed. Kathryn A. Bard and Steven Blake Shubert, 864–6. London: Routledge.

Garbrecht, Günther and Heinz-Ulrich Bertram (eds.). 1983. *Sadd el Kafara.* Mitteilungsheft des Leichtweiss-Instituts 81. Braunschweig: Technischen Universität Braunschweig.

Godley, Alfred D. 2004. *Herodotus*, Volume 1: *Books I–II.* Cambridge, MA: Harvard University Press.

Harris, James R. 1961. *Lexicographical Studies in Ancient Egyptian Minerals.* Berlin: Akademie Verlag.

Jacques, François and Bernard Bousquet. 1984. "Le cataclysme du 21 Juillet 365: phénomène régional ou catastrophe cosmique?" In *Tremblements de Terre Histoire et Archèology*, eds. Bruno Helly and Alex Pollino, 183–198. IVémes rencontres internationales d'archéologie et d'histoire d'Antibes 2–4 Novembre 1983. Valbonne: Association pour la promotion et la diffusion des connaissances archéologiques.

Johnson, Diane and Joyce Tyldesley. 2014. "The Metal That Fell from the Sky." *Ancient Egypt* 14(4): 43–7.

Jones, Horace L. 1959. *The Geography of Strabo*. Volume 8. Cambridge, MA: Harvard University Press.

Karakhanyan, Arkadi and Ara Avagyan. 2011. "Archaeoseismological Investigation in the Temple of Amenhotep III and the Surrounding." *Annales du Service des antiquités de l'égypte* 85: 277–305.

Kebeasy, Rashad M. 1990. "Seismicity." In *The Geology of Egypt*, ed. Rushdi Said, 51–9. Rotterdam: A. A. Balkema.

Kelly, Gavin. 2004. "Ammianus and the Great Tsunami." *Journal of Roman Studies* 94: 141–67.

Krichak, Simon O., Marina Tsidulko, and Pinhas Alpert. 2000. "November 2, 1994, Severe Storms in the Southeastern Mediterranean." *Atmospheric Research* 53: 45–62.

Lipinska, Jadwiga. 1967. "Names and History of the Sanctuaries built by Tuthmosis III at Deir el-Bahri." *Journal of Egyptian Archaeology* 53: 25–33.

McCoy, Floyd W. and Grant Heiken. 2000. "The Late-Bronze Age Explosive Eruption of Thera (Santorini), Greece: Regional and Local Effects." In *Volcanic Hazards and Disasters in Human Antiquity*, ed. Floyd W. McCoy and Grant Heiken, 43–70. Geological Society of America Special Paper 345. Boulder: Geological Society of America.

Meneisy, Mohamed Y. 1990 "Vulcanicity." In *The Geology of Egypt*, ed. Rushdi Said, 157–72. Rotterdam: A. A. Balkema.

Murphy, Kim. 1994. "New Flooding in Egypt Threatens Historic Tombs." *Los Angeles Times*, November 5, 1994. <http://articles.latimes.com/print/1994-11-05/news/mn-58761_1_southern-egypt>.

Rackham, Harris. 1967. *Pliny—Natural History*, Volume 2: *Books III–VII*. Cambridge, MA: Harvard University Press.

Ramsey, Boniface. 1997. *John Cassian: The Conferences*. New York: Paulist Press.

Ritner, Robert K. and Nadine Moeller. 2014. "The Ahmose 'Tempest Stela,' Thera and Comparative Chronology." *Journal of Near Eastern Studies* 73(1): 1–19.

Rolfle, John C. 1986. *Ammianus Marcellinus*. Cambridge, MA: Harvard University Press

Said, Rushdi. 1981. *The Geological Evolution of the River Nile*. Berlin: Springer Verlag.

Sethe, Kurt. 1910. *Die altaegyptischen Pyramidentexte*. Volume 2. Leipzig: J. C. Hinrich.

Siebert, Lee Tom Simkin, and Paul Kimberly. 2010. *Volcanoes of the World*. 3rd ed. Washington: Smithsonian Institution.

Stanley, Daniel J., and Harrison Sheng. 1986. "Volcanic Shards from Santorini (Upper Minoan Ash) in the Nile Delta, Egypt." *Nature* 320: 733–5.

Strudwick, Nigel. 1995. "News from Luxor. January 16, 1995." *Egyptology Resources*, <http://www.fitzmuseum.cam.ac.uk/er/lxr/luxor.html>.

von Beckerath, Jürgen. 1966. "The Nile Level Records at Karnak and Their Importance for the History of the Libyan Period (Dynasties XXII and XXIII)." *Journal of the American Research Center in Egypt* 5: 43–55.

Wiener, Malcom H. and James P. Allen. 1998. "Separate Lives: The Ahmose Tempest Stela and the Theran Eruption." *Journal of Near Eastern Studies* 57(1): 1–19.

Bunbury, Chapter 14—The Fickel Nile . . .

Adams, B. 1995. *Ancient Nekhen: Garstang in the City of Hierakonpolis*. Egyptian Studies Association Publication 3. New Malden: SIA Publishing.

Bristow, C. S., and N. Drake. 2006. "Shorelines in the Sahara: Geomorphological Evidence for an Enhanced Monsoon from Palaeolake Megachad." *The Holocene*, 16(6): 901–11.

Bubenzer, O. and H. Riemer. 2007. "Holocene Climatic Change and Human Settlement Between the Central Sahara and the Nile Valley: Archaeological and Geomorphological Results." *Geoarchaeology International* 22: 607–20.

Bunbury, J. M., A. Graham, and M. A. Hunter. 2008. "Stratigraphic Landscape Analysis: Charting the Holocene Movements of the Nile at Karnak through Ancient Egyptian Time." *Geoarchaeology* 23: 351–73.

Bunbury, J. M., A. Graham, and K. D. Strutt. 2009. "Kom el-Farahy: A New Kingdom Island in an Evolving Edfu Floodplain." *British Museum Studies in Ancient Egypt and Sudan* 14: 1–23.

Bunbury, J. M. 2010. "The Development of the River Nile and the Egyptian Civilization: A Water Historical Perspective with Focus on the First Intermediate Period." In *A History of Water*, Series II, Volume 2: *Rivers and Society: From Early Civilizations to Modern Times*, ed. T. Tvedt and R. Coopey. London: IB Tauris.

Conway, D. and M. Hulme. 1993. "Recent Fluctuations in Precipitations and Runoff over the Nile Sub-basins and their Impact on Main Nile Discharge." *Climate Change* 25(2): 127–51.

Gunn, B. 1927. "The Stela of Apries at Mitrahina." *Annales du Service des antiquités de l'Égypte* 27: 211–37.

Hassan, F. 1986. "Holocene Lakes and Prehistoric Settlements of the Western Faiyum, Egypt." *Journal of Archaeological Science* 13(5): 483–501.

Hassan, F. 2005. "A River Runs Through Egypt." *Geotimes* (April, 2005), <http://www. geotimes.org/apr05/feature_NileFloods.html>.

Hassan, F. (ed.). 2002. *Droughts, Food and Culture: Ecological Change and Food Security in Africa's Later Prehistory*. New York: Kluwer Academic/Plenum Publishers.

Herodotus. 1998. *The Histories*, ed. Carolyn Dewald and trans. Robin Waterfield. Oxford: Oxford University Press.

Hillier, J. K., J. M. Bunbury, and A. Graham. 2007. "Monuments on a Migrating Nile." *Journal of Archaeological Science* 34: 1011–15.

Hoffman, M. A., H. N. Barakat, R. Friedman, H. A. Hamroush, D. L. Holmes, J. McArdle, and J. O. Mills. 1987. "A Final report to the National Endowment for the Humanities on Predynastic Research at Hierakonpolis, 1985–86." (NEH Grant No. RO-20805-85.) Earth Sciences and Resources Institute, University of South Carolina, Columbia, SC.

Hoffman, M. A., H. A. Hamroush, and R. O. and Allen. 1987. "The Environmental Evolution of an Early Egyptian Urban Centre: Archaeological and Geochemical Investigations at Hierakonpolis." *Geoarchaeology* 2 (1): 1–13.

Jeffreys, D. and A. Tavares. 2012. "Memphis, A City Unseen." *AERAgram* 13(1): 2–7.

Kropelin, S., D. Verschuren, A.-M. Lezine, H. Eggermont, C. Cocquyt, P. Francus, J.-P. Cazet, M. Fagot, B. Rumes, J. M. Russell, F. Darius, D. J. Conley, M. Schuster, H. Von Suchodoletz, D. R. Engstrom. 2008. "Climate-Driven Ecosystem Succession in the Sahara: The Past 6000 Years." *Science* 320/5877: 765–8.

Kuper, R. and S. Kropelin. 2006. "Climate-Controlled Holocene Occupation in the Sahara: Motor of Africa's Evolution." *Science* 313/5788: 803–7.

Macklin, M. G., W. H. J. Toonen, J. C. Woodward, M. A. J. Williams, C. Flaux, N. Marriner, K. Nicoll, G. Verstraeten, N. Spencer, and D. Welsby. 2015. "A New Model of River Dynamics, Hydroclimatic Change and Human Settlement in the Nile Valley Derived from Meta-analysis of the Holocene Fluvial Archive." *Quaternary Science Reviews* 130: 109–23.

Said, R. 1962. *The Geology of Egypt.* Amsterdam: Elsevier.

Said, R. 1981. *The Geological Evolution of the River Nile.* New York: Springer-Verlag.

Said, R. 1993. *The River Nile: Geology, Hydrology and Utilization.* Oxford: Pergamon Press.

Stanley, D. J. and A. G. Warne. 1993. "Recent Geological Evolution and Human Impact." *Science* 260: 628–34.

Van Neer, W., V. Linseele, and R. Friedman. 2002. "Animal Burials and Food Offerings at the Elite Cemetery HK6 of Hierakonpolis." In *Egypt at Its Origins: Studies in Memory of Barbara Adams*, ed. S. Hendrickx, R. Friedman, K. Cialowicz, and M. Chlodnicki, 67–130. Leuven: Peeters.

Wendorf, F. and R. Schild. 2013. *Holocene Settlement of Egyptian Sahara*, Volume 1: *The Archaeology of Nabta Playa.* New York: Springer Science+Business Media.

Woodward, J. C., M. G. Macklin, M. D. Krom, and A. J. Williams. 2007. "The Nile: Evolution, Quaternary River Environments and Material Fluxes." In *Large Rivers: Geomorphology and Management*, ed. A. Gupta, 261–92. Chichester: John Wiley and Sons.

David, Chapter 15—Illness from Afar . . .

Aufderheide, Arthur C., and Conrado Rodriguez-Martin. 1998. *The Cambridge Encyclopedia of Human Paleopathology.* Cambridge: Cambridge University Press.

Bietak, M. 1996. *Avaris. The Capital of the Hyksos. Recent Excavations at Tell el-Daba'a.* London: British Museum Press.

Black, F. L. 1975. "Infectious Diseases in Primitive Societies." *Science* 476: 515–20.

Boessneck, J. 1976. *Tell el-Dab'a III Die Tierknochenfunde 1966–1969.* Untersuchungen des Osterreich Archäologischen Institut (UZK), Abt. 5. Akademie der Wissenschaft, Cairo.

Breasted, James H. 1930. *The Edwin Smith Surgical Papyrus.* 2 vols. Chicago: University of Chicago Press.

Bruce-Chwatt, L., and J. de Zulueta. 1980. *The Rise and Fall of Malaria in Europe: A Historico-epidemiological Study.* London: Oxford University Press.

Bynum, W. F., and Roy Porter (eds.). 1993. *Companion Encyclopaedia of the History of Medicine.* 2 vols. London: Routledge.

Cockburn, Aidan, Eve Cockburn, and Theodore A. Reyman (eds.). 1998. *Mummies, Disease and Ancient Cultures.* 2nd ed. Cambridge: Cambridge University Press.

Cockitt, Jennifer, and Rosalie David (eds.). 2010. *Pharmacy and Medicine in Ancient Egypt.* BAR International Series 2141. Oxford: Archaeopress.

David, Rosalie (ed.). 2008. *Egyptian Mummies and Modern Science.* Cambridge: Cambridge University Press.

Davis, D. H. S., A. F. Hallett, and M. Isaacson. 1975. "Plague." In *Diseases Transmitted from Animals to Man*, ed. W. T. Hubbert, W. F. McCulloch, and P. R. Schnurrenberger, 147–73. Springfield, IL: C. C. Thomas.

Dewing, H. B. (trans.). 1914. *Procopius: History of the Wars*, Volume I: *The Persian War*. London: Heinemann.

Dols, M. W. 1974. "Plague in Early Islamic History." *Journal of the Oriental Society* 3: 371–84.

Drancourt, M., and D. Raoult. 2002. "Molecular Insights into the History of Plague." *Microbes and Infection* 4(1): 105–9.

Dzierzykray-Rogalski, T. 1980. "Paleopathology of the Ptolemaic Inhabitants of Dakhleh Oasis (Egypt)." *Journal of Human Evolution* 9: 71–4.

Dzierzykray-Rogalski, T. and E. Prominska. 1994. "A Further Report on Pharaoh Siptah's Handicap (XIXth Egyptian Dynasty)." *HOMO* 45 (Supplement), S45.

Ebbell, B. 1937. *The Papyrus Ebers*. Copenhagen: Levin & Munksgaard.

Gardiner, Alan H. 1961. *Egypt of the Pharaohs*. London: Oxford University Press.

Geller, Markham J. 2010. *Ancient Babylonian Medicine: Theory and Practice*. Oxford: Wiley-Blackwell.

Goedicke, H. 1984. "The Canaanite Illness." *Studien zur Altägyptischen Kultur* 11: 91–105.

Goyon, J.-C. 1974. "Sur les formule des rituels de conjuration des dangers de l'année." *Bulletin de l'Institut français d'archéologie orientale du Caire* 74: 79–83.

Guy, M. W., W. A. Krotoski, and A. Cockburn. 1981. "Malaria and an Egyptian Mummy." *Royal Society of Tropical Medicine and Hygiene* 75: 601.

Győry, H. 2010. "*J3dt rnpt* or the 'Pestilence of the Year.'" In *Pharmacy and Medicine in Ancient Egypt: Proceedings of the Conferences Held in Cairo (2007) and Manchester (2008)*, ed. Jenefer Cockitt and Rosalie David, 81–4. Oxford: Archaeopress.

Harris, James E. and Kent R. Weeks. 1973. *X-Raying the Pharaohs*. New York: Charles Scribner's Sons.

Harris, James E. and Edward F. Wente (eds.). 1980. *An X-Ray Atlas of the Royal Mummies*. Chicago and London: University of Chicago Press.

Henschen, F. 1966. *History and Geography of Diseases*. New York: Delacorte Press.

Hillson, Simon W. 1980. "Chronic Anaemias in the Nile Valley." *MASCA Journal* 1: 172–4.

Hoffmeier, J. K. 1996. *Israel in Egypt: The Evidence for the Authenticity of the Exodus Tradition*. Oxford: Oxford University Press.

Hopkins, D. 1980. "Ramses V: Earliest Known Victim?" *World Health* (May, 1980): 220.

Houlihan, P. F. 1996. *The Animal World of the Pharaohs*. London: Thames and Hudson.

Hoyte, H. M. 1993. "The Plagues of Egypt: What Killed the Animals and the Firstborn?" *Medical Journal of Australia* 158(10): 285–6.

Jones, W. H. S. (trans.). 1923. *Hippocrates*. 2 vols. London: Heinemann and New York: Putnam.

Kozloff, Arielle P. 2006. "Bubonic plague during the reign of Amenhotep III?" *KMT* 17 (3): 36–46.

Krotoski, W. A. 1980 Untitled. *Paleopathology Newsletter* 31: 7–8.

Kurt, A. 1995. *The Ancient Near East c.3000–330 BC*. London: Routledge.

Lang, Philippa. 2013. *Medicine and Society in Ptolemaic Egypt*. Leiden: Brill.

Leca, A-P. 1988. *La médecine égyptienne au temps des pharaons*. Paris: Roger Dacosta.

Lefebvre, G. 1956. *Essai sur la médecine égyptienne de l'époque pharaonique*. Paris: Presses universitaires de France.

Leitz, C. 2000. *Magical and Medical Papyri of the New Kingdom*. London: British Museum Press.

Lewin, Peter K. 1984. "'Mummy' Riddles Unravelled." *Bulletin of the Electron Microscopy Society of Canada* 12(3): 3–8.

Lichtheim, Miriam. 1975. *Ancient Egyptian Literature*, Volume 1: *The Old and Middle Kingdoms.* Berkeley: University of California Press.

Lichtheim, Miriam. 1980. *Ancient Egyptian Literature*, Volume 3: *The Late Period.* Berkeley: University of California Press.

Marr, J. S. and C. D. Malloy. 1996. "An Epidemiologic Analysis of the Ten Plagues of Egypt." *Caduceus* 12(1): 7–24.

Miller, R. L., S. Ikram, G. J. Armelagos, R. Walker, W. B. Harer, and C. J. Schiff. 1994. "Diagnosis of *Plasmodium falciparum* Infections in Mummies Using the Rapid Manual *Para*Sight™-F test." *Transactions of the Royal Society of Tropical Medicine and Hygiene* 88: 31–2.

Milne, J. G. 1914. "The Sanatorium at Deir el-Bahri." *Journal of Egyptian Archaeology* 1: 96–8.

Mitchell, J. K. 1900. "Study of a Mummy Affected with Anterior Poliomyelitis." *Philadelphia Medical Journal* 6: 414–15.

Møller-Christensen, V. 1967. "Evidence of Leprosy in Earlier Peoples." In *Diseases in Antiquity: A Survey of the Diseases, Injuries and Surgery of Early Populations*, ed. Don Brothwell and A. T. Sandison, 295–306. Springfield, IL: C. C. Thomas.

Møller-Christensen, V. and D. R. Hughes. 1966. "An Early Case of Leprosy from Nubia." *Man* 1: 242–3.

Moran, William L. 1992. *The Amarna Letters.* Baltimore: Johns Hopkins University Press.

Nunn, John. 1996. *Ancient Egyptian Medicine.* London: British Museum Press.

O'Neill, Y. V. 1993. "Diseases of the Middle Ages." In *The Cambridge World History of Human Disease*, ed. K. F. Kiple, 270–9. New York: Cambridge University Press.

Panagiotakopulu, E. 2004. "Pharaonic Egypt and the Origins of Plague." *Journal of Biogeography* 31: 269–75.

Patoul Burns, J., Jr. 2001. *Cyprian the Bishop.* London: Routledge.

Pritchard, J. B. 1955. *Ancient Near Eastern Texts Relating to the Old Testament.* Princeton: Princeton University Press.

Ruffer, Marc A. 1910. "Remarks on the Histology and Pathological Anatomy of Egyptian Mummies." *Cairo Scientific Journal* 4: 1–5.

Ruffer, Marc A. and A. R. Ferguson. 1911. "Note on an Eruption Resembling That of Variola in the Skin of a Mmummy of the XXth Dynasty." *Journal of Pathology and Bacteriology* 15: 1–3.

Rutherford, Patricia. 2008. "DNA Identification in Mummies and Associated Material." In *Egyptian Mummies and Modern Science*, ed. Rosalie David, 116–32. Cambridge: Cambridge University Press.

Sandison, A. T. 1972. "Evidence of Infective Diseases." *Journal of Human Evolution* 1: 213–24.

Sandison, A. T. and Edmund Tapp. 1998. "Disease in Ancient Egypt." In *Mummies, Disease and Ancient Cultures*, ed. Aidan Cockburn, Eve Cockburn, and Theodore A. Reyman, 38–58. 2nd ed. Cambridge: Cambridge University Press.

Sallares, G., S. Gomzi, A. Richards, and C. Anderung. 2000. "Evidence from Ancient DNA for Malaria in Antiquity." Abstract in *Proceedings of the 5th International Ancient DNA Conference, Manchester.*

Scheidel, Walter. 2001. *Death on the Nile: Disease and the Demography of Roman Egypt.* Mnemosyne, Supplements 228. Leiden, Koln: Brill.

Sigerist, H. E. 1951. *A History of Medicine*, Volume 1: *Primitive and Archaic Medicine.* New York: Oxford University Press.

Smith, Grafton E. 1912. *The Royal Mummies.* Catalogue général des antiquités égyptiennes du Musée du Caire. Cairo: Imprimerie de l'Institut français d'archéologie orientale.

Smith, Grafton E. and Warren R. Dawson. 1924. *Egyptian Mummies.* London: George Allen and Unwin.

Smith, Grafton E., and Douglas E. Derry. 1910. "Anatomical Report." *Archaeological Survey of Nubia Bulletin* 6: 9–30.

Strouhal, E. 1996. "Traces of Smallpox Epidemic in the Family of Ramses V of the Egyptian 20th Dynasty." *Anthropologie* 34: 315–19.

Tiradritti, Francesco. 2014. "Of Kilns and Corpses: Theban Plague Victims." *Egyptian Archaeology* 44: 15–18.

Weeks, Kent R. 1998. *The Lost Tomb.* London: Weidenfeld & Nicolson.

Wegner, Josef. 2015. "A Royal Necropolis at South Abydos: New Light on Egypt's Second Intermediate Period." *Near Eastern Archaeology* 78 (2): 68–78.

Winlock, Herbert E. 1945. *The Slain Soldiers of Neb-Hepet-Re Mentu-hotp.* New York: Metropolitan Museum of Art Egyptian Expedition.

Ziegler, H. 1998. *The Black Death.* Harmondsworth: Penguin.

INDEX

Page numbers in italics indicate illustrations.

Ancient Egyptian Terms (Transliterations)
Note: Egyptian words with anglicized spellings, as well as all other foreign words, are included in the main index.

MAIN INDEX

Abu Ballas trail, 6, *7*, *40*
Abu Simbel, temple at, 140
Abydos, tombs at, 64, 120, *184*
Actiuim, naval battle of, 34
Adapa and the Southwind, 210
Admonitions of Ipuwer, 25, 284
Aegean
    domination of, 30
    exchange with, 31
    goods, dispersal of, 27
    importance of, 32
    influence of, 148
    as literary setting, 13
    place names, topographical lists of, 16
    religious beliefs and practices, 229–237
    scarabs, 161
Aegeans, 68, 73
Aegean Sea, 242
Aegean wars, 26
Africa, circumnavigation of, 16–17
Africa, East, 57
African imports to Egypt, 39
African tectonic plate, 242
afterlife, beliefs concerning, 203–204, 213
agriculture, 259, 266–267
Aha, King, 117, 119
Ahhotep, tomb of, 139–140
Ahmose, son of Ebana, 99
Ahmose I, 250
Akestor, King (from Cyprus), 148
Akhenaten, mother of, 83
akhet ("horizon"), 231
Akhimenru (TT 404), 282
Akhu (demon), 214
Akkadian language, 85, 171, 185
ʾalep (letter), 193
Alexander the Great, 34, 268
Alexandria, 34, 246, 268
Algeria, 152
alphabet, invention of, 190–192
alphabets, examples of, *191*
Amarna, glassware at, 177
Amarna, religion of, 210
Amarna Diplomacy (Cohen and Westbrook), 11
Amarna Hymn, 71–72

Amarna Letters
    Anatolia and Tigris-Euphrates region covered
      in, 6–7
    Babylonia, communication with, 12
    cuneiform tablets, 171, 172
    diplomacy content of, 85–87, *86*
    international correspondence, 209
    material goods covered in, 88–89
    plague references in, 283
Amduat, 5
Amenemhat I, 124
Amenemhat II, 96, 104, 124–125
Amenemhat of Beni Hassan, 97
Amenhotep I, 29, 56
Amenhotep II, 129, 215
Amenhotep III
    Aegean diplomatic mission during reign of, 32
    ailments, curing, 272
    construction by, 265–266
    correspondence, 172
    scarabs, 153, 163
    statues, 244, *245*
    topographical lists from reign of, 16
    trade during reign of, 129
Amenhotep IV, 229
Amenhotep son of Hapu, 168–169
Amka, battle of, 283
Ammianus Marcellinus, 244, 246
amulets, Egyptian-style, 144, *145*
amulets, seal, 149
Amun (god), 172, 222–223, 229–230
Amun-Re (god), 72
Amun temples, 223–224
Anat (goddess), 198, 215, *216*, 217
Anatolia
    Egyptian knowledge of, 8
    Hittite empire in, 189
    roadways in, 51
    scarabs in, 151
    as *terra incognita,* 6–7
    writing system, 188–189
animals from wet climate, 259, 262–263, 267
ankh ("life") sign, 187, *187*, 211, *212*, 231, 233
Ankhtifi (warlord), 25
Anopheles mosquitoes, 275